Date Due

MEDIEVAL LITERATURE
and FOLKLORE STUDIES

FRANCIS LEE UTLEY

MEDIEVAL LITERATURE and FOLKLORE STUDIES

Essays in Honor of Francis Lee Utley

Edited by JEROME MANDEL *and*
BRUCE A. ROSENBERG

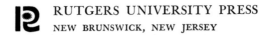
RUTGERS UNIVERSITY PRESS
NEW BRUNSWICK, NEW JERSEY

Contents

Preface

This volume was planned in 1965 when both of its editors were finishing their work for the Ph.D. at Ohio State University under the benevolent guidance of Francis Lee Utley. At that time we had planned to honor him at his retirement from teaching. But since he has subsequently decided not to retire, we have delighted ourselves in preparing this jubilee volume in honor of his 65th birthday.

One needs no occasion to honor a man thrice awarded a fellowship from the John Simon Guggenheim Memorial Foundation and who was at various times president of the American Folklore Society (1951–1952), the American Name Society (1966), and the College English Association (1969). After study at the University of Wisconsin (AB, 1929; MA, 1934) and Harvard (Ph.D., 1936) where he was a Dexter Fellow, he joined the Department of English at the Ohio State University where he has served for more than thirty years, with occasional years as visiting professor at Columbia, Harvard, Padua, and the University of California both at Los Angeles and at Berkeley. His energy and enthusiasm for matters medieval, linguistic, folkloric, onomastic, biographical, bibliographical, anthropological, and pedagogic are recorded in the many books and articles he has written. In prose noted for its grace and wit, Professor Utley reveals not only his own delight in the making of language to convey idea but shows himself the very antithesis of the remote scholar.

The editors of this book, especially, and no doubt many of those whose essays appear here have a special interest in honoring Francis Lee Utley. He made us so much better than we would have been without him. Some of the most distinguished scholars of medieval literature and of folklore, who have known him as teacher, colleague, and friend, are helping us to celebrate Professor Utley's birthday. Their original contributions to the study of the Middle Ages and Folklore appear here in a splendid variety of approaches and techniques, of continuations, summations, and beginnings. Since no single book could reflect Professor

Utley's universal taste and catholic interests, we have allowed his philosophy to dictate the subject of this book. Some of the contributors are considered folklorists, others medievalists—but for Professor Utley there is little difference between folklore and medieval literature. In his life and through his students he has shown that medievalists are more than amateur folklorists and that competent folklorists know a lot about the Middle Ages. We think it the ultimate tribute to Professor Utley's professional life that folklorists consider him one of their number and medievalists count him among their own.

As an act of praise is an act of love, this book must stand as public witness to the editors' affection and gratitude for a man who taught us more than we could learn. We join his many friends, both those represented here and those for whom there was not room, in wishing him well on this birthday.

Jerome Mandel
Bruce A. Rosenberg

MEDIEVAL LITERATURE
and FOLKLORE STUDIES

ARTHUR G. BRODEUR

Beowulf: One Poem or Three?

The theory of the composite origin of *Beowulf,* most rationally presented by Schücking,[1] and effectively controverted by Chambers,[2] has
recently been revived by Francis P. Magoun, Jr.[3] Since Magoun based
his case on grounds different from Schücking's, he felt no need to cite
the older scholar's arguments in support of his own, or to mention the
opposing evidence brought forward by Chambers. Like Schücking, however, he centers his case, in his paper *"Béowulf A', a Folk-Variant,"*
upon that portion of the poem known as "Beowulf's Return."

Magoun considers the greater part of this section (specifically 2009b–
2176, including most of the hero's report to Hygelac and the fourteen
lines that relate his presentation to Hygelac and Hygd of the gifts
given him by Hrothgar and Wealhtheow) as "an insertion by an anthologizing scribe of a variant (*A'*) which, though giving a far shorter
version of the *fabula* in question, included what seemed to him like a
lot of curious and interesting features not in" the main narrative of
Part I. This inserted *"A' "* is, in Magoun's opinion, an independent oral
poem which the anthologizing scribe "soldered" to *"A"* (that is, to the
main body of Part I) composing in his own words only the "neatly
soldered joints"—and presumably sacrificing "the original ending of
A . . . likewise no doubt the original beginning of *A'.*"[4]

The presence of previously unrevealed detail in Beowulf's report to
Hygelac is indubitable, but it is only one example of a narrative procedure characteristic of all parts of the poem. Klaeber observed that
(in *Beowulf*) "different parts of a story are sometimes told in different
places, or substantially the same incident is related several times from
different points of view." Thus, "The brief notice of Grendel's first
visit in Heorot (122 ff.) is supplemented by a later allusion containing
additional detail (1580 ff.)."[5] I have pointed out, in another context,

3

that whenever our poet retells what he has told before, he gives each telling its peculiar interest, tone, and function.[6] A notable instance is his repeated retellings of Hygelac's fall in Frisia (1202–1214a, 2354b–2366, 2501–2508a, 2910b–2921), each of which contains details not found in the others. The same is true of the three distinct relations of the wars between Geats and Svear (2379b–2396, 2472–2489, 2922–3007a). In every retelling, added details, or shifts in emphasis reflect both the poet's need in a specific context and the personal feeling of the teller. In each instance the action or situation is first narrated by the poet; in later narrations the speaker is one of the personages of the poem. This is a technique so consistently used by the poet that we must regard it as deliberate; it is powerful in its impact, and it lends itself nicely to characterization.

Inevitably, given the poet's fondness for this technique, we should expect Beowulf's report to Hygelac to contain "curious and interesting features" which the poet had not told before. These features not only feed the interest of the poet's audience, they also appear to have been chosen for their immediate effectiveness in the setting of Hygelac's court. For Beowulf's audience in his uncle's hall is a special one, personally and emotionally concerned, as the eighth-century audience for which the poet first recounted Beowulf's troll-killings was not. The poet, with the instinct of the true artist, so managed his story that upon each audience it exerted an appropriately telling effect.

Addition of striking detail in his report to Hygelac affords, therefore, no evidence for a song, or a version, different from that represented by the poet's earlier account. Discrepancies between the two accounts are a different thing, and Magoun believes that he has found them. He tells us that Beowulf's account of his reception at Heorot

differs greatly from what was told before. He says that as soon as he got to Lejre and Hróthgár understood his intentions . . . the latter seated him by a single unnamed son (1. 2013) and that Wealhthéow passed among the company and distributed gifts. But in *A* neither Wealhthéow nor the boy(s) appear at all on this occasion, Wealhthéow not until 1. 612b of the first banquet (ll. 491 ff.), the two boys, not one boy, named Hróethríc and Hróthmund, not before the big dinner (ll. 1008 ff.), where they are mentioned in 1. 1189 and where it is merely remarked that Béowulf was at a given moment sitting beside them, not that he had been placed there as part of the seating arrangements. *A′* is here not at all like *A*.[7]

Let us consider first the number of the boys. As Klaeber recognized in his glossary, *sunu* (2013) may be either singular or plural; and he is supported by Sievers.[8] If it is plural, then there is no discrepancy here between *"A"* and *"A′"* in the matter of number: in both the poet's direct narrative and Beowulf's report Beowulf is seated by Hrothgar's sons. The only differences are: (1) that in the main narrative the moment at which the poet chose to mention this fact is not the same moment in the narrative sequence at which Beowulf reports it to Hygelac, and (2) that in the report the names of the boys are not given.

There are sound reasons for the first difference. There is nothing that precludes a poet, oral or lettered, from using any element in his story at the point or points at which it seems to him to have most value. The poet knew, better than his critics, that specific information is most effectively imparted at the point at which it has most relevance and force. Now, it is significant that the very scene in which Hrothgar's sons first appear, and are named—that of the feast in celebration of Beowulf's victory over Grendel—is the same scene at which Hrothulf is first mentioned, and in which Wealhtheow assumes personality and character. In 612 ff., when she first appears, she is no more than a gracious lady performing her duty to her guests: She enters only after the men's business (Beowulf's greeting to Hrothgar, the latter's reply, and the flyting with Unferth) is concluded; her second entrance (1162 ff.) is mentioned immediately after the scop has sung of Finn, Hildeburg, and Hengest. It is directly followed (1163b ff.) by a clear intimation that the peace and good faith then prevailing between Hrothgar and Hrothulf will end disastrously—a catastrophe which has already been hinted in 1017b–1019. It is in 1017a that Hrothulf is first named. From 1173b to 1191 (or even to 1201) and from 1215 to 1231 Wealhtheow holds the stage, and in two deeply anxious speeches appeals first to Hrothulf's loyalty and sense of gratitude, then to Beowulf, in the hope of assuring the safety of her sons. It is in this immediate context that the boys are named, and that we are told that Beowulf was sitting by (or, more exactly, between) them.

Surely this entire scene is one carefully designed whole. First, the staging (1008b–1019): with the *comitatus* seated at the feast—with special mention, of course, of the two royal kinsmen, Hrothgar and Hrothulf—followed by a statement of present decorum and good faith, and a contrasting hint of future dissension and treachery (1018–1019). Then, after the gift-giving, and as example of the entertainment, the scop's heroic song, stressing early the tragedy of Hildeburg, and surely conveying to the poet's audience the ultimate, and similar, tragedy of Wealhtheow.[9] Then, after a second intimation of calamity for her and those she loves (1163–1168), she makes her delicate and gracious appeal to Hrothulf which, if she trusted him, she need not have made. Then, turning at once to Beowulf, the mightiest of men, who sits between her sons, she seeks from him assurance of his protection for them. This is the spot at which they should first be named, the place at which they assume dramatic importance.

Once more, we must remember that this first account was designed for one audience (the poet's) and Beowulf's report for another (Hygelac). Hygelac has just reminded the hero that he had urged him to let Hrothgar settle his own feud with Grendel. Therefore it is entirely appropriate that the hero should inform Hygelac that the Danish king had received him with all honor, seating him beside the young princes, as soon as he understood that his guest had come to deliver the Danes from Grendel's ravages. But in any case a poet is surely entitled to communicate specific details of his story at any point which he finds appropriate. Certainly there was no occasion, in the report to Hygelac, to repeat the earlier context (1188–1191) in which the boys had been named, and in which it is most important that they should be named.

It is quite true that in the first section Wealhtheow does not appear upon the scene until after Beowulf's retort to Unferth; whereas in Beowulf's report her entrance seems to be earlier. Nevertheless her first appearance, in *"A,"* occurs in precisely the same scene as that in which the hero has his first audience with Hrothgar. The order of events in 402–620 is this: Beowulf enters Heorot, greets Hrothgar, and asks permission to confront Grendel. Hrothgar replies, with a gracious welcome and an account of his sufferings; there is feasting followed by the flyting between Unferth and Beowulf. After an affirmation of Hrothgar's confidence that Beowulf can overcome the monster, Wealhtheow passes mead cups.

It should be noticed that Beowulf, in his report, concentrates his first mention of all the members of the Danish royal family (except, of course, Hrothulf) within 15 lines: Hrothgar (2010), his sons (2013), Wealhtheow (2016), Freawaru (2020–2023). The reason is obvious: the poet, in Beowulf's report, has to compress into the brief space of 153 lines all that the poet had told to his audience in 1482 lines.

Magoun also finds it "odd that nothing was said in *A* about the very existence of Princess Freawaru, not to mention her name." [10] Surely there was no need to mention Freawaru in the poet's direct narrative of Beowulf's adventures in Denmark, since she plays no part in the main story. If he had told us, there, of her betrothal to Ingeld and the revival of the feud between Danes and Heathobeardan, the tale of the hero's monster-slayings would have been obstructed by matter impertinent to it. Her "very existence" has relevance only to the Ingeld Episode.

Through Wealhtheow's appeal for Beowulf's support for her sons, and through his promise to bring a thousand thanes to Hrothgar's aid if foes should assail him, Beowulf has in effect committed the Geats to an alliance with Hrothgar; and he has virtually involved Hygelac in this pledge (1822–1835). It therefore becomes his manifest duty to pass on to Hygelac his misgivings that the ancient quarrel between Danes and Heathobeardan will break out afresh, and that Hrothgar may require Geatish help. He had no comparable knowledge of Hrothulf's future revolt; as the poet has told us, at the time of Beowulf's visit to Denmark, Hrothulf's loyalty to his uncle was yet unbroken: each was faithful to the other. The hero's report of Freawaru's betrothal, and his warning that trouble may come of it, are in exactly the proper place. Here, again, there is no discrepancy between the two accounts, but there *is* a most significant and dramatic addition in Beowulf's report.

Magoun maintains that the account of Beowulf's combats with Grendel and Grendel's dam "in *A'* differs quite drastically from what is in *A.*" In 739–745a the Geatish warrior devoured by Grendel is not named; in the report to Hygelac he is called Hondscio. Again, in 2085 ff., Beowulf describes Grendel's *glof,* which had not been mentioned earlier. Beowulf tells Hygelac that Grendel had intended to thrust him and other Geats into this *glof,* but failed to do so "because in a rage Beowulf stood straight up (1. 2092), a point at variance with *A* (ll. 745b–749), where it is clear that Beowulf is lying down." [11]

Now the mention of Hondscio by name and of the *glof,* in Beowulf's report, differ from the earlier account only in that they supplement it with specific detail. In the original narrative of the fight with Grendel, the poet was concerned with Beowulf's peril and Beowulf's valor; the devouring of any one of his men furnished a sufficient climax to the poet's carefully calculated design for terror.[12] But upon his return to his uncle's court Beowulf must account for the missing thane, whose name Hygelac certainly knew, and for whose non-appearance he would expect an accounting. Naming him, describing his horrible death, and following this almost immediately with a vivid description of the monstrous glove and Grendel's intention to stow Beowulf and all his men in it all enhance, for Hygelac, the effect of cumulative terror achieved by even more grisly effects in the earlier narrative. Once more the two accounts, closely similar in their strategy, are accommodated to two different audiences. Again in Beowulf's report, we have additions rather than discrepancies.

I find no discrepancy between 2091b and 745 ff. Beowulf tells Hygelac that, after devouring Hondscio, Grendel took hold of Beowulf himself; 746 ff. tell us the same thing. In 747a ff. the poet says that Beowulf was *at that moment* on his couch, but immediately grappled with Grendel and rose to his feet. In the earlier account, as in the report to Hygelac, what caused Grendel's defeat (and consequently his powerlessness to put Beowulf and his men in the *glof,*) was not the hero's first grip of Grendel's arm, but his *rising* and grappling closely with the troll. This is obvious from a collation of 2091b–2092:

> hyt ne mihte swa,
> syððan ic on yrre   *uppriht astod,*

with 758–761:

> Gemunde þa se goda   mæg Hygelaces
> æfenspræce,   *uplang astod*
> ond him fæste wiðfeng;   fingras burston;
> eoten wæs utweard,   eorl furþur stop.

The two accounts are completely consistent. In his report, Beowulf merely omits to say that he *had been* lying down; but this is implied in the line *syððan ic on yrre   uppriht astod.*

"In *A',*" Magoun tells us, "the hero cuts off Grendel's mother's head, in *A* (ll. 1588–1590) he cuts off Grendel's. One may well imagine that there were two traditions as to whose head was cut off . . . and that the singer of *A* was basically a Grendel's head man, the singer of *A'* a Grendel's mother's head man." [13] Magoun failed to observe that, in 1565–1568, we are specifically told that Beowulf ended his fight with Grendel's mother by cutting off *her* head even before he decapitated Grendel:

> yrringa sloh,
> þæt hire wið halse   heard grapode,
> banhringas bræc;   bil eal ðurhwod
> fægne flæschoman . . . .

Magoun finds other discrepancies in the account of the "banquets" in Heorot: what is told of the banquet after the defeat of Grendel "in *A'* is quite different from *A* and much of what is said of the corresponding banquet in *A* is in *A'* transferred to the banquet which follows the death of Grendel's mother." Again: "In *A'* the major banquet comes after the slaying of Grendel's mother and with it lavish presents; on the corresponding occasion in *A* (ll. 1783b–1784) no presents are given though they are promised for the next morning." [14] Actually, neither in the main narrative ("*A*") nor in Beowulf's report to Hygelac ("*A'* ") *is there any mention of a banquet after the death of Grendel's dam.* In the poet's story a banquet would have been quite out of place: the Danes, believing Beowulf slain, are in a despairing rather than a celebrating mood, until Beowulf's appearance with Grendel's head comes with the suddenness of a clap of thunder. There is, then, no justification for the view that "the varied arrangements of the banquets and present-giving would seem to reflect two traditions, one knowing it as in *A,* the other as in *A'*." [15]

Magoun tells us: "In *A* the gifts receive much attention (ll. 1020–1053a, 1193b–1200) whereas in *A'* they are disposed of in three verses (ll. 2102–2103b) the big presents come later (ll. 2142–2176)." Herein he has misunderstood the poet's purpose and method. In the earlier narrative, it is true, the gifts given Beowulf after the defeat of Grendel are listed and described at length; after the slaying of Grendel's dam, Hrothgar promises to give gifts on the morrow (1783b–1784); and though the promise is kept, we are told only that Hrothgar gave him "twelve treasures" (*maþmas twelfe*) which are not described. In his report to Hygelac, the hero says merely that Hrothgar had given him many rewards after the killing of Grendel (2101–2103b), and "many treasures" after the killing of Grendel's dam; again the gifts are neither specified nor described (2142–2143). But *all* the gifts given him are listed and described, in the poet's words (except for Beowulf's account of the war-gear that had once been Heorogar's) in 2152–2176.

The poet's method of procedure in his original account and in "*A'* " is identical. Just as in 1020–1053a, 1193b–1200, he had described Hrothgar's gifts in detail, as they were given to the hero, so now, in 2152–2166a and 2172–2176, the poet again enumerates and describes the gifts as Beowulf gives them to Hygelac and Hygd. This complete uniformity between the earlier and later accounts—the describing of the gifts only as they are bestowed—is evidence that a single poet

composed the whole of Part I (1–2199). And this is done for a purpose: As the original bestowal of the gifts upon Beowulf was testimony to the hero's valor and to Hrothgar's munificence, so Beowulf's
giving them to his beloved uncle and lord stresses the love and loyalty
between them—which is the theme sounded and re-emphasized in the
closing lines of Part I.

Magoun argues that there are "some remarkably close similarities
and some very marked differences" between the two accounts in the
nature of the gifts. He regards *eofor* (2152) as "somewhat uncertain"; but whether we take *eofor heafodsegn* as a three-member compound (which seems unlikely) or, with Klaeber, take the combination
as asyndetic parataxis [16] the banner or standard in question—which
the poet terms *segen gyldenne* (1021a) and in a variation *hroden
hildecumbor* (1022a; MS *hiltecumbor*)—is surely to be thought of as
of much the same type as the beautiful specimen from Sutton Hoo,
but surmounted by the figure of a boar rather than that of a stag.
Magoun admits that "the next four gifts are in *A* and *A'* identical and
are introduced in the same order." [17]

The first real discrepancy, in Magoun's view, is that "In l. 1021
these [gifts] are given Béowulf by Hróthgár, in l. 2147b Béowulf
says in effect that he was allowed to select them (*on minne selfes
dóm*)." [18] But 2146b reads: *ac he me (maðma)s geaf,* which certainly
signifies "giving" as plainly as the *Forgeaf* of 1020; moreover *selfes
dom* does not necessarily carry the implication of "selection" among
a presumably more extensive number of gifts brought out and displayed. If the poet had meant any such thing, he would presumably
have said so more explicitly. In 895 *selfes dome* carries no suggestion
of selection: *þæt he beahhordes brucan moste/ selfes dome. . . .*
The meaning here seems to be "to do with according to his own judgment"; and I take this to be the meaning of *on minne selfes dom* in
2147b. That is, Hrothgar left Beowulf free to dispose of the gifts as
he wished; this interpretation is supported by the verses immediately
following (2148–2149a): *ða ic ðe, beorncyning, bringan wylle,/
estum geywan.* Surely there is no discrepancy here.

In the matter of the horses given Beowulf, Magoun finds what seems
to him a striking inconsistency: "In *A* there are eight with gold-plated
bridles (ll. 1035–1037a), and all are presented at the same time along
with one most handsome saddle . . . that was Hróthgár's personal
possession. In *A'* there are seven horses and they are given in two
installments, first four (ll. 2163 ff.) and no harness, then (ll. 2174b–

2175a) three finely saddled horses given him by Wealhthéow." [19] Here, too, the discrepancy is imaginary. Hrothgar gave Beowulf eight horses; there is neither any statement nor any intimation anywhere in the poem that they were given in two installments, nor that any of them were given by Wealhtheow. Magoun has misread the text: what 2163–2166, 2172–2175a actually say is that Beowulf gave four of his horses to Hygelac *and three to Hygd:*

> feower mearas
> lungre, gelice   last weardode,
> æppelfealuwe;   he him est geteah
> meara ond maðma . . . .

> Hyrde ic þæt he þone healsbeah   Hygde gesealde,
> wrætlicne wundurmaððm,   ðone him Wealhtheow geaf,
> ðeodnes dohtor,   þrio wicg somod
> swancor ond sadolbeorht.

Þrio wicg is the object, not of *geaf,* but of *gesealde.* The disposal of the eighth horse is suggested by Klaeber's question, in his note to 2172a: "How many of the presents did Beowulf keep for himself?" The answer is one horse, presumably that which bore Hrothgar's war-saddle. Here the poet can be charged with no more than the omission of very insignificant detail.

It surprises Magoun that "If *A*'s *hrægl* is *A"*'s *hildesceorp* and if *A* knew the connection with Heorugár, . . . he makes no mention of it when *hrægl* is referred to." [20] An interesting point, and not without weight; though it may be worth remembering that Hrothgar gave Beowulf *two* corselets (*byrnan,* 1022b; *hrægl,* 1195a). If either of these is identical with the *hildesceorp* of 2155a, it must be remembered that in 1020–1045 the poet is primarily concerned to communicate the splendor, rather than the history, of Hrothgar's gifts; and that the giving of the *hrægl* in 1195 is immediately linked with both the tragic passages in which Wealhtheow appeals to Hrothulf and to Beowulf to protect her sons, and the first report of Hygelac's death. In short, when he mentions either of the corselets in his direct narrative, he is more immediately concerned with more important things. But in Beowulf's report, where there is nothing to interrupt or detract from the hero's presentation of the gifts to Hygelac, he can very appropriately begin his presentation speech with the history of the corselet—which Hrothgar has commanded him to do in any case (2156–2157).

"It is equally curious that A' knows nothing of the remarkable magic sword (ll. 1588 ff., 1677) of which so much is made in A." [21] Why curious? The one appropriate place for it is precisely the place selected by the poet: in the direct narrative of the hero's combat with Grendel's dam, the issue of which is decided by its edges—and at the moment when Beowulf places it in Hrothgar's hands. This last is one of the two most powerful and dramatic moments of the first part of the poem, skillfully signalized by the break between *Hrothgar maðelode* (1687a) and the first words of his speech (1700 ff.). This gap is filled by a description of the writings or pictures on the hilt and guards, among them a representation of God's destruction of the giants, which deliberately echoes 1679b–1680: *hit on æht gehwearf/ æfter deofla hryre Denigea frean.* There is no such dramatic situation in Beowulf's report to Hygelac; there the whole combat with Grendel's dam is summed up in seven lines, which tell all that Hygelac needs to know.

In his comment on the "feasts" in Heorot, Magoun observes: "As in A there is said to have been singing but in A there is mention of only one particular song, the Finn Episode, while in A' there seems to be both traditional songs (*feorran reahte*, l. 2106b) and lyrics (ll. 2108b–09). This last is a small matter but not small at all is the difference in the identification of the singer who in A is Hróthgár's court scop . . . , in A' the Scielding king himself." [22]

The singer at the feast following Grendel's defeat is indeed Hrothgar's scop, who evidently sang several traditional songs (*gid oft wrecen*, 1065b) of which only the lay of Finn and Hengest is reported in detail. The "songs" mentioned in Beowulf's report are not specified at all; indeed they may not have been songs, though 2107–2108a seem to imply that Hrothgar sang: *hwilum hildedeor hearpan wynne/ gomenwudu grette.* . . . Beowulf says that *þær wæs gidd ond gleo* (2105a), that Hrothgar "touched the harp," and *hwilum gyd awræc soð ond sarlic* ("told a true and grievous tale" [or "saying"]) and lamenting his loss of youth and strength, recalled with emotion many things (2108b–2114). The meaning of *gidd ond gleo* is uncertain: it may denote minstrelsy and song, or merely conversation and mirth; and we cannot be sure that 2105a refers to Hrothgar's actions as described in 2105b–2114. *Gidd* (*gyd*) may denote song, or merely formal, solemn speech; and the sole evidence that Hrothgar sang is the statement that he "touched the harp"; but this is set off from all that follows (as each of Hrothgar's actions here is set off from the next) by *hwilum . . . hwilum . . . hwilum*. This adverb serves to indicate alternate or successive acts. If we interpret these acts as Beowulf reports them in terms of the poet's narrative in 1709a–1778a, we shall discover the probable nature of Hrothgar's utterances, and see that there is perfect congruence between the two accounts. The *gyd . . . soð ond sarlic,* and the *syllic spell,* surely refer to Hrothgar's tale of the tyranny and greed of Heremod, and the woe which he brought upon his people and himself; these are the things that Hrothgar *feorran rehte* and *rehte æfter rihte.* That 2105b ff. allude, not to traditional songs or lyrics, but to the contents of Hrothgar's long monologue in 1709–1778 is proved by Beowulf's specific emphasis upon the Danish king's lament for his lost youth and strength, so impressively set forth in 1769–1778a. That *gyd,* in 2108b refers to that magnificent monologue, and not to the singing of songs, is clearly implied in 1723b–1724a: *Ic þis gid be þe/ awræc wintrum frod.* Observe how beautifully these verses accord with 2108b–2109a, 2113b–2114 of Beowulf's report: *hwilum gyd awræc/ soð ond sarlic, . . . hreðer inne weoll,/ þonne he wintrum frod worn gemunde.*

So far, then, I can find no actual discrepancies between the two accounts, and there is no ground for assuming two distinct traditions contained in independent songs pieced together by an anthologizing scribe. The evidence points clearly to well-controlled, carefully structured composition by a single poet.

So far; but there is one striking discrepancy, which I have already discussed elsewhere.[23] In his earlier narrative, the poet placed Hrothgar's monologue after the death of Grendel's dam; but in his report to Hygelac, Beowulf places it at the feast following the defeat of Grendel. This is the kind of lapse of memory much more likely to be made by a single poet working with complex material, and faced with the necessity of retelling, in drastically condensed form, what he had earlier told at great length, than by two poets working with different traditions. In Beowulf's report the poet had to let his hero account for two different, yet basically similar situations: similar in that, in each, Hrothgar is filled with gratitude and joy at his deliverance from a monster, and is moved to express his gratitude in "wise words." Such lapses are far from rare in extended narrative: any publisher's editor can cite examples from authors' manuscripts, and there are many instances in published works.

In his later paper Magoun argues that the Second Part of *Beowulf* (*"Béowulf B"*) was "originally an independent work like *A'* soldered on to what precedes. . . . Such a view can in fact do no more than remove from the literary scene the conception of an unknown and unknowable poet or singer who composed the *Béowulf* of the editions in a single and continuous effort." [24] Unhappily it would substitute for the conception of one poet that of three, equally unknown and unknowable.

Magoun advances three general arguments before considering specific details. First:

Seldom if ever does a folk-singer, composing extemporaneously without benefit of writing materials, compose a cyclic poem, that is, sing in a single session or series of sessions a story which he or she feels is a unit dealing with several consecutive events in a character's life. Oral singers normally sing episodically, treating of some discrete body of material, be it the ten months [*sic*] of the Trojan War in the *Iliad* or Völundr's kidnapping and escape in the Eddic *Völundarkiða*. . . . In view of a general lack of cyclic composition in oral singing the apparent cyclic character of the *Béowulf* material in Brit. Mus. Ms Cotton Vitellius A. XV is *a priori* immediately suspect. [25]

This argument is obviously dependent upon the assumption that the author of *Beowulf* was a "folksinger, composing extemporaneously without benefit of writing materials"—an assumption by no means universally accepted, and which many competent critics reject. It is quite true that the Germanic heroic lays known to us (the *Finnsburg Fragment,* the *Hildebrandslied,* and the heroic lays of the *Elder Edda*), which were composed orally, are not cyclic, but deal with a single situation, or at most with two closely related situations. They were short songs, and the type to which they belong was fixed before the age of writing. When two or more such lays (for example, the Sigurd lays of the *Edda*) deal with the same legendary story, each represents a strictly limited action: generally they treat different phases of the story, or treat it from different points of view. Magoun cites *Reginsmál* and *Fáfnismál* as instances of "two songs making up a little cycle and . . . likely enough concatenated by the scribe of the Codex Regius." [26] Right enough; one might also cite *Guðrúnarhuöt* and

Hamðismál. Beowulf, on the other hand, is a very long poem, not only longer than any known lay, but utterly different in pace and in narrative manner. Indeed, it is almost as different from the typical heroic lay as the relevant parts of *Paradise Lost* are from *Genesis B.*

Magoun's second general argument is that there is an "extraordinarily large time-gap between *Béowulf A-A'* and *Béowulf B.*" [27] True; and deliberately and properly so, as Tolkien and Malone have made clear to us.[28] In fact, this "general argument" is made up of a series of particulars, each intended to support the others: the time-gap is great; Part I "ends up with a somewhat curious miscellany of remarks (ll. 2177–99) that seems only casually to concern what precedes or follows";[29] Part II begins in "an almost jolting fashion"; 2200 "would seem to represent a transition verse substituted by some anthologizing scribe" for "some original verses more appropriate for starting a brand new story";[30] 2200 is "so very mechanical."[31]

This amounts to saying that 2177–2199 are incoherent in themselves and unrelated to the rest of the poem; and that 2200 is a crude interpolation substituted for some hypothetical lines which would have introduced the line sequence 2201 ff. more effectively—and perhaps have filled, or softened the effect of the time-gap. But Magoun concedes that "apart from verse 2200 the rest of the opening passage may well be original";[32] and he should have seen that both syntactically and lexically 2201 ff. depend upon 2200. Whether that line is jolting and mechanical or not is beside the point: it is a vital part of its context. In 1–2199 the poet has told us all he had to tell of Beowulf's earlier career; now, to implement his "opposition of ends and beginnings," he must sweep away the machinery and setting for his hero's youthful exploits to clear the stage for the old king's heroic end. In Tolkien's words: "the poem was not meant to advance, steadily or unsteadily. . . . In its simplest terms it is a contrasted description of two moments in a great life, rising and falling; an elaboration of the ancient and intensely moving contrast between youth and age, first achievement and final death."[33] Line 2200 cannot be separated from the rest of the sentence of which it is a part. It tells us that many years have elapsed since the action of Part I; and the lines immediately following report, with utmost brevity, the major events that had occurred in those years—the deaths of Beowulf's uncle and cousin, and the consequences of those deaths: Beowulf has become king, and has now reigned for fifty years. The conclusion of this long sentence intimates (2210b) that in consequence of a dragon's ravages the hero's long life and reign must end. This transitional passage, bridging the gap between Part I and Part II, achieves its purpose—with breathless haste indeed; but later on (2354–2400) that haste is compensated by a satisfyingly expanded account.

I cannot agree with Magoun's estimate of 2177–2199. I find the passage neither curious nor a miscellany; surely it has the clearest connection with what precedes and follows. Lines 2177–2183a draw a purposeful contrast between Beowulf, the strong and noble champion, gentle toward his hearth-companions, and Heremod (though the latter is not named, the implication is obvious) composed in recollection of Hrothgar's monologue (cf. 1713: *breat bolgenmod beodgeneatas,* with 2179b–2180a: *nealles druncne sloh/ heorðgeneatas . . .*). In similar vein, in 2166b–2171, the poet implies a similar contrast between Beowulf and Hrothulf. The closing lines of Part I relate the presentation by Hygelac of a sword and the gift of a splendid estate to Beowulf, and assert strongly the affectionate relation between Hygelac and his loyal nephew. The relation of this to what precedes is clear; it bears a definite relation to what follows. In Part I Beowulf is portrayed as valiant champion and faithful thane to Hygelac; in Part II he is, first, self-sacrificingly loyal regent for the dead Hygelac's son, and then wise and protective ruler of his people. As Part I ends with a strong affirmation of the loyal love of Beowulf and Hygelac each to the other, so Part II opens with the announcement of the deaths of Hygelac and Heardred, which alone could end that relationship. But since it was founded in love, loyalty to Hygelac lives on undiminished in Beowulf's heart, as 2434b, 2490–2506a eloquently attest. Thus 2177–2199 form a very real link between the entire scene in Hygelac's court and the action of Part II, in which Beowulf, as king of the people once Hygelac's, must act as their champion, as earlier he had been Hygelac's thane.

"Furthermore," Magoun continues, "if we had to do with a singer who had set out to compose a cyclic song about Beowulf's career, it might strike one as odd that he did not include between Béowulf *A-A'* and *B* the story of Hygelac's death in the Rhineland, a story . . . with which the *B*-singer in particular shows himself so familiar."[34] But the poet *does* mention Hygelac's death in 2201, which—especially in view of Magoun's rejection of 2200—is as close to a position between Part I and Part II as possible. A fuller version has already been given in 1202–1214a; line 2201b is a clear allusion to that earlier account, and takes for granted the audience's familiarity with it. Later on (2354b–2379a) the poet, following his consistent practice of reverting to important aspects of the story which he has told before, once more recalls Hygelac's fall, and tells us of Beowulf's heroic resistance to the Franks, his escape home, Hygd's offer to him of the crown, and his refusal to deprive Heardred of his inheritance. Just as 2201b is a back-reference to 1202–1214a, so 2202–2206 look forward to 2378b–2390, which narrate the whole story of Heardred's accession, his rash involvement in the dynastic quarrels of the Svear, his death, and Beowulf's accession to the throne. This is the same kind of retrospect and anticipation which is characteristic of the whole poem: this uniform narrative procedure affords the strongest evidence that both parts were composed by the same author. A further account of Hygelac's last battle is put in the hero's mouth (2490–2508a); and we are told of it again when Wiglaf's Messenger informs the Geats of Beowulf's death, and ascribes to Hygelac's Frisian raid the hatred felt by Franks and Frisians for the Geats. Each of these four accounts has its own tone and emphasis; each presents details not earlier reported. The poet's procedure is exactly the same as that employed in Part I, in the three several accounts of the slaying of Grendel and his dam; each omits certain details already told; and each presents details not earlier reported. Far from indicating plural authorship, these all illustrate a consistent narrative manner, which points to single authorship.[35]

Turning to "specific features which seem to me to confirm a view . . . which led me to think of the *B*-singer as an altogether different person from the *A* or *A'* singer," Magoun notes first the contrast between the treatment of the Scylding dynasty in 4–63 and the accounts of the Hrethling dynasty in 2354–2379a, 2379b–2390, and 2426–2443.[36] The contrast is indeed marked; and so it should be. In 4–63 the poet was concerned to set the stage for the major action of Part I. Broadly speaking, this passage is a true Germanic genealogy, with brief comment on each of the Scylding kings, and a longer and very beautiful description of the funeral ceremonies of Scyld, the founder of the line. In its listings and characterizations of the successive members of a dynasty it reminds us of *Ynglingatál*. It is an introduction, so framed as to impress upon the audience the glory and power of the Danes, culminating in Hrothgar's reign and the building of Heorot. This is as it should be: for it is in Hrothgar's reign and in Heorot that Beowulf is to manifest his valor and strength. The purpose of this genealogy is to enhance the hero's glory, by furnishing his exploits with an appropriately splendid background and *mise-en-scène*.

In Part II the situation is quite different. There the closest approach to true genealogy is in 2428–2443, in which Beowulf speaks of Hrethel and his sons. But here the purpose is not genealogical, but emotional and elegiac: it is not the poet who speaks, listing members of a dynasty; it is the hero, expressing his love and gratitude to Hrethel, sorrowfully recalling the tragic killing of Herebeald by Hæthcyn, and Hrethel's broken-hearted death. The elegiac tone is carried further, into his telling of the death of Hæthcyn, and reaching its climax in his recollection of the fall of Beowulf's beloved uncle Hygelac. And this fulfills a dual purpose: it gives us a glimpse into the hero's heart, and informs us how Beowulf came to the throne, and how faithfully, until Heardred's death, he performed his duty to Hygelac's son. The assistance which he gives Eadgils against Onela is, in effect, an act of vengeance for Heardred—the hero's last service to his uncle's son.

So much Beowulf, and the poet, tell us. The long speech of Wiglaf's Messenger contains no genealogizing at all: its exciting and highly personalized narrative of Hæthcyn's raid into Sweden, initially successful and then disastrous, and of the vengeance taken for Hæthcyn's death, is delivered with strict impartiality and is intended to account for that embittered hatred of the Geats by the Svear which will ultimately result in the ruin of the Geatish nation. The opening lines of the speech make this clear: they foretell "a time of strife, when the death of the King (Beowulf) becomes openly known to Franks and Frisians," the former have not forgotten Hygelac's raid; the Svear still have Ongentheow's death to avenge.

The information given us about the Scylfing dynasty is, similarly, not genealogical in any proper sense; it is given us, by necessity, to account for the stages in that long feud which progressively weakened the Geats, and culminated in their end as a nation after Beowulf's death. Moreover the apprehension of the fatality overhanging the Geats is first felt in Beowulf's monologue (2426–2508a), and as the poet, Wiglaf, and the Messenger develop the theme of the feud with the Svear, this apprehension works upon our minds cumulatively, as the intimations, in Part I, of tragedy impending over the House of Hrothgar do not. It is fitting, therefore, that the treatment of the Scylding dynasty in Part I, and that of the Hrethlings and Scylfings in Part II, should have been managed quite differently.

Magoun feels that "the *B*-singer is obviously far more interested in the Rhineland episode than in the Heorot adventure . . . when Béowulf reminisces about the former strength of his grip, he thinks of the time when he crushed the Frank Dæghrefn to death (ll. 2501–8a), not of Grendel." [37] But this—so far as it is true—is evidence, not of different authorship, but of the poet's proper concern for time, place, and circumstance. The action of Part II is separated from Beowulf's adventures in Denmark by approximately sixty-five years; the scene of Part II is the Geatish homeland; its matter is Beowulf's last fight and death, and their tragic consequences: it is on these matters that the interest of poet and audience alike is focused. In Part II, the troll-killings of Part I are matter for only minor interest; but the significance of Hygelac's death for the story of the hero and the tragedy of his people is still matter of consequence. The two brief allusions (2351–2354a, 2521) in Part II to the combats with Grendel and his dam—once in the poet's words, once in Beowulf's—are sufficient to show that neither had forgotten them. The poet was too great an artist to encumber the narrative of his hero's death with long-drawn reminiscence of deeds which belonged to Beowulf's long-past youth.

Moreover it is right that, *in the context of his personal recollection of Hygelac's fall,* Beowulf should think of having killed Dæghrefn with his hands since, in slaying the Frankish champion, he was avenging Hygelac. [38] But Magoun has forgotten that Beowulf *does* call to mind his killing Grendel with his hands. Only ten lines after recalling his victory over Dæghrefn, he explains his intent to use weapons against the dragon, not because he no longer possesses the strength of his youth, but because the dragon holds resources which make it impossible to come to handgrips with him (2518b–2524a):

> Nolde ic sweord beran,
> wæpen to wyrme, gif ic wiste hu
> wið ðam aglæcan elles meahte
> gylpe wiðgripan, *swa ic gio wið Grendle dyde;*
> ac ic ðær heaðufyres hates wene,
> (o)reðes ond attres; forðon ic me on hafu
> bord ond byrnan.

Magoun notes that there occur in the poem only six instances of A-verses "in which the second measure is filled out with the masc. acc. sing. *þone* of the demonstrative *sé,* giving in effect an unusual postpositive use of the article." [39] These six are: *uhthlem þone* (2007); *eorðweard þone* (2334b); *grundwong þone* (2588a); *freoðwong þone* (2959a); *wælhlem þone* (2969b); and *goldweard þone* (3081b).

Magoun finds no other instances of this type of A-verse anywhere in Anglo-Saxon poetry. "It is striking," he observes, "that five of these six examples occur in *Béowulf B,* only one (l. 2007b) in the far shorter *Béowulf A',* and none at all in the quite long *Béowulf A. . . .* These formulaic systems—for so such verses may be described—would seem to be somehow characteristic of the *B*-singer's verse-making habits and thus to set him off from the *A*-singer and the singers of other recorded Anglo-Saxon songs." [40]

But in view of the rarity of this type of A-verse, the distribution of its occurrences does not appear very significant. It appears once in the 168 lines of *"Beowulf A' "*; five times in the 982 lines of *"Beowulf B"*—that is, once in every 196 lines of Part II; but it does not occur at all in the 254 lines between 2334 and 2588, nor in the 370 lines between 2589 and 2959. Would Magoun maintain that these 254 and 370 lines respectively are *not* the work of the poet of *"Beowulf B"*? Since this type of A-verse never occurs at all except in *Beowulf,* in the whole surviving poetic corpus, the lack of any instances in 1–2006 appears quite meaningless. Moreover, in the six instances noted there is good reason for the postposition of the article. Klaeber pointed out that "Type A admits in the second foot a short stressed syllable. . . . There occur several very doubtful instances of a short stressed syllable in the first foot." [41] To have placed the article in its usual position before the substantive compound would, in all six cases, have resulted in a very rare and dubious verse. The transposition of the article may very well have been deliberate, to avoid bad verse. Much more and much stronger metrical and stylistic evidence must be produced before Magoun's view can be accepted. As Chambers wrote concerning Schücking's argument from unusual uses of moods and tenses: "Now a large number of instances like this last might afford basis for argument; but they must be in bulk to prove anything." [42]

It is interesting, moreover, that in each of the six verses in question the substantive compound constituting the first foot is found only in *Beowulf.* I have pointed out elsewhere that compound *hapax legomena* in *Beowulf* exceed, both in number and in proportion, those in any other poem.[43] Since this type of A-verse, and the key-word in all six cases as well, appear only in *Beowulf,* may we not ascribe them to the personal taste of the poet?

Magoun finds evidence for difference of authorship in the conflicting statements about Beowulf's youth (2183–2188a, 2430–2434).[44] They *do* conflict; but their mutual inconsistency does not prove that both were not made by the same poet. The conflict means, at most, that the poet drew upon two different traditions. In Part II, all of which Magoun ascribes to the *"B*-singer," there are two "Different and contradictory accounts of the early history of the treasure" guarded by the dragon: [45] ll. 2231–2270; 3069–3075. Does this require us to break up Part II into *"Beowulf B"* and *"Beowulf B'"*?

The difference between the two statements about Beowulf's youth poses a difficult problem. Stories of heroes whose great achievements come suddenly, after a period of youthful sluggishness, are not uncommon in folktale and legend; a very striking case is that of Offa I. That a hero who testifies to his own youthful exploits as Beowulf does (415–424a, 2426–2427a), and whose heroic qualities are manifested to us throughout the poem, should be described by the poet as inglorious in youth, has troubled scholars and given rise to various explanations. One problem is that of chronology: at what point in Beowulf's early life are we to place the inglorious period? Malone's view, that it "presumably came in his young manhood," after his first boyish exploits,[46] and after Hrethel's death, has the great merit of resolving the major inconsistency between the two passages: if we follow Malone, we can accept both Beowulf's own assertion that Hrethel held him in as high esteem as any of his own sons, and gave him treasure and feasting, and the poet's statement that the Geats long held Beowulf in slight esteem and that their king thought him "not worthy of much on the mead-bench." The heart of 2183b–2188a is: *swyðe wendon þæt he sleac wære,/ æðling unfrom.* This calls to mind Saxo's account of Offa's youth: *Hic Uffo coæuos quosque corporis habitu supergressus, adeo hebetis ineptique animi principio iuuentæ existimatus est, ut priuatis ac publicis rebus inutilis uideretur.* If we accept Malone's view the analogy is imperfect, for Offa, like most male Cinderellas, passed through an originally inglorious period into one of great glory, not through a sequence of glorious early youth, inglorious later youth, and heroic manhood.

Malone's time-scheme raises problems of its own, which have been discussed by Bonjour.[47] But what concerns us here is not to decide between their views, but to face the issue raised by Magoun: the discrepancy between 415 ff., 2430 ff., on the one hand, and 2183–2188a on the other. This troubled Klaeber, who felt that "the motive of the sluggish youth is, somewhat awkwardly, added to his (Beowulf's) person," [48] and Miss Bartlett regarded it as artistically unjustified.[49] Could the same poet have given us two widely contrasting accounts of his hero's youth?

The problem has been somewhat complicated by Magoun's shift of

ground between 1958 and 1963; in his earlier paper he had set the
bounds of *"A'"* as from 2009b to 2176; but in *"Béowulf B"* he wrote:
"It seems to me hard to assign these verses (2183b–2189), to decide
whether they form part of *Béowulf A* (with *A'* wedged in between)
or of *Béowulf A'* or whether they are altogether separate. . . ." [50]
Now, if the lines about the sluggish youth belong to *"A',"* they have
no relevance whatever to the question of one "singer" for 1–2009a and
another for 2200–3182; the inconsistency would be between Magoun's
"A'" and *"B."* To regard them as "altogether separate" would raise
the rather grotesque phantom of still a fourth *Beowulf* "singer," or
leave us with the slippery issue of interpolation.

I have elsewhere explained the inconsistency in question in these
terms: "the author's fondness for contrast misled him into attempting
to enhance Beowulf's heroism in young manhood by setting it off
against an imagined sluggishness in youth. The flaw lies in the total
absence of anything outside this passage to support a tale of the hero's
earlier inactivity. It seems probable that a 'male Cinderella' tradition
had associated itself with the figure of Beowulf, and that the poet,
knowing of it, made the mistake of using it . . . the only error of
taste is to be found in the tale of Beowulf's sluggish youth, which is
out of harmony with the hero's character and career as these had already been represented." [51]

Today I give far greater weight to the views of Malone [52] and
Bonjour, who have seen the problem more clearly. Both perceived that
the poet's deliberate contrast between Beowulf and Heremod, implied
in 2179–2183a, does not end there, but extends through 2189. The
contrast is twofold: (1) Beowulf, unlike Heremod, "did not slay his
drunken hearth-companions; his was not a savage spirit, but, brave
in battle, he maintained with greatest strength the ample gift which
God had given him"; and (2) Heremod was a mighty prince, of whose
promising beginnings great things were expected; but he became greedy
and tyrannical and brought calamity on his people; Beowulf, on the
other hand, conducted himself graciously and nobly once he had out-
grown his early sluggishness. "Thus we have indeed a poor beginning
followed by a prodigious ascent contrasted with a brilliant promise
ending in a miserable downfall!" [53]

This is surely right. In the *Comments* added, in 1962, to his earlier
paper, Bonjour justly concludes that the story of Beowulf's inert youth
is "artistically justified in its immediate context"; and that "the deliberate effect of surprise, far from being detrimental to our opinion of

the hero, makes his ascent the more extraordinary and skilfully serves to enhance his glory." [54] I now fully agree with Bonjour that "The flaw therefore lies not in the poet's use of the sluggish youth motive as such, but in his later allowing Beowulf to make a statement that cannot possibly agree with it." Bonjour concurs with me that the poet, "although, for the most part, he has seen his story whole, and managed it with remarkable unity and consistency . . . , could, at times, become so fascinated with the moment that, in his desire to achieve a particular effect here and now, he could forget or ignore what he had told us before." [55]

But there is a possibility of yet another resolution of the problem— a solution adumbrated by Malone, and very clearly suggested (see notes 52–54) by Bonjour, to whom, in the following, I am deeply indebted. The account of the hero's sluggish youth is given by the poet for a purpose admirably stated by these two scholars; but 2430 ff. are spoken by Beowulf himself, and express his love for and gratitude to King Hrethel. This passage is, moreover, an integral part of his fond recollections of his Hrethling kinsmen, and sets forth, with deep sympathy, his sorrow at their tragic fates. In the course of this long monologue Beowulf gives great attention to the tragedy which cost the life of Hrethel's eldest son, and caused the old king to die of grief. The elegiac passage on the old man whose son is hanged (2444–2462) is a kind of mourning in parable for Hrethel's tragedy; *Swa Wedra helm* (2462b) makes this clear. Beowulf was deeply indebted to Hrethel for his fostering; and 2428 ff. acknowledge his gratitude in terms which suggest that he may have felt the old king's kindness to him disproportionate to his deserts.

Now if we turn back to 416–424a, it appears probable that Beowulf is there narrating his sudden transformation from the sluggish youth to hero; his insistence that the wise warriors among the Geats had themselves looked on as he returned victorious from this exploit, and recognized his strength, strongly suggests this. Lines 2426 ff. would, then, resolve the inconsistency between the lines on the sluggish youth and 2430 ff. The less we try to chop the poem into separate songs, the more we look at it as a whole, the more coherence and excellence it assumes.

Magoun concedes that "there is one great unity, namely, the consistency of the hero's character. Everywhere his nobility, courage, gentleness, youthful strength and eagerness to leave behind a fair name (*dóm*) emerges." In the following sentences, however, he presses his view of the oral composition of *Beowulf*: "In a lettered work such consistency would ordinarily point to the consistent conception on the part of a single poet and, if applied to the *Béowulf* material, would strongly suggest unity of authorship. In an oral, folk tradition, however, such an offhand conclusion can scarcely be drawn, for in such a tradition the basic familiar character will normally be the same everywhere and among all singers." [56]

But oral composition of *Beowulf* has not been proved; it has merely been asserted on the evidence of the formulaic character of its diction. But we should heed Claes Schaar's caution in using such evidence: "the proposition that 'all formulaic poetry is oral' does not follow, either logically or psychologically, from the proposition 'all oral poetry is formulaic' "—a point which should be self-evident, and which has recently been strongly reinforced in an admirable article by Larry D. Benson.[57] Moreover, consistency of characterization in the *Kalevals* and in Yugoslav minstrel poetry, which Magoun cites as illustrative evidence, has little bearing on characterization in *Beowulf*, which is definitely *not* a folk poem.

For that matter, uniformity in "the basic conception of an important character" is by no means universal: consider the very different representations of Hrothulf in *Beowulf* and Hrólfr in *Hrólfssaga*, of Hagen in the *Kudrun-Waltharius* and Hagen in the *Nibelungenlied*, of Guðrún in the Eddic lays against Kriemhilt in the *Nibelungenlied*, or of Attila in South German against Scandinavian tradition. Magoun's view that "the consistency of Béowulf's character throughout the preserved material is in itself no argument for unity of authorship, no more in fact, than is the high degree of consistency in the style, diction, and syntax of the poetic corpus in general" [58] is anything but sound. All Old English poetry is formulaic in greater or less degree; but apart from formula there are marked and significant differences in style and diction between one poem and another; and the richness and beauty of the diction and style of *Beowulf* set it apart from all other poems in the corpus. *Exodus*, for all the formulas that it shares with *Beowulf*, or with other poems, is unique in the vivid, and often startling, sharpness of its figures and turns of phrase. *Juliana* differs markedly in style and rhetoric from *Judith*; *Andreas*, for all its borrowings from *Beowulf*, could never be mistaken as by the author of *Beowulf*. *Elene* and *Crist II*, both by Cynewulf, show no "high degree of consistency" in diction or style; and *Phoenix*, in virtue both of its subject and its sources, stands by itself.

Finally, Magoun sees no evidence of single authorship in the consistency of Hrothgar's "prophecy" (1845b–1853a) with the account of Beowulf's accession to the throne in Part II: "To me it only points to the fact that almost any singer who knew any part of the *Béowulf* material was likely . . . to know all parts. . . . This prophecy has no bearing one way or the other on the question of unity of authorship." [59] This amounts to saying that, though an occasional inconsistency in a long poem is proof of multiple authorship, consistency has no value as evidence for single authorship—which is obviously absurd. Moreover, this speech of Hrothgar's is not prophecy at all: Hrothgar says, not "If Hygelac dies, you will become king, provided you see fit to accept the throne"; but "I hold it likely that, if Hygelac dies and you survive, the Geats will have no better to choose as king, if you wish to accept." Of course the poet knew a tradition that the throne had been offered to Beowulf after Hygelac's fall, and even this early in his story meant to use that tradition in Part II. The clause *gyf þu healdan wylt/ maga rice* significantly underlines this intention, and points to a single author; for in 2373 ff. we are told that Beowulf refused the throne which Hygd offered him and loyally served as regent and protector for Heardred until the latter's death. By framing Hrothgar's speech as compliment rather than as prophecy, the poet gave greater force to his later revelation of Beowulf's unselfish loyalty. In this, as in all his other anticipations of events to come, there is not only congruity, but fine artistry as well—an artistry so consistently displayed as to argue strongly for unity of authorship.

I deplore Magoun's characterization of *Beowulf,* or of any of its parts, as a "folk-poem." The English and Scottish traditional ballads are folk poems; *Beowulf* is not. The sluggish youth, the marvelous feats of swimming, the combats with trolls, are the stuff of folk tradition; but the over-all poem, in setting, tone, and manner, and in its consistent exemplification of the Germanic courtly code, is aristocratic rather than popular. The scenes at the Danish court, and the treatment of the feud between Geats and Svear, rest primarily upon old heroic lays and genealogical material; indeed, the main sources are traditional, but the tradition is courtly, not of the folk. The Germanic heroic lays themselves were not folk poems, but court poems, composed by trained scops in the service of princes; they illustrated the courtly code, which was based upon, and reflected, the relations between Germanic prince and *comitatus,* between kinsman and kinsman, and between retainer and lord. They were created and sung both to delight and to instruct

courtly audiences; their themes, and their point of view, were aristocratic. There should have been no need to point this out; Heusler has
made it abundantly clear.[60]

As I wrote some years ago:

Richard Meyer long ago observed that poetry so traditional and heroic
in theme must both concern itself with an ideal and represent this ideal
as typical. The tendency toward idealization affected the poetic vocabulary,
and influenced it toward typical rather than toward individual or repre-
sentational expression. In the heroic lays and eulogies which Germanic
poets were called upon to compose, the situations were typical; the themes
commonly illustrate the ideal relation between warrior and lord, or those
conflicts of duty or of interest which might confront an honorable warrior.
The resolutions inevitably tended to become stereotyped. This poetry
exemplified and maintained the warrior's code, and expressed an ideal of
conduct conditioned by the nature of the Germanic social order.[61]

Under these conditions, and under the pressure of the brevity of its
form, compelling concentration upon a single, central situation, the
heroic lay exhibited its personages typically rather than as clearly de-
lineated individuals. Aside from that group of Eddic lays which Ker
felicitously called "Northern Heroides," I do not know of a single
heroic lay, or heroic fable preserved by chroniclers, which achieves
any real characterization. But in *Beowulf* three persons at least are
clearly and warmly characterized: Beowulf, Hrothgar, and Wealhtheow. Without any physical description, these three stand vividly before our eyes; they are deeply human, as the personages of the lays
are not; they are the creations of a gifted artist. Moreover, the poet
has given personality to Hygelac and Wiglaf as well, though they are
not so fully rounded as the hero and the Danish king and queen. To
have achieved his rich characterization of the hero, the poet had to
carry him through his whole life, even to his heroic end; and it is
worth noting that Hygelac is given additional depth of character
through Beowulf's loving recollection of him in Part II. If the text
as we have it had been a composite of three once-distinct songs, pieced
together by a scribe, and resting in some degree upon different traditions, the solidity of characterization which we admire today could
never have been attained. And there would have been more, and more
disturbing, inconsistencies.

F. G. CASSIDY

A Symbolic Word-Group in *Beowulf*

It has been said that *Beowulf* is bound together by a "unifying technique" which "permits the Christian and pagan elements to coexist meaningfully within the framework of the poem." [1] The hero, clearly depicted in terms of Germanic warrior and dragon-killer (and compared with Siegfried and others) exhibits at the same time virtues belonging to the Christian hero. His life and times are anachronistically, but as if naturally, set in a Christian world (in which, however, pagan beliefs hang on) where both he and the wise old King Hroðgar speak of God as Christians would. Yet because of the absence of emphasis on Christian doctrine, or of any direct mention of Christ (long since noted), the God of *Beowulf* has been called an "Old Testament God." At the same time, the hero's broad resemblance to a Christ-figure can hardly be denied: he is a protector, a purger of hellish monsters; he dies for his people, who sum him up as "mildest of men and gentlest among kings of the world." [2]

As Klaeber once well put it, the Christian interpretation of the main story is "delicately kept in the background." [3] One may suppose that otherwise the poet's "unifying technique" would have broken down. Yet perhaps he saw no need to be more overt. His audience [4] were certainly people who might have been expected to catch Christian allusions—at least the better-known ones—those main ideas of the "Christian story" which churchmen had diligently dwelt on over a period of centuries not only in literal terms but through the secondary means of symbol and tropology.

The Anglo-Saxon clergy and missionaries who attained any degree of learning were familiar with the Bible, the main writings of the Church fathers, and the lives of the saints. By the time of Bede they had accessible, in addition, a good many works of secular Roman liter-

ature, history, and philosophy in one form or another, as full originals
or in anthologies.[5] Even the least learned knew, through Church usage
and sermons, the Pentateuch, the Psalter, and the Gospels as the basic
lore of Christianity. Nevertheless, they obviously clung also to the
traditional Germanic literature, heroic tales and lays, presented and
probably composed orally on established lines with the aid of thematic
structures and verbal formulas. Had it not been for the custom which
Alcuin condemned [6]—still too much alive at the end of the eighth
century to suit him—Caedmon would never have been able, a century
and a half before, to compose his inspired songs. For whether or not
he was the first to pour Christian wine into Anglo-Saxon poetic
bottles, he must necessarily have known the model of heroic verse in
order to adapt it to his uses. Not because song was unfamiliar to him
did he quit the singers at the monastery table, but from timid reluctance to take his turn with the harp. Once the angelic messenger
overcame this timidity and furnished him a subject, Caedmon knew
the proper form to put it into and had no further trouble.

The extent to which his model had already been adapted to Christian use may never be known.[7] But certainly there were many set
phrases in early Latin Christian writing and ceremonial usage which
could have been converted with very little change into Anglo-Saxon
poetic formulas. St. Ambrose's series of epithets for the sun furnish
an example: it is the world's eye, the day's joy, the beauty of heaven,
the grace of nature, greatest of creations [8]—a series reminiscent of
that in *Brunanburh*: God's bright candle, glorious star, noble creation.
By the time this poem was composed, these and others had long since
become cliché.

Our contention in the present paper is that a number of words
hitherto taken to be merely literal in *Beowulf* and other compositions,
formed, for the Christian Anglo-Saxon audience, certain collocations
through association with each other in idea and doctrine; hence, that
when one or more are introduced in the poetry, even in contexts not
overtly Christian, one should suspect the possibility of a second, symbolic or tropological meaning. A good many examples may be found
in Old English poetry,[9] but at present we may limit ourselves to
Beowulf and to a single group of associated words, the first of which
is *sun*.

Though the sun is not made much of in *Beowulf,* the three direct
mentions of it have symbolic overtones. The first is in the Creation
song (92–98) : the sun and moon were "established by the Almighty,

luminaries as lights for land-dwellers." This is intended to be taken
literally, and Klaeber derives it from the perfectly literal *ut lucerent
super terram* of *Genesis* 1 : 17.[10] Even so, the *Beowulf* poet has made
a significant change: it is not merely the earth that is to be illuminated,
but people. The sun (and moon) understood as *leoman to leohte landbuendum* raises a distinct echo of "a light to lighten the gentiles" (in
Simeon's song *lumen ad revelationem gentium*) [11]—hence an allusion
to Christ.

Lest this appear far-fetched, let us remember that the establishment
of the sun as tropologically referring to Christ had occurred certainly
by the second century. In Egypt, Babylonia, Greece, and Rome sun-
worship had flourished before the Christian era. The early Church,
rather than try to uproot it, subsumed it to the Christian purpose. The
sun could not be fully identified with Christ; it is carefully distinguished as a creation: made, not—as Christ—begotten. Nevertheless
there were powerful parallels: it is God's most splendid creation and,
as the source of light, essential to life; and light and life are taken
both literally and spiritually. (God also created light—even before the
sun: *Genesis* 1 : 3–5.)

The substitution of the first day for the Hebrews' seventh day testifies to the power of sun worship. What became the Lord's Day (*dies
dominicus,* whence Italian *Domenico,* Spanish *Domingo,* French
Dimanche, etc.) had been Late Latin *dies solis,*[12] which went into
Germanic languages as *Sunday* and its cognates. Churchmen justified
this change as referring to Christ's resurrection "on the third day,"
the day of crucifixion being the first. But the sun was also a symbol
of resurrection, hence the connection was undeniable. The Romans
celebrated on December 25th the "birthday of the unconquered sun"
(*solis invicti*) ; [13] to this, from the third century, the Church opposed
the feast of the Nativity, in which "the Sun of Righteousness went
forth from the virgin cloud." [14]

Further evidence from early Christian symbol and iconography [15] is
plentiful. Syrian Christians placed a cruciform anagram over the doors
of their houses combining *light* and *life* through their Greek forms
Φ
ZΩH as a name of God, a beneficent and protective talisman.[16] The
C
letters *jhwh,* Jahweh, surrounded by a sun-nimbus were another early
Christian symbol of God.[17] Representations of the Transfiguration
(*Matthew* 17 : 2) are

based on a Roman iconographic formula that goes back to a time before the
flowering of Christian art. It is a formula used to represent the Sun rising
in the sky. . . . It was the Christians who added the aureole or oval disk
of light. The aureole, which shows the illuminated air around the entire
person, is of the same origin as the luminous frame around the head of a
figure, for example, the personified Sun. This nimbus probably comes originally from Mazdean Persia.[18]

The cross, too, is frequently depicted in an aureole of light; similarly
in the monstrance where the Host is exhibited, once again making the
connection with Christ.[19]

Among the Old Testament texts that were taken as prophecies of
Christ, the great favorite seems to have been that of *Malachi* 4:3:
"But unto you that fear my name shall the Sun of righteousness
arise with healing in his wings." [20] The phrase "Sun of righteousness"
became a common epithet for Christ, "arise" was taken for the resurrection, the wings are angelic, and healing is in the Savior's role.[21]
Often used also was: "The Lord [is] clothed in light as with a gar-
ment," [22] which found frequent iconographic expression. But another,
the prophecy of Isaiah, might well come to mind with the passage of
Beowulf 94 on the light of the sun and moon, since it moves from the
luminaries to their Creator, the literal to the spiritual: "The sun shall
be no more thy light by day; neither for brightness shall the moon
give light unto thee; but the Lord shall be unto thee an everlasting
light, and thy God thy glory." [23]

As to the New Testament, evidence from the Gospels is specially to
be seen in *John* 1:9, where Christ is called *lux vera, quae illuminat
omnem hominem,* and *John* 8:12, where Jesus acknowledges this metaphor: *Ego sum lux mundi; qui sequitur me non ambulat in tenebris,
sed habebit lumen vitae.* In the last two words the collocation is again
made between *light* and *life* which we saw before as an anagrammatic
talisman.[24] Christ is the light to enlighten all people, the tropological
reflection of the sun: *leoma to leohte landbuendum.*

The second reference to the sun in *Beowulf* (l. 606) is in the hero's
prophecy that he will deliver the Danes from Grendel's power before
another day dawns:

> Gaeþ eft se þe mot
> to medo modig siþþan morgenleoht
> ofer ylda bearn oþres dogores,
> sunne sweglwered suþan scineð!

Here the sun, "light of the morning," is "clothed in splendor" and if it has no part in the actual deliverance, it will at least announce it or make it manifest. This role for the sun, furthermore, has just been prepared a few lines earlier (569b–570a) where, swimming against Breca at night, Beowulf has killed a number of sea monsters. These will now no longer trouble seafarers. Here the deliverer is himself delivered: *Leoht eastan com,/ beorht beacen Godes. . . .* The *leoht* is of course the sun, here God's token or sign.[25] One feels a certain shock to find the pagan *wyrd* turning up immediately after this in the famous gnome: *Wyrd oft nereð/ unfaegne eorl,   þonne his ellen deah!* And yet (noting *nereð* and *Nergend,* an epithet for Christ) is this not the precursor and perhaps foreshadowing of our present "God helps him who helps himself"?[26] May not even *wyrd* be a token of God? In Alfred's *Boethius* it is at least a force subject to God's will.[27] One finds it hard to believe that a Christian poet could have meant it in the full pagan sense.

The last mention of the sun in *Beowulf* refers to the belief that evil forces lurk in darkness and cannot come out while it is light. So with Grendel:

> wiste þæm ahlæcan
> to þæm heahsele   hilde geþinged,
> siððan hie sunnan leoht   geseon meahton,
> oððe nipende   niht ofer ealle . . .
> scriðan cwoman.

The fear of dark is universal; its association here with diabolical creatures would have special force for Christians. It echoes the preceding passage: as Beowulf once at night in a great swimming exploit destroyed monsters, we expect him now to perform the same. Night falls and the evil creatures can come out, but Beowulf confidently awaits the decision of God (685b–687). When morning comes (837) his success is manifest.

The sun was described above as a light coming "from the east, bright beacon of God."[28] This it literally is, but it is not the only bright beacon. The epithet is transferred (2776b–2777a) to the splendid banner which Wiglaf, entering the dragon's cave after the fight, finds and takes out to show to the dying Beowulf: *segn eac genom, beacna beorhtost.*[29] In glosses from at least the eighth century, *beacen* and *tacen* were regularly employed to translate *vexillum* and *signum* [30] —and, as here, we find it equated with *segn,* the English loan-form of *signum.* This word *segn* or *segen* will bear further scrutiny. In *Beo-wulf* it is always used of a kingly banner and, whenever described, is golden.[31] But this of the dragon's, also standing high over the treasure, and "all-golden," is magically handwoven so that it gives off light by which Wiglaf can see everything—it is indeed a beacon, and of the brightest. If we are to look for Christian overtones anywhere it should be here, where the miraculous light-giving property is attached to the *segen.* Though no mention is made of a banner in the Grendels' lair (1570–1572a), there is magical illumination, of which *leoma* and *leoht* are used; it is compared to the light of the sun under the common epithet "heaven's candle": *efne swa of hefene   hadre scineð/ rodores candel.* This light is part of the Power which saved Beowulf by means of the gigantic sword providentially at hand (1553b–1555).[32]

The point at which the beacon, *segen,* and *vexillum* come together is, of course, in the famous sign seen by the Emperor Constantine and adopted as his battle-banner: *In hoc signo vinces.* In *Elene* [33] the story appears as follows: Constantine, before the day of battle, awakes to find a messenger, surrounded by light, who tells him (as the shades of night glide away) not to fear, but to look to heaven where he will see the sign of victory (*sigores tacen*). He looks up and sees a splendid tree of glory over the heavens' roof, adorned with gold and shining gems. On it is lettered, *Mid þys beacne ðu . . . feond oferswiðesð* (92b, 93b). This *tacen* or *beacen* is *Cristes rode* (103b); Constantine commands his soldiers at once to raise the *heorucumbul* and to carry the holy tree before them among their enemies: *beran beacen godes* (105–109a). It is referred to as a *segn* (124a)—and after the battle the emperor acknowledges (162b–163) that this, God's *beacen,* gave him the victory. So *beacen* comes to mean, among other things, the cross. We find this sense again in *Crist* 1065, *seo hea rod ryht aræred rices to beacne,* and 1086, *beacna beorhtast,   blode bistemed.*[34] The cross that Constantine saw is, in all essentials, that which appears in the *Dream of the Rood:*

> syllicre treow
> on lyft lædan   leohte bewunden,
> beama beorhtost: all þæt beacen wæs
> begoten mid golde;   gimmas stodon. . . .

Farther on it is a *fuse beacen,* with six other epithets. Here the group of associated words comes full circle.

The point I would emphasize is that though *beacen* did not every-where have Christian reference to the sun, to Christ, or to Christ's cross, it had it so frequently that one cannot well meet the word with-out wondering whether in this instance it may not have more than literal meaning. The development of an adjective *beacniendlic,* "allegor-ical," and a verbal noun *beacnung,* "a speaking by tropes or figures, *tropologia,*" [35] proves a contemporary awareness: it is not one which we are reading in from the present day.

Last of the places in which *beacen* is found in *Beowulf* is toward the very end. In his dying words the hero has asked that a high burial mound be built for him at the sea's edge on Whale's-ness, which sea-farers may call "Beowulf's barrow" and which may guide them through dark or mist (2802–2808). After his funeral this is done: ten days are spent in building *beadurofes becn.* Now this word may mean no more than (very literally) *tumulus,* on a headland a con-spicuous landmark. But it is also a memorial intended to remind the passing wanderer or seafarer of the hero's exploits, his fame. Hence Beowulf becomes a symbol: He stands as a model of heroic behavior, a beacon guiding men to the noble life. If, finally, for reasons already referred to, he is to be taken as a sort of Christ-figure, covert allusion is made to this through *beacen* with its established tropological force.

Our reading of such parabolic hints must, however, be made with considerable caution.[36] The fact that certain words acquired or were loaded with secondary symbolic reference of Christian portent means neither that they were thereby deprived of their literal or non-Christian meanings, nor that every instance of their use perforce included the secondary symbolic reference. The latter should be seen as potential—ready to be used by the poet when he chooses, and to be understood by the hearers or readers only when some clue to it is clearly present in the context. Such a clue is often, though not necessarily, verbal; it may be given, for example, simply by parallelism of incident or character. In parable fashion: "He that hath ears to hear, let him hear."

Some in the Anglo-Saxon audience, and some today, will hear sooner than others, and agreement as to the poet's intent is not always to be expected. The game of literary allusion is still a good one of which many a modern author avails himself. Indeed, today a further dimension has been added since some authors admit to alluding un-consciously as well as consciously, and the hearer's unconscious may be equally involved in a sort of multiple echo set reverberating by a telling word or phrase. Something of the same sort was certainly pos-

sible for those words or phrases in Old English which, strongly established, often formulaic and hence recurrent, formed a network with
others, partly through the need for poetic variation. The words *sunne,
leoht, beacen,* and *tacen* [37] constitute such a group. Any one of them
may suggest or trigger any of the others—they "go in and out of each
other" and when two or more appear together it is a clear hint to look
beyond the literal meaning. In *Beowulf* they are used to keep the
Christian coloring, though present, unobtrusive enough not to clash
with the imaginative picture of a pagan world of the past presented
in favorable, even admirable terms.

"Melancholy," from the Augsburg Calendar (*ca.* 1480)

KEMP MALONE

A Reading of *Beowulf* 3169–3182

Beowulf ends with a passage that makes trouble for the student first of all because its text is defective. Lines 3169–3182 come on the verso of folio 201, a leaf of the unique MS damaged not only by fire (along with the other leaves of the codex) but also by wear and tear, and the two Thorkelin transcripts of 1787 (commonly called A and B) help us less than might have been expected, though of course we should be worse off without them. The MS text, supplemented where this is wanting or illegible from A and B, runs thus:

13	þa ȳbe hlæw riodan
14	hilde deore æþelinga bearn ealra twelfa woldon
15	:::: cwiðan kyning mænan word gyd wrecan &ȳb we:
16	sprecan eahtodan eorl scipe & his ellen weorc duguðū
17	demdon swa hit ḡde:: bið þ mon his wine dryħ wordū
18	herḡ ferhðū freoḡ þon he forð scile ofl ?chaman
19	:::: weorðan swa begnornodon geata leode hlafordes
20	:::re heorð ḡ neatas cwædon þ he wære wyruldcyning
21	mann? mildust & mondrærust leodū liðost &lof
22	geornost.

Here *w* stands for the runic letter *wynn* and the ampersand replaces the MS abbreviation for *ond*. The colon denotes a letter wanting or illegible; the question mark, a letter the identity of which is in dispute. The macron represents the MS stroke marking abbreviation: set over a vowel sign it indicates that the letter so marked is to be followed by *m*; set over *g*, by *e*; set over *n*, by *ne*; drawn through the ascender of *h*, by *ten;* and drawn through that of *þ*, by *æt*.

Since Wanley entered our codex in his MS catalog of 1705, made well before the Ashburnham House fire (in which Cotton Vitellius

A.xv was badly scorched), we might have hoped to find a better text
of our passage in his explicit, but alas, he gave no explicit for *Beowulf*.
Thorkelin's edition of 1815 does not help us either, but N. F. S.
Grundtvig in the notes appended to his Danish paraphrase of the poem
gave the readings *Of lic-haman* 18 and *mon-þwærust* 21.[1] For him
these were emendations, for his paraphrase, like Thorkelin's edition,
was based on the A and B transcripts, which agree in reading *oflac
haman* and *mondrærust* (the latter in B corrected from an earlier
mond . . . rust). Grundtvig's *þ* had a long career; not until Zupitza's
Autotypes of 1882 was it replaced by the *ð* of today's texts, the letter
which A and B presumably misread as *d*.

At some time between 1815 and 1820 J. J. Conybeare[2] collated
Thorkelin's edition with the MS text and among his readings we find
lichaman 18 in agreement with Grundtvig, though we cannot tell
whether he took this to be the form that stands in the MS or gave it
this form by emendation, since he did not mark emendations as such.
He also read *cyningnes* 20 and *Mannum* 21 for Thorkelin's *cyning* and
Monne (taken from B; A skipped both words). J. M. Kemble in his
edition of 1837 (based on the MS text) agreed with Grundtvig and
Conybeare in reading *lic-haman*. With Grundtvig he also read *mon-
þwærust* but bracketed its *on-þwæ;* seemingly in his day the *m*, now
gone, was still in the MS. He was the first to read *ḡ-defe* 17 (with *efe*
bracketed), *cyninga* 20 (with bracketed *a*), and *manna* 21, the readings now usual. I will not list his misreadings, unhappy emendations,
and false quantities. Benjamin Thorpe did not bring out his *Beowulf*
edition till 1855, but as early as 1830 he had collated Thorkelin's edition with the MS and his text was based on this collation. He contributed the reading *hryre* at the head of line 20.

The word ending line 15 clearly begins with *wynn,* but A and B
took the letter for insular *s*, a mistake easy to make. Thorpe also misread it thus, and Kemble mistook it for *f*. The A scribe could not
make out the next letter but B read it as *e*; so also Kemble[3] and
Thorpe.[4] Thorkelin in his edition read the word as *se* and Thorpe
emended this to *worn* to get the alliteration needed with *wordgyd* and
wrecan. C. W. M. Grein in his *Bibliothek* of 1857 changed Thorpe's
worn to *wer* (*ver* in his orthography) by striking the *n* and going
back to the old reading *e* for the second letter. By this roundabout
route the *wynn* of the MS made its way into the editions.

At the head of line 15 Grein supplied *ceare* and this reading proved
popular with the editors, though the sense it gives is not altogether

satisfactory. Stylistically one would expect a word varying as well as alliterating with *kyning* and *cenne,* accusative of *cene* "brave" (modern *keen*), would seem a better solution. Another possibility is *ceorl* in its poetic sense "fighting-man, hero." Note the poet's application of it (2972) to the aged king Ongentheow of Sweden in his heroic last fight. But a word of five letters would have to be written small to fit into the space in the MS, or so I judge. I supply *life* at the head of line 19.[5]

Conybeare's reading *cyningnes* 20 makes no sense as it stands and we can therefore hardly explain it as an emendation he made of the MS's *cyning.* It seems more reasonable to think he was copying something he saw in the MS (though it is now wanting) when he added *nes* to *cyning.* The only three-letter word that would fit this context is *his* (at least, this is the only word that occurs to me). Given the damaged state of the MS text here, we may conjecture that Conybeare's *n* stands for an *h* which had lost its ascender and that his *es* is a misreading of a blurred or otherwise hard-to-make-out *is.* If so, his *Mannum* (i.e., *mannū*) is right and Kemble's *manna* is wrong.[6]

Ordered by lines of verse our text reads thus:

> 3169 Þa ymbe hlæw riodan hildedeore,
> æþelinga bearn, ealra twelfa;
> woldon cenne cwiðan, kyning mænan,
> 3172 wordgyd wrecan & ymb wer sprecan.
> Eahtodan eorlscipe, & his ellenweorc,
> duguðum, demdon, swa hit gedefe bið
> 3175 þæt mon his winedryhten wordum herge,
> ferhðum freoge, þonne he forð scile
> of lichaman, life, weorðan.
> 3178 Swa begnornodon Geata leode
> hlafordes hryre, heorðgeneatas:
> cwædon þæt he wære wyruldcyning
> 3181 his mannum mildust & monðwærust,
> leodum liðost, & lofgeornost

[Then round the barrow rode battle-bold ones, sons of athelings, twelve in all; they were minded to mourn for the brave one, bewail the king, make elegy, and have their say of the man. They lauded (his) heroism and made much of his deeds of daring, (his) virtues, as it is fitting that one praise one's lord and friend in speech, love (him) in spirit when he shall be (gone) forth from the body, from life. So the people of the Geatas, the hearth-fellows, made moan for the fall of (their) lord: they said that he would be the earthly king mildest and kindest to his men, gentlest to (his) people, and most eager for a good name.]

I end with a few comments. The form *twelfa* 3170 is commonly emended to *twelfe* to make it agree with conventional Old English orthography and this is well enough, but I reckon it better editorial practice to let the scribe's misspellings stand (though calling attention to them, of course) in cases like this, where the slip of the pen tells us something about his own speech, as against that of the earlier scribe whose text he was copying. It seems altogether likely that writing *-a* for *-e* exemplifies the late Old English leveling of weak final vowels, a change hidden by the standard spelling that the scribe learned in school, but brought to light by occasional departures from this spelling. I take *duguðum* 3174 for a dative of accompaniment, varying the accusative plural *ellenweorc* 3173. Though Klaeber took it for an adverb meaning "highly," I have not found the adverbial use elsewhere and must record my skepticism. Since *mon* 3175 does not alliterate, it is to be taken as the indefinite pronoun; cf. *man* 1175 and *mon* 2355. Indefinite use with alliteration, as in line 25, calls for the rendering "a man" rather than "one." The phrases *wordum herge* 3175 and *ferhðum freoge* 3176 make a pair, the one giving the outward expression, the other the inward feeling. Both befit the true mourner, and neither would be enough alone. The distinction drawn in 3178–3179 between the people as a whole and the *dright* or body of retainers is kept in the lines that follow, where *mannum* has the technical sense "men of the *comitatus*." This sense is also to be presumed in line 2080, where *leofes mannes* varies *mærum maguþegne* 2079 (compare *Andreas,* 246, and *Maldon,* 205), and seems the sense most fitting in 201, 1835, 1943, 1994, and 2533. In my rendering "would be" for *wære* 3180 I am of course taking it for a subjunctive in meaning as well as in form; that is, as more than the conventional subjunctive usual in indirect quotations. Grammatically, "was" would be an equally defensible translation.

W. T. H. JACKSON

Problems of Communication in the Romances of Chrétien de Troyes

It is a notorious fact of the literary history of the Middle Ages that the heroes of the national epics are inarticulate. They are, apparently, incapable of conducting rational conversation with their fellows, for their speech consists of rather lengthy statements of policy, gasconades about deeds either past or contemplated, or mere statements calculated to keep the action going. It is perhaps not too much to say that Charlemagne's problems in the *Chanson de Roland* stem from his inability to obtain a consensus from men who were incapable of nice argumentation or even a true exchange of ideas, and that much of the obscurity of the *Nibelungenlied* owes its origin not to a contamination of sources but to the incapacity of its characters to handle even the simplest of subordinate clauses.

How different is the romance! *Facundia,* the power of smooth and polished speech, is of the very essence of the characters. They are engaged in constant discussion not only of their own actions and reasons for action but also of the theoretical principles that guide their conduct. If there is no one available for such discussion, the characters are perfectly happy to talk to themselves, with a generous infusion of such abstractions or mythological beings as love, Cupid, their own hearts, their own eyes, and above all sorrow. Needless to say, the principal topic of their dialogues and monologues is love.

The earlier romances are instructive on the subject. Vergil has little to say on the love affair between Aeneas and Lavinia, and that little hardly leads us to believe that there was a true love affair. The author of the French *Roman d'Enéas,* on the other hand, shows us a developing passion. It cannot be conducted through the medium of dialogue, since the two potential lovers are separated by opposing armies and a castle wall. The dialogue/monologues, if such they may be called—for they are addressed to the other person even though they cannot be heard—are not analyses of love so much as anticipation of its delights. They are highly sensuous imaginings rather than esthetic evaluations.

It is to Chrétien de Troyes that we turn when we think of the love monologue and love dialogue as principal instruments of exposition in the romance, and it is fatally easy to assume that his technique is the same in all his romances, when in fact this is far from being the case. Chrétien does not treat love in the same way in all his works. Indeed, there is good reason for believing that each of those works is an attempt to study the love-phenomenon in a different way, and that his romances have as a principal object the exposition, not always sympathetic, of the various ways in which love can be treated. Perhaps we can throw some light on this problem by examining the different ways in which the love dialogue appears. In making this brief study I shall assume, perhaps unwisely, that Chrétien makes extensive use of irony in his Arthurian romances and that we are not bound to take all his remarks seriously.

It can hardly be denied that in Chrétien's *Erec* we are presented with love in its simplest and most attractive form. Erec's failure to realize the importance of service as an attribute both of love and the knightly life does not affect Enid's attitude to him. Her complaint, which her half-bemused husband overhears and mishears, has no relation to her own honor and standing in society; and throughout the poem her actions are guided by one principle and one only—her husband's safety, prowess, and honor. There is little in her attitude which could be called courtly. She calls for no service; she exacts no tribute of adulation. Of all Chrétien's heroines she is the most attractive and least demanding.

How is this most desirable of brides wooed? How does Erec fall in love with her? When she first appears she is dressed virtually in rags—and if the descriptions are to be believed and if such a thing is possible, clothes made the woman even more in the Middle Ages than they do now. But, as Chrétien shrewdly observes, the outside was poor but the inside was beautiful. If we assume, as I think we may, that this description reflects what Erec observes, we have a man struck by a girl's simple beauty, and this impression is confirmed by the author's comment: Erec was overcome with admiration. But there is no wounding of the heart through the eyes, none of the agonizing which accompanies the first sight of the beloved in other poems. Apart from normal salutations, they do not exchange a word, and this is not because Erec is so stricken that he cannot speak but because the real business of life goes on—Enid is taking his horse to the stable.

The wooing of Enid as shown by Chrétien must have been much closer to a normal wooing in noble families than were those which we usually find in twelfth-century romances. Erec needs Enid so that he may enter the contest for the silver sparrow hawk. She is surpassingly beautiful and deserves the honor. If her father agrees to her going, Erec will marry her and, to establish his right to do so, he tells of his birth and parentage. Enid is not asked for her opinion of the transaction. She is merely "very happy at being given this courteous knight and she well knew that he was a king and that she herself would be a crowned queen and loaded with honors." After the victory, Erec refused all offers of new fine clothing for Enid. The queen is to see her as she is and then herself make Enid beautiful. The contrast between the ladies of Arthur's court and Enid could hardly be more pointed. It is to Enid, the simple, unspoiled girl that Arthur gives the ceremonial kiss of the White Stag. In all this time Chrétien records no direct speech between the lovers, except of a most trivial nature, no love dialogue, no monologue on passion and the nature of love. They admire one another intensely, but their feelings are not verbalized. Chrétien is here, presumably deliberately, departing from the established tradition of love analysis by dialogue. We are invited to judge the lovers by their acts, not by their words. Now it is perfectly possible to argue here that Erec's love sinks into mere sensuality and that Chrétien intends by such a portrayal of love to indicate the lack of those social and spiritual features that should attend love in its higher sense. But even if we grant this, the fact remains that Enid's love is and remains a high and pure devotion and that Erec is brought to a realization of the nature of love not by discussion but by the evidence of Enid's devotion to him presented when she could not possibly believe that he was a witness to it. It is this conviction that there is such a thing as selfless love that causes him to undertake the adventure of the *Joie de la cort*. Mabonograin is the victim of precisely the love that Erec has avoided—a love of demanding service in which the male lover is utterly deprived of free will—and Erec has avoided it because of the nature of Enid. She expresses that nature clearly and frankly in her monologues, and I can find no hint of irony in them.

Here, surely, more than anywhere, Chrétien portrayed his ideal lady and he did so without using the love dialogue at all, or indeed any of the artificial concepts of service normally expressed in that dialogue.

In *Cligès* we are provided with a total contrast. Although the work is a romance of chivalry, the concentration is entirely on the love-phenomenon. The first half of the poem is full of dialogue and internal monologue, and the descriptions of love given in these passages have made the work a *locus classicus* for "courtly love." Now the early discussions of love by Alexander and Soredamurs, which are naturally monologues, since neither dares to address the other, appear at first sight to be well within the tradition set out in the *Roman d'Enéas*. They describe the devastating effects of love's passion. Yet closer examination reveals that it is the effect of love, not of the beloved, which is being examined. Alexander assembles in his first love monologue almost every cliché and every figure which had by this time become the stock-in-trade of the troubadour, of what Kolb has called "die Mystik des Auges und des Herzen." [1] This untutored youth, Alexander, discusses eyes, light, mirror, arrows with a glibness which belies his previous innocence of love. When he does describe his love, however, it is in figures of significant sensuality. In all this there is little of what we could describe as love. The concentration is entirely upon a formalized analysis of his own feelings, which proves in the end to have little of service or even of reverence, as the last figure of the arrow shows, but to be thinly disguised urgings of the flesh. Soredamurs is equally concerned with self, for she says little of the man who has inspired her love but a great deal of her own position and the attitudes she must take. The scene in which Alexander understands that his shirt has been sewn with a hair of his beloved—surely one of the funniest in Arthurian literature—reduces the lovers' posing to its true level of inanity. For why should there be all this anguish? The two are of marriageable age, there are no impediments of social position, and when Queen Guinevere in pity brings them together, they are betrothed at once. One can only ask why the more direct methods of Erec and Enid would not be effective in this case. Are we to think that Alexander and Soredamurs are capable of *fin amors* and that Erec and Enid are not? If we take the indications of Chrétien's sympathy as a guide, the reverse would appear to be true, for he clearly regards the passion of Alexander and Soredamurs as laughable. The love monologues, then, would appear to be parody, parody of those we find in the *Roman d'Enéas* and still more of the sentiments of the troubadours. There arises a formal question—is the love monologue/dialogue itself an indication of parody, of a lack of serious belief in the love affair? I do not mean to imply, of course, that any dialogue between lovers indicates parody but that the formal monologue on love's symptoms and the formal dialogue of total submission may well be such an indication.

Fenice reveals her passion not to Guinevere but to Thessala, a specialist in black magic, who neatly sets up for her the very reverse of the Tristan love potion, for instead of making love inevitable, it makes it impossible. There is no real communication between Cligès and Fenice. Each allegedly is deeply in love with the other but for months their relationship is a kind of *amor de lonh,* both physically and spiritually. Cligès, we are told, fears rejection and hence does not communicate his love to his lady, but Fenice has, without his knowledge, already insured that there can be no true love between husband and wife and indeed no love at all. Their first dialogue is again couched in formal terms, this time the separation of heart and body motif which is found so often in the *chanson de croisade.* The dialectic is complex; the hearts, after much meandering, are finally in place; and now Fenice reveals to Cligès her true relations with her husband, not without a repetition of her earlier statement that she will refuse to be an Iseut la blonde. His suggestion that she go with him to Britain is rejected because she would then be regarded as an adulteress—far better to be an adulteress than to be thought of as one.

From now on the love affair between Cligès and Fenice is a series of deceits and technicalities, all of which are designed to preserve the fine distinction between being an adulteress *in esse* and an adulteress *coram publico.* Fenice has a nice taste in these matters which seems to accord ill with the power of love to deprive its victims of their rational faculties. Here, surely, is the ultimate absurdity of this secret love, the necessity of concealing it from the *jaloux.* Poor man, he does not even know that he has reason to be jealous. Preservation of the intact status of her body is very important for Fenice, and the scene in which the doctors are prevented from roasting it by a thousand angry ladies is an excellent commentary by Chrétien on female values. After all, Fenice was allegedly dead. Yet all the deception is in vain. The lovers do have to flee to Arthur's court in the end, and Arthur is perfectly prepared to take their side until the problem is solved by the emperor's death. All has come out right in the end— the lovers are united and adultery is justified. The trappings of love are here, but not true love itself. In the last resort, each of the lovers is concerned only with bodily satisfaction and with reputation, not with true service to each other or to their neighbors. Their communication, for all its elaborate figures, never rises above the lowest level, and their love, for all its dialectic, is sensual indulgence in an elaborate tomb.

In the *Chevalier de la Charrette* the communication is of a very different kind. Nowhere do we find love analyzed in dialogue or monologue. Lancelot's musings are the contemplations of a mystic rather than the analyses of the love dialecticians. The communication between Lancelot and the queen is of a direct and peremptory nature. The queen commands and Lancelot obeys. His reception in the tower after the incident in the cart is notoriously cool, but the amount of conversation between the two is small. Lancelot is utterly unable to understand the queen's disdainful attitude toward him, for he has performed service for her, as several third parties remind him. There is no analysis of love between the two, only a statement of Lancelot's service to the queen. When the two lovers meet again, the problem is stated with a minimum of words: "You waited two steps." Lancelot asks for pardon and receives it. A rendezvous is made for the evening, and the two spend the night together. It is the fact of physical love which is important here, not discussions of the love theory. The rendezvous is, of course, more reminiscent of the *alba* than of the *canzon*, but this meeting is less characteristic of the love between Lancelot and Guinevere than is the stream of commands that pass from the queen to her knight. This romance is the story of love-service pushed beyond reason. It is not a love that can be expressed in dialogue, because dialogue should mean verbal communication on a rational level, and such communication does not exist between Lancelot and Guinevere. Nor is it the kind of "courtly love" that we found in *Cligès*, for there the love was at least mutual. In the *Lancelot* there is little evidence of true love on the part of Guinevere. She grants rewards to Lancelot, but she never says that she herself is in love, nor does she ever discuss the subject with anyone else. Lancelot's love expresses itself not in dialogue or indeed in any kind of verbalization but in action. He seeks the queen and finds her and in tournaments he wins or loses completely at her command. If service is the mark of the perfect lover, then Lancelot bears that mark. Yet this love is one-sided and ill-balanced. As Fenice and Cligès were in communication only on the level of sensual indulgence and discussed their relationship only from the point of view of making Fenice available without a technical loss of honor, so the love of Lancelot and Guinevere is discussed only from the point of view of service and reward. This is not to say that Lancelot's love was not sincere. He is, perhaps, the most deeply involved of all Chrétien's heroes, but his involvement is not expressed verbally. It is very significant that on the one occasion when Lancelot is shown thinking about love, we are not made party to his thoughts. Yet this absence of love monologue or love dialogue does not indicate the kind of love we find in *Erec*. The queen is the very opposite of Enid, for she uses her lover entirely to reinforce her personal sense of power. Communication through dialogue would thus be an impossible means of communication, for it implies give and take, compromise, and the possible recognition of another point of view, all of which would be quite impossible for the queen whom Chrétien portrays. The command is more natural.

It is, perhaps, in *Yvain* that the use of the love dialogue is most effective and most subtle. The love-problem is presented to us in this work, as in *Erec*, as a conflict between two aspects of the knightly life, but it is not, as has so often been stated, merely the reverse side of the *Erec* coin. Laudine's love for Yvain is never the same as that of Enid for Erec, either before Yvain departs on his tour of adventure or after his return.

Yvain's reaction on first seeing Laudine is not unlike that of Alexander on seeing Soredamurs. He is, he declares, hopelessly entangled in love. The first words of his monologue are: *Por fol me puis tenir,* and he is much nearer the truth than the cliché of the love monologue might indicate. Yvain follows the usual lines of the internal debate— his lady may hate him, he fears to approach her, her beauty is remarkable and should not be marred by sorrow. But this time, as Chrétien coolly remarks, Yvain is not a mere prisoner of love, bound in silken chains, but an actual prisoner in a space bounded by very substantial stone walls. His love is indeed mad by any logical standards, since he desires and knows he desires a lady whose husband he has just killed. Now according to Andreas Capellanus and certain Provençal and French lyric poets, the husband was an impediment, a jealous man who was better out of the way; Yvain has already put the husband out of the way but is liable to find him a more effective bar to love when dead than he ever was when alive. Yet once again social convention proves its strength. How can a widow accept her husband's murderer as a lover? (We have not yet reached the point of discussing

Yvain as a husband.) At this point Yvain is as obsessed with his desires as were Alexander or Cligès. He has no thought of any larger issue or indeed of the lady's feelings. His desire is to possess beauty, and his monologue reveals that he thinks of the death of Laudine's husband merely as an impediment to desire and Laudine's possible objections to receiving him as being based formally on the fact that he had killed her husband.

Now in the dialogue between Lunete and Laudine that leads to the introduction of Yvain to his mistress, the word "love" does not occur. Lunete does not ask that her mistress should love Yvain but that she should take him as the defender of the fountain, as her lord, because he is clearly the best available candidate. This is a dialogue of reasoned matrimony, not of love, and it is very reminiscent of Erec's "wooing" of Enid. Laudine's monologue is a rather casuistic proof to herself that her acceptance of the killer of her husband is a reasonable thing to do. A far cry, indeed, from the lovers in the *Roman d'Enéas* and *Cligès*. Again there is no mention of love, but when Lunete appears again, the question of rank and lineage is raised. Once the qualifications of Yvain—as a husband, not as a lover—have been determined, Laudine is impatient for his arrival. Laudine's description of her impatience is remarkable for its *double entendre,* its play with the vocabulary of love and medieval actuality. Yvain accepts the prison in its "love" sense, but Lunete knows better. He is taking his chance of actual prison if he does not please his mistress.

Yvain makes the formal acknowledgment of complete submission to Laudine. She asks whether this extends to her killing him. He says that it does. Now in the formal love dialogue such a remark would be perfectly acceptable, since to kill him would mean simply to make him die of love. But Laudine does not mean this. She means actual physical death. The love dialogue is being parodied in a grim tone. The parody continues as Laudine questions the reasons for his decision to come to her, carefully eliciting from him the required answers—his heart has made him do so, and his heart was forced by his eyes, and his eyes by her beauty, and all this led to a "love which is the greatest possible, so that my heart can not be separated from you and go elsewhere, so that I can think of nothing else, so that I love you more than myself, so that I would live or die according to your wish." And what is the reply to this passionate declaration? "And you would undertake to defend my fountain?" No word of love, simply of peace between them. There is considerable stress on the formal nature of the union, on the ceremony before the barons which made Yvain their lord. And Chrétien adds significantly: "the lady thought it more honorable to take a husband with the approval of her people, even though she would have done so without their prayers, at love's command." She has never said that she loves Yvain, any more than Enid had said that she loved Erec. There is no love-musing, no display of feelings, nor are we told at any time of love. The stress is rather on the externals of courtly entertainment. (It is perhaps significant that Gawain becomes Lunete's chevalier, promising her unstinting service, but is far away when she needs him.) Yvain's request to be allowed to go on an adventure tour is granted by Laudine before she knows what she will have to promise, and when she sets the term and says that her love will turn to hate if he exceeds it, she is merely continuing the contract on which all their relations have been based. Yet she is more thoughtful than Yvain, for she gives him a ring to preserve him from harm.

Yvain's adventures are mere games, but they are sufficient to make him forget his deadline. Just before the arrival of Laudine's messenger he is depressed by the thought that he has exceeded his leave, and well he may be, for events show that Laudine has been far more concerned about their separation than has Yvain, with all his protestations of eternal fidelity and love. His madness and thus separation from his earlier life is the introduction to a new and completely different phase of existence. During this period his attitude toward love is different. He is in despair and when he says that he will die if he cannot be reconciled with Laudine, he is speaking the literal truth. There are no shams, no dialogues of the sorrows of love, only a genuine desire to serve. The failure of Laudine to recognize him is not one more instance of the common medieval lack of visual memory. He is a different man, and his dialogue with Laudine is carried on in the person of the Chevalier au Lion, not that of Yvain. His request to her to intercede for him with his lady can be couched directly because he is not speaking as Yvain, and she can answer directly because she does not know that she is speaking to her husband and lover. There is, of course, irony in the condemnation of the hard-hearted mistress of the Chevalier au Lion, but Laudine is acting in precisely the same manner that Yvain had urged when he first made his exaggerated declarations of service. Now that he does indeed serve all women who need help, he need no longer make such protestations. His ultimate return is made in his new person and with the true humility that is characteristic of it. The dialogue is very far from the standard form. Laudine says that she is "entirely at his disposal; she would be willing to do what he wants and wishes only to do him good so far as she can." These words are addressed to the new Yvain, to the Chevalier au Lion, but they are to be applied to the old Yvain, to Laudine's husband. Laudine understands this perfectly well when it is revealed to her who the Chevalier au Lion really is and this is why she cries out that she has been tricked. Their agreement had again been reached on a utilitarian basis—the need to defend the fountain—and Laudine makes it clear that she is still not sure of Yvain's love and that there will always be a lingering doubt in her mind. But Yvain's repentance, which is not a declaration of love, is accepted.

At the end of the poem Chrétien has brought his hero to an understanding of the function of knighthood in the world and has also raised him to a degree of moral responsibility and social awareness far superior to that of the Arthurian court represented by Gawain. The relation with Laudine, which began with a totally conventional "falling-in-love," has thus served its purpose in bringing about the maturity of the hero. It may also be argued that his personal relationship to Laudine also shows more maturity, since he no longer thinks of her in terms of beauty only but as a woman to whom, as to the other women he has helped, he owes a knightly duty. Yet Chrétien still does not show us any true communication between the two. Laudine accepts Yvain as her lord again, although she says that only her oath is making her do so. She does not say that she loves him and it is far from certain that she understands what he has learned since his madness and "rebirth." Her relation to him, in other words, is still formalistic. She feels that he has broken the agreement they made and that he should be punished. There is no evidence in Chrétien's poem that Yvain and Laudine will be happy ever after or even that Yvain's love-service has gained his mistress' love at all. He can only hope.

Hartmann von Aue, who wrote a German version of *Yvain* which keeps very close to Chrétien's poem, obviously felt that this lack of love and total reconciliation was a defect in the poem, for he added a scene in which Laudine flings herself at Iwein's feet and begs his forgiveness. The poem thus ends in total harmony, and the conventions have been satisfied. For the German hero, love-service has brought not only maturity but the love of his wife, and love is shown as merely one factor, if a major one, in bringing about the development of the hero. Laudine, for Hartmann, simply must accept her husband after he has fulfilled the necessary conditions. Chrétien prefers to leave the matter to the imagination of his audience.

Since Chrétien never completed the *Perceval,* it would be unfair to draw conclusions about the love of the hero for Blancheflur. Yet it is worth noting that the conversation between the two is almost all of a very practical nature. They discuss what services the young Perceval can render, and the lady apparently gives herself to him in exchange for the promised services. In the Gawain incidents there is, of course, a great deal of parody. In the incident with the little girl, the communication with Gawain is entirely formal conversation, in that with the sister of the king of Gavalon it is all action. Only in the long negotiations with the scornful damsel do we see the expanded love dialogue and it is, of course, largely an exercise in futility, since the participants are working from different premises. Gawain never muses over his love for the proud damsel—indeed, he never says that he loves her—but he accepts her commands as Lancelot does those of Guinevere. His conversation with her concerns those commands. Her conversation with him reflects her concern for the defiling of her body which is really the cause of her unrelenting behavior toward Gawain. She proves in the end not to be the cruel mistress who exacts service from her knight but a woman who has suffered from the system, who knows very well what the approach of a knight means. Her apparent demand for unremitting and dangerous service is in effect an attempt to prove to Gawain, the perfect knight, that if a woman really demands service she can bring about the death of her knight, not his glory, just as the cousin of Perceval had done for her lover. It is worth observing that there is a strong resemblance between Erec and Enid and Gawain and the proud damsel, with the roles, of course, reversed.

What conclusions can we draw? To me it is clear that Chrétien uses the love dialogue, the characteristic of early romances, only when love is not sincere in his sense. In other words, if Alexander and Soredamurs, Cligès and Fenice are courtly lovers, then Chrétien wants no part of courtly love. His real lovers never indulge in the love monologue or love dialogue when they are truly in love. The unregenerate Yvain is full of words and mouths his statements with the best, but the repentant, experienced Chevalier au Lion does not. Enid loves without words. Laudine loves true service, and the dialogue is reshaped in her mouth to practical ends. Neither Lancelot in his infatuation nor Gawain in his patient endurance indulges in words about love. Each demonstrates by his actions his devotion to his mistress, besotted though that emotion may appear to be. On the basis of the use of dialogue, certain divisions of Chrétien's romances become clear. There are two in which love is commanded: the *Chevalier de la Charrette*, in which it is commanded for a woman's ego and is unhealthy and suspect; and the Gawain incidents in *Perceval* in which it is commanded by a lady who has suffered and who later repents of her commanding. Dialogue and monologue flourish in *Cligès* and yet, in spite of the many words, the only concern of the participants is bodily satisfaction. Love brings them no nearer to maturity. Finally there are two in which love is founded not on fine phrases but on the gradual evolution of mutual understanding. In both of these it is not love, courtly or otherwise, which is the prime force, but social needs and mutual help. The successful marriages are those in which the lovers do not protest too much.

Communication between lovers in Chrétien's romances is thus not quite so fluent as it may seem at a first reading. It would not be far from the truth to say that much of the verbalizing is non-communication, since it consists of a series of shams, of fronts which prove to be unreal or, at best, evidence of a kind of love which Chrétien regards as unhealthy. Real communication in words is rare. None of the "true" lovers succeeds in expressing to the other what his or her feelings are. Had they been able to do so, much grief would have been averted, but the maturity which comes from suffering would not be attained. For Chrétien, the communication of real love, as distinct from the formalized games of the court, apparently came through action and through indirect communication of affection. He clearly mistrusted the rhetoric and dialectic of earlier romances as a method of representing love in its higher aspects and used them principally to parody the type of love he rejected. If we are right in assuming that he regarded married love as that which best fulfilled the aspirations of both man and woman, then we must also assume that he felt that such love needed no elaborate verbal communication. True love expressed itself in mutual trust, not in the artifices of cunningly wrought words.

T A U N O   F .   M U S T A N O J A

The Suggestive Use of Christian Names in Middle English Poetry

Some years ago Professor C. A. Bodelsen made a statistical study of a number of Danish surnames, to find out what sort of qualities the popular imagination associated with those names.[1] The results were interesting. The men whose surnames were Poulsen or Paulsen, for example, were mostly imagined to be thin, quiet, and distinguished, while the Olsens and Hansens were mostly thought to be fat, jaunty, and undistinguished. Strikingly enough, Professor Bodelsen himself had that mental picture of men whose name was Olsen, although he did not remember anyone who was particularly fat and knew several who were thin.

There does seem to be a tendency to associate certain names with pleasant, noble, and romantic notions and certain names with notions that are less pleasant, less noble, and less romantic. *Nomen est omen*— a name is an omen. Why, for example, do popular novelists tend to use names of certain types for their heroes and heroines and names of different types for their villains? And why is the use of pseudonyms so common in certain spheres of public life? Why do movie stars so often have fictitious names; why does a French pop singer assume an English name? Surely to win additional popularity under a catchy, suggestive name, a name that has a pleasant sound and is likely to arouse agreeable associations—a name that sells.

A great deal has been written about proper names, but no one has so far proposed a definition that takes into account all their distinctive characteristics. From appellative origins they have developed into what many writers consider to be mere signs or labels, with no function beyond that of identification. The view that proper names have no

51

meaning was first formulated by John Stuart Mill, who believed that "a proper name is but an unmeaning mark which we connect in our minds with the idea of the object."[2] To Mill, proper names are strictly denotative: they denote individuals but give no information about them; whereas common nouns are connotative, they imply properties connected with or characteristic of the individual.

But it is only in theory that proper names are purely denotative. In a context of living speech there are no proper names without connotative associations, real or imagined. The associations are usually quite vague and purely contextual. In certain circumstances, however, they may develop into regular semantic meanings or shades of meaning. As a result of such a development the proper name may eventually come to be used as a common, appellative, noun. A case in point is *Jack,* used not only as a Christian name but as a common noun expressing many things, such as a mechanical device for raising heavy objects. The transition from proper to common names is in fact a universal phenomenon, found in many, perhaps all, languages of the world.[3]

In literature the suggestive use of proper names has always been a popular stylistic means of implying mental associations of various kinds.[4] The present paper is an attempt to examine the Christian names of characters in Middle English poetry from that angle. Owing to the limitations of space, names and their occurrences have been included on a selective basis to prevent the paper from becoming a mere list. For the same reason the interesting evidence of the sixteenth century had to be left out; it is to be hoped that this does not create the impression that there existed any breach of continuity between the Middle English and Tudor periods.

It is also to be regretted that the study could not be extended to cover parallel uses from other European countries. The inclusion of the medieval poetry of France would have been particularly illuminating in this respect—the *pastourelles,* for example, that highly conventional genre fashionable in southern and northern France in the twelfth and thirteenth centuries. The *pastourelle* is essentially a debate between a knight—the poet—and a shepherdess, a young country girl, as unsophisticated as she is lovely. The knight requests her love, but, having a regular *ami,* she mostly refuses. The girl's name varies. It may be *Aélis, Alinete, Emmelot, Isabel, Jehannete, Margot,* or *Perronnele* but most frequently it is a pet form of *Marie,* such as *Mariete, Marion,*

Marot, Marotele, or *Maroie.* Her regular friend is most often *Robin,*
or *Robinet, Robeçon,* or *Robeçonnet,* all pet forms of *Robert.*

"To sing about Robin and Aélis became synonymous with singing
and dancing in a ring," says Alfred Jeanroy in his monumental work
on the origins of French lyric poetry.[5] But it was with Marion that
Robin was mostly linked in the popular imagination. The two characters became the traditional pair of rustic lovers in a pastoral setting.
A typical country lad and lass—young, unsophisticated, light-hearted
and light-headed, always ready for flirting and love-making; the kind
of people who give more thought to dancing and caroling than to
church-going. The author of a poem of religious instruction writes in
despair:

> On dist souvent mainte chançon
> De Robin et de Marion,
> Mès tout ce ne vaut un bouton:
> A ce faire no temps perdon.[6]

[Many songs are sung of Robin and Marion, but all that is not
worth a button; it is a mere waste of time.]

Robin and *Marion* occur in John Gower's French work *Mirour de
l'Omme,* in the same suggestive sense, but elsewhere in English poetry
their nearest equivalents are *Jankin* and *Malkin.* The author of the
thirteenth-century *Lutel Soth Sermun,*[7] who has no tolerance for sinners, would send all backbiters, robbers, deceitful peddlers and bakers
and brewers to hell, and priests' wives too, and

> þeos prude ȝunge men
> þat luvieþ Malekin
> And þeos prude maidenes
> þat luvieþ Janekin.
> At chirche and at cheping,
>   hwanne heo togadere come,
> Heo runeþ togaderes
>   and spekeþ of derne luve.
>   (53–60)

The girls, the author goes on, pay no attention to masses or matins,
"for Wilkin and Watkin are in their thoughts." And Robin will take
Gilote (Jill) to the alehouse, and in the evening she will go with him.

All these names are used in a sense suggestive of "any frivolous young man" and "any flighty girl."

Forms and General Occurrence of Medieval Christian Names. Before proceeding further, however, a brief discussion of the formal characteristics and the general occurrence of medieval English Christian names seems necessary. The names with which the present paper is concerned occur mostly in a hypocoristic or pet form (*Robin, Marion, Hobbe, Hicke, Cis, Malkin,* etc.). An implication of familiarity is inherent in such forms, and there may also be an element of affection. Pet names are derived from the full forms of the names in various ways, often by shortening. Some are formed by aphaeresis or the omission of the initial syllable, such as *Colle* for *Nicole,* the early English and French form for *Nicholas.* The more common method, apocope, or cutting off the final syllable, accounts for names like *Cesse* or *Sisse* for *Cecilia, Gib(be)* for *Gilbert,*[8] *Gill* or *Jill* for *Gillian* (from *Juliana*), *Kate* and *Kitte* for *Katharine, Simme* for *Simond, Tomme* or *Thomme* for *Thomas, Watte* for *Walter,*[9] and *Will* for *William.* Syncope, or omission of a syllable in the middle of the word, occurs in *Phip* for *Philip.* The shortening is frequently combined with a phonetic change. In a number of instances this is obviously due to a more or less regular phonologic development (*Herry* for *Henry,* for example, must be due to a denasalization of *en* before *r*). Mostly, however, there is a substitution of one consonant by another, as in *Hicke* for *Richard, Hobbe* for *Robert, Hogge* for *Roger,* and *Malle* for *Mary.*

In some instances the development of the pet name is difficult to account for. Thus *Jack,* used in England for *John* since the thirteenth century, may not, after all, come from French *Jaques,* Latin *Jacobus,* as one would assume. E. W. B. Nicholson believes that *Jack* is a shortened form of *Jankin* where *an* has become denasalized and shortened (*Jakin*).[10] P. H. Reaney (*A Dictionary of British Surnames,* p. 180, s.v. *Jakins*) cites *Jakin de Lagefare* from 1202 but doubts the validity of Nicholson's explanation, which, he believes, does not easily account for such early forms as *Jacce* or *Jake* (1195–7). He suggests the French *Jaques* as a likelier source.

Another difficult name is *Malkin.* Reaney (*A Dictionary of British Surnames,* p. 212, s.v. *Malkin*), the *Oxford Dictionary of English Christian Names* (pp. 93–94, s.v. *Mary*) and some other authorities take it to be a diminutive of *Mall,* for *Mary.* Skeat (in his edition of *Piers Plowman,* II, p. 29) cites *Promptorium Parvulorum,* which says,

"Malkyne, or Mawt, propyr name, Molt, Mawde : *Matildis, Matilda*."
The *NED* (s.v. *Malkin*), C. T. Onions [11] and Herbert Koziol [12] accept
this latter view. Ernest Weekley [13] believes that *Malkin* has more to
do with *Mary* than *Matilda*. C. W. Bardsley [14] suspects that Malkin
was a pet form for *Mary* in the North of England and for *Matilda* in
Norfolk and southeast England generally, but does not produce evidence to support his theory. He also hints at the possibility that the
use of the name *Malkin* for Maid Marian, the mistress of Robin Hood,
was because of the identification of Maid Marian as Matilda, daughter
of Lord Fitzwalter.[15] But the identification is late and therefore not
very helpful in settling the *Matilda/Mary* problem. It would seem that
Malkin came to be associated in the popular imagination with both
Mary and *Matilda,* through the familiar forms *Mall* and *Mald.*

A common method of deriving pet forms from names is the addition of a diminutive suffix. The basic function of such a suffix is to
indicate a lessening in size, amount, or quality, but it is widely used
also to express various subjective and emotional attitudes of mind, such
as affection, fondness, endearment, irony, derision, and contempt.

The use of diminutives seems to have a close connection with national characteristics. They are very common in the Slavonic languages,
especially in Russian. A striking peculiarity of the German language
spoken in Austria is the abundance of diminutives. They are very popular in the Romance languages too, particularly in Spanish, Portuguese,
Italian, and Rumanian, but somewhat less so in French. And in English they are quite rare. Practically all the diminutive suffixes in Middle
English were borrowings from the continent, mainly from France. The
French suffix *-el* accounts for *Peronelle (Pernel)* ; *-et* for *Colett, Gillet,
Jonet(te)* ; *-in* for *Colyn, Hogyn, Malyn, Robin; -on* for *Alison* and
Beton; and *-ot* for *Annote, Gilote, Katelote,* and *Kalote.* The most pop-
ular diminutive ending used with Christian names was, however, *-kin,*
imported from the Low Countries. In the literature examined for the
present paper it occurred in such names as *Dawkyn* (for *David*),
Hawkyn (probably for *Henry,* through *Hal*), *Jankin* (for *John*),
Malkyn (*Makyn,* for *Matilda* and/or *Mary*), *Perkyn* (for *Pers,
Peter*), *Symkyn* (for *Simond*), *Tomkyn* (for *Thomas*), *Wat(e)kin*
(*Wadekin,* for *Walter*), and *Wil(e)kin* (for *William*).

A striking feature of Middle English Christian names is that they
are practically all importations from France. Only a few native names
survive, such as *Edmund, Edward,* and *Alfred.*[16] Many French names
are, of course, originally Germanic : thus *Alice* comes from *Adalhaidis,*

Gilbert from *Gisilbert, Richard* from *Ricohard, William* from *Willi-helm,* etc. In *Robert* we may have the Old English *Hreodbeorht,* which after the Norman Conquest merged into the French *Robert,* originally from old Germanic *Hrodebert.* Some of the diminutives which end in *-kin* seem to have come from the Low Countries as such (*Jankin, Hankin,* etc.). In twelfth-century London the commonest French names were *Geoffrey, Gilbert, Henry, Hugh, John, Nicholas, Peter, Ralph, Richard, Robert, Roger, Stephen, Walter,* and *William* for men and *Agnes, Alice, Christine,* and *Maud* for women.

It is, perhaps, illuminating to see the frequencies of the commonest Christian names in medieval Paris, for men and women. The following list [17] is based on the taxation roll for 1292:

		%			%
Jehan	2020	13.3	Jehanne	223	1.5
Guillaume	1181	8.1	Marie	128	0.9
Pierre	798	5.5	Emeline	107	0.7
Robert	648	4.5	Agnes	100	0.7
Nicholas	403	2.8	Aalis	99	0.7
Richart	399	2.8	Perronele	94	0.6
Thomas	336	2.3	Maheut	76	0.5
Raoul	301	2.1	Ysabel	76	0.5
Jehannot	294	2	Marguerite	72	0.5
Estienne	260	1.8	Jehannete	65	0.4

After *Estienne* the commonest male names were *Henri, Simon, Geffroi, Rogier, Jaques, Gautier, Adam, Hue, Guillot, Phelippe, Michiel, Re-naut, Giles,* and *Robin.*

Semantic Development of the Names. In the names chosen for the present discussion the denotative (purely identifying) element is or seems to be weakened and a connotative element makes itself felt. The shift is noticeable in two directions:

(1) The identifying use gives way to a vague generic use in the sense "a typical representative of the kind of people to whom a name of that kind is usually given." A further weakening of the denotative element results in the use of the name for an ordinary, average person and, eventually, as a rough equivalent of "any man," "any woman."

(2) The person or persons to whom the name has been given come to be associated with certain qualities, real or imagined, with the result that the name as such becomes suggestive of those qualities. In the

majority of cases the implications are pejorative. The name may eventually become a common noun.

Generic Use. A passage frequently quoted as an example of Christian names used in a vaguely generic sense occurs in John Gower's *Vox Clamantis*:

> Watte vocat, cui Thomme venit, neque Symme retardat,
> Betteque Gibbe simul Hykke venire iubent:
> Colle furit, quem Geffe iuuat, nocumenta parantes,
> Cum quibus ad dampnum Wille coire vouet.
> Grigge rapit, dum Dawe strepit, comes est quibus Hobbe,
> Lorkyn et in medio non minor esse putat:
> Hudde ferit, quos Iudde terit, dum Tebbe minatur,
> Iakke domosque viros vellit et ense necat. . . .
>
> (Book I, 783–790) [18]

Gower is describing the Peasants' Revolt of 1381. The use of the names is purely stylistic, to present a vivid cross-section of the composition of the peasant army. It is interesting to compare Gower's list with the names in John Ball's letter to the peasants of Essex:

Iohon Schep, som tyme Seynte Marie prest of ȝork . . . greteth wel Iohan Nameles, and Iohan þe Mullere, and Iohon Cartere, and biddeþ hem þat þei bee war of gyle in borugh, and stondeth togidre in Godes name, and biddeþ Peres Plouȝman go to his werk and chastise well Hobbe þe Robbere, and takeþ wiþ ȝow Iohan Trewman and alle his felawes and no mo. . . .[19]

Iohan Nameles, "John Nobody," is interesting because it implies that *John,* a common Christian name, is here used approximately in the sense of "any man." The fact that no less than five of the seven personal names in the letter are *John*s suggests a special stylistic use. *Hobbe the Robbere*—considering the explicit mention of Piers Plowman—is probably a reference to Langland's poem, where *Robert the Robber* occurs in the A-text, Passus V, 233 and in B, Passus V, 469.

The stylistic use of personal names in a vaguely generic sense is characteristic of some lively scenes in *Piers Plowman.* Here is a description of Reason (Conscience in the A-text) preaching:

> He bad wastours go worche and wynne here sustinaunce
> Thorw som trewe trauail, and no tyme spille.

He preide Purnele here porfil to leue
And kepe hit in here cofre for catell at hure nede.
He tauhte Thomme Stowe to take two staues,
And fecche Felice home fram wyuen pyne.
He warnede Watte hus wif was to blame,
For hure hefd was worth half mark and hus hod nat a grote.
He bad Bette go kutte a bowh other tweye
And bete Beton thermyd bote hue wolde worche.[20]

(C-text, VI, 127–136)

There is another passage where Glutton—as the personification of Gluttony—on his way to church is tempted to enter the ale-house of Beton the brewster:

Thenne goth Gloton yn, and grete othes after.
Sesse the sywestere sat on the benche,
Watte the warynere, and hus wif dronke,
Thomme the tynkere and tweye of hus knaues,
Hicke the hekeneyman and Houwe the neldere,
Claryce of Cockeslane, the clerk of the churche,
Syre Peeres of Prydie and Purnel of Flaudres

.   .   .   .   .

A ropere and a redyngkynge and Rose the disshere,
Godfray the garlek-mongere and Griffyn the Walish

.   .   .   .   .

Clemment the cobelere cast of hus cloke

.   .   .   .   .

Hicke the hakeneyman hitte hus hod after
And bad Bette the bouchere to be on hus syde.[21]

(C-text, VII, 361–379)

Most of the names in these two passages seem to be used in a vaguely generic sense; some are used suggestively and will be discussed later in this paper. A feature common to them all is that they are part of an allegory. Their conventional character is suggested by their alliterative structure: *Betone the brewstere, Sesse the sywestere, Watte the warynere, Thomme the tynkere, Hicke the hakeneyman, Claryce of Cockeslane, Peeres of Prydie, Godfray the garlek-mongere, Clemment the cobelere,* and *Bette the bouchere.* That the names are conventional is further suggested by the freedom with which the scribes altered them. The B-text, Passus V, lines 109–111, for example, read:

> Awey fro þe auter þanne turne I myn eyghen
> And biholde how Eleyne hath a newe cote.
> I wisshe þanne it were myne and al þe webbe after.

For line 110 the A-text (V, 91) has "And beholde how Heyne haþ a newe cote." For *Heyne,* a male name, one manuscript has *Herry,* one *Hoge,* one *Hyk;* one has *he* and one *an hyne.*

Similar semi-generic uses of Christian names are to be found in many poems of the period. In *The Tournament of Tottenham* [22] there are several names of that kind:

> In a story as we rede
> Of Hawkyn, of Herry,
> Of Tomkyn, of Terry
>
> .   .   .   .
>
> þer hopped Hawkyn,
> þer daunsed Dawkyn,
> þer trumped Tomkyn,
> And all were trewe drynkers.
>   (5–7 and 15–18)

A relatively advanced stage in the weakening of the denotative element seems to be exemplified in the following quotations from a few fourteenth- and fifteenth-century poems. Thus in *A Satire on the Consistory Courts* [23] the names *Magge* and *Malle* seem to mean little more than "women" (who want to marry a reluctant peasant). The conventional character of the names is suggested by the alliteration which links them together: [24]

> þer stont up a ȝeolu mon, ȝeȝed wiþ a ȝerde,
> And hat out an heh þat al þe hyrt herde,
>   And cleopeþ Magge ant Malle;
> Ant heo cometh bymodered ase a mor-hen
>
> .   .   .   .   .
>
> Ant saith, "by my gabbyng, ne shal hit so gon,
>   Ant þat beo on ou alle;
> þat þou shalt me wedde ant welde to wyf."
>   (55–64)

And in the following passage from Chaucer's Friar's Tale the personal names approach the meaning "any man":

"This false theef, this somonour," quod the Frere,
"Had alwey bawdes redy to his hond. . . .
He hadde eek wenches at his retenue
That, wheither that sir Robert or sir Huwe,[25]
Or Jakke, or Rauf, or whoso that it were
That lay by hem, they tolde it in his ere."
                    (D 1338–1339, 1355–1358)

In *Piers Plowman* the name *John* is a symbol for "an ordinary man":

Ac many a Iustice an Iuroure wolde for Iohan do more
Than *pro dei pietate*
                    (B-text, VII, 44)

The pet name *Jack* is common in a more or less generic function, just as are its French and German cognates, *Jean*[26] and *Hans*.[27] The beginnings of the extensive use of these three names as common nouns are clearly discernible in medieval texts. Here is a passage from Gower's *Confessio Amantis*:

Whil that a man hath good to yive,
With grete routes he mai live
And hath his frendes overal

.   .   .   .

Thei seie, 'A good felawe is Jacke.'
Bot whanne it faileth ate laste,
Anon his pris thei overcaste,
For thanne is ther non other lawe
Bot 'Jacke was a good felawe.'
                    (Book V, 7747–7756)

In *Gramercy Mine Own Purse*,[28] preserved in the fifteenth-century MS Sloane 2593, *Jack* has the same meaning:

Quan my purs gynnyght to slak,
And ther is nowt in my pak,
They wil seyn, 'Go, farwil, Jak,
Thou xalt non more drynke with us.'
                    (stanza 2)

The low social status of the name is implied in the sixteenth-century proverb "Jacke would be a gentleman if he could speake Frenche."[29]

An early instance of its occurrence for inanimate things is *Jack of Dover* in:

> And many a Jakke of Dovere hastow soold
> That hath been twies hoot and twies cold,
> (The Cook's Prologue, A 4347–4348)

where it obviously refers to warmed-over food, possibly a twice-cooked pie or some kind of fish.[30] It is clear that at this early date the development of *Jack* into a lexical Jack of all trades—a *Johannes fac totum* or *Jean-fait-tout*—is already under way.

Suggestive Use. The background of the suggestive use of proper names is complex and highly variable, and therefore difficult to analyze. The best thing one can do is to call attention to a few salient features in the names available for the present study. Young people, for example, were customarily referred to by diminutive forms of their baptismal names; so those forms were naturally associated with qualities characteristic of youth. Thus *Jankin* and *Malkin* came to symbolize light-hearted and light-headed young people. Priests often had the name *John* and the title *sir* was commonly prefixed to their names; so *sir John* became a conventional name for a priest and was saturated with various mental associations aroused by that profession in the popular mind.

Many other factors played a part in the suggestive use of medieval names. That of sound and letter symbolism has been occasionally referred to, but the exact role of this factor is not easy to define. Religious, historical, and literary traditions must also be taken into account; one need only think of such names as *Adam, Eve, Herod, Judas, Hercules, Caesar,* and *Ganelon* and, particularly, the symbolical names of the Blessed Virgin:

> þou ert Iudith, þat fayre wyf
>
> . . . .
>
> þou ert Hester, þat swete þynge
>
> . . . .
>
> þou erte þe ryȝte vayre Rachel.[31]

Punning. Popular etymology and word-play—punning—has to be taken into consideration as a background influence. Thomas Wright, in *The Political Songs of England,* pp. 46–51, prints a Latin satire on the vices of great people during the reign of Henry III. The anony-

mous author mentions "four brothers," Robert, Richard, Gilbert, and
Geoffrey, whose names he explains in the following way:

> Competenter per *Robert, robbur* designatur,
> Et per *Richard, riche hard* congrue notatur;
> *Gilebert* non sine re gilur appellatur;
> *Gefrei,* si rem tangimus, in *jo frai* commutatur.[32]

Here, *Richard* is explained as meaning a *rich, hard* man. In *The Battle
of Lewes* [33] the name is connected with *trichard,* "trickster":

> Richard, þah þou be euer trichard,
> Tricchen shalt þou neuer more!
> (burden)

   The habit of interpreting names by popular etymology is illustrated
in the account which Mainerus, the scribe of a three-volume Bible
written in England in the twelfth century and now in Paris, gives of
his family.[34] Among the names explained is Mainerus' second brother:
*Secundus dicebatur Robertus, quia a re nomen habuit; spoliator enim
diu fuit et praedo* ("The second was named Robert because it was a
natural name for him; for he had long been a robber and plunderer").[35]
The name *Robert* was in fact commonly associated with robbers in
medieval England. In *Piers Plowman*:

> Robert the robbere on *reddite* lokede.[36]
> (B-text, V, 469; A-text, V, 233; *Robyn* in MS W)

The C-text has *Roberd the ryfeler,* which is the same thing. John Ball's
letter, quoted above, mentions *Hobbe the robbere,* using a common pet
form of *Robert. Piers Plowman* also speaks of *Robertes knaves* (C-
text, I, 45), who seem to have been marauding vagabonds. They apparently caused a great deal of trouble in the fourteenth century, and
there are several references to them as *Robert's men.* The *NED* (s.v.
Roberdsmen) cites *Peres the Ploughman's Crede,* which refers to
"Robertes men" (line 72), and two royal statutes, of 1331 and 1383,
written in French, in both of which the reference is to "Roberdesmen."
Skeat (*Piers Plowman,* II, 7) quotes Sir Edward Coke, who assumes
that *Robert's men* were originally the followers of Robin Hood in the
reign of Richard I.
   In *York Play* VII, *Sacrificium Cayme and Abell* of the fifteenth

century, Cain addresses Abel abusively as *robard iangillande,* "jangling robber." *Robard* may stand simply for "robber," with the second syllable showing contamination with the French pejorative suffix *-ard* (cf. *dochard,* "dotard, fool" and *mobardis,* "clowns," in the same collection of plays). But the possibility that it stands for *Robert* (with the normal development of *-ert* into *-art*) in the sense "a robber" is by no means excluded. The editor, Lucy Toulmin Smith, suspects that it is shortened from *Roberdsmen* or *roberdes knaves.*

John M. Steadman has argued that *Symkyn,* the name of the miller in Chaucer's Reeve's Tale, is a pun on the Latin adjective *simus,* "flat-nosed, snub-nosed." [37] More recently Dennis Biggins has suggested another Latin-English word-play on the same name. He believes that the name is a pun on the Latin noun *simia,* "ape." [38] In the tale, the miller is described in the following way:

> Round was his face, and camus was his nose;
> As piled as an ape was his skulle—
> (A 3934–3935)

and Biggins also calls attention to line 3927 (*pipen he koude* . . . ; cf. also A 565), where he sees a possible analogue of some marginal drawings in medieval manuscripts in which an ape is playing a bagpipe.

An interesting and obviously rather complex instance of punning is exemplified in Chaucer's Friar's Tale:

> an old wydwe, a ribibe (D 1377)
> Heere woneth an old rebekke (D 1573)

Ribibe and *rebekke* are disparaging terms for "old woman" in these contexts. *Rebekke* may contain an echo of the Biblical name *Rebecca,* which is mentioned in the marriage service, as Skeat reminds us in his note on D 1377; but this is speculation. There is an evident connection with the French verb *rebéquer,* "to reply sharply or impertinently"; cf. French *madame Rébecca* and Switzerland German *Rebeck,* "shrewish woman." [39] But the ultimate origins of the two words are *rebeck* (medieval Latin *rebeca*) and *ribibe,* Old French *rebebe,* both being western variants of the Arabic word *rebab* for a three-stringed fiddle. [40]

Robin. Robin and Marion are the favorite pair of rustic lovers in Old French pastoral poetry. A reflection of this literary convention occurs in John Gower's *Mirour de l'Omme,* in a passage on Fornication, the first of the five daughters of Lechery:

> Om fait de ce pecché les mals
> Plus commun es jours festivals
> Q'en autre jour de labourer
>
> .   .   .   .   .
>
> Qant Robin laist le charuer
> Et Marioun le canoller.[41]
>   (8653–8660)

Another echo of the French tradition is obviously Henryson's pastoral poem *Robene and Makyne,* which begins:

> Robene sat on gud grene hill
> Kepand a flok of fe. . . .

In the following two passages:

> That he that whilom was so gay,
> And of the daunce joly Robyn,
> Was tho become a Jacobyn . . .
>   (*Romaunt of the Rose,* 7452–7454)

> From hazelwode, there joly Robyn pleyde,
> Shal come al that that thow abidest heere—
>   (*Troilus and Criseyde,* V, 1174–1175)

the references to "jolly Robin" may be allusions to the same tradition, but that is not absolutely certain. These references seem to be paralleled, to some extent at least, in the following passage from Gower's *Mirour:*

> Ne say qui dance ne qui jouste,
> Mais bien say, qant sa large jouste
> Ly moignes tient tout plein du vin,
> Par grant revell vers soi l'adjouste
> Et dist que c'est la reule jouste;
> Ne croi point de saint Augustin,
> Ainz est la reule du Robyn
> Qui meyne vie de corbyn.[42]
>   (20881–20888)

In the *Lutel Soth Sermun*:

> Robin wule Gilot
> leden to þen ale.
> (73–74)

Here Robin is an ordinary country lad, like Jankin and Wilkin, and behaves like one. He is obviously in a different category from Robin *the rybaudour* of *Piers Plowman* (C-text, IX, 75), whose words were "rusty."

Jankin. Robin and Marion have no clear counterpart in Middle English poetry, but Jankin and Malkin provide a fairly good parallel. The indignant author of the *Lutel Soth Sermun* speaks disapprovingly about young men who love Malkin and young women who love Jankin; here the two characters typify very ordinary country lads and lasses. "Jolly Jankin" is a prominent figure in a fifteenth-century parody on the Mass whose burden runs:

> 'Kyrie,' so 'kyrie,'
> Iankyn syngyt merie
> with 'Aleyson.' [43]

Jankin figures in a number of other songs too, such as:

> Ianekyn of Londone
> Is loue is al myn.[44]

> Saue þin Iankyn lemman dere,
> Saue Iankyn lemman dere,
> saue þin onlie dere.[45]

The Wife of Bath's Prologue is a natural setting for Jankin. In fact it has room for two Jankins. In her long lecture the Wife scolds her husband for being suspicious when their apprentice Jankin is "squiering" her:

> And yet of oure apprentice Janekyn,
> For his crispe heer, shynynge as gold so fyn,
> And for he squiereth me bothe up and doun,
> Yet hastow caught a false suspecioun.
> I wol him noght, thogh thou were deed to-morwe!
> (D 303–307)

The other Jankin was a former "clerk of Oxenford," who:

> me thoughte he hadde a paire
> Of legges and of feet so clene and faire
> That al myn herte I yaf unto his hoold.
> He was, I trowe, a twenty wynter oold,
> And I was fourty. . . .
>
> (D 597–601)

In The Summoner's Tale Jankin is the eloquent squire of a country gentleman (D 2288 and 2293), and in B 1172 the Host addresses the Parson derisively as *Jankin* ("O Jankin, be ye there?").

In Lydgate's *London Lyckpeny* [46] "Some songe of Jenken and Julyan for there mede" (line 83). *Jenkin and Julian* is a prototype of *Jack and Jill* (see *Jack,* below).

Wilkin. In the thirteenth-century *Lutel Soth Sermun* girls neglect church services because they have only boys in their minds:

> Masses and matynes
> ne kepeþ heo nouht,
> For Wilekyn and Watekyn
> beoþ in hire þouht.
>
> (69–72)

Wilekin is the cleric who, through the services of Dame Sirith, a go-between, becomes the lover of a merchant's wife in the fabliau of Dame Sirith.

Jack. With *Jack* the erotic associations are not particularly prominent. In *A Midsummer Day's Dance* [47] it is the name of a holy-water clerk who seduces a girl; in another lyric printed by Robbins [48] Jack likewise has an affair with a girl. Jack may be called *Jack Reckless* [49] or *Jack the juggler* (*Piers Plowman,* C-text, IX, 71), but he is also a man to whom girls are likely to say "Farewell, Jacke; þin loue is pressyd al in þi pake." [50] But in practically all the contexts where *Jack* is mentioned this name seems to mean little more than "a fellow" or "a man." Chaucer uses *Jack* as a contemptuous epithet in The Miller's Tale: "'Go fro the wyndow, Jakke fool,' she sayde" (A 3708). And in a couple of political poems William de la Pole, Duke of Suffolk, murdered in 1450, is referred to as Jackanapes:

> Iack napys, with his clogge,
> Hath tied Talbot, oure gentil dogge. [51]

Jenkin and Julian is obviously a prototype or a variant of *Jack and Jill*, which is found in a macaronic poem on *Friars, Ministri Malorum*:

> þei weyl assaylle boyth Iacke and Gylle,
> Licet sint predones.[52]

Jack and Jill turn up also in the *Towneley Mysteries* ("for Iack nor for Gille").

John. *Jankin* and *Jack* are pet forms of John, which in *Piers Plowman* (B-text, VII, 44) is used to typify an ordinary man. In medieval French literature a cuckold often has the name *Jean,* as in the fabliau *Des trois dames qui trouverent l'anel;*[53] in John Heywood's *Mery Play betwene Johan Johan the Husbande, Tyb his Wyfe, and Syr Jhan the Preest*[54] the cuckolded husband and the priest have that name. Perhaps Chaucer had this implication in mind when he gave the name *John* to the carpenter in The Miller's Tale.

Sir John and Other Names of That Type. "The honorary title of Sir was given to priests down to a late period," Edward L. Cutts writes and gives examples from Shakespeare.[55] A comparable title used with the names of members of religious orders was *dan* (*daun*). John was apparently a common name among clerics, and *sir John* and *daun John* became conventional and often suggestive names for priests and members of religious orders. *Sire Johan* and *sire Geffray* are two worldly priests in *Piers Plowman,* B-text, XV, 120 ("Sire Johan and sire Geffray hath a gerdel of syluer"). Whether the *sir John* whose amorous inclinations form the subject matter of two short fifteenth-century poems printed by Robbins (*A Betrayed Maiden's Lament* and *Our Sir John*) is a priest or a layman it is difficult to say; Greene, commenting on one of the two poems, believes that "Sir John is probably the village priest or at any rate a cleric."[56] In The Nun's Priest's Prologue the Host "with rude speche and boold" addresses the Nun's Priest: " 'Com neer, thou preest, com hyder, thou sir John!' " (B 4000). The derisive tone of the Host's words is particularly clear from his use of the singular pronoun *thou.* Robinson (p. 198) refers to the recurrence of the name in the same context ("this sweete preest, this goodly man sir John," 4010) and believes that *John* was the priest's actual name. But this is only an assumption, and it is equally possible that in both instances the name is used conventionally for a typical priest. In *The Tale of the Basyn,* preserved in a manuscript of the fifteenth century, *Sir John* is a lecherous priest

("Hit is a preest men callis sir John," 78) whose amorous relationship with a married woman comes to an ignominious end.[57] A greedy
mendicant friar in The Summoner's Tale is *frere John* (D 2171), and
in The Shipman's Tale *daun John* is a young monk who pays for the
love of a rich merchant's wife with money borrowed from her husband. The Host, in The Monk's Prologue, addresses the Monk by
these words:

> by my trouthe, I knowe nat your name.
> Wher shal I calle yow my lord daun John
> Or daun Thomas, or elles daun Albon?
> (B 3118–3120)

He does learn the Monk's real name because on a later occasion
(B 3982) he addresses him as *daun Piers*. The Friar's Tale is about
a summoner who

> hadde eek wenches at his retenue,
> That, wheither that sir Robert or sir Huwe,
> Or Jakke, or Rauf, or whoso that it were
> That lay by hem, they tolde it in his ere.
> (D 1355–1358)

Sir Robert and *sir Huwe* were probably priests, as Robinson (p. 705)
assumes,[58] and so is probably *sire Piers of Prydie,* who in *Piers Plowman* (C-text, VII, 367) is found in the less respectable company of
Purnel (Peronelle) of Flaundres.

A word-play on *sir Robert* is perhaps involved in a euphemistic fifteenth-century poem to which its modern editor has given the title
Love in the Garden.[59] A girl had asked to have grafts of a pear-tree
yielding pear-jonets (an early ripening kind of pear) inserted into her.
A year later she had occasion to say that "it was a per Robert but non
per Ionet." The exact implication is not clear, but it is just possible
that there is an allusion to *sir Robert* as a type of a lecherous cleric.

Other Male Names. Evan (ȝyvan, *Yevan*), the Welsh form of *John,*
occurs in *Piers Plowman* (in the C-text only) in a passage describing
a Welshman:

> Then was ther a Walishman was wonderliche sory,
> He highte 'ȝyuan ȝeld-aȝeyn-if-ich-so-muche-haue.' . . .
> (VII, 309–310)

The name is obviously used in a suggestive sense. Another Welshman, *Griffyn* [60] *the Walish,* is mentioned passingly (C-text, VII, 373) and in a much more colorless way. *Colin* and *Colle,* both pet forms of *Nicholas,* are the names of two typical rascals in a song against the retinues of great people: [61]

> Of rybaudȝ y ryme and rede o my rolle,
> Of gedelynges, gromes, of Colyn and of Colle,
> Harlotes, hors-knaues. . . .
>
> (1–3)

It is impossible to say whether the two names are here used generically or whether they—either alone or when used together as an alliterative group—had pejorative associations of the kind implied in the passage quoted. Another alliterative group of names, *Diggon and Dobin,* occurs in *Mum and the Sothsegger* [62] ("Degon and Dobyn, that mennys doris brastyn," III, 362). Skeat (*Piers Plowman,* II, 302) believes that the two "common names for country bumpkins" are here used "in contempt of the upstarts who used to burst in men's doors and rob them"; and he adds that Spenser has *Diggon* and *Hobbinol* in his *Shepherdes Kalender* for September.

It would be interesting to know what the author of *Piers Plowman* had in mind when he chose *Haukyn* as the name of his "active man." Did he associate it with some idea he wanted to express? It seems idle to speculate on this point; perhaps it was chosen simply because it was a common name, in accordance with the author's consistent attempt to handle a moralizing allegoric theme in a concrete and realistic way. Besides, the form *Haukyn* has been called in question, by Ingrid von Bonsdorff, who thinks that the name was not *Haukyn* but *Hankyn.* The latter name, from *Hannekin,* came to England with merchants from the Netherlands, just as *Jankin* did. [63]

Hubert is the name of the magpie in *The Man in the Moon* ("hupe forþ, Hubert, hosede pye!" 37), and it is the name of Chaucer's Friar ("This worthy lymytour was cleped Huberd," A 269). Charles Muscatine has a note on this line, [64] where he says that "while a personal allusion is possible, I should like to suggest that *Huberd* may be an ironic allusion to Hubert *l'escoufle* [the kite] in the Old French poems of the Renart tradition."

The "Crooked Rib." Like their male counterparts, feminine names often occur in a more or less generic sense, to give an additional realistic touch to the stylistic treatment. Many of the names in *Piers Plow-man,* for example, seem to be used mainly for that purpose. Any special associations that names like *Betone the brewstere, Felice* (Tom Stowe's wife), *Letice at the style,* or *Rose the regratour* may have aroused in a contemporary audience have become obscured in the course of the centuries that have elapsed since. Often, however, this is not the case. In the *Ludus Coventriae,* for example, there is frequently a descriptive epithet to give a certain suggestiveness to the name; there are many names like *Betrys belle, fayr Jane, Kate kelle, Kytt cakelere, Letyce lytyl-trust, Luce lyere, Megge mery-wedyr,* and *Tyffany twynkelere.*

No one knows better than the "onlie begetter" of the present jubilee volume that female names are used fairly frequently in Middle English poetry to suggest ideas of various kinds. Apart from the names where the allusions are purely or predominantly literary, historical, or Bibli-cal (and which for lack of space cannot be included in the present dis-cussion),[65] there are many where the allusions are more or less topical. The range of the implications is not particularly wide, nor are they rich in nuance. They deal mostly with sexual behavior and are more or less derogatory. The gallery of characters ranges from very or-dinary women (often of the lower middle class) and unsophisticated country girls to prostitutes and procuresses.

Alis, Alison. The name comes from the old Germanic name *Adal-haidis* through Old French *Aalis, Aélis.* Songs about the *bele Aélis* were common in medieval France, where, to quote Jeanroy once again, "chanter de Robin et d'Aéliz" became synonymous with singing and dancing in a ring.[66] *Alis* and its pet form *Alison* are commonly asso-ciated with love and flirting in Middle English poetry. The poet who wrote the Harley lyric beginning "Bytuene Mersh and Averil" sings of his love for Alysoun, who is the "fayrest may in toune"; this Alysoun, of course, may have been a real living person. In "Jolly Jankin," the "I" is obviously a girl named Alison:

> 'Kyrie,' so 'kyrie,'
> Jankyn syngyt merie
> With 'Aleyson.' [67]

Here *Aleyson* is a pun on *(kyrie) eleyson.* The choice of *Alison* as the name of the carpenter's pretty young wife in Chaucer's Miller's Tale can hardly be accidental. And it is thoroughly natural that the Wife of Bath, who was every inch a woman, as one might say, should also have that name: she is referred to both as *dame Alis* and *Alisoun.* It is a little confusing that her gossip has exactly the same name.

Malkin. The etymology of this name is discussed briefly above. In The Nun's Priest's Tale Malkin is a very ordinary country lass, obviously a maid-servant:

> Ran Colle oure dogge, and Talbot and Gerland,
> And Malkyn, with a dystaff in hir hand.
>
> (B 4574)

In the *Ludus Coventriae* a contemptuous epithet is attached to that name (*Malkyn Mylkedoke,* 123,10). "Merry" *Makyne* (*Malkyne*) in Robert Henryson's *Robene and Makyne* is an echo of the shepherdesses of French pastoral poetry, but she is more than that: the angry author of the thirteenth-century *Lutel Soth Sermun* would send to hell all the "arrogant young men who love Malkin." In the early fourteenth-century *Interludium de Clerico et Puella* [68] a clerk tries in vain to win the love of "mayden Malkyn" and finally has to resort to the services of a go-between. Malkin's maidenhood, by the way, appears to have been proverbial, in one sense or another. It is referred to in *Piers Plowman* and in Chaucer's Man of Law's Introduction:

> 3e ne haue more meryte in masse, ne in houres,
> Than Malkyn of hire maydenhode that no man desireth.
>
> (*Piers Plowman,* B-text, I, 181–182)

> It wol nat come agayn, withouten drede,
> Namoore than wole Malkynes maydenhede
> Whan she hath lost it in hir wantownesse.
>
> (*Canterbury Tales,* B 28–31)

The two references, as Frederic G. Cassidy points out,[69] differ in meaning. There is no doubt about Malkin's wantonness in the Chaucer passage; in the *Piers Plowman* one there does not seem to be any implication of that kind: Malkin is still in possession of her maidenhood because no man has desired her. John Heywood alludes to the topic in "there was no mo maydens but Malkyn tho" (*tho,* "then").[70]

Joan, Jane, Janet. In a fragmentary love lyric (dance song?) of the fourteenth century the color of the girl's hair has caught the fancy of her lover: "Al gold, Ionet, is þin her." [71] In an Anglo-Norman poem written in Winchester on the 15th of September, 1293, and preserved in Harley MS 2253, *Johane* is a virtuous girl; it is only after the persistent teasing of a wanton friend, Gilote, that she gives up her chastity and takes a lover.[72] But the clear allusions in two parallel references, in *Piers Plowman* ("Ionette of the styues," C-text, IX, 71) and the *Towneley Plays* ("ye Ianettys of the stewys, and lychoures on lofte," 378,350) seem to suggest that the diminutive form *Janet* tended to be associated with loose sexual attitudes.

   Gill, Jill, Gilote. *Gilote* is a diminutive of *Gill,* which is a pet form of *Gillian,* from *Juliana.* The characters of the *Towneley Plays* include *Jelian Jouke,* "Gillian Clown" (377,317), *Gylle* or *Jelott,* the wife of Mak the sheep-thief (131,359; 126,316), and another *Gille,* who is Noah's wife (29,219). The *Ludus Coventriae* has *Gylle fetyse* (123,18). The *Middle English Dictionary,* s.v. *gil,* cites passages where *Gill* occurs as an appellative noun in the sense "girl, woman."

   The name *Gilote* makes its appearance in English literature in the thirteenth century. The author of the *Lutel Soth Sermun* complains that "Robyn wule Gilot leden to þan ale/ And sitten þer to-gederes and tellen heore tale." He will pay for her ale, and she will go with him in the evening. In *Gilote et Johane,* the Anglo-Norman poem dated 15 September, 1293, referred to above,[73] *Gilote* is a wanton young woman preaching a gospel of free love. The name becomes eventually an appellative noun meaning "a loose, wanton woman." It somehow seems to have become connected with *giggelot* (*giglot*) "flighty, giddy girl or woman," though the precise nature of that connection remains obscure.

   Katherine, Kate, Kit, Kalote, Katelote. The name of the dreamer's wife in *Piers Plowman* is *Kitte* (e.g., "Kytte my wyf and Kalote my daughter," B-text, XVIII, 426; C-text, XXI, 473). Occasionally the name means nothing more than "wife," as in "ich may nat come for a Kytte, so hue cleueth on me" (C-text, VIII, 304). The *Ludus Coventriae* has *Kate kelle* (123,15) and *Kytt cakelere* (123,17). *Kalote,* the name of the dreamer's daughter, is enigmatic because its etymology is unknown. It seems very unlikely that it has ever been used as a proper name, though Skeat believes it has.[74] As a common, appellative noun in the sense "a woman of low standing or of loose character" it has occurred since the late Middle English period (e.g., "a genttyll woman, or a callot, men wyll deme thow arte"[75]). The *NED,* s.v. *callet,* mentions three suggested etymologies: (1) French *caillette,* "a frivolous, prattling woman," (2) Old French *calotte,* "a kind of small cap or headdress," and (3) Gaelic or Irish *caile,* "girl."

There is something to say for all the three suggestions. It is perhaps worth noticing that in *Ludus Coventriae* a female character has the name *Kate kelle,* for *kelle* is probably a northern form of Middle English *calle* "a net for the hair, a kind of headdress" (though it might also be a Scandinavian loan).

A. E. H. Swaen believed that *kalote* was originally a Gypsy word.[76] He connected it with the *kelavdí* of Greek Gypsies, used in the sense "a prostitute" or "concubine." The word was brought to Britain by the Gypsies and underwent the natural phonetic changes. For the chronology of the English word Swaen relied on the *NED,* in which the earliest example dates from *ca.* 1500, and accordingly did not know of the earlier occurrences of the word. His theory is not applicable to *Kalote* in the two versions of *Piers Plowman* because the Gypsies did not arrive in Europe until the early fifteenth century, and the earliest record of their being established in Britain dates only from 1505. The theory, though a fascinating one, must therefore be regarded as an unsuccessful attempt to explain the etymology of the word *kalote.*

But Swaen, without knowing it, rendered a useful service to students of *Piers Plowman* when he called attention to the repeated occurrence of *kalote* in conjunction with *Kit.* He quotes Ben Jonson's masque *The Gypsies Metamorphosed*[77] ("to sett *Kitt-Callot* forthe in prose or ryme," 252) and an example in the *NED* (from 1532) in which Sir Thomas More refers to Luther and his wife Katharina von Bora as "Frere Luther and Cate calate his nunne." To these is to be added "Kyt calot my coosyn" in John Heywood's *Dialogue Containing Proverbs* (x, 181).[78]

This compels us to see the line in *Piers Plowman* in a new light. It seems that the author is playing upon the combination *Kit kalote,* which must have had at least some proverbial currency even as early as the late fourteenth century. He splits the phrase and makes *Kit* his wife and *Kalote* his daughter.

In a recent study Professor George Kane has argued convincingly that the dreamer in *Piers Plowman* is identifiable with the poet; so we may assume that "the poet was . . . implying that the Dreamer was— to some indeterminable extent—made in his own image."[79] The same reserved identification has been made by Morton Bloomfield: "Will is both William Langland and every Christian man."[80] What about the dreamer's wife and daughter? Did they have their counterparts in real life too? As far as the daughter is concerned, what has been said about the word *kalote* in the present discussion and, particularly, about the more or less proverbial character of the alliterative combination *Kit kalote* suggests strongly that her name at least is fictitious. The case of the wife might be different—after all, *Kit* is a real proper name—and the possibility that the author had a wife whose name was Katherine is not to be excluded; but it is at least equally possible that her name, too, is a pure fabrication.

But one also wonders whether in some vague, indefinable way *Kalote* might not be connected with *Katelote,* a name which occurs in Gower's *Mirour de l'Omme,* line 20,678, in a passage where the poet criticizes worldly priests for running after women: "O prestre, q'est ce courte cote? L'as tu vestu pour Katelote, Pour estre le plus bien de lui?" (Have you put on this short jacket [81] to win the favor of Katelote [who here represents the type of women coveted by priests]?) *Katelote* is obviously a pet form of *Katherine;* the name *Cathelot* occurs for *Catherine* in thirteenth-century Paris taxation rolls.

Peronelle, Pernel, Purnel. Peronelle was a common name in the Middle Ages. It had a relatively high frequency in the taxation rolls of Paris round about 1300. In several rolls it holds the third place after *Jehanne* and *Marie.* Reaney (s.v. *Parnall*) mentions *Peronelle* (*Pernel*) as one of the most popular of early English girls' names, recorded since the thirteenth century. In some passages of *Piers Plowman, Peronelle* is criticized for her pride ("Purnele proute-herte," C-text, VII, 3) or her fondness of gay dresses ("til . . . Purneles porfil be put in the whuche," C-text, V, 111; "he preide Purnele here porfil to leue/ And kepe hit in here cofre," C-text, VI, 129). *Pernel prane* ("prawn") is a character in the *Ludus Coventriae. Peronnele,* like *Marion, Aalis,* and *Emmelot,* is a shepherdess in some early French *pastourelles,* and her connection with them obviously contributes to early association with passing *affaires d'amour.* Gautier de Coinci, prior of the religious house of Vic-sur-Aisne in France, who wrote his famous miracles of the Virgin in the early part of the thirteenth century, describes some Sodomites who are drawn rather "to Perrotin than to Perronnele." In *Mum and the Sothsegger* ("if Pernell preisid the plytis bihynde," III, 156) the implication is that she is the kind of woman whose company is sought by medieval dandies and that she is a lady of easy virtue. In "dame Purnele a prestes file" (*Piers Plowman,* C-text, VII, 135) the noun *file* no doubt means "concubine, wench" (as Skeat says), and the same explanation applies to "that that . . . Priestes on aparail and on Purnele spenen" (C-text, XVIII,

71) and probably to "Syre Peeres of Prydie and Purnel of Flaundres" (C-text, VII, 367), who sit together in an ale-house instead of attending Mass. Skeat quotes a passage from Henry T. Riley's *Memorials of London* [82] according to which streetwalkers by night were especially "Flemish women." The name becomes eventually a common noun used in a pejorative sense; see *NED,* s.v. *Parnel* and *Pernel.*

Other Names with Pejorative Implications. The ancient regulation quoted by Riley in his *Memorials* goes on to say that prostitutes were "to keep themselves to the places thereunto assigned, that is to say, to the stews on the other side of Thames, and Cokkeslane." [83] This seems to place *Claryce of Cockeslane* (*Piers Plowman,* C-text, VII, 366) in the same category with *Ionette of the styues* (C-text, IX, 71), and likewise "of Shordyche dame Emme" (B-text, XIII, 340).

The etymology of the name *Sirith* is obscure; it is impossible therefore to say whether it was chosen as the name of the female go-between in *Dame Sirith* for any implications that may have been inherent in it. Her "colleague" in the *Interludium de Clerico et Puella* is *mome Helwis,* i.e., *Héloïse,* a name which may have been chosen for its suggestiveness based on the love story of Abélard and Héloïse, well known in the Middle Ages.

*

The suggestiveness of a personal name may owe something to sound and letter symbolism (that most elusive factor) as has been claimed and, in instances like *Jack and Jill* (see p. 351, note 24), to the name's phonetic and syntactic structure. Normally, however, it depends entirely on contextual factors and has no connection with the form of the name. Owing to its nature, it is often extremely difficult or even impossible to define it in a satisfactory way, as will have become apparent from the present attempt to examine it in a number of Middle English poems. The study was complicated by the considerable distance in time and the uneven quality of the surviving texts. In the circumstances the writer had to proceed with great caution in his interpretations, to say too little rather than too much and to leave a great deal to the judgment of his readers. This seemed to be the only sound policy in a matter in which much inevitably depends on subjective attitudes and impressions.

Epithets attached to medieval Christian names—precursors of modern surnames—often provided useful clues to the suggestive element. The most helpful of them were the nicknames which described mental, moral, and physical peculiarities. These occur in many texts, particularly in the Mysteries; there are names like *Jack Reckless, Perkin Reveler, Robert Runabout, Sim Small Faith, Kit Cackler, Lettice Little Trust,* and *Meg Merryweather.*

Diminutives and other pet forms of Christian names are common in the texts studied. A pet form suggests familiarity, and its social prestige is always lower than that of the full name. Chaucer, who had a sharp eye and a sensitive ear for manifestations of social vanity, makes skillful use of the pet/full name variation in The Reeve's Tale. The narrator, the Reeve, who has no love for millers, consistently refers to the miller of Trumpington as *Symkyn.* The two Cambridge students address him as *Symond,* for politeness or diplomacy, or for other reasons. His wife, who has never got over "hire kynrede and hir nortelrie/ That she hadde lerned in the nonnerie," uses both forms in her confusion when she is suddenly awakened from her sleep:

Awak, Symond! the feend is on me falle.

.   .   .   .   .

Help, Symkyn, for the false clerkes fighte!
(A 4288 and 4291)

The associations aroused by the various kinds of pet forms are usually pejorative to a varying extent. The quality most frequently hinted at is loose moral conduct, particularly in the sphere of sexual behavior. As usual, the targets are mostly women. The present study of suggestive names in Middle English texts confirms once again the truth of the Italian proverb which Francis Utley quotes at the beginning of his *Crooked Rib,* that brilliant study of medieval satire on women: *In men every mortal sin is venial; in women every venial sin is mortal.*

The suggestive use of ordinary personal names in literature is, of course, essentially a stylistic device. Among the works studied for the present paper none makes a more effective use of it than *Piers Plowman.* The reason is not difficult to see: a desire to give vividness and pungency to that moralizing allegory by tying it firmly to the concrete world of everyday life.

WILLIAM MATTHEWS

Caxton and Malory: A Defense

As long ago as 1737, John Lewis protested that scholars had not dealt as well with William Caxton as his service to letters warranted; in evidence he cited judgments that the books Caxton printed were of little value and also John Bale's observation that the printer was not entirely stupid or benumbed with sloth, *vir non omnino stupidus aut ignavia torpens.*[1] Now, after two more centuries of similar disparagements, a new biographer might well be inclined to echo Lewis' protest. Seemingly there is something about Caxton and his work that prompts even admirers to tarnish their praise with censure. Isaac Disraeli gathered most of the objections into one comprehensive attack: that being a mercantile printer, mindful of his commercial interests, Caxton left the glory of restoring the classical writers of antiquity to the learned printers of Italy; that he was an indifferent translator, a prolix genius of lax verbosity, who was almost a foreigner in his native idiom; that most of his publications were fabulous histories or spurious writings of the monkish ages, when they were not trivial productions that pandered to the ignorant readers of his own country.[2] Most critics are very far from such thoroughness; their strictures mingle with cautious praise. Thus Holbrook Jackson, while lauding Caxton as an amateur of letters who helped lay the foundations of literary English and the popular acceptance of books, blankets his faint praise under specific complaint: that Caxton was artless as a printer and had no sensitivity for types or type-pages; that rather than being a craftsman, he was a businessman in a hurry.[3]

Such criticisms are not groundless. Caxton certainly was a fifteenth-century English businessman catering to a public of merchants and their offspring as well as to nobles. The books he printed are in English and no one would claim that many of them are masterpieces. His types and typesetting compare poorly with those of the best of the continental printers. He produced translations in rapid succession, several a year sometimes, and they were prone to be hurried and excessively literal. And although, as Kellner, Roberts, Byles, and Bühler have argued,[4] he was sometimes a better writer than he was prepared to admit, much of his independent writing is distressingly subservient to the flatulent fashions of contemporary France. The only serious objection that can be raised against the complaints is that they cloud simple recognition of the solid accomplishment of a modest man who labored steadily in the cause of literature and education, who deeply honored and respected good writers and good books, and who published one great classic, Malory's *Le Morte Darthur,* that might have gone unknown for over four centuries had it not been for his love of England and literature.

On one score, however, there does seem to be an agreement of regard: that Caxton's character was admirable. Blades, after declaring that Caxton nowhere shines forth pre-eminent, pays tribute to his character, "a character which attracted the love and respect of his associates—a character on which history has chronicled no stain—a character which . . . retained to the last its innate simplicity and truthfulness." Byles avers that "in his original writings he shows the quiet strength, the modesty, the insistence on the highest standards of excellence, that characterize a great man." Aurner declares that his outstanding traits were "modesty, simplicity, and almost childlike absence of affectation." And Bühler sums up: "His nature was a gentle one, utterly devoid of the slightest trace of venom." [5] These and other such personal tributes are responses to Caxton's record as a businessman and to the record of his work as translator, editor, and publisher, which appears in prologues and epilogues and the works themselves. The estimate is general; so far as I know there is only one important disagreement.

This disagreement is related to one further complaint that has often been raised against his work: that his texts were poor and that as an editor he made free to make whatever changes he thought fit. The criticism was raised even in his own day, when one reader of the first edition of the *Canterbury Tales* told him it was a bad text. In Berthelet's 1532 edition of Gower's *Confessio Amantis,* it is objected against Caxton's edition that it varied in many places from the manuscripts and omitted "lines and columns, ye and sometymes holle pages." And a few years before, Gavin Douglas attacked his version of the *Aeneid*

with full Scottish downrightness: "The two are na mare like than the
Devil and Sanct Austin." It might be replied, of course, that it was
by no means easy for a fifteenth-century printer to come by the best
text, that Caxton, a devout admirer of Chaucer, hastened to print a
second edition from the text that his critic thought better, and that his
Eneydos is not translated from Virgil but from a French romance.
Yet there is some basis for the criticisms: Caxton does seem to have
been content to work with such texts as came readily to hand and to
translate such books as were within his own capacity.

The most damaging and frequently cited expression of this criticism, however, was made by Churchill Babington in his edition of
Higden's *Polychronicon.*[6] Facing Higden's Latin, Babington prints
John Trevisa's translation and an anonymous translation, and in abundant footnotes to the Trevisa he records changes that Caxton made in
his edition of 1482. In his preface he makes forceful comment on
Caxton's "manipulation" of Trevisa. The spelling, vocabulary, grammar, and sentence structure are so greatly changed, he declares, "that
the English is no longer the language of the 14th, but of the 15th
century." As a result, he felt "compelled to observe that his edition is
not of much critical value," while in a footnote he quoted approvingly
the observation of a writer in the *Christian Remembrancer,* that Caxton "exercised the part of editor of his various productions, by no
means after the fashion of Madden and Forshall. . . . *He cared
nothing for philology;* his books were printed for the sake of their
matter, and he was not willing to allow the interest of the subject to
suffer from the presence of obsolete spelling, *though he is strangely
inconsistent in his orthography."* These comments, together with the
list of words that Caxton had modernized, have served to support a
widely held view that Caxton, in C. S. Lewis's phrase, was a "creative
editor" who felt free to doctor his texts.

Examination of the instances in Babington's preface and footnotes
and comparison of numerous lengthy sections of the Trevisa and
Caxton texts indicates that while there is truth in what Babington
says—Caxton is an unlikely candidate for a founding member of the
Early English Text Society—his changes are by no means so drastic
as they might seem merely from looking at Babington's collection of
examples, and certainly not so radical and free-wheeling as the tradition from Babington has assumed. A random sample may be cited to
show Caxton's dealing:

Trevisa	*Caxton*
Also it is i-rad in Cronicis Anglorum þat Mordredus, Arthur his nevew, desirede for to regne, but he dradde onliche Cerdicus, and ʒaf hym oþer townes for to favoure hym ; Cerdicus assented þerto, and restored his province and contrayes wiþ newe Saxons, and was i-crowned at Winchestre in þe manere of mysbeleved men. But at Londoun, Mordredus was i-crowned kyng of Bretouns, but the yle of Wight left to Withgarus the nevewe of Cerdicus. But þe storie of Britons telleþ þat Arthur fauʒt afterward wiþ Mordredus and slouʒ hym, and was i-slawe, and i-buried in þe vale of Avalon bysides Glastonbury. Aftirward his body and þe body [of his wif] Gwenvere were i-founde in þe second kyng Henries tyme, and i-translated into þe chirche, about the ʒere of oure Lord enlevene hondred and foure score; so seiþ Giraldus, distinctione prima, capitulo 18⁰, þat was on lyve and handelede Arthur his bones. (Book V, cap. vi)	Also it is rad in Cronicis Anglorum that mordredus Arthurus nevewe desyred for to regne but he dradde only Cerdicus and yaue him other townes for to fauoure hym. Cerdicus assented therto and restored his prouynce and countryes with new saxons and was crowned at Winchester in the maner of misbileuyd men, but at London mordredus was crowned kynge of Britons, but the yle of Wyght left to Withgarus the nevew of Cerdicus. But the storye of Brytons telleth that Arthur fought afterward with mordredus and slough hym and was slayne and buryed in the vale of Avalon besides Glastingbury. Afterward his body and the body of his wyf Gwenner were founden in the second Harryes tyme and translated in to the chirche aboute the yere of our lord enleuen honderd four score, so seyth Giraldus distinctione prima capitulo decimo octavo, that was tho a lyue and handled Arthurs boones.

Not all the text shows so few changes as this, and to illustrate the extreme of Caxton's changes, here is the shorter of two passages that Babington cites as especially gross examples of how Caxton occasionally recast part of a sentence—he forgets Caxton might have used a different MS:

Trevisa	*Caxton*
þat he schulde wende out of þat lond in to a stede whider an aungel hym wolde lede, and by suche ledyng he com in to Scotlonde. (I, p. 393)	that he should go in to a place whyder an angel wolde lede hym, and so he cam into Scotland

Babington lists only thirteen of such recastings in Volume I, however, and in eleven of them the recasting is considerably less. Certainly

Caxton's editorializing stopped short of any additions or omissions beyond an occasional small detail (commonly for clarification), and just as certainly it entailed no radical rewriting, no interference with Trevisa's matter, style, or intent, and very little with his syntax. The one lengthy addition that Caxton does make is a continuation of the history from 1357 to 1460, and this is set apart and given its own separate table of contents—for reasons thoroughly characteristic: "For I dar not presume to sette my booke ne ioyne hit to his" because his own history was not scholarly enough and because his own "rude symplenesse and ignorant makyng ought not to be compared, set, ne ioyned to his boke"—Caxton's consistent humility toward his authors is almost touching. The alterations that he did venture frequently, often a dozen or more to a page, lie in spelling (e.g., *morwe* to "morow," *lafte* to "lefte," *londes* to "landes"), morphology (e.g., *i-seide* to "said," *leste* to "lasted," *seygh* to "saw," *i-dreynt* to "drowned"), and the occasional substitution of familiar words for older or dialectal ones (e.g., "part" for *deel,* "fledde" for *fliȝ,* "taken" for *bynome,* "eggs" for *eyren*). Such changes certainly result in Trevisa's fourteenth-century southwestern English taking on the color of the London English of Caxton's time.

To assume that editorialization as extensive as this was Caxton's normal practice, however, is quite unjustified. Trevisa was a special problem. Few linguistic tales are more familiar than the tall story that appears in Caxton's preface to *Eneydos* about the northern merchant who landed at a southern port and asked for *eggs,* only to be told by the goodwife that she could not speak French. Caxton's comment— what should a man in these days now write, *eggs* or *eyren?*—represents his dilemma as an editor when he was faced with preparing for his audience a text that employed local language of a former time. His response in Trevisa's case was for *eggs,* but it is quite typical of him that in proem and epilogue he lauds his author, belittles himself, and honestly explains what he had done. Not only had he added an eighth book and set it apart, he had also included a table of contents. Moreover, he had "a lytel embelysshed fro tholde makyng," having endeavored "to wryte fyrst ouer all the sayd book of *polycromion,* and somwhat haue chaunged the rude and old englysshe, that is to wete certeyn wordes which in these dayes be neither vsyd ne vnderstanden." What he did was no more than what other copyists of his time did; what is typical of him is that he reported his doings and gave his justifications.

Such indeed was his usual practice. The prologues and epilogues that he attached to many of his books usually explain the essence of what he had done in each case. Only those to the *Polychronicon* report that he had modernized the language, and it may be assumed that that was because it was the only time he did so extensively. Elsewhere he declares, for example, that he had not presumed "to correct or enpoigne onythinge" (*The Game and Playe of the Chesse*); that he had followed every word of the copy he had received from Lord Rivers, "as his secretaire can recorde" (*Moral Proverbes*); that he had followed his author "as nygh as I can or may, not chaungyng the sentense, ne presumyng to adde ne mynusshe onything" (*Jason*); that he had taken a translation that came into his hands and "diligently after my little understanding corrected it" (*Tullius of Olde Age*); that in assembling his *Golden Legend* he had worked from a Latin, a French, and an English text and had written "one oute of the sayd thre bookes, which I haue ordryd otherwyse than the said englysshe legend is"; that he had first refused Lord Rivers' plea that he oversee and correct his lordship's translation of *The Dictes and Sayengs of the Philosophres* for fear he might "apaire it," but later had checked it, and finding that it omitted some of Socrates' remarks about women, he had added them after the epilogue, not knowing whether his lordship had omitted them deliberately or because they were lacking from the manuscript from which he translated. These and other such notes are not the utterance of an editor of free-wheeling type; they display remarkable punctilio—something that is emphasized by his habitual request that his readers correct his defaults. Apart from the complaint (which Caxton reports) about the first edition of the *Canterbury Tales* and the objections that Margaret of Burgundy brought against the English of *The Recuyell of the Historyes of Troye,* we do not know how Caxton's own readers responded. But the response of modern editors generally bears Caxton out. "His translation is almost a literal one" (Mary Noyes Colvin), "Caxton takes no liberties with his subject-matter" (A. T. P. Byles), "Caxton seldom departs from his original" (Oliver H. Prior), are judgments on individual works that are summed up by H. S. Bennett's dictum: "Caxton humbly followed his original for the most part." [7] This applies to his translations, but there is no reason to think differently of his work as editor and publisher of English texts. Here and there in prose texts, changes in the spelling, morphology, even vocabulary, of the copy might occasionally have been made by the typesetters or Caxton himself, for such changes were part of the tradition of copying. Presumption, however—serious changes in matter or style, anything that clearly ran counter to the author's intention—was apparently taboo; and if a text was one that demanded extensive changes, as Trevisa's was, then the proceeding and the reasons were to be clearly set out.

In 1485, Caxton published the noble and joyous book entitled *Le Morte Darthur*. In the preface he reports the occasion of the publication and what he did in editing the copy. Many noble and divers gentlemen, he states, had often asked him why he had not printed the history of the Grail and of Arthur, and had urged him to print the history of the king and his knights, together with the history of the Grail and of the death of Arthur. They had tried to persuade him by reminders that Arthur had been born in Britain and been king of it, and that there were in French divers and many noble volumes concerning him. After mentioning the doubts expressed by some people whether Arthur ever existed [8] and the contrary reasons why he himself "coude not wel denye but that there was suche a noble kyng named Arthur," Caxton continues:

And many noble volumes be made of hym and of his noble knyghtes in Frensshe, which I have seen and redde beyond the see, which been not had in our maternal tongue. But in Walsshe ben many, and also in Frensshe, and somme in Englysshe, but nowher nygh alle. Wherfore, suche as have late ben drawen oute bryefly into Englysshe, I have, after the symple connynge that God hath sente to me, under the favour and correctyon of all noble lordes and gentylmen, enprysed to enprynte a book of the noble hystoryes of the sayde kynge Arthur and of certeyn of his knyghtes, after a copye unto me delyverd, whyche copye syr Thomas Malorye dyd take oute of certeyn bookes of Frensshe and reduced it into Englysshe.

After stating that he had set the book in print "accordyng to my copye," Caxton adds: "And for to understand bryefly the contente of thys volume I have devyded it into twenty-one bookes, and every book chapytred." Having listed these books, their topics, and the numbers of their chapters, he concludes: "The somme is twenty-one bookes whyche conteyne the somme of fyve hondred and seven chapytres."

These statements, so similar to reports on editorial procedures with his other books, would seem to represent a straightforward and credible accounting. Moreover, Sally Shaw in summarizing her comparison of his text with that of the Winchester manuscript pays it marked respect: "Above all his text is careful and accurate; and most of what appears to be editorial liberties, especially the substitution of modern equivalents, are either perfectly justifiable or too slight to cause serious objection." [9] In his introduction to his edition of Malory,[10] however, Eugène Vinaver maintains that Caxton deliberately misled readers about the nature of Malory's work. In effect, according to him, the copy from which Caxton printed consisted of several noble volumes: these were not physically separate, but each was marked off by an explicit, eight separate tales in one manuscript, the "works" which Malory wrote at intervals during a period of several years. Caxton, to satisfy the demand of his patrons and to effect editorial economy, printed them all as a modern book, deleting most of the explicits and giving the book the general title of *Le Morte Darthur* in order to make it seem to be a whole rather than a collection. This book he meant to be read as a work of moral edification, and to avoid an undesirable discrepancy he excised from the explicits (and particularly the first of them) elements that indicated that the author was a prisoner.

Before proceeding to details, some general observations may be ventured on Caxton's behalf. First: that he clearly says what he did in dividing his material. Second: that his preface tells us all that we know about his patrons and their wishes and from that it is by no means clear that they wanted a book "in the modern sense": all that is certain is that they wanted the stories of the Grail and of Arthur and his knights and the death of Arthur. Third: that it is far from certain that Caxton intended the work for moral edification. Although his preface stresses the book's moral value, it seems likelier that he read the book so and thought it was so intended than that he had any mind to impose his own piety on Malory. Malory's designation of himself as a "knyght presoner" does not appear in Caxton, but it is improbable that it is missing for any moral reason. In Malory's narrative the term is applied only to prisoners of war, and it is only our lately learned knowledge of the imprisonment of Sir Thomas Malory of Newbold Revel on charges of theft, rape, attempted murder, and so on, that lends any unsavory connotation to the term. There is no reason at all to think Caxton knew anything of this turbulent knight, and even if he did, it now is seriously questionable whether it was that knight who wrote the book.[11] Caxton was fond of including in his prefaces small details about his authors, and since he says nothing of Malory's being a prisoner, the most reasonable explanation may be that the information did not appear in his copy. Fourth: the theory that Malory's works were written over a period of several years is based on the supposition, now seriously questioned, that Malory spent the last decade of his life in Newgate prison. Fifth: since the explicits in Malory largely correspond to explicits in the works he was translating, they are not very convincing evidence of the kind of separateness that his editor claims. Sixth: that Caxton would even have thought it possible to deceive his audience in this way is something that might be questioned. His copy was not a manuscript in the modern sense; it was a copy of a published work, and he was not to know what copies of it might be available to his patrons—there may be significance in his statement that he printed the book "under the favour and correctyon of al noble lordes and gentylmen." It is certainly very improbable that he would have thought of deceiving future scholars and readers.

The editor claims, however, that what Caxton did "may be inferred from Caxton's own statement"; that when the printer refers to "many noble volumes in Freynsshe" and to "suche as have late ben drawen oute bryefly into Englysshe," he indicates that his own copy must have consisted of "many noble volumes"; [12] something that is supported by his never referring to them "otherwise than in the plural." To another reader, however, the matter may not seem so clear. The only "noble volumes" to which Caxton refers in his preface are the French books he had seen and read while he was abroad—and four years earlier, before ever he knew of Malory, he had used similar terminology about French writings on Arthur and his knights.[13] Nowhere does he say that his copy of Malory consisted of many noble volumes; when he does refer to it, it is in the singular, "thys book," "thys volume" which he had printed. While Caxton indicates the plural nature of the French sources, he does not, as it seems to me, indicate anything of the same kind about his copy of Malory.

There remain the explicits, and also the incipits which serve to indicate the major divisions of the narrative. Those from which the editor argues appear in the two texts as follows:

Winchester	*Caxton*
Here endyth this tale, as the Freynsshe booke seyth, fro the maryage of kyng Uther unto kynge Arthure that regned after hym and ded many batayles.	Explicit liber quartus Incipit liber quintus
And this booke endyth whereas	

Winchester

sir Launcelot and sir Tristrams com to courte. Who that woll make ony more lette hym seke other bookis of kynge Arthure or of sir Launcelot or of sir Trystrams; for this was drawn by a knyght presoner, sir Thomas Malleorre, that God sende hym good recover. Amen.

Explicit

Here endyth the tale of the noble kynge Arthure that was emperour hymself thorow dygnete of his hondys.

And here folowyth afftyr many noble talys of sir Launcelot de Lake

Explicit the noble tale betwyxt king Arthure and Lucius the Emperour of Rome

Explicit a noble tale of Sir Launcelot du Lake

Here folowyth Sir Garethis Tale of Orkeney that was callyd Bewmaynes by Sir Kay
And I pray you all that redyth this tale to pray for him that this wrote, that God sende hym good delyveraunce soon and hastely. Amen.

Here endyth the tale of Sir Gareth of Orkeney.

Caxton

Thus endeth the fyfthe booke of the conqueste that kynge Arthur hadde ageynste Lucius the Emperoure of Rome/ and here foloweth the syxth book whiche is of syr Launcelot du lake

Explicit the noble tale of syr Launcelot du lake whiche is the vi book

Here followeth the tale of syr Gareth of Orkeney that was called Beaumayns by sir kay and is the seuenth book

Thus endeth this tale of syr Gareth of Orkeney that wedded dame Lyones of the castel peryllous/ And also syr Gaherys wedded her syster dame Lynett/ that was called the damoysel saueage/ And syr Agrauayne wedded dame Laurel a fayr lady and grete and mighty

Winchester	*Caxton*
	landes with grete richesse gaf with them kyng Arthur that ryally they might lyue tyl their lyues ende
Here begynnyth the first boke of Syr Trystrams de Lyones, and who was his fadir and hys modyr, and how he was borne and fostyred, and how he was made knyght of kynge Mark of Cornuayle.	Here foloweth the viii book the which is the first book of sir Tristram de Lyones/ & who was his fader/ and his moder & hou he was borne and fosteryd/ And how he was made knyghte
Here endyth the secunde boke off syr Trystram de Lyones, whyche drawyn was oute of Freynshe by sir Thomas Malleore, knyght, as Jesu be hys help. Amen.	Here endeth the second book of syr Tristram that was drawen oute of Frensshe in to Englysshe
But here ys no rehersall of the thirde booke.	But here is no rehersal of the thyrd book/ And here foloweth the noble tale of the Sancgreal that called is the hooly vessel and the sygnefycacyon of the blessid blood of our lord Jhesu Chryste/ blessid mote it be/ the whiche was brought in to this land by Joseph of Armathye/ therefor on al synful souls blessid lord haue thou mercy
But here folowyth the noble tale off the Sankegreall, whyche called ys the holy vessell and the sygnyfycacion of blyssed bloode off our Lord Jesu Cryste whyche was brought into thys londe by Joseph of Aramathye.	
Therefore on all synfull, blyssed Lorde, have on thy knyght mercy. Amen.	Explicit liber xii/ Et incipit Decimustercius
Thus endith the tale of the Sankgreal that was breffly drawy[n] oute of Freynshe—which ys a tale cronycled for one of the trewyst and of the holyest that ys in this worlde— by Sir Thomas Maleorre, knyght.	Thus endeth thistory of the Sanggreal that was breuly drawen oute of Frensshe into Englysshe/ the whiche is a story cronycled for one of the truest and the holyest that is in thys world/ the whiche is the xvii book/
O, Blessed Jesu, helpe hym thorow hys myght! Amen.	And here foloweth the eyghtenth book
And bycause I haue loste the very mater of Shevalere de Charyot I depart from the tale of sir Launcelot	And by cause I haue lost the very mater of la chevaler du charyot/ I departe from the tale of sir

Winchester	*Caxton*
and here I go unto the morte Arthur, and that caused sir Aggravayne	Launcelot/ & here I goo unto the morte of kynge Arthur/ and that caused syre Agrauayne
And here on the othir syde folowyth the moste pyteuous tale of the Morte Arthure Saunz Gwerdon par le Shyvalere Sir Thomas Malleorre, Knyght.	Explicit liber xix And here after foloweth the moost pytous history of the morte of kynge Arthur/ the whiche is the xx book
Jesu ayede ly pur voutre bone mercy! Amen.	
[Explicit lacking; manuscript defective]	Here is the end of the hoole book of kyng Arthur and of his noble knyghtes of the Rounde Table, that whan they were hole togyders there was euer an hondred and forty/ and here is the ende of the deth of Arthur/ I praye you all jentylmen and jentelwymmen that redeth this book of Arthur and his knyghtes from the begynnyng to the endyng/ praye for me whyle I am on lyve that God sende me good delyveraunce/ & whan I am deed I pray you all praye for my soul/ for this book was ended the ix yere of the reygne of King Edward the Fourth/ by sir Thomas Maleore, knyght, as Jesu helpe hym for hys grete myght/ as he is the servaunt of Jhesu bothe day and night

Comparison of the two columns indicates the following procedures on Caxton's part—always assuming his copy had exactly the same incipits and explicits as Winchester. First: the omission of repetitious statements. Second: the omission from all but the last explicit of reference to Sir Thomas Malory. Third: the omission from all but the last explicit of the author's prayers for deliverance or for God's mercy. Fourth: the addition of book-numbers. All three types of omission could fairly be ascribed to a printer's bias toward system and economy; the essential information is left for the emphatic position at the end of the work. The omission of the whole of the first explicit that appears in Winchester, however, is something quite different. In fact it is so different from Caxton's dealing with the others, that it seems to me very unlikely to be his own doing.[14]

These omissions apart, the incipits and explicits are very similar in both texts. It is true that Caxton's versions do not always have exactly the same form as Winchester's, but they are close enough—and sufficiently longer than Caxton's usual book-explicits—as to make it unlikely that Caxton intended to obliterate the major narrative-divisions in his copy; had that been his intention he could easily have replaced them all by his own brief book-number explicits. In all but two cases, however, he combines his own book-division system with the "tale" or "history" divisions that Winchester uses: the third explicit in Winchester, for example, "Explicit a noble tale of Sir Launcelot du Lake" is matched by Caxton's "Explicit the noble tale of syr Launcelot du lake whiche is the vi book."

And if with these eight major divisions Caxton sticks reasonably close to his copy, so too does he with his further divisions into books. The incipits and explicits listed above, upon which Vinaver largely bases his charges against Caxton, are by no means the only such marks of division in the Winchester manuscript. For example, early in Malory's work these occur:

Winchester	*Caxton*
the Booke of Balyne le Saveage that folowith nexte aftir; that was the adventure how Balyn gate the swerde	the book of Balin le Savage, that foloweth next after, how by aduenture Balin gat the swerd. Explicit liber primus. Incipit liber secundus.
Thus endith the tale of Balyn and Balan, two brethirne that were borne in Northumbirlonde, that were two passynge good knyghtes as ever were in tho dayes. Explicit.	Thus endeth the tale of Balin and of Balan, two brethren born in Northumberland, good knights. Sequitur iii liber.

These are the first of the incipits and explicits of the Winchester manuscript, and they correspond to Caxton's own first incipit and explicit and also to his division of Books I to III. It is perhaps worth remark, in view of Caxton's terminology, that Winchester's first incipit also uses the term "book." But what is more noteworthy is that the correspondence between Winchester's divisions and Caxton's which is indicated in this first instance continues throughout the work. All but two of Caxton's book-divisions, in fact, correspond to explicits-cum-incipits in Winchester (Books 1–9, 12, 13, 19, 21) or to comparable indications of changes of subject, such as "Now leave we . . . and speke we of . . ." or "Now turnyth this tale unto . . ." (10, 11, 14–17).[15] The two exceptions are Book 18, which ends (as also does the Winchester manuscript) with the famous analogy between love and summer, and Book 20, where the narrative shift from the siege of Benwick to Mordred's conspiracy is so striking that a new book seems imperative.

For Caxton's division of these books into chapters, there is less authority in the Winchester manuscript. But there is still a good deal. In that manuscript the material between incipit and explicit is divided into sections by means of a large capital or an indentation at the beginning of a new section. Caxton's chapters often correspond to these indications: of the eighteen chapters in his Book VI, for example, seven correspond to large initials in Winchester and three to indentations. For two additional chapters, the manuscript has sidenotes corresponding to Caxton's chapter-headings. The chapter-headings themselves must be largely Caxton's work, his method of indexing and summarizing the outlines of the narrative "for to onderstonde bryefly the contente of thys volume." But there is enough agreement between them and the occasional sidenotes in Winchester to suggest that similar notes in his own copy might have confirmed him in adding these more systematic indications of subject. Here, for example, are the correspondences for Book VI:

Winchester	*Caxton*
The deth of Terquyn by sir Launcelot	9. How syr Turquyn was slain and how syr Launcelot bad syr Gaheris delyver al the prysoners.
Here sir Launcelot slew Perys de Forest Saveage	10. How syr Launcelot rode with the damoysel and slewe a knyght that distressid al ladyes and also a vylayn that kept a bridge.
Here sir Launcelot slew two Gyauntes in the castel of Tyntagil	11. How syr Launcelot slewe two geauntes and made a castel free.

Winchester	*Caxton*
Here sir Launcelot bete iii knyghtes and rescowed sir Kay	
Here sir Launcelot with one spere smote downe sir Sagramour sir Ector sir Uwayne and sir Gawayne	13. How syr Launcelot justed ayenst four knyghtes of the Rounde Table and overthrewe theym.
Here sir Launcelot heled sir Melyot de Logrys with sir Gylberde the Basterdis swerde	15. How sir Launcelot cam into the Chapel Peryllous and gate there of a dede corps, a pyece of the cloth and a swerde.
Here sir Launcelot made sir Pedyvere bere the dede body of the lady to Quene Gwenyvere	17. How syr Launcelot overtoke a knyght which chased hys wyf to have sleyn hyr, and how he sayd to hym.

In sum, what Caxton did in organizing his copy for printing seems to have been very much what he said he did. In accordance with his practice with other books (e.g., *Charles the Grete* and *The Book of Fayttes of Armes and of Chyualrye*), but also with a good deal of authority from his copy, he systematically divided the narrative into books and chapters. He preserved the major explicits and incipits largely in their original form, and he made his book divisions correspond to narrative divisions indicated in his copy. Yet although the procedure seems quite aboveboard in its details, its effect is certainly somewhat different from the effect of the Winchester manuscript. Caxton's systematic terminology and his division into books and chapters make Malory's work seem visually more solid and four-square than it seems in Winchester, and his many chapter-headings tend to lessen the effect of the major explicits in indicating the eight-part division of the narrative. The divisions are there, of course, for except for Book V the narrative is unchanged; but the external pointers to the division are less striking. This effect may have been unintended, but it is a concomitant of Caxton's understanding that he was publishing a book, a volume. Whether he was misrepresenting the form of his copy depends on what was his understanding of how that copy was made up.

Vinaver assumes that Caxton understood the copy's organization in exactly the same way as he himself does, and that in publishing his volume he deliberately misrepresented his text. Apart from his dealings with the explicits, he contrived this, so Vinaver charges, by imposing upon his copy a single general title. The charge relates to Caxton's colophon:

Thus endeth thys noble and Ioyous book entytled le morte//Darthur/ Notwythstondyng it treateth of the byrth/ lyf/ and/ actes of the sayd kyng Arthur/ of his noble knyghtes/ of the rounde table/ theyr meruay-lous enquestes and aduentures//thacheuyng of the sangreal/ & in thende the dolorous death &/ departyng out of thys world of them al/ whiche book was reduced in to englysshe by syr Thomas Malory knight as afore// is sayd/ and by me deuyded into xxi bookes chapytred// and/ enprynted and fynysshed in thabbey westmestre the last day//of Iuyl the yere of our lord mcccclxxxv   Caxton me fieri fecit

At various times Vinaver terms this colophon a stratagem, a subter-fuge, Caxton's most ingenious device. He also terms part of it Caxton's "famous apology" however, and argues that the colophon is both an acknowledgment of what Caxton did to his copy and the means by which he has misled scholars and critics. The charge is so grave and so seriously at odds with Caxton's general reputation for simple hon-esty that it warrants some examination.

The last explicit in Malory makes a distinction between the whole book and that part of it which deals with the death of Arthur. "Here is the ende of the hoole book of kyng Arthur and of his noble knyghtes of the Round Table . . . ," he writes, "And here is the ende of the deth of Arthure." In the next sentence a similar allusion is made to "this book of Arthur and his knyghtes from the begynnyng to the endyng." [16] If these remarks indicate titles—although they may merely indicate subjects—then it could be argued that whereas "The Deth of Arthur" would be the title of the last section, the title of the whole book would be something like "The Whole Book of King Arthur and his noble knyghtes of the Round Table."

Caxton's colophon begins, "Thus endeth thys noble and Ioyous book entytled le morte//Darthur/ Notwythstondyng it treateth of the byrth/ lyf/ and/ actes of the sayd kyng Arthur/ of the noble knyghtes . . ." etc. Taken with Malory's last words, it affords evidence, in Vinaver's view, both of Caxton's deception and his apology for it.

There is something very peculiar, however, in reporting an offense and at the same time apologizing for it—particularly when the offense was deception, and a deception that was persisted in. Elsewhere Vinaver stresses details that Caxton has omitted, supposedly to further his deception. Had deception been really his objective, it surely would have been simple to omit from Malory's last explicit the few phrases that might have been interpreted as contradicting the general title *Le Morte Darthur*. In these circumstances, Caxton's colophon takes on the air, not of a "famous apology" but of an explanation of his copy. Moreover, if the "Notwythstondyng" was meant to qualify the preceding statement, as it may well have been, the explanation seems tinged with perplexity. Caxton had just printed Malory's statement that the whole book was about King Arthur and the 140 noble knights of the Round Table. Ten lines later, he himself writes of this noble and joyous book entitled *Le Morte Darthur,* obviously referring to the whole book, but going on in the statement beginning "Notwythstondyng" to indicate the peculiarity of the title in view of the varied subjects of the book. It is easy, of course, to read into such phrases meanings that may not have been intended, but in this case it does seem possible that rather than obscuring a distinction, Caxton was puzzling over an apparent discrepancy.

If this reading is sound, then it would follow that it was not Caxton who imposed this title on the whole book, but that there was something in his copy that led him to think that Malory's own title for the whole book was *Le Morte Darthur*. This is a guess, but possible support for it may be found in Malory's own narrative.

Early in Malory's work, just before the story of Balin, there occurs a brief account of Merlin's prophecy that Arthur would be killed by a boy who had just been born on May Day. This being a form of the Herod story, Arthur proceeds to send for all noblemen's sons who had been born on that day, intending to destroy them. Among those who were sent was Mordred, the offspring of King Lot's wife and Arthur himself:

And so was Mordred sente by kynge Lottis wyff. And all were putte in a shyppe to the sea; and som were four wekis olde and som lesse. And so by fortune the shyppe drove unto a castelle, and was all to-ryven and destroyde the moste party, save that Mordred was cast up, and a good man found hym, and fostird hym tylle he was fourtene yere of age, and than brought hym to the courte, as hit rehersith aftirward and towarde the ende of the MORTE ARTHURE.[17]

This is Malory's text as it appears in the Winchester manuscript. Caxton differs slightly in making the cross-reference read, "as it rehearseth afterward, toward the ende of the deth of Arthur." [18] At this point Malory was summarily translating from the *Suite du Merlin,* and the lines in that romance which correspond to the end of the foregoing quotation run:

Et li sires fist retenir l'enfant et metre avoc Sagremor son fil; se les fist ensi norrir ensemble, et dist que se Dieus les amendoit tant qu'il venissent en l'aage de estre chevalier, il les feroit faire chevaliers ensemble. . . . Ensi trouva Mordrec secours et aide apriès le peril de la mer. Mais or laisse li contes a parler atant et retourne au roi Artu(s).[19]

Apart from the condensation of the narrative, Malory's main change is the insertion of the detail about Mordred's coming to court at fourteen "as hit rehersith aftirward and towarde the ende of the MORTE ARTHURE."

In point of fact, Mordred's coming to court at the age of fourteen—or at any age—does not appear anywhere in Malory. It seems likely, therefore, that at the time Malory wrote this detail and cross-reference he either thought there was such an incident later in his French sources or that he meant to insert such an account himself. In the one case, he was wrong; in the other, he must later have forgotten. But the most interesting detail in the statement is where the episode was to appear: toward the end of the *Morte Arthure.* According to what that title refers to, the last section or the whole book, two possible interpretations suggest themselves: that the episode would come toward the end of the last section or toward the end of the whole book.

It is fairly easy to judge between these alternatives. At the beginning of the final section, Mordred is no stripling of fourteen, just come to court; he is a mature knight who had performed various adventures and was now ready to put his malevolence to effect. Toward the end of the section he is dead, slain in the last great battle. A place "toward the end" of the whole work gives much wider scope for bringing Mordred to court at appropriate age. If logic means anything, therefore, Malory's cross-allusion must refer to the whole book under its general title, *Morte Arthure.*

Whether Malory's work is a series of separate tales or a single book with an over-all construction is now a matter of scholarly dispute. Vinaver holds to his theory of separateness; but Brewer and other

critics have pointed out the many ways in which Malory loosely binds
the parts of his narrative into a whole; and Lumiansky and Moorman
have argued that the work is firmly constructed as a unity, written to
develop a single tragic conception. Caxton proffered no such theme,
though he read *Le Morte Darthur* as a moral work. Having read the
many noble volumes in French, he knew well enough that his copy was
a reduced form of various French romances. But there is no reason to
think that he believed this copy represented anything but a whole book,
which began with Arthur's birth and ended with his death and the
passing of the Round Table—"the whole book of Kyng Arthur and
of his noble knyghtes of the Round Table" and "this book of Arthur
and his knyghtes from the beginning to the endynge" to use Malory's
last words. Nothing in Caxton's career or in his handling of this book
supports the opinion that he would have deliberately deceived his readers. If he was wrong and the copy he divided into 21 books and 507
chapters was in fact eight distinct works, then it must still be assumed
that his error was committed in innocence and that his editing was
done with intent to help rather than to deceive. As for the title, Caxton
gives none, for he has no title page.

Printer's mark of William Caxton, Westminster

MARGARET SCHLAUCH

Thomas Usk As Translator

Problems of fourteenth- and fifteenth-century literary prose (what we might call *Kunstprosa*) have attracted much attention in recent years, but there are still many to be investigated. Perhaps the most mannered of prose stylists among Chaucer's contemporaries was Thomas Usk, best known for his *Testament of Love,* a long philosophical piece, partly autobiographical, written in Boethian-Chaucerian vein. I have already attempted an analysis of Usk's style in some typical original parts of this work.[1] However, not all of Usk's writing in the *Testament* was original. Years ago it was pointed out by George Sanderlin [2] that Book III was closely modeled on an ambitious work of St. Anselm entitled *De concordia praescientiae et praedestinationis.*[3] Source relationships were at the time carefully indicated. It became clear at once that, in general, Usk treated his source with a certain freedom upon occasion, though by no means always. By comparisons in detail it may be possible to deduce something about his linguistic and stylistic technique in those parts where he functioned as a more or less faithful translator.

It should be remembered from the start that we have no manuscript copy of Usk's *Testament*; our sole authority is the text mistakenly included in Thynne's edition of Chaucer's works (1532).[4] Here the introduction of current sixteenth-century spelling, plus printers' fallibility, have together given rise to some internal textual obscurities, which were probably not all Usk's fault.

For instance, Anselm has: *Quare si necesse est me peccare ex voluntate, intellego me cogi aliqua occulta vi* (509 A), but *TL* as we have it changes the sense by omitting *if:* "wherfore necessitè is me to love of wil" (112; the substitution of *love* for *peccare* and other verbs is typical; see below). The full stop appears after *wil* in Thynne's print. Anselm makes a clear statement: *quoniam Deus non fallitur nec videt*

97

nisi veritatem sive ex libertate sive ex necessitate eveniat (513 C), but *TL* is ambiguous here: "for god is not begyled, ne he seeth nothing wheder it shal come of libertè or els of necessitè" (119; is it possible that an expression like *but trouthe* has been dropped out after *nothing?*). Again Anselm writes: *nec praedestinatio excludit liberum arbitrium nec liberum arbitrium adversatur praedestinationi* (521 A), but in *TL* we find: "presence and predestinacion in nothing disacorden" (143). It seems doubtful that Usk wrote "presence" (perhaps rather "prescience"?), since later in the same sentence he correctly renders the *liberum arbitrium* and *praescientia* of Anselm as "free choice" and "before weting" respectively. Anselm gives a complete and logical comparison: *sicut est ratio instrumentum ratiocinandi quo utimur cum ratiocinamur; et visus instrumentum videndi, quo utimur cum videmus* (534 C), but this becomes nonsense in *TL* by omission of an essential part: "right as reson is instrument of resons which ye usen whan ye loken" (130). Did Usk's eye skip a line here, or his scribe's, or the printer's? We do not know.

Another general fact to be borne in mind is the difference in purposes between the two authors. St. Anselm is concerned with a very general problem: the reconciliation of divine omnipotence and foreknowledge with the occurrence of evil deeds, specifically of sins committed by acts of free will. Usk, on the other hand, is concerned with only one sort of event, namely the act of falling in love, whether literally or allegorically. He asks: Is this fore-ordained or not? Accordingly, he substitutes for Anselm's *peccare* and cognates such words as "love" and "lover," as here:

Sed dices mihi: Non removet tamen a me necessitatem peccandi, quoniam Deus praescit me peccaturum, vel non peccaturum . . . (508 A).	(Usk speaks:) God before wot me in service of love to be bounden to this Margarite-perle, and therefore by necessitè thus to love am I bounde . . . (112).
Sic itaque si dico, necesse est peccaturum, vel non peccaturum sola voluntate, sicut Deus praescit, non est intelligendum quod aliquid prohibeat voluntatem quae non erit, aut cogat illam esse quae erit . . . (509 B).	Right so, if I say, thorow necessitè is thee to be a lover or els noon; only thorow evil, as god beforn wete. It is nat to understonde that any thing defendeth or forbit thee thy wil, which shal nat be; or els constrayneth it to be, which shal be . . . (112).

Elsewhere Usk several times renders the colorless word *res* by *love* (e.g., Anselm, 509 f.; *TL,* 113 f.), in accordance with his general purpose. The shift is carried out in relation to other words too, for instance here:

Nam si dico: *Cras seditio futura est in populo,* non tamen necessitate erit seditio (511 A).	For if I say, 'to-morrow love is comming in this Margarites herte,' nat therfore thorow necessitè shal the ilke love be (115).

When he wishes to do so, Usk is quite capable of translating his source very closely. Here is an example:

Lignum enim non est semper necessitate album, quia aliquando priusquam fierit album, potuit non fieri album; et postquam est album potest fieri non album: lignum vero album, semper necesse est esse album . . . (510 A-B).	For a tree is nat alway by necessitè white. Somtyme, er it were white, it might have be nat white; and after tyme it is white, it may be nat white. But a white tree evermore nedeful is to be white . . . (114).

Sometimes fidelity to St. Anselm betrays Usk into non-English constructions, for instance when he copies directly the accusative with infinitive for indirect speech: *intellego me cogi* (508 A), "I understand me to be constrayned" (112); *saepe dicimus necesse esse* (509 A), "often we sayn thing thorow necessitè to be" (112); *si dico* cras esse futurum ortum solis (511 A), "as if I say, 'to-morowe be comminge the rysinge of the sonne' " (115); *si hoc modo dicimus Deum praedestinare malos* (520 A), "if in that manner be sayd, god toforn have destayned . . . badde" (142; but here "have" may be a subjunctive).

Occasionally however Usk replaces the Latin infinitive with an English *that*-clause: *Ponamus itaque simul esse . . .* (507 B), "Nowe I suppose that they mowe stande togider" (111); *Ponamus itaque simul esse et praescientiam Dei . . . et libertatem arbitrii* (507 B), "Nowe I suppose that they mowe stande togider: prescience of god . . . and libertè of arbitrement" (111; the use of the proleptic pronoun *they* is interesting). In a number of cases Anselm himself employs a different construction for indirect discourse, namely a *quia*-clause with indicative mood, which Usk is able to follow quite literally with the corresponding English construction: *Ergo sciendum est* quia *saepe dicimus necesse esse quod nulla vi esse cogitur* (509 A), "thou shalt wel understande, *that* often we sayn thing thorow necessitè to be, that by no strength to be neither is coarted ne constrayned" (112; emphasis added). Yet it will be noticed here that a conventional accusative with infinitive is embodied within the *quia*-clause, and here too *TL* follows Anselm closely.

A shift from an impersonal to a personal construction is sometimes found: *Cognosci potest etiam non omnia quae praescit Deus esse ex necessitate* (512 C), "thou shalt understonde that, right as it is nat nedeful, god to wilne that he wil, no more in many thinges is nat nedeful, a man to wilne that he wol" (116; here the sense is expanded and modified). Elsewhere *TL* usually follows the Latin model: *necesse est esse peccaturum* (509 B), "thorow necessitè is thee to be a lover" (112). Usk even changes a personal to an impersonal construction: *Forsitan dicis: Nondum aufers a corde meo vim necessitatis* . . . (508 C), "whan it is said, 'th[r]ough necessitè it is me in love to abyde'" (112). Other minor liberties are taken in the English version. A passive construction may be made active: *velut homo homini facit injuriam unde ab illo occiditur* (521 A), "as if a man another man wrongfully anoyeth, wherfore he him sleeth" (143). Or a negative statement may become a positive one: *et necesse est Deum non esse injustum* (509 A-B), "and it is necessitè, god to be rightful" (112). However, such deviations are relatively unimportant.

Stylistic aspects of Usk's relation to his source are more interesting than the grammatical. We know from his original writing in *TL* that Usk liked verbal repetition, play with cognate forms (*adnominatio*), and the like. Now it happens that St. Anselm himself frequently employs verbal repetition, but his primary purpose is clarity, not decoration, as can be seen in a passage such as this which Usk follows fairly closely:

Nam, non semper scribo aut volo scribere: et, sicut, dum non scribo aut non volo scribere non est necesse me scribere aut velle scribere; ita necesse non est ut aliquando scribam, vel velim scribere . . . (514 C-D).	Lo! somtyme thou wrytest no art, ne art than in no wil to wryte. And right as while thou wrytest nat or els wolt nat wryte, it is nat nedeful thee to wryte or els wilne to wryte (122).

Or this:

Voluntas quidem justitiae est ipsa justitia; voluntas vero beatutidinis non est beatitudo: quia non omnis habet beatitudinem, qui habet ejus voluntatem (528 B).	Wil of rightfulnesse is thilke same rightfulnesse, as here-to-fore is shewed; but wil of blisse is not thilke blisse, in whom the wil therof is abydinge (140).

The use of tautological doublets and near-synonyms is a trick of style very characteristic of Usk's original prose, where it appears primarily to serve the purposes of decoration rather than clarification. In the Latin of St. Anselm, Usk found but few instances to follow: e.g., *factor et autor . . . malorum operum* (517 C), "maker and auctor of badde werkes" (123). When he introduces his own, the purpose is sometimes (but not often) to offer an explanation: *coactionem vel prohibitionem* (509 A), "coaccion, that is to sayne, constrayning, or els prohibition, that is, defendinge" (112). But elsewhere the device seems to stem rather from Usk's delight in words, a trait shared by other writers of late Middle English prose. Sometimes alliteration reinforces the effect:

nulla prohibitione (509 A)	neither coarted ne constrayned (112)
prohibeat (509 B)	defendeth or forbit (112)
ad ratiocinandum (534 A)	to knowe and to prove (129)
praedestinatio (512 A)	presence and predestinacion (143)
haec enim favet spiritui concupiscenti adversus carnem (537 C)	This helpeth the spirit to withsitte the leude lustes of flesshly lykinge (139).

Inversions in word order are occasionally suggested to Usk by Anselm's text:

hoc ipsum namque praescit Deus (509 B)	That same thing, forsooth, god before wot (113)
Rectitudo quidem . . . nullius mali causa est (527 C)	This rightfulnesse . . . of none yvel is it cause (139)

But more often we find inversions introduced by the translator, in accordance with his marked stylistic preference elsewhere in *TL*:

sed quando consentit concupiscenti adversus spiritum (528 A)	but whan to flessly lustes it consenteth ayenst reson of soule (140)
Perdito igitur instrumento volendi justitiam, id est, rectitudinem, nullo modo nisi per gratiam reddatur, potest voluntas instrumentum velle justitiam (540 A).	Wherfore yet I say, . . . whan instrument of evil *lost hath* rightfulnesse, in no maner but by grace *may he* ayen retourne *rightfulnesse to wilne* (141, italics added).

There is an especial concentration of inversions in a passage (141, ll. 142 ff.) which begins:

but rightfulnesse was so yeven that man *might it lese,* which if he *not lost had,* but continually [might] *have it kept,* he shulde have deserved the avauncement in-to the felowschippe of angels, in whiche thing if *he that loste,* never by him-selfe forward *shulde he it mowe ayenward recovre* . . .

and so on (italics added). Some of Usk's inversions were, of course, sanctioned by traditional usage from Old English on and are therefore from the historical point of view quite normal, although already optional. It may be said, however, that Usk employed both these and others with exceptional frequency. Chaucer did not favor them to this extent.

Because the purpose and literary form of *TL* were so different from those of Anselm's *De concordia,* Usk had to introduce passages of dialogue and modes of expression unknown to his original. These include chiefly the conversations between the author and his interlocutor, the Lady Margaret. A typical interpolation is this:

Tho liste me a litel to speke and gan stinte my penne of my wryting, and seyde in this wyse.

'Trewly, lady, as me thinketh, I can allege authoritees grete, that contrarien your sayinges' (119, nothing to correspond in Anselm, 513 C).

Other interpolations are various. St. Anselm had made a concise contrast between saints in eternity, where there is neither past nor future but only the present, and the mutable human condition based on free will. Usk expanded this by a parenthetical remark heightened by alliteration and a concrete reference to a time span of 7000 years:

Hoc quippe propositum, secundum quod vocati sunt sancti, in qua non est praeteritum, vel futurum, sed tantum praesens, immutabile est, sed in ipsis hominibus ex libertate arbitrii aliquando est mutabile (515 D).

This purpos, after whiche they ben cleped sayntes or holy in the everlasting present, wher is neither tyme passed ne tyme comminge, [but ever it is only present, and now as mokel a moment as sevin thousand winter; and so ayenward withouten any meving is nothing lich temporel presence for thinges that there is ever present]. Yet amonges you men, er it be in your presence, it is movable thorow libertè of arbitre-

ment (120; square brackets introduced to show added material, italics
to show alliteration).

It will be noticed that Usk makes the last sentence a bit livelier by
introducing the second personal pronoun you/your into St. Anselm's
impersonal statement. In a long interpolated sentence about astronomy
(120, ll. 144–151) Usk makes use of the same second person possessive
pronouns—"your transitory times, your temporal presence, your tymes"
—much as did Chaucer in his *Astrolabe,* as well as other writers of
scholarly texts in the vernacular. The conventional linguistic device
helped no doubt to establish a sense of direct contact between author
and student-reader.

A freely adapted sentence will show how readily Usk heightened
word-play and *adnominatio* upon occasion:

Dubium utique non est quia voluntas non vult recte nisi quia recta est. Sicut namque non est acutus visus quia videt acute, sed ideo videt acute quia acutus est (523 C).	It is no maner doute, that wil wol not love but for it is lovinge, as wil wol not rightfully but for it is rightful it-selve. Also wil is not lovinge for he wol love; but he wol love for he is lovinge; it is al oon to wilne to be lovinge, and lovinges in possession to have (137 f.).

Briefly it may be said that Usk could be a literal translator when he
wanted to be; he could omit, condense, expand or modify according
to his special purpose; and that when he treated his source most freely
he evinced most clearly the rhetorical traits characteristic of his original formal writing. He was, in short, a very conscious experimenter
in the medium of fourteenth-century English prose.

Emperor on Horseback

HELAINE NEWSTEAD

Some Observations on King Herla
and the Herlething

Among the many marvels recounted by Walter Map in the miscellany known as *De Nugis Curialium,* the story of King Herla has attracted the attention of diverse scholars largely because of the assumed connection of his name with the traditions of Harlequin and the Wild Hunt.[1] The interest in this element of the story, however, has overshadowed other features in Walter Map's treatment that are equally significant and worthy of study.

First of all, as James Hinton pointed out many years ago,[2] Walter Map relates the story as an exemplum to illustrate the restlessness of the court. It is preceded by a lengthy discourse in which the court of his own day is compared to hell:

> The rolling of flames, however, the thickness of the shadows, the rankness of the rivers, the loud gnashing of the teeth of demons, the shrill and woeful groans from troubled spirits, the foul crawling of vermin, vipers, and snakes and every manner of creeping thing, and the godless roarings, the stench, the strident wailings, the awfulness—methinketh, should I try to set all these forth one by one by means of allegory, I lack not comparisons among the courtiers, but this matter demandeth a longer time than I see is at my service.

He concludes that "the court is a place of punishment. I say not, however, that it is hell (which doth not follow), but it is as nearly like it as a horse's shoe is like a mare's."[3] Later, after referring to himself as the "Tantalus of this hell," he introduces the story of King Herla with this statement: "That there was but one court similar to this of ours we learn from old stories. These tell us that Herla, the king of the very ancient Britons. . . ." [4] The story of Herla's adventures should be read in this context.

King Herla was led into a compact with a pygmy king riding on a goat, who proposed that he attend Herla's wedding on condition that Herla attend his a year later. At Herla's wedding feast, the pygmy king arrived with a multitude of splendidly garbed retainers who served a feast of unparalleled magnificence. Reminding Herla of his promise, the pygmy king and his retinue vanished at cockcrow. A year later, he suddenly appeared and demanded that Herla attend his wedding according to the pact. Herla, with his retainers, followed the pygmy king into a dark cavern in a cliff that led into a hall that seemed to be illuminated not by sun or moon but by many lamps. After the sumptuous wedding, Herla and his company departed laden with gifts of "horses, dogs, hawks, and all things befitting venery and falconry." [5] The pygmy king escorted his guests to the darkness and gave Herla a small bloodhound warning them not to dismount until the dog should leap from the arms of its bearer. When Herla emerged into the sunlight, he asked an old shepherd for news of his queen. The shepherd replied that he could scarcely understand Herla's British speech since he was a Saxon and that he knew of no queen of that name save the wife of Herla, an ancient British king, who was supposed to have disappeared with a pygmy into the cliff some two hundred years earlier. Herla's sojourn seemed to him to have lasted only three days. Some of his retainers, ignoring the pygmy's warning, dismounted and at once crumbled to dust. Herla then forbade anyone to touch earth before the descent of the dog, but since it never descended, Herla and his army wandered without rest. But finally in the first year of King Henry's coronation, the troop was seen less frequently. Then it was seen by many Welsh sinking into the Wye at Hereford. "But from that hour that wild march ceased, just as if these rovers had handed over their wanderings to us for their own peace." [6]

At a later point in the text, he mentions apparently the same troop of wanderers, here called Herlethingi:

Gatherings of those troops of night-wanderers whom men call Herlethingi were very famous in England up to the time of Henry II, our present king, an army of infinite wandering, of the maddest meanderings, of insensate silence, in which appeared alive many who were known to be dead. This band of Herlething was last seen on the borders of Wales and Hereford in the first year of King Henry II, at high noon, in the same guise in which we wander abroad, with chariots and beasts of burden, with pack-saddles and bread-baskets, with birds and dogs, with men and women running side by side. Those who first saw them aroused with shouts and trumpets the whole neighborhood against them. After the manner of that most watchful nation (the Welsh), many bands fully equipped with arms came at once, and because they were unable to extort a word from the strange troop in reply to their words, they prepared to exact a reply with their darts. But the visitors, rising into the air, suddenly disappeared.

From that day this troop hath been nowhere seen, since seemingly it hath bequeathed to us foolish folk its errant ways, through which we wear out garments, lay waste provinces, break our bodies and those of our beasts, and are never free to find a cure for our sick souls.[7]

Despite the inconsistencies in the two accounts of the wandering army, the whole story, including the adventure with the pygmy king, is colored by Walter's invective against the restless court of his own day, made explicit in his conclusion that the court had inherited the compulsive wandering of Herla's company after its recorded disappearance in the first year of Henry II's reign. The comparison of the court to hell in the introductory passage is also developed in the description of the Herlething, who included many known to be dead. Similar implications occur in the description of the pygmy king: "just such a man as Pan is pictured, with glowing face, enormous head, and a red beard so long that it touched his breast (which was brightly adorned with a dappled fawn skin), a hairy belly, and thighs which degenerated into goat-feet."[8] Although the king was generous and benevolent in his actions, the details of his appearance and the comparison with Pan would have suggested the demoniac to Walter's contemporaries.

Walter Map's purpose has shaped the story and directed its emphasis. Although the Herlething are generally identified with the Wild Hunt, Walter's version lacks some typical features. The Herlething are represented as a troop of the dead, who are classified as "night-wanderers," though they were last seen at high noon haunting the Welsh marches in uncanny silence and refusing to reply to those who encountered them before they vanished into the air. They are not said to be engaged in hunting. The Wild Hunt, however, is a noisy crew, whose nocturnal appearances [9] are typically associated with the clamorous accompaniments of the chase, especially the baying of hounds. Walter's version resembles the experience in Normandy of the Eng-

lish priest Gualchelm in 1092 reported by Ordericus Vitalis, in which
he saw and spoke with a vast company of damned souls, many of
whom he recognized. After hearing their cries and lamentations and
witnessing their sufferings as they passed by, he concluded that they
must have been the "familia Herlechini," of whose fame he had heard
often, presumably in England.[10] In both stories the names of the mysterious company are similar and in both the apparitions are represented
as the spirits of the dead, with no reference to hunting. The same
tradition is reflected in a letter by Peter of Blois dated in 1175 in
which he includes an unflattering comparison of English courtiers to
the "milites Herlewini," a curious anticipation of Walter Map's idea.[11]

The story of King Herla is connected with the separate account of
the Herlething not only by the same purpose, but also by the localiza-
tion and date. King Herla's company was last seen sinking into the
Wye at Hereford; similarly the Herlething made their last appearance
on the border of Wales and Hereford, but instead of sinking into the
river they vanished into the air. The event is dated in both variants
in the first year of Henry II's reign. King Herla's mad wanderings
are noted, but there is no explicit reference to hunting. Yet a significant trace of such a tradition is preserved in the parting gifts that
Herla's pygmy friend bestowed upon him: "horses, dogs, hawks, and
all things befitting venery and falconry." This detail suggests that in
an earlier form of the story Herla was indeed the leader of the Wild
Hunt. Since Walter Map was intent upon the invidious comparison
with the contemporary court, it is not surprising that he showed no
interest in Herla's use of his hunting equipment.

The story of Herla's adventure with the pygmy king is actually
independent of the traditions about the Wild Hunt. As E. S. Hartland
pointed out long ago,[12] the supernatural lapse of time in fairyland is
the principal motif of that tale. Like other visitors to an Otherworld
realm, Herla is lavishly entertained for three days, as he supposes, but
learns after his departure that he has been absent for two centuries.
Those of his followers who disregard the pygmy's warning against
dismounting instantly crumble to dust.

The motif of the supernatural lapse of time is ubiquitous, as Hartland's collection of examples shows, but Walter's story has its closest
affinities with Celtic tales of similar type.[13] In some of these tales the
visitor suffers no ill effects from his sojourn, but in others, as in
Walter Map's story, death or disaster results if a warning from the
supernatural host is unheeded.[14] The normal conclusion of this tale is

the revelation of the lapse of time and the disintegration of the dis-
obedient followers. Obviously Herla and the rest of his retainers must
also be dead after two centuries, but they avoid the terrible fate of
their fellows by their ceaseless wandering.

The tradition of the Wild Hunt seems, then, to be originally distinct from the experience with the pygmy king. We cannot now know
how they came to be combined, but we may hazard a guess. Many
stories about the Wild Hunt include an explanation of its cause. The
Wild Hunt is sometimes a punishment for failure to keep a fast day,
for hunting on Easter Day, for disturbing church services, for suicide,
unshriven death, parricide, and other sins.[15] In a similar way, the
adventure with the pygmy king and his parting gift of hunting equipment may have been attached to King Herla to account for his leader-
ship of the Wild Hunt.

The name Herla remains a puzzle, and the elaborate but inconclusive
arguments to explain its origin are too complicated for brief recapitu-
lation. A few facts, however, can be established. First, Herla is not
the name of any British or Welsh king, nor is he otherwise known to
history or legend. But the name of the Wild Hunt seems to be more
familiar: Walter Map's Herlethingi, the "familia Herlechini" of Ordericus Vitalis, and the "milites Herlewini" of Peter of Blois suggest
that the Wild Hunt was known in England under such a polysyllabic
name in the twelfth century. The name seems to be English. Hinton's
suggestion [16] that Herlething is a mistake for Herleking, "King Herla,"
has been accepted and developed by several scholars.[17] The form
Herlewine has also been interpreted as "Herle-wine," meaning "household of Herla." [18]

But the reverse process is also conceivable. If the originally independent story of the pygmy king was attached to the tradition of the
Wild Hunt in order to explain the wanderings of the company, the
name of its leader, Herla, may possibly have been derived from one
of the names of the Wild Hunt current in the twelfth century. The
polysyllabic form of the name may also be connected, as Kemp Malone [19] has proposed, with the name Herelingas recorded some four
hundred years earlier in the Old English *Widsith*. The Herelingas are
generally identified with the Harlung brothers, whose death by hanging is related in Germanic legend.[20] Malone points out that death by
hanging would have meant in the old Germanic religion consecration
to Woden, who also appears as leader of the Wild Hunt. But unfortunately, tempting though the suggestion may be, the reference to the

Herelingas in *Widsith* gives no hint of such a legend, and there is no evidence that this story of the death of the Harlungs circulated in England.[21] The form of the name, however, and similar place names in England [22] imply the existence of some tradition in the days when *Widsith* was composed, but it is too shadowy to be identified with any confidence. The connection with the Herelingas, though possibly significant, remains tenuous since the resemblance of the names is not supported by other evidence.

Walter Map's story is thus a composite of traditions about the Wild Hunt and a tale about a mortal's visit to the Otherworld realm of a pygmy king and its dire consequences. Walter himself did not make the original combination, but he evidently knew two variants of the Wild Hunt tradition, one without the story of the pygmy king. His own contribution seems to have been the embellishment of the story with details suggestive of hell and damnation and the witty conclusion, in both variants, that the doomed wanderers bequeathed their restlessness to the English court of his own day. Yet the didactic purpose and the learned allusions do not obscure the vivid immediacy of the supernatural encounters. Like his friend and learned colleague, Giraldus Cambrensis, and other scholarly clerics of the twelfth century, Walter Map was deeply interested in manifestations of the marvelous. Some tales he gathered from books, others from oral tradition. Just as Giraldus recounted tales he had heard in Brecon and Pembroke, the regions most familiar to him,[23] so Walter Map may originally have heard the stories of King Herla and the Herlething in the neighborhood of Hereford, his early home, where he localizes them.

R. E. KASKE

Gawain's Green Chapel and the Cave at Wetton Mill*

In *Sir Gawain and the Green Knight,* the climactic meeting between Gawain and his mysterious adversary is preceded by a detailed description of the "green chapel" with some of its topographical surroundings:

> And þenne he wayted hym aboute, and wylde hit hym þo3t,
> And se3e no syngne of resette bisydez nowhere,
> 2165 Bot hy3e bonkkez and brent vpon boþe halue,
> And ru3e knokled knarrez with knorned stonez;
> þe skwez of þe scowtes skayned hym þo3t.
> þenne he houed, and wythhylde his hors at þat tyde,
> And ofte chaunged his cher þe chapel to seche:
> 2170 He se3 non suche in no syde, and selly hym þo3t,
> Saue, a lyttel on a launde, a lawe as hit were;
> A bal3 ber3 bi a bonke þe brymme bysyde,
> Bi a for3 of a flode þat ferked þare;
> þe borne blubred þerinne as hit boyled hade.
> 2175 þe kny3t kachez his caple, and com to þe lawe,
> Li3tez doun luflyly, and at a lynde tachez
> þe rayne and his riche with a ro3e braunche.
> þenne he bo3ez to þe ber3e, aboute hit he walkez,
> Debatande with hymself quat hit be my3t.
> 2180 Hit hade a hole on þe ende and on ayþer syde,
> And ouergrowen with gresse in glodes aywhere,
> And al watz hol3 inwith, nobot an olde caue,
> Or a creuisse of an olde cragge, he couþe hit no3t deme
>   with spelle.

* This study was made possible by a Grant-in-Aid from the American Council of Learned Societies.

2185   "We! Lorde," quoþ þe gentyle knyȝt,
        "Wheþer þis be þe grene chapelle?
        Here myȝt aboute mydnyȝt
        þe dele his matynnes telle!"

        "Now iwysse," quoþ Wowayn, "wysty is here;
2190   þis oritore is vgly, with erbez ouergrowen;
        Wel bisemez þe wyȝe wruxled in grene
        Dele here his deuocioun on þe deuelez wyse.
        Now I fele hit is þe fende, in my fyue wyttez,
        þat hatz stoken me þis steuen to strye me here.
2195   þis is a chapel of meschaunce, þat chekke hit bytyde!
        Hit is þe corsedest kyrk þat euer I com inne!"
        With heȝe helme on his hede, his launce in his honde,
        He romez vp to þe roffe of þe roȝ wonez.
        þene herde he of þat hyȝe hil, in a harde roche
2200   Biȝonde þe broke, in a bonk, a wonder breme noyse. . . .
2217   "Abyde," quoþ on on þe bonke abouen ouer his-hede,
        "And þou schal haf al in hast þat I þe hyȝt ones."
        Ȝet he rusched on þat rurde rapely a þrowe,
2220   And wyth quettyng awharf, er he wolde lyȝt;
        And syþen he keuerez bi a cragge, and comez of a hole,
        Whyrlande out of a wro wyth a felle weppen. . . .[1]

Though no one would argue that a poetic description of this kind
must necessarily mirror an actual piece of terrain, the present passage
does seem to push the imagination inevitably in that direction. For one
thing, the chapel and its setting not only are unparalleled in the rest
of medieval literature, but are in fact singular to a really remarkable
degree—an effect greatly heightened by the unusual fullness and spe-
cificness with which they are described. Again, there is a surprising
air of homely literalness about some of the details: *nobot an olde
caue,/ Or a creuisse of an olde cragge* . . . (2182–2183). And finally,
the chapel which is the central feature of this elaborate topographical
picture remains altogether functionless in the confrontation that follows; no one goes into or comes out of it, and it is not mentioned
again in the remainder of the poem. In themselves, of course, such
hints can hardly provide more than interesting speculation; what they
do suggest is that if we can find a precise and complex enough pattern
of correspondences between the poet's description of the green chapel
and some actual locality (preferably within his supposed dialect area),

there will be good reason for suspecting either topographical inspiration or some sort of deliberate topographical allusion.[2]

Among the various prototypes that have been suggested for the green chapel, probably the most familiar is the cave at Wetton Mill (also known as Nan Tor), proposed by Mabel Day in a passage which must by now have come under the eyes of thousands of students of the poem:

If Wales, which lay behind Sir Gawain, is excluded, the nearest mountain country to Wirral is the Staffordshire moorland. Now, just at the bottom of the valley where the Hoo Brook runs into the Manifold at Wetton Mill, Staffs., there stands, above a weir, a striking cave projecting from the hillside after the manner of a flat-topped dormer window. According to Plot [*The Natural History of Stafford-Shire* (Oxford, 1686)], its name was Thursehouse or Thursehole, *i.e.* fiend's house. It has a large entrance at the end and a smaller hole at each side of it. If Sir Gawain, approaching as he would from the west, came down from Butterton Moor by the Hoo Brook, he would see it on the left beside the weir when he reached the bottom of the valley. The bank on which the Green Knight stood would be the cliff just below the Hoo Brook on the opposite side of the Manifold to the Green Chapel. From the top of this cliff a passage, mentioned by Plot and still traversable, communicates with a cave at the foot, the "hole" of l. 2221. Issuing from thence, the Green Knight crossed the Manifold to the level ground in front of the mill, where the Beheading Game took place. If this identification is correct, we may infer that the West Midland poet in his earlier life had some connection with Wetton Mill. There is no castle in the neighbourhood, but there is no reason why there should be one. The poet, writing a story in which a castle was an integral part, introduced a description of a place known to him, but it does not follow that this was near a castle.[3]

Though promising so far as it goes, this summary account—particularly in the absence of supporting pictures—is apt to strike an interested reader as tantalizing rather than convincing. The purpose of the present article is to offer a fuller analysis of the similarities between the green chapel and the cave at Wetton Mill, along with photographs of the cave and some of its surroundings.

We must, to begin with, abandon the potentially significant name "Thursehouse" or "Thursehole," which according to Day is used of this cave by the seventeenth-century topographer Robert Plot—a belief which has subsequently found its way into interpretation of the poem.[4] The relevant passage in Plot's *Natural History* is as follows:

There is also another *Thurshouse* or *Thursehole,* sometimes call'd *Hob-hurst Cave,* near *Wetton* mill (where the *Manyfold* falls first into the ground, on the *Easterly* side of the dry Chanell,) which goes into a great *Mountain,* from the mouth to the further part, about 44 yards and is in the middle, as near as I could guess, about 30 foot high, the *roof* being supported by a rough *natural pillar,* which also in a manner divides it into several *partitions* or *rooms:* where I was shewed in the *roof,* the natural *effigies* of a *Man* with a *curled beard,* looking out of a *hole,* not very unlike what it was said to represent, though I suppose wholy casuall, and never designed by *nature.*[5]

The general dimensions of this cave as reported by Plot, his description of it as going "into a great *Mountain,*" and the natural pillar by which it is supported, are all strikingly inappropriate for the cave at Wetton Mill. What they clearly describe is the much more impressive landmark now known as "Thor's Cave" (presumably by way of a folk-etymology from *Thurse* to *Thor's*), on the same side of the Manifold about three-quarters of a mile to the south.

As can be seen in the accompanying photographs (Figs. 1–3), the cave at Wetton Mill is in a stone outcropping, generally knoll-like in shape, protruding from the slope of a low, grass-covered hill. The large hole at the center leads into a chamber about twenty-five feet across at its widest point, and about thirty-five feet from the rear wall to the point where the cave-like entrance ends. This chamber was evidently covered at one time by a natural roof which has since collapsed, leaving it open to the sky; the greatest distance from the floor to the outer surface of this one-time roof (that is, to the upper rim of the present hole) is about twenty or twenty-five feet. In addition to this central entrance and chamber, the outcropping is riddled with a multiplicity of smaller holes and tunnels, one of which leads from the central chamber to another entrance on the left side, not visible in the photographs.

The correspondences between this curious formation and Gawain's green chapel are, I think, more numerous and exact than is likely to be gathered from Day's brief sketch. Gawain's initial impression of the chapel itself is of *a lawe as hit were;/ a balȝ berȝ* (2171–2172). Allowing for the inadequacy, figurative quality, or other obliquity clearly implied by *as hit were,* it seems possible to understand *lawe* here as "structure somehow knoll-like," and *balȝ berȝ* as "bulging structure somehow knoll-like"—a description that would fit the shape of the outcropping at Wetton Mill well enough. The *hole on þe ende and on ayþer syde* (2180) can, as Day suggests, be taken most obviously as referring to the large central opening and the smaller ones on either side of it; or, if emphasis is supposed to fall more strongly on the fact that one hole is on an "end" and the other two on adjacent sides, the hole on the left in the accompanying photographs—which occupies a somewhat protruding spur of rock and is set at a quite different angle from the large opening (Fig. 2)—might be thought of as the *hole on þe ende,* with the large opening to the right of it and the distinct hole on the left side of the outcropping (not visible in the photographs) as the two *on ayþer syde.* The descriptions of the chapel as *ouergrowen with gresse in glodes aywhere* (2181) and *vgly, with erbez ouergrowen* (2190) are obviously accurate, as is the statement that it *al watz holz inwith* (2182). The peculiar and apparently self-contradictory picture *nobot an olde caue,/ Or a creuisse of an olde cragge, he couþe hit nozt deme . . .* (2182–2183) would be accounted for rather well by the structure of the cave at Wetton Mill, if we can assume that the roof had already fallen in by the fourteenth century; while the large central entrance and the short roofed passageway beyond it are completely cave-like, the central chamber in its roofless condition might be thought of plausibly enough as a "crevice of an old crag." There is, however, enough "roof" left on all sides of this central aperture to allow for Gawain's climbing *vp to þe roffe of þe roz wonez* (2198)—a simple matter from the uphill side of the outcropping, the top of which amply justifies the description *þe roz wonez.*

The situation of the green chapel also corresponds extraordinarily well to that of the cave at Wetton Mill. The phrase *bi a bonke* (2172), which I take to mean "on a slope" (as in line 511, *bi bonk*), agrees perfectly with the position of the cave; and the difficult expression *a lyttel on a launde* (2171), which I would render "a little way off, in an open space," seems at least reasonably compatible with it (Fig. 3). Gawain's walking around the chapel (2178)—an action that on the face of it may seem difficult to imagine, since most caves lead into the sides of hills—creates no problem with regard to the outcropping at Wetton Mill, which can be walked around easily in a few minutes. The chapel is described as standing

> þe brymme bysyde,
> Bi a forz of a flode þat ferked þare;
> þe borne blubred þerinne as hit boyled hade.
> (2172–2174)

Fig. 1. Cave at Wetton Mill

Board's of Buxton

Fig. 2. Cave at Wetton Mill

Board's of Buxton

Fig. 3. Wetton Mill

Fig. 4. Hole at foot of Ossom's Crag

117

At the foot of the brief slope bearing the cave at Wetton Mill runs the small, swift River Manifold, really a broad brook rather than a river; at the spot where it comes closest to the cave there is a cluster of submerged rocks, creating a small audible rapid that gives somewhat the appearance of boiling. If the disputed word *forʒ* (2173) should be understood as *fors,* "waterfall," [6] it may be worth noticing that the Hoo Brook, which runs into the Manifold at Wetton Mill, has a miniature waterfall perhaps two feet high, apparently natural, only a few yards from the spot where it joins the Manifold; line 2173 might then be rendered, "Near the waterfall of a stream [*i.e.,* the Hoo Brook] that flowed there." However that may be, the Manifold itself seems about the right width to make effective the Green Knight's hopping over it on his axe (2232)—much too broad for jumping, but narrow enough so that one can picture its being vaulted by a creature of slightly more than human prowess. The floor of the Manifold Valley can be accurately described as *a bent þat brode watʒ aboute* (2233); the situation of the cave, on its low hill within the valley, accords with the earlier remark of Gawain's guide that he will find the chapel *in þat slade* (2147); and if Gawain is to be thought of as approaching the Manifold Valley by way of the Hoo Brook, he would see the cave as his guide predicts (with apparently both topographical and symbolic significance), *on þi lyfte honde* (2146).

On the other side of the Manifold some three hundred yards south of the cave at Wetton Mill, at the point where the river passes under a stone bridge, is the high rock known as Ossom's Crag. Running through this rock is a slightly spiralling vertical tunnel, described by Plot as "at least 40, if not 50 yards high," [7] which, as Day says, "communicates with a cave at the foot" (Fig. 4). If my analysis of the cave at Wetton Mill has been convincing, this prominent crag and tunnel will of course provide the *cragge* and *hole* on the opposite side of the stream (2221) by which the Green Knight descends to meet Gawain. The face of Ossom's Crag in which the exit of the tunnel appears is, to be sure, at right angles to the front of the cave at Wetton Mill, so that the hole itself cannot be seen from the cave; this very feature, however, when viewed from the direction of the cave, produces an angle or nook in the wall of the cliff, which seems quite credible as the *wro* (2222) out of which the Green Knight "whirls" after emerging from the hole. Ossom's Crag is considerably higher than the cave at Wetton Mill, justifying the references to *þat hyʒe hil* (2199) and *þe bonke abouen ouer his hede* (2217); its top has a dis-

tinct rim with an apparent declivity behind it, thus providing an ideal
stage for the Green Knight's unseen whetting of his axe (2199 ff.).
So far as I can see, the only adjustment needed to bring Ossom's Crag
and the cave at Wetton Mill into convincing correspondence with the
setting in this part of the poem would be a reduction of the three
hundred level yards between them—a change that strikes me as one
of the more likely kinds in the complex process of turning fact into
fiction.

To whatever extent the preceding argument has carried conviction,
it implies that the *Gawain* poet either lived in or was somehow personally familiar with the northeastern corner of Staffordshire. This
is certainly a plausible enough locality for the dialect of *Sir Gawain
and the Green Knight* as we have it; and a recent statement by Angus
McIntosh places its dialect in striking proximity to Wetton Mill:

Let us suppose that one takes the trouble to plot on maps as much
as possible of the dialectal information available in localised documents
which come from various parts of S Lancashire, Cheshire, SW Yorkshire,
W Derbyshire, N Staffordshire and N Shropshire. If one then examines
the language of *Gawain and the Green Knight,* it eventually becomes clear
that this text, as it stands in MS Cotton Nero AX, can only *fit* with
reasonable propriety in a very small area either in SE Cheshire or just
over the border in NE Staffordshire. That is to say, its dialectal characteristics *in their totality* are reconcilable with those of other (localised)
texts in this and only this area.[8]

Professor McIntosh does, to be sure, cite the cave known as Lud's
Church (discussed below) as lying precisely within his proposed dia-
lect-area; but the cave at Wetton Mill is not significantly distant, lying
only about nine miles southeast of Lud's Church.[9]

This cave or fissure called Lud's Church, which has been suggested
by Ralph W. V. Elliott as the original of the green chapel,[10] merits
our attention as probably the most important rival of the cave at
Wetton Mill. Its terrifying cave-like entrance, leading to a great open
crevice, accords perfectly with the ambiguity between cave and crevice
already noticed in lines 2182–2183. Like the cave at Wetton Mill, it
can be accurately described as *þe roȝ woneȝ* (2198), and as *ouergrowen with gresse in glodes aywhere* (2181) and *with erbeȝ ouergrowen* (2190). And as Professor Elliott hints, the very name "Lud's
Church"—current as early as the seventeenth century[11]—may well
point to an earlier reputation as a demonic "chapel." In most other

particulars, however, it seems to me to fit the description of the green chapel much less closely than does the cave at Wetton Mill. For example, it is not easy to think of Lud's Church even figuratively as a *lawe* (2171) or a *balȝ berȝ* (2172). Again, in the poem Gawain first walks around the chapel (2178), and later climbs to the roof of it (2198). It would be difficult to walk around Lud's Church, which is in the side of a rather steep hill; and in any case, walking around it would necessarily involve climbing to the "roof" of it—actions which in the poem are obviously thought of as distinct. I am not even sure that Lud's Church can be said to have *a hole on þe ende and on ayþer syde* (2180), at least in the most obvious sense of the words; what it has is a prominent central entrance and, running at right angles to it on either side, a long deep crevice which at each end disappears into the ground.

Further problems are created by the immediate surroundings of Lud's Church. Far from being *in þat slade* (2147) and *þe brymme bysyde* (2172), it is in fact so far up the ridge and so far from the valley that neither the Black Brook nor the River Dane is visible from it. Nor can any sign of Lud's Church be seen from the bottom of the valley, so that the account of Gawain riding down the valley and catching sight of it *a lyttel on a launde* (2171) after a brief search would, in this setting, be virtually impossible. The terrain below Lud's Church—unlike that below the cave at Wetton Mill—includes nothing that could be described as *a bent þat brode watz aboute* (2233). And finally, there is no cliff on the other side of either the Black Brook or the Dane high enough to provide a basis for the picture of Gawain standing on top of the green chapel, listening to a voice from beyond the brook *on þe bonk abouen ouer his hede* (2217). Such criticisms, of course, take no account of the alchemy that can be wrought by the poetic imagination, and I suppose it is always possible that the green chapel and its environs represent a blending of two or more actual places; the point of the present comparison is that if this part of *Sir Gawain and the Green Knight* does somehow reflect a particular landscape to a recognizable degree, the cave at Wetton Mill seems in all ways a more likely candidate than Lud's Church.

But, it may be pertinently asked, even if we accept the cave at Wetton Mill as the original of Gawain's green chapel, what does that finally contribute to our understanding of the poem? Antiquarian interest aside, how does the knowledge that the *Gawain* poet thought of the green chapel as an actual place have any more significance than, say, our knowledge that Laȝamon thought of the cliff called Redstone near Areley Regis as an actual place? Let us recall that Gawain's itinerary from Camelot until some time before he arrives at Bertilak's castle is clearly meant to be geographically accurate: northward through Wales, then eastward past the "isles of Anglesey" and along the north coast of Wales, and finally over a ford into Wirral (691–701). It seems unlikely that his further adventures before reaching the castle (709–735) are, in terms of literal geography, intended to bring him all the way to the northeastern corner of Staffordshire. In the geography of medieval romance, however, such telescopings are an established convention; witness for example the famous obliteration of the English Channel in Chrétien's *Yvain* and elsewhere. May it not be that our poet, writing in northern Staffordshire, has employed this convention in an original way and climaxed a slightly distanced journey of Gawain through Wales and Wirral by introducing a local landmark of sinister repute, meant to be recognized by his immediate audience? Such a device—whether the local landmark is to be identified as the cave at Wetton Mill or as Lud's Church—would relieve the green chapel of at least some of its apparent functionlessness, contribute slyly to an already evident suggestion of universal applicability in Gawain's humiliation by the Green Knight, and add another facet of allusion to this most carefully fashioned of all medieval romances.

Lovers and Imp, from *Der Seelentrost* (Augsburg, 1478)

ALBERT C. BAUGH

Convention and Individuality in the Middle English Romance

Middle English romances, like medieval romances in other languages, abound in conventional elements. Their very subject matter is standardized, consisting as it does of deeds of knightly prowess, whether in large-scale battles or in individual combats with other knights. When the hero is opposed by a giant or dragon, the effect is much the same. This goes for even those romances that concern an historical character, such as Alexander or Richard the Lion-Hearted, or treat pseudo-history, as in the case of the Troy story. These are made up mostly of battles, combats, and other exploits requiring physical strength and courage. By those who concern themselves with the theory of improvisation the armed encounter is known as a theme, whether it be an individual combat or a battle, which in the romances is generally a series of individual combats. The description of such an encounter follows a conventional pattern: the opponent approaches, the hero takes note of him, he leaps into the saddle, he spurs his horse, he shouts an angry defiance or orders his opponent to yield, he rides against the foe, the knights meet head-on, and so forth. I have elsewhere listed and illustrated forty-nine of these components.[1] Any particular description seems to be but a selection from this storehouse of commonplaces, some of which are like interchangeable parts. The vocabulary and phrasing are likewise to a large extent conventional, stock phrases and clichés which the poet and the reciter equally had on the tip of his tongue. They are sometimes whole lines like "Dead he felled him in the field" or "There began a great bataile." More often they are convenient short phrases of a common metrical pattern, suitable for beginning or ending a line. It is little wonder that to the student of the medieval romances conventionality seems to be their most prominent characteristic.

Yet the presence of so much that is conventional may keep us from seeing what is individual and at times quite original. As we read the Middle English romances, we come now and again to one that has a stylistic character which seems to be due to the author rather than to the traditions of the genre. We may feel that what is distinctive is something he could hardly have derived from his source, but we are not in a position to prove it. Few, I believe, doubt that we have an example of this in *Sir Gawain and the Green Knight,* whether or not a developed French original lies behind this poem. In the same way one feels that a real poet was at work on the long poem which goes by the unfortunate name of *Gest Historiale of the Destruction of Troy,* and that the author of the so-called *Laud Troy Book* was an excellent craftsman. Since they both relied mainly on Guido della Colonna, it is reasonable to assume that the narrative and stylistic qualities noticeable in these poems are their own. One would like to know how much of the well-knit structure and lively style of *Havelok* is due to the English poet. Again, when one reads the tail-rime romances, *Sir Degrevant* stands out for its stylistic individuality, a quality that is largely responsible for its being one of the best of the group. But we have no direct source for either of these works. It is only when we have a romance that is closely dependent on a French original, and when that original has been preserved, that we are able to watch the English author at work and appraise his individual contribution to the final result. Fortunately we are able to do this in a number of cases, such as *Bevis of Hampton, Octavian, Libeaus Desconus, Ipomedon,* and a few others. Where, as in some of these, we have several English versions, it is possible to carry the comparison further. In a single short paper it is impossible to examine all the romances mentioned, and in the present study I shall confine myself to the first two.

Bevis of Hampton belongs to the type of story in which the hero is forced into exile but in the end returns home to avenge himself on those who have wronged him and recover his heritage—the so-called exile and return motif. In order to provide a setting for the discussion that follows, it will be well to recall some of the more important events of the narrative while omitting the innumerable small adventures that add considerably to the novelty and interest of the story. Bevis' father, the earl of Southampton, is murdered at the instigation of his wife, who marries the murderer. To get rid of Bevis the mother orders the boy's uncle, Saber, to put him to death and, when she learns that her commands have not been carried out, turns the boy over to some foreign merchants to be carried to a far-off land. They present the handsome youth to Ermin, a Saracen emperor. Ermin's daughter Josian, after the manner of Saracen princesses in romance, falls in love with the hero, especially after he has successfully defended her against a king named Brademond who has come to marry her, by force if necessary. In the fighting Bevis has stopped Brademond from carrying off two of Ermin's knights, for which they show their gratitude by falsely reporting to Ermin that Bevis has lain with Josian. The English poet is outraged by this perfidy. They lied, he says; he only kissed her once. But Ermin is easily taken in and sends Bevis to Brademond with a letter that contains secret instructions to put Bevis to death. Upon receiving the letter from Bevis, Brademond has him seized and thrown into prison, a deep cave or pit full of vipers. Bevis, however, survives. He languishes there for seven years until he finally manages to escape. Meanwhile Josian's hand is sought by another king, Yvor of Monbrant. Though she is compelled to submit to the marriage, she maintains her chastity by means of magic. Bevis, after his escape, fights off his pursuers, killing Brademond himself and subsequently others, including a giant. Going in search of Josian, he learns that she is married to Yvor. Disguised as a palmer he succeeds in carrying her off during Yvor's absence. But before they make good their escape, Josian and Bevis have many strange adventures, to some of which the author manages to give a humorous cast. Bevis eventually succeeds in getting back to England, defeats and kills his stepfather, and recovers his earldom. His mother kills herself by jumping off a tower. Here the original story may well have ended. But the author is reluctant to stop. Perhaps his audience cried out for more. In any case, the romance continues with incidents, sometimes trivial, for a space half as long as all that has preceded. It is apparently for the purpose of doubling the exile and return theme, but perhaps also to enlarge Saber's part in the story and allow Bevis finally to dispose of Yvor. In the end he again returns to England, recovers his heritage a second time, and triumphs in a final battle over opposition aroused by the king's steward. In the course of this part of the romance Bevis' sons have each won kingdoms. Bevis and Josian are allowed to spend the last twenty years of their lives in peace, dying in each other's arms.

As is well known, *Bevis of Hampton* was told four times in French verse, in some versions at great length. A very brief examination suffices to show that the three continental texts are not related to the English romance. There is an Anglo-Norman version, however, that is so close to the English as to leave little doubt that it was the source of the English poem. For example, the Anglo-Norman poem is in laisses. Up to a certain point (line 415) the laisses are invariably short, generally six lines with an occasional divergence to five or seven. The effect, as I have shown elsewhere,[2] is that of a poem written in six-line mono-rimed stanzas. From this point on, the laisses are generally much longer, in an extreme case running to 187 lines and eventually changing from rime to assonance. Now the English poem undergoes a similar change of meter. Up to approximately the same point in the story the English poem is in six-line stanzas (romance sixes) and, generally speaking, one stanza renders one laisse. But then the English poem changes to couplets. The incidents and the sequence of incidents are, almost without exception, the same throughout, the English reproducing many small and quite casual details. But while the English poet follows his French text with considerable fidelity, he is not a slavish translator. When he comes to an episode that warms his imagination, he gives his pen free rein. There are certain episodes, for example, common to both versions, that are designed to reveal Bevis' prowess and, since they are witnessed by Josian, to further inflame the princess' love for the young knight. One of them is a fight with a wild boar that has proved too much for the Saracen knights. It recalls Tristan's fight with the dragon, since in both cases another tries to steal the trophy and take credit for the achievement. In the Anglo-Norman poem the adventure is told briefly and in a quite matter-of-fact way. The boar opens its mouth wide in anticipation of devouring Bevis; Bevis hurls his spear in the open mouth and it reaches the heart. He then cuts off the head to present it to the emperor. Here is the Anglo-Norman account:

> Boefs vint a bois pur quere le sengler,
> mes il le trova mult tost, ne li estoit doter;
> le sengler lui vist si comença a griffer,
> e sa grant gule commença baier,
> com c'il vosist tretut Boefs devorer.
> Boefs tost le vit si brocha son destrer
> e tint la launce tut red, dunt li fer fu enter;
> en la goule overte ferist le sengler
> e la point lui fist de ci que a quer tocher,
> e lui sengler tost murt saunz nul demurer;

e Boefs tret le espeie, le chef li va couper
e prent le tronson de sun espé, ke il out fet debruser,
la teste a sengler fet desus ficher.   (437–449)

It is interesting to note what the English poet does with this:

Þo Beues in to þe wode cam,
His scheld aboute is nekke a nam
And tide his hors to an hei þorn
And blew a blast wiþ is horn;
Þre motes a blew al arowe,
Þat þe bor him scholde knowe.
Þo he com to þe bor is den,
A seȝ þer bones of dede men,
Þe bor hadde slawe in þe wode,
Ieten here flesch & dronke her blode.
'Aris!' queþ Beues, 'corsede gast,
And ȝem me bataile wel in hast!'
Sone so þe bor him siȝ,
A rerde is brosteles wel an hiȝ
And starede on Beues wiþ eien holwe,
Also a wolde him haue a-swolwe;
And for þe bor ȝenede so wide,
A spere Beues let to him glide;
On þe scholder he smot þe bor,
His spere barst to pises þore;
Þe bor stod stille aȝen þe dent,
His hyde was harde ase eni flent.
Now al to-borste is Beues spere,
A drouȝ his swerd, him self to were,
And fauȝt aȝen þe bor so grim,
A smot þe bor and he to him.
Þus þe bataile gan leste long
Til þe time of euesong,
Þat Beues was so weri of fouȝte,
Þat of is lif he ne rouȝte,
And þo þe bor was also,
Awai fro Beues he gan go,
Wile Beues made is praier
To god and Mari, is moder dere,
Whaþer scholde oþer slen:
Wiþ þat com þe bor aȝen
And bente is brostles vp, saunfaile,

Aȝen Beues to ȝeue bataile;
Out at is mouþ in aiþer side
þe foim ful ferli gan out glide;
And Beues in þat ilche venev,
þourȝ godes grace & is vertv
Wiþ is swerd out a slinte
Twei toskes at þe ferste dent;
A spanne of þe groin be-forn
Wiþ is swerd he haþ of schoren.
þo þe bor so loude cride,
Out of þe forest wide and side,
To þe castel þar þat lai Ermin,
Men herde þe noise of þe swin;
And, alse he made þat loþeli cri,
His swerd Beues hasteli
In at þe mouþ gan þreste þo
And karf his hertte euene ato:
þe swerd a breide aȝen fot hot
And þe bor is heued of smot,
And on a tronsoun of is spere
þat heued a stikede for to bere.
þanne a sette horn to mouþe
And blew þe pris ase wel kouþe,
So glad he was for is honting.   (771–831)

The English poet has evidently seen a boar hunt, knows the procedure, and has a command of the technical terms of the chase. Such episodes are of course stock themes, but he has the knack of creating suspense. The moment when the boar, weary from the contest, starts to slink off and then returns to face his antagonist again is a nice touch.

Although here and throughout I speak of the Anglo-Norman version as the source of the English romance, I should make it clear that I am not necessarily referring to the actual manuscripts from which Stimming edited the text.[3] The two manuscripts that have come down to us are both defective, and in those portions that are found in both manuscripts there are considerable verbal differences. Moreover, there are places where the text is evidently corrupt, as the editor recognized, and in the last third of the romance the narrative is sometimes confused and incoherent. The version that the English poet knew was doubtless contained in a better manuscript than those that we have. In my discussion of the relation of the English romance to this Anglo-

Norman source, I' have tried to avoid drawing any inferences that might be invalidated by the faulty character of the French text.

It is not generally acknowledged that we have in English not one romance of *Bevis of Hampton* but at least three. There is the version in the Auchinleck MS, the oldest surviving manuscript, which Kölbing prints as his main text.[4] But there is a version represented by four manuscripts (ESNC in Kölbing's designation) which differs greatly from the Auchinleck text not only in lines and couplets but in long passages throughout. And there is the version in the Chetham MS and two early printed editions. These versions are not independent renderings of the French, but seem definitely to go back to a common original, probably much like the version in the Auchinleck MS. They contain details and incidents not found in the French but which are present in the Auchinleck version. The Chetham version in particular differs so much from the Auchinleck and the more closely related second version that the variants could not be recorded in the ordinary way. In Kölbing's edition the text is printed separately at the foot of the page. It is in couplets throughout, but the difference in meter does not begin to explain the differences in wording. It is clearly an independent telling of the story, the narrative of someone who knew the story well, probably from having heard it recited more than once. The version he had heard was essentially the Auchinleck version. He remembered lines and couplets but was far from having the romance by heart. So he retold the story in his own words, reproducing the incidents in sequence and sometimes in small details, and, as just remarked, incorporated lines and couplets where his memory enabled him to do this. Even when the Auchinleck version changes to couplets the Chetham version shows the same independent wording. If my interpretation of the evidence is correct, both of the latter versions represent the story as told by different minstrels, from memory, who resorted to improvisation and independent composition when their memory failed. They would make an interesting study in themselves. Here I must confine myself to the version in the Auchinleck MS.

The question to which I wish to address myself is: How does the English poet use his source and to what extent does he contribute to the final result by his own literary personality? As I remarked above, he is faithful to his original throughout the whole course of the story and observes the sequence of incidents, both major and minor. That he was capable of expanding an incident in his own way has been shown in the episode of the boar hunt. But his method of telling the story involves more than the elaboration of his original. It is characterized by many small changes which reveal him not as a translator bent on finding words to clothe an idea in his original, but an author who relates incidents in his own way. When Bevis is on his way to Brademond to deliver the letter which contains his own death warrant, he comes to a temple in which Mahomet is being worshipped by a great multitude. In the Anglo-Norman text he dismounts, enters the temple, seizes the image of Mahomet, and hurls it at a priest, killing him, after which all the other priests flee. In the English, after slaying the priest he "threw their gods in the fen and laughed all the people to scorn." The point I wish to make is not that the English poet exaggerates this crude display of Christian hatred for the infidel, which is a commonplace in romance, but that he is not simply translating the French text. Soon after, when Bevis presents himself before Brademond the king greets him courteously. Bevis bids him read the letter at once *"ou jeo vus couperai la teste."* This time the English poet gives Bevis better manners:

> God þat made þis world al ronde,
> Þe saue, sire king Brademond,
> And ek alle þine fere,
> Þat i se now here,
> And ȝif þat ilche blessing
> Likeþ þe riȝt noþing,
> Mahoun, þat is god þin,
> Teruagaunt & Apolin,
> Þe blessi and diȝte
> Be alle here miȝte! (1373–1382)

These brief passages are chosen almost at random. They are not major incidents, but they suffice to show the English adapter's independent visualization of a scene.

His personal qualities come out also in little touches that create or heighten a humorous effect. Bevis has a marvelous horse, Arondel, one of the few horses in literature distinguished by a name. Arondel is unusually intelligent and high-spirited, and will allow no one but Bevis and Josian to ride him. By his behavior on numerous occasions he becomes one of the characters of the poem. When Bevis is sent to Brademond with the secret letter, he is persuaded to leave Arondel behind with Josian. Now it will be recalled that while Bevis is suffering his long captivity in Brademond's prison Josian is forced to marry

Yvor of Monbrant. When the two journey to Monbrant Josian takes the horse with her, wishing to see that it is properly cared for. One day, to show his "grant hardement," Yvor decides to ride the famous horse; but when he goes to the stable Arondel kicks him in the chest so that he falls and fractures his skull against a wall. Such is the account in the Anglo-Norman version, and it was much too colorless for the English poet. As he relates the incident, Josian's father presents Arondel and Bevis' equally famous sword Morgelay to Yvor at the time of the wedding. Riding back to his kingdom, Yvor thinks to make a show of his greatness by riding Arondel into his capital city. The spirited horse, however, soon realizes that it is not Bevis on his back and becomes unmanageable. He runs away, and, to make the unfortunate Yvor's plight the more ludicrous, races with him through woods and thorn bushes before pitching him off on his head:

> þat hors wel sone vnder-ȝit,
> þat Beues nas nouȝt vpon is rigge.
> þe king wel sore scholde hit abegge.
> He ran ouer dich and þorn,
> þourȝ wode & þourȝ þekke korn;
> For no water ne for no londe,
> Nowhar nolde þat stede astonde;
> At þe laste a þrew Yuor doun
> And al to-brak þe kinges kroun,
> þat al is kingdom wel vnneþe
> Arerede him þer fro þe deþe;
> And er hii miȝte þat hors winne,
> þai lauȝte him wiþ queinte ginne.   (1514–1526)

The author was evidently pleased with his handling of this incident, for later on in the story he has one who was an eyewitness of Yvor's experience relate it again for Bevis' entertainment.

This is not the only instance in which the English poet saw the humorous possibilities in situations not exploited in his source. When Bevis succeeds in carrying off Josian while Yvor is out hunting, one of the king's numerous followers sent in pursuit is a giant named Ascopard, who catches up with them. Before the two fight, Bevis asks him his name, where he comes from, and whether all the people in his country are as large as he is. In the French he replies to the last of these questions by saying that at home he was known as the dwarf. All this reappears in the English poem, but with an amusing addition.

Although thirty feet tall, he says that among his own people he was so small that every one picked on him and he had to run away. The fight that ensues is not by any means one-sided. Ascopard's club is like the trunk of an oak tree, but he is finally downed and Bevis is about to cut off his head. At this point Josian intercedes, and, in the French, suggests that Bevis spare him, provided he will swear homage and become Bevis' man. In the English this becomes:

> 'Sire,' ʒhe seide, 'so god þe saue,
> Let him liuen & ben our knaue!'

The idea of a thirty-foot page is new. In both of these cases the addition or modification is a subtle one, but they testify to the English poet's sense of the incongruous.

A contribution of another kind which the English poet makes is his skillful way of supplying circumstances that bring about a convincing sequence of events and better motivate the action. This structural skill may be seen in the episode in which Bevis, having escaped from Brademond's prison, sets out in search of Josian. Up to a certain point the French and the English are quite close. Bevis meets a knight whom he has known before and from him learns that Josian is married to Yvor. He proceeds to Yvor's city of Monbrant. When he arrives at the gate of the castle, according to the French, he enters as a palmer and by chance hears Josian lamenting the disappearance of Bevis. The lament is important at this point, since it assures him that in spite of her marriage to Yvor, which he has no way of knowing was forced upon her, she is still loyal to him. But his hearing her at the moment when he arrives is pure coincidence, and while we are accustomed to the intervention of chance in medieval romance, in this case it is somewhat less than convincing. The author seems like one who has a story to tell, but is not a story-teller. The whole incident, including Josian's lament, is reported factually in seven lines. It is not so in the English poem. The English poet first accounts for Bevis' disguise. Outside the town he meets a palmer and questions him about the king and queen. He learns that Yvor is out hunting with all his knights and that Josian is in her bower. He asks the palmer to exchange clothing with him, gets off his horse, and helps the palmer to put on the unfamiliar armor while he takes the palmer's staff and pilgrim cloak. The palmer rides off "as a king." When Bevis comes to the castle gate he sees there

many palmers from many lands. He asks them what they are all doing
there. They tell him how kind the queen is to all palmers, how she
feeds them and gives them *"riche wede"*:

> For a kniȝtes loue, Beuoun,
> þat was i-boren at Souþamtoun.

She would make a rich man of any one who could bring her tidings
of Bevis. Bevis asks at what hour she does this, and is told *"be-twene
middai & noun"*:

> Hit nas boute ȝong dai;
> A þouȝte þat he wolde er þan
> Wende aboute þe barbican,
> For to loke & for to se,
> How it miȝte best be,
> ȝif he þe castel wolde breke,
> Wher a miȝte best in reke;
> And also a com be a touret,
> þat was in þe castel iset,
> A herde wepe and crie;
> þederward he gan him hie.

It is, of course, Josian lamenting the loss of Bevis. The little episode
shows the difference between one who is content to report facts and a
poet who can visualize a scene and clothe the facts with suitable dialogue and circumstantial detail.

While the incident I have described shows off the English poet to
advantage, it is not necessary to my thesis that this be so. The individuality of the story-teller may be manifested in the way he chooses to
relate an incident, whether or not his way is better. We may find an
example of what I mean in the continuation of the episode just related.
As the Anglo-Norman poem tells it, Bevis, upon hearing Josian's
complaint, enters the castle and asks her for food. When she has served
him she asks him where he was born, and upon being told that he was
born in England, inquires whether he has ever heard of Bevis of
Hampton. He tells her that Bevis is in England and married to a
woman *"bele e coluré, unkes plus bele de ly fu trové."* Josian sinks to
the floor in a swoon. When she comes to, she keeps thinking how
much the palmer resembles Bevis. She even calls her squire, who con-

firms her impression, and she confesses to the palmer that if it were
not for his palmer's dress she would say that he was Bevis. The palmer
brushes the statement aside and asks to see Bevis' horse, which he has
often heard about. The horse is within earshot, and when it hears
Bevis' name mentioned it breaks its chains and comes running into the
court. The palmer rides it and his identity is evident. The narrative
here is a better example of what the author of the Anglo-Norman
poem is capable of, although the first part of this incident is rather
conventional. It is a commonplace of romance, just before a happy
reunion, for the heroine to be told that her lover (or husband) is dead
or lost to her, and to swoon. The latter part—the behavior of Arondel
—taxes one's credulity. But on the whole the incident is well managed,
the dialogue is natural, and the appeal to the marvelous is one of the
conditions we must accept in medieval romance. Both the conventionality and the improbability, however, are avoided by the English poet,
who shifts the emphasis. For him the climax of the episode is the
palmer's ability to ride Arondel, that spirited and strictly one-man
horse, and he gets to it quickly. When Josian visits the group of
palmers at her accustomed time, Bevis has taken his place among them.
After feeding them she asks her usual question: Does any one among
them know Bevis of Hampton? All reply in the negative except the
"new" palmer, who remains silent. "What about you?" she asks. Bevis
does not mislead her.

> 'þat kniȝt ich knowe wel inouȝ!
> Atom,' a seide, 'in is contre
> Icham an erl and also is he;
> At Rome he made me a spel
> Of an hors, men clepede Arondel:
> Wide whar ichaue iwent
> And me warisoun ispent,
> I souȝt hit boþe fer & ner,
> Men telleþ me þat it is her;
> ȝif euer louedestow wel þat kniȝt,
> Let me of þat hors haue a siȝt!'

As Josian leads him to the stable, she keeps looking at him closely, is
impressed at his resemblance to Bevis, and, as in the French, is confirmed in her impression by her squire. When Arondel hears Bevis'
voice—not the mere mention of his name—he behaves as in the French

romance. Josian warns the palmer that Arondel has been the bane of many a man who tried to take him. The palmer says he can do it; he rides him and is recognized. Both versions tell the story well. It is not a question of which is better. My point is that the English poet, finding the episode in his source, narrates it in his own way.

A distinguishing characteristic of the English poet is his concern for plausibility. Where the treatment of an episode in his source is markedly improbable, he alters it. In the French, for example, when Bevis and his men make the expedition to England to wreak vengeance on Bevis' stepfather, the latter by chance sees them land and rides toward them. He inquires who they are. Bevis replies that his name is Gyraut (Gerraud) and that he is from France. So far the incident follows a common pattern in romance. But at this point the king's credulity seems extreme. "Are you a soldier?" he asks. Upon receiving an affirmative reply, he at once, without further investigation, offers to hire the strangers to make war on a *"vylen"* who is causing him much trouble. It is, of course, Bevis' uncle Sabaoth (Saber). They agree on the price. The king shall furnish Bevis' ship with food and drink and give arms to all his men. Thus equipped, Bevis and his men sail to Saber's castle on the Isle of Wight. In the English poem the episode is more plausibly managed. Bevis and his men reach England and make their way to a hill a mile out of Southampton. Bevis calls for a volunteer who can speak French and who will carry a message to the king, saying that his master will fight for him if the king will give him his "hire." The messenger meets a porter at the castle gate, who conducts him to the king. Matters are arranged so that that night Bevis and the king dine together. After asking the visitor's name and learning that he is called Gerard, the king explains the situation to him. His wife, before he married her, was married to an earl, by whom she had a son. He was a proud young wretch, like his father, who came of *"leþer blode."* They called him Bevis. As soon as he was of age, he sold his heritage to the king and *"spente his panes in scham & schonde."* Afterward he fled England. Now, he has an uncle here, on the Isle of Wight, named Saber, who claims his inheritance and causes the king much trouble. If Gerard (Bevis) will slay him in the field, the king says he will gladly pay his hire. Bevis says his men are unarmed. If the king will fit out his ship, arm his knights with weapons and horses, and supplement his hundred knights with a hundred of the king's

> y schel swere þe an oþe,
> þat i schel ʒeue swiche asaut
> On þat ilche Sabaaut
> þat wiþ inne a lite while
> þow schelt here of a queinte gile!

Thus Bevis avoids perjuring himself. But what of the hundred knights furnished by the king, who might well be expected to interfere with Bevis' *gile*? The poet has not forgotten this possibility:

> In þe schipe þe kniʒtes seten, y-wis,
> On of here, anoþer of his.
> Whan þai come amidde þe forde,
> Ech þrew is felawe ouer þe bord;
> Of þemperures kniʒtes euerichon
> Wiþ inne bord ne leuede non.   (3027–3032)

To take another example, greater plausibility is clearly behind the deliberate change which the English poet makes in another episode. When Josian, against her will, is married to Yvor, she has no intention of yielding her body to him. In the French she has a magic girdle of silk, which, when worn *desus son vestement,* has the power of keeping any man from approaching her bed. This is retained in the English version of the Chetham MS, so that it may have been in the English archetype. But to the poet (or reciter) responsible for the Auchinleck version this was not convincing. In an age when people slept without nightclothes of any kind this device lacked plausibility. So he substitutes a magic ring:

> 'Ac for þe loue þat was so gode,
> þat I louede ase min hertte blode,
> Ichaue,' ʒhe seide, 'a ring on,
> þat of swiche vertu is þe ston:
> While ichaue on þat ilche ring,
> To me schel noman haue welling,
> And, Beues,' ʒhe seide, 'be god aboue,
> I schel it weren for þe loue!'   (1467–1474)

A similar situation occurs a little later. When Bevis goes to England for the first time to recover his heritage, he leaves Josian in Cologne in the care of an uncle, the bishop, and her giant page Ascopard. While he is gone Josian is wooed by an earl and again forced into an unwilling marriage. In the Anglo-Norman version she hangs the unwelcome husband in bed on their wedding night, using her silk girdle as the noose. There is no explanation of how she is able to do this, and the silk girdle hardly seems sufficient for her purpose. The English poet devises a much more circumstantial account of the incident. After the wedding feast the earl has her conducted to her bed and then, accompanied by a great gathering of wedding guests, offers her much wine *for to maken hire dronke a bedde.* She asks him as a favor to send all his friends away, *"þat noman se our priuete"*:

> 'Wimmen beþ schamfast in dede
> And namliche maidenes,' ȝhe sede.

He grants her request, ushers them all out, *and schette þe dore wiþ þe keie.* He returns and sits down on the side of the bed to take off his shoes:

> 'Me schon i mot me self of drawe,
> Ase y neuer ȝet ne dede.'

The bed has curtains *on raile tre* for privacy. Josian has meanwhile knotted a *towaile* and, seizing the opportunity, slips it around his neck and pulls him up by the *raile tre*:

> Be þe nekke ȝhe haþ him vp tiȝt
> & let him so ride al þe niȝt.

Descriptions of battles and combats of all kinds were the stock in trade of those who recited romances, and doubtless of many who wrote them. Whenever the author of the English *Bevis* comes to such an episode his account bears little relation to his source. Bevis' final encounter with Yvor is an excellent example of such independence. Coming near the end of the romance, this is an important feature of the story. Yet in the Anglo-Norman poem it is very brief. The antagonists exchange blows. Yvor's horse is killed and, lest his own horse suffer the same fate, Bevis dismounts. Yvor strikes him on the helmet, in return for which Bevis cuts off Yvor's head. *Le cors chet a terre, le alme a Belsabu.* That is all. The whole encounter takes twenty lines. For the English poet such an encounter offers a major opportunity to display his skill. The combatants ride at each other; each one's lance pierces the other's shield, but their byrnies withstand the blows. On the second clash their saddle girths break and both fall to the ground. They attack each other now with falchions, and the fire bursts out as from a burning brand. Thus they battle from prime to undern. All who witness the fight agree that they never before saw such a contest between Saracen and Christian. At mid-day Yvor strikes a mighty blow on Bevis' helmet, cutting off the gold crest and splitting the visor. The sword cuts off half of Bevis' beard, but the flesh is not hurt. The onlookers again cry out. Bevis is angered and with his famous sword Morgelay cuts deep into his opponent's shoulder, so that Yvor falls to his knees. But he jumps up and attacks Bevis furiously, cutting away a quarter of his shield. In return Bevis cuts Yvor's shield in two, severing his left hand at the wrist. Nevertheless Yvor continues to fight *ase he wer wod,* Bevis managing to protect himself with his shield. Bevis now cuts off Yvor's right arm at the shoulder. At that, Yvor, on the point of death, calls on his gods to save his soul. Bevis, with Christian charity rather than irony, urges him to address his prayers to God and to Mary and be christened; otherwise he will suffer without end the pains of Hell.

> 'Nay,' queþ Yuor, 'so mot y þen,
> Christene wile ich neuer ben.'

Upon hearing this, Bevis unlaces Yvor's ventail, cuts off his head, *and on his spere he hit piʒte.* The Christians rejoice, the Saracens flee. This vivid and circumstantial narrative—five times the length of the episode in the French original—owes practically nothing to that original. The English poet, when he comes to an incident like this, has no need for a source. He has, as it were, thrown the book away.

The independence and originality of the author of the English *Bevis* may be exemplified by one final adventure, the last in which Bevis (now with his two sons) figures. It is his second return to England to claim his inheritance, this time from King Edgar. In the Anglo-Norman source this part of the story is disposed of quite briefly, and the author shows only a general knowledge of the geography of the country. He knows that the Isle of Wight is separated from Southampton by a body of water and he knows where London is. That is about all. In contrast, the English poet makes this part of the story a major incident and, while doing so, shows an intimate knowledge of London. As he follows the action through various streets and districts, all named, he imparts to his narrative a verisimilitude that is rare in this type of literature. Bevis returns to England, leaving his forces at Southampton and his wife at Putney, and presents himself humbly before the king at Westminster. He asks to have his earldom restored. The king consents, to the great satisfaction of all the barons except the *"stiward of þe halle."* The latter shows his enmity toward Bevis in an angry speech, in which he accuses Bevis of having killed the king's son. Although Bevis is *wroþ,* he rides with six knights to London and finds lodging at an inn in Tower Street. Meanwhile the steward, with sixty knights, also makes his way to London and, when he gets to *Chepe,* rouses the Londoners against Bevis. In a speech in which he claims to be bearing the king's orders he urges them to seize the traitor for treason. On learning from the taverner what the tumult is about, Bevis and his six followers arm themselves against the mob and in the fighting that ensues Bevis kills the steward. He sets out for *Chepe* (in the Caius MS he goes by way of Goose Street). The mob pursues him, and his six companions are killed in the fighting. Although now alone, Bevis defies his attackers. New crowds pour out *boþe of lane and of strete.* It is not necessary to recount Bevis' acts of prowess and the contribution made by his horse Arondel, but by evensong he has killed five thousand. Nevertheless, a false rumor reaches Josian at Putney that Bevis has been slain and she calls upon her sons, Guy and Miles, to avenge their father's death. The sons ride in all haste until they reach London gate, where they overpower the defenders and burn the gate. *Be twene Bowe and London ston* the fighting reaches its climax. They ride up just in time to rescue their father from a *Lombard.* In winning the victory they kill so many Londoners that all the Thames is red. After the fighting has ended they go to Leadenhall, send for Josian, and enjoy a feast that lasts a fortnight. Of all this there is not a word in the French romance.

Enough has been said, I hope, to show how the English poet, while following his source closely in plot and in the sequence of episodes that make up that plot, succeeds in fashioning his materials into something fresh and distinctive. As we read the English *Bevis,* we are inclined to accept as a matter of course many of the incidents which I have chosen for illustration. Indeed, when we are reading any romance known to be based immediately or ultimately on some antecedent version, we are prone to assume that a passage that arouses our interest has most likely been taken over from its source. It is only when we are fortunate enough to have that source and can read the English romance alongside its French original that we are brought to realize that we are having to do with a poet and story-teller who was in his larger or smaller way drawing on his own creative powers, that while content to take his material where he found it, was not content merely to turn his text from one language into another, but was moved to use his imaginative gifts and narrative skill to arouse and hold the interest of his listeners. In the process he succeeded in stamping more or less conventional material with literary qualities of his own.

In turning to *Octavian,* the second of my two examples, I hope to show wherein its individuality lies, how in one English version this quality was all but lost, and how in the other it was enhanced by a story-teller who realized the potentialities of his source.

Unlike *Bevis of Hampton,* the romance of *Octavian* exists in a single early French version,[5] the only manuscript of which is the work of an Anglo-Norman scribe. Basically it is the story of an accused queen, of the type most familiar in Chaucer's Man of Law's Tale. After fifteen childless years the wife of Octavian, emperor of Rome, gives birth to twin boys. Through the machinations of the emperor's mother he is led to order all three to be burned at the stake, but at the last moment relents and sends them instead into exile. They are left in a forest filled with wild beasts. While the mother sleeps, the children are carried off by friendly animals, one by an ape, the other by a lioness. Both animals suckle the respective infants and protect them. The rest of the story relates the wanderings of the hapless queen and the subsequent adventures of the two children. In the end all are brought together, not without the usual series of coincidences: identities are established, and the emperor and his queen are easily reconciled. On this basic story, however, are grafted several novel features. There are wars and battles between Christian and Saracen that give the two sons, when they have grown up, a chance to distinguish themselves. There is a Saracen princess, who is not only beautiful enough to win the hero's love but is unusually resourceful. What is most important, there is added a fourth component which gives the romance its distinctive character, and of which more in a moment. These various elements, it may be said, are well integrated, and, once the author gets past the preliminaries leading to the queen's banishment, his narrative style becomes lively and vivid. He makes excellent use of circumstantial detail, allows his characters, especially the Saracen princess, to indulge in moments of introspection in the manner of Chrétien, and manages to make of an unwieldy conglomerate a natural and straightforward succession of events.

What gives the romance its distinctive quality is the character of Climent le vilain, who is both absurd and lovable. He is really not a *vilain,* but a simple-hearted bourgeois who has made money as a butcher and money-changer. He is on a pilgrimage to the East at the time the queen's infant son is carried off by the female ape. The child is rescued from the ape by a knight, but the rescuer is immediately attacked by a band of thieves who force him to give up his horse and the infant. Later they offer the child for sale and Climent buys it. The bourgeois engages a nurse, brings the boy back to Paris, and tells his wife that it is his illegitimate son. She loves the child and brings it up with her own. When he is old enough to learn a trade, Climent decides to make a butcher of him and sends him with two beeves to be butchered. Instead Florent trades the animals for a hawk. His foster father is upset, but accepts his loss when he sees how fond the boy is of his prize. A little later Florent, sent to change £40, sees a beautiful horse, which he covets. The owner asks £30 for it, but Florent says the price is too low and gives him the forty. Both ride away quickly, each fearing that the other will go back on his bargain. The bourgeois again accepts his loss philosophically. His wife is convinced that Florent is no son of the butcher; his tastes, she says, show that he is of gentle birth.

Many subsequent incidents are designed to reveal Climent not as an indulgent father but as a comic character. He is a real personality. Generally the weakest point in medieval romance is characterization. The heroes are ideal knights, heroines are beautiful but types, giants are unbelievably big and hideous, but are not individuals. Even in so gifted a story-teller as Chrétien de Troyes, except for a few major figures, the personages perform their functions in producing the story. By contrast Climent is a bourgeois with a consistently bourgeois attitude, which is brought out in a series of episodes with comic overtones. Paris is besieged by the sultan and a huge army. His champion is a fifteen-foot giant who picks up his opponent and carries him off under his arm. Florent, Climent's foster son, is determined to meet the monstrous antagonist in spite of all Climent's attempts to dissuade him. Climent can provide only his own old and rusty armor. His sword is so rusted in its scabbard that it takes the combined strength of Climent and his other son to pull it out, and when it finally comes loose both are sent sprawling. During the fight Climent is up on the wall shouting encouragement when Florent gets in a good blow, weeping and praying when he is hard-pressed. After Florent has conquered the giant and cut off his head, the king promises to knight him. Climent begs him not to, saying that he wishes to make the young man a money-changer. When the king offers to make Climent a knight as well, the bourgeois declines. He doesn't want to be a knight. He wants to rest, count his deniers, eat fat capons, drink good wine, at night embrace and kiss his wife. Florent is knighted amid great festivity. The place is swarming with minstrels, which Climent considers an unnecessary expense. He drives them away with his *baston: Por le cor dieu, sont ce or noces?* During the banquet he gathers up all the guests' cloaks and locks them in a room to make sure they pay their reckoning. Only when the king assures him that he will pay for everybody does he agree to restore the cloaks. Even the previous scene in which Florent is being clad as a knight in preparation for the dubbing is made to contribute to the revelation of Climent's personality. He insists, as the young man's father, in putting on his spurs. But he has trouble doing it and gets them on backward. In the easy social atmosphere that prevails, the king offers to help him. He accepts the offer with the wry confession that he does not know his business (*Car ie ne soi pas mon conroi*). He treats the king of France with a familiarity that is laughable. The French *Octavian* is *The Shoemakers' Holiday* of medieval romance.

This highly distinctive romance, or a version much like it, is the source of two Middle English redactions, known respectively as the Southern and the Northern versions.[6] They are clearly independent of each other. While telling the same basic story, they differ in what they tell and what they omit. The Southern version relates how Octavian, at the end of five years as emperor, is urged by his barons to marry. They suggest the daughter of Dagobert, king of France. So he journeys to Paris, secures her father's consent, and they are married by the pope. There is nothing of this in the Northern version or in the French *Octavian*. The new empress is named Florence, a name that does not occur in the French or in the Northern English text. In the Southern version the emperor begets on his wife twins in the first year. In the French they are childless for fifteen years, while in the Northern English version they are childless for seven years and succeed in having children only after they have founded a *ryche abbey* in honor of the Virgin. And so one might go on. Sarrazin notes only a few correspondences between the two English versions contrary to the French and thinks they are obvious realistic touches.

The Old French *Octavian* runs to 5371 lines, more than twice the length of either English romance, yet all three tell the same story with only such minor differences as we have mentioned. One might conjecture the existence of a shorter version in French, no longer known. But one would probably have to assume two such shorter versions if one wished to believe that each English author was following more or less closely his source. All this is possible, but seems unlikely. The only other version of the story in French is a late *chanson de geste* preserved in several manuscripts of the fifteenth century and a still later redaction of these in prose. The *chanson de geste* runs to over 16,000 lines, more in some manuscripts, and agrees in general with the romance as far as the romance extends. But it continues with an interminable account of the adventures of the two sons, of the younger Octavian and then of Florent. It certainly does not offer us a shorter form of the story. When we observe that a German version of the tale, preserved in a Volksbuch, follows closely the French romance, it seems likely that the form of the French poem which the English authors knew, and to which they refer, approximated that of the version that has come down to us.

This is not to say that either English author was translating from a manuscript that lay before him. The evidence is very much against such a supposition. There are practically no verbal parallels. And it may be added that the small number of passages (perhaps two score) which Sarrazin thought it worth while to cite from the French in his notes correspond only in the general idea, not in wording. Each English author seems to have forgotten on occasion the name of a character given in the French text, and each omits episodes and details which are lively and effective, and which would have added nice touches to his narrative if he had included them. It will be remembered that when Florent goes to fight the sultan's giant champion he is wearing his foster father's old and rusty armor. He makes a rather ridiculous appearance. In the French this is made much of. As he rides through Paris to the gate, he is soon followed by a crowd, jeering and shouting taunts. "Make room for the hardy bachelor. What a helmet and what a shield! It is the knight Arthur, who will kill any one he meets." And so on. The Southern English version says merely that many people laughed (*Many man loʒ*), the Northern that *alle þat about þe chylde*

stode,/ Laghed as they were wode,/ And skornyd hym that tyde. There
are numerous other minor but effective scenes that do not appear in
the English versions. When the pilgrim ship on which the banished
queen is a passenger puts in at an island, some of the crew go ashore
and discover a child being cared for by a lioness. It is one of the
queen's lost children. When she learns of this and goes to investigate,
the friendly animal allows her to take up her child, but follows her
back to the ship, and when she goes aboard leaps on board too. The
consternation among the crew makes a fine episode in the French
romance, with seamen jumping overboard, leaping over one another
in their effort to escape, knocking each other down, climbing the mast
and rigging—all told with vigor and humor. Later, when one of the
seamen makes advances to the queen and tries to embrace her by force,
the lioness tears him to pieces. The rest of the crew throw the dead
body overboard, observing that he got what he deserved. All this is
left out entirely by the Southern English version, and all that is left
of it in the Northern version is the statement that forty of the crew
jumped overboard. The order of incidents is often different, and everything seems clearly to indicate that both English reciters are telling
from memory a story which they have heard or read, which they know
quite well in its main outlines, but of which they have no written text
to follow or refer to.

As far as the comparison of the English versions and their source
goes, there can be no question as to the superiority of the Old French
romance. But for my present purpose this is less important than the
contrast between the two English narratives. The creator of the Southern version is a competent versifier, but a less than mediocre story-
teller. He seems to have remembered only the main elements of the
plot. He leaps from one episode to another, often fails to explain what
happens in between, and as a result leaves his audience puzzled. One
needs often to know the French romance to understand the relation
of incidents in the English. But what is most to his discredit is his
complete failure to appreciate the character of Climent and the unique
contribution that the bourgeois makes to the story. The humorous and
satirical elements of the French romance have almost completely disappeared, and, except for the impounding of the guests' cloaks at the
banquet, the most important incidents in which the butcher's character
is revealed are not included. This feature of the original had simply
not registered with him. Any incident in which Climent figures is
reported in a factual way without overtones. He tells his story me-

chanically and without inspiration. While I am of the opinion that too often we have attributed English romances to minstrel authorship, with insufficient evidence, I am inclined to believe that in the Southern *Octavian* we have a minstrel performance, and, in this case, a rather pedestrian one.

By contrast the author of the Northern version, though he is telling a condensed story in which, as we have seen, a number of nice touches in the French have dropped out, nevertheless responds to the humor inherent in the character and behavior of *Clement the Velayn,* who is here described as a burgess of Paris. Indeed, at times he finds ways of enhancing an incident. Thus when Florent is being armed, in the French it is Climent and his son who try to pull the rusty sword out of the scabbard. The English poet has Clement and his wife pull against each other. When it finally comes loose and both tumble to the ground, the scene is the more absurd. Again, at the festivities after the dubbing of Florent, Clement not only drives off the minstrels and impounds the guests' cloaks, but the English author better motivates these actions by explaining that the bourgeois thought he would have to bear the expense of all the entertainment:

> Clement so sorye was þat daye
> For all þaire costes, þat he solde paye,
>   That he gane wepe wele sore;

and when the king persuades him to return the cloaks, saying that he would pay for all the guests' *mete, . . . Clement þore of was fulle blythe.* But he still doesn't understand courtly ways:

> Whene þe folke alle had etene
> Clement hade noghte forgetyne,
>   His purse he openede thore:
> Thritty florence forthe keste he
> And said: "Hafe here for my sone and me . . ."

and he adds that they are all he will pay for. These touches are additions by the English poet. He enters fully into the spirit of the original. The incidents in which Clement figures, however, are not the only evidence of the English poet's humorous bent. When the sultan is camped outside the walls of Paris, it will be remembered, he has a giant who offers to fight all comers. The English poet has him go up to the city fortifications and lean on the top of the wall to issue his challenge. Again, the giant has promised to bring to the sultan's daughter, for whom he experiences unrequited love, the head of the French king. After Florent has nullified this boast, he carries the giant's head to the princess:

> 'Damesele,' said Florent, 'faire and free,
> Wele now gretis thi lemane the,
>   Of þat he the byhete;
> Lo here, an heuede i hafe þe broghte,
> The kynges of France ne es it noghte,
>   For it were fulle euylle to gete!'

Recognizing the head, she remarks that he was as good as his word. Since he couldn't get the king's head, he had sent his own. It is things like this that we remember when the commonplace and conventional are forgotten.

It has not been my purpose in this paper to deny, or even to play down, the large part that convention plays in the Middle English romance. It is rather to show that there is also creative originality, not merely in the *Gawain* poet and the authors of a few other romances where it has been recognized, but in humbler poets in whom it has generally gone unnoticed. If we could study more of the English romances in relation to their sources, as we can read Chaucer's *Troilus* against the background of the *Filostrato,* we might be able to add to the number of those who impressed their own individuality on the material that they inherited from the general body of romance tradition. It is hoped that the two cases that I have presented may help to redress too great a critical imbalance.

EUGÈNE VINAVER

From Motive to Ornament

The concept of invention varies from one period of literary history to another. To apply intelligence to the matter in hand, to go in search of stories waiting to be redeemed by ordered elucidation, such was, I believe, the essential task undertaken by the most inventive French romance writers of the twelfth century, and the flowering of the genre in the subsequent centuries was a clear measure of their success. It was in order to describe this process in what we would now call "compositional" terms that Chrétien de Troyes coined the phrase *une moult bele conjointure,*[1] which meant, so far as we can tell, a skillful arrangement of the narrative, the adoption of an effective organizing principle capable of giving the narrative shape and substance, either by revealing the hidden motives and reasons behind the facts of the story or by relating these facts to one another in an intelligible way.

Chrétien proudly proclaimed the superiority of this method over the crude manner of ignorant story-tellers who went about reciting their stories *devant rois et devant contes* in a disjointed and, as he thought, "corrupt" fashion.[2] Few modern readers and critics would disagree with him. For his is the method which we still use in academic discourse, and which we still expect any imaginative writer to use in a novel or a play. We might, however, be less inclined to press for its acceptance if we knew more about the history of medieval fiction; if we realized, for instance, what happened when in the thirteenth century the romantic matter inherited from Chrétien de Troyes and from his near contemporary, Robert de Borron, was elaborated into a vast composition, the Vulgate Cycle of Arthurian romances. The Cycle was built up in accordance with this same method of adaptation applied on a hitherto unknown scale. Like their predecessors, thirteenth-century romance writers wanted to make their stories articulate, to place

them in a "causal" perspective; but out of their sustained and pro-
longed efforts to organize their material in a coherent fashion there
arose something so vast and so complex that in our modern age it has
until recently defeated every attempt to discover any coherent principle behind it. The tangled branches of the forest in which knights-
errant wandered, fought, and wandered again no longer let the light
through; elucidation, carried to such extremes, practiced with such
consistency, plunged the whole scene into what appeared to be chaos
and darkness.

How did this happen? How did medieval romance in its search for
illumination become ostensibly a genre in which some of the most
clear-sighted readers of today can see nothing but endless confusion?
Part of the answer lies in the distinction we often fail to make between two concepts, that of clarity and that of simplicity or brevity.
We tacitly assume—the confusion can be traced back to the Renaissance and beyond—that in order to be clear one has to be simple and
economical. Historically and logically, these are by no means identical
notions. *Brevitas* was in classical rhetoric one of the *virtutes narra-
tionis.* If we are to believe what Socrates says in *Phaedrus,* the art of
brevity was invented by the very founders of Greek rhetoric, Teisias
and Gorgias; and it certainly proved valuable for judicial and political
oratory, where brevity and relevance were, and still are, not only virtues, but matters of practical necessity. The story of how in the end,
through the powerful agency of Roman rhetoric, the structure of a
judicial or political discourse became part of an artistic ideal has often
been told, as well as the story of how, as a result, we came to believe
that brevity in a work of literature was a merit and prolixity a fault;
and how the principle formulated by Horace in his *Ars poetica—brevis
esse laboro*—came to be recognized as a universal principle of literary
composition. What is not so well known is that in the Middle Ages
the situation was very different from what it is in our age of tame and
unquestioning neo-scholasticism. Medieval treatises on the art of poetry
may extol the advantages of *brevitas,* especially in narrative poetry
and in the epistolary genre, but from the end of the twelfth century
onward they insist more and more on the necessity of combining
brevitas with its converse, *dilatatio,* which is one of the forms of amplification. Curtius remarks that about the year 1200 poetic theory
offers a choice between the two procedures: an author can draw the
subject out, or he can dispatch it as briefly as possible; and it so
happens that the former method receives more attention than the

latter. The reason for this is not, as Curtius thought, that "there was more to be said about *amplificatio* than about *abbreviatio*," [3] but that the writers of the time, conditioned as they were by their own literary experience, were better able than any of their classical masters to appreciate amplification as a form of art: not simply as a means of making the story more explicit, nor as a concession to the reader's intellectual curiosity, but as something valuable and attractive in itself, regardless of its explanatory function; as part of the artist's contribution to a further sophistication of the theme.

The seemingly irrational behavior of certain Arthurian characters is sometimes the result of this kind of elaboration. One such character is Arthur's versatile and treacherous sister, Morgan le Fay. Lucy Allen Paton speaks of her as a character endowed with a "wide range of capacities," and Mark Twain's protagonist refers to these in unequivocal terms. "I have seen," he says, "a good many women in my time, but she laid them all over in variety." "She may be," to quote Roger Sherman Loomis, "Arthur's tender nurse in the island valley of Avilion, or his treacherous foe. She may be a virgin, or a Venus of lust. In her infinite variety she enthralled the fancy of the Middle Ages, and has lived on to our day not only in literature, but in folklore. As the Fata Morgana, she still evokes the mirages of the Straits of Messina." [4] A character whose versatility can strike with equal force three such different observers is clearly the product of a complex imaginative process. For Loomis, Morgan was "manifestly a creature of tradition rather than invention." I prefer to think that she was both, and that in her case as in that of many other characters of Arthurian romance, the more we can discover about the nature of the "invention," the less likely we are to overestimate the importance of the "tradition."

One striking example of spontaneous invention is the part assigned to Morgan in what is known as the *Suite du Merlin*—a work written soon after the Vulgate Cycle as a prelude to some of its branches.[5] In the *Suite* the adventures inspired by Morgan begin when one day Arthur is hunting a stag in the forest of Camelot with Accalon, the lover of Morgan, and Urien, her husband.[6] The three companions see a magnificent ship gliding toward them at the river's edge, its decks hung with shining silks. They are joyfully greeted and invited to come aboard by twelve maidens who clothe them in rich attire, entertain them with a royal feast, and then take each one of them to a bedchamber. When the next day they awake they are all three in quite other places: Urien in the arms of his wife, Morgan; Arthur in a prison black as pitch; Accalon in a meadow near a spring, still wearing the robe the maidens gave him the night before. As each intrigue develops, the three-fold mystery becomes more and more involved. First, Accalon sees a dwarf appear in front of him in the meadow. The dwarf is carrying a sword—it happens to be Arthur's own sword —and he gives it to Accalon saying it is a gift from Morgan le Fay. When Accalon asks him to explain the meaning of it all, he replies: "These are the adventures of Britain or the enchantments of this land." [7] And so they are, for when we next see Arthur in prison we discover that he is there because his captor needs a champion to fight for him, and Arthur agrees to take the fight upon himself in order to obtain his release and that of all the other prisoners. One of the ladies of Morgan le Fay suddenly appears at a window. She brings Arthur what he thinks is his sword, but it is only a replica. The real sword is in Accalon's hands, and it is Accalon whom Arthur has to meet in single combat the next day. He fights with all his strength, but the counterfeit weapon is soon shattered and Accalon calls upon Arthur to admit defeat. Arthur replies that he would rather die than sur- render; "and he would have been killed," the author tells us, "had it not been for the Lady of the Lake who appeared just at that moment, cast a spell upon Accalon and made the good sword drop from his hand onto the grass." [8] Arthur seizes it, recognizes it, and tears the scabbard away from Accalon, whose wounds immediately begin to bleed. For such is the magic power of the scabbard that whoever car- ries it can never lose a drop of blood in battle. With his last breath Morgan's unhappy lover asks Arthur to forgive his involuntary treachery: he did not know that he would be fighting his own king. Morgan's plans, however, are not so easily defeated. She tries to murder her own husband, Urien, in his sleep. Her son, Yvain, sees her approaching Urien's bed with a sword, disarms her and threatens to kill her. As if to comfort herself for this new setback she goes to the place where Arthur is spending the night, creeps into his tent while he is asleep, and steals the magic scabbard once more from him. Arthur gives chase and Morgan, feeling her strength running out, hurls the scabbard into a lake from which it will be taken only for Gawain to wear in his fight with the sorcerer Naborn, and no one will know what becomes of it after this. Arthur will never set eyes on it again. In the final phase of the battle of Salisbury Plain there will be no charmed weapon to prevent Mordred from wounding him to the death.

Nothing like this series of episodes had been thought of by the authors of the Vulgate Cycle. The elaborate machinations culminating in the removal of the magic scabbard from Arthur were invented by a later writer who was apparently intent on producing a work that would pave the way for the main events of the *Queste del Saint Graal* and of the *Mort Artu*—the two concluding branches of the Cycle. But the long succession of plots, ruses, and attempted assassinations inspired by Morgan was clearly out of all proportion to its explanatory function. Indeed, to seek its *raison d'être* in its usefulness as a preparation for the final catastrophe would be to condemn it outright. All the intrigues of Morgan outgrow—and are deliberately made to outgrow—their relevance, whether we judge their relationship to the story in dramatic or in discursive terms. How, then, are they to be justified?

So far as the story of Arthur's death is concerned, the same question may be asked with reference to some of the other seemingly superfluous additions to the original narrative. Neither Geoffrey of Monmouth [9] nor Wace [10] had tried to explain the downfall of Arthur's kingdom. To them it was a natural consequence of a military disaster, of an accident of warfare which in other circumstances could have been avoided. But as soon as the story ceased to be a chronicle and became a romance, that is to say part of the Arthurian prose cycle, it acquired a motivation of a different and characteristically complex kind. The disaster was accounted for not in terms of any one particular cause, but in terms of several concurrent causes. It was made clear, to begin with, that at the close of the quest for the Holy Grail divine protection had been withdrawn from Arthur and from Lancelot and that neither Arthur nor Lancelot could thenceforth save Arthurian chivalry from destruction.[11] By classical standards this would have been an adequate explanation, but in a thirteenth-century cyclic romance there was room for more. And so the Wheel of Fortune was introduced to show that the disaster had to come in any case as a result of Arthur's rise to excessive heights of success and fame. A third line of motivation, implicit in the action and the characters, was the notion that disaster came in the wake of divided loyalties—a theme developed in such a way as to bring out the insoluble conflict of "two goods," one symbolized by Lancelot's allegiance to Guinevere, the other by his fidelity to Arthur and Gawain. The resulting conflict tears Arthur's kingdom apart at the moment of its gravest peril. Finally a fourth motive was added at a still later stage: Mordred, Arthur's nephew, was made the child of his incest, and Arthur's death at Mordred's hands became a retribution for his sin. It stands to reason that in order to justify this multiplication of motives and antecedents we must not think of them as being dramatic necessities. Not only are all of them except one redundant by the standards of classical or neo-classical dramatic composition, but their multiplicity is contrary to any recognized view of action in a novel or a play. In real life two reasons may be better than one, but if Brutus or Othello had more than one reason for doing what he does, the whole dramatic edifice would collapse like a house of cards. We are here brought face to face with a conception of artistic propriety which has little relation to any literary theory that we are familiar with. Most of us have been slow to grasp this contrast, and I confess that it was not until I came to consider the next stage in the motivation of Arthur's death—that which involves Morgan le Fay —that the nature of this motivation became for the first time apparent to me.

What Morgan le Fay does is to carry the process one step further, but far enough to make us realize what exactly has been happening to the story all along. Of all Arthurian characters she is the one who conspires most consistently and most effectively against our preconceived notions of literary form. Her intrigues never spoil the story; on the contrary, they add considerably to the interest of the episodes in which they occur. But to do them justice we must recognize as legitimate one quality which they share with many other motivating themes in the Arthurian world, namely their dramatic superfluity. They are obviously even less necessary for the understanding of the tragic ending of the Arthurian epic than any one of the four themes introduced in the Vulgate: the Grail quest, the Wheel of Fortune, the clash of loyalties, and Arthur's incest; and more than in the case of any of these, we must think of Morgan's intrigues—if we are to understand them at all—in nondramatic terms, preferably in pictorial terms. For what after all are these arabesque-like conspiracies if not an interlace practiced with consummate skill? A triptych is placed before the reader at the outset: the adventure develops along three different lines until the lines begin to cross and the entire pattern converges upon the fate of the magic scabbard and that of the king himself. The resulting fabric of interwoven events is the work of a sorceress whose object is to involve us in situations of the greatest intricacy, not in order to make the final resolution of the action more acceptable, but in order to give us the kind of pleasure we experience in discovering through patient observation the shape of an ornament on a richly decorated page of a liturgical manuscript of the eleventh, twelfth, or thirteenth century.

The test of an ornament is, of course, its fitness. It must occupy a space, fulfill a purpose, be adapted to the material in which it is executed and to the process *by* which it is inserted into the general framework. Art historians tell us that while the forms of ornament are often derived from nature, repose is best secured by some remoteness from nature, some transfiguration of natural forms; for the artist's problem in ornamentation is primarily one of *design*. The same is true of the ornamental complexity of Arthurian romance. Each individual element of it may be drawn from the common stock of tradition and may even seem to conform to the pattern of ordinary human behavior. Jealousy, revenge, conflicting loyalties, human passions, good and wicked, all these things may be present; but they undergo a transfiguration which for most of the late medieval writers represents the essential logic of the story: a logic of the same kind as that which brings forth the figures of animals in an inhabited scroll or the ornamental foliage growing out of the animals' heads in certain decorated initials, or the decorative border which from the thirteenth century onward frequently dominates the whole design of the page. These things do not have to be transparent to be enjoyed, any more than the adventures of Britain and "the enchantments of this land." We must be grateful to Morgan le Fay and the other magicians, good and evil, for having revealed to us this unsuspected world: a world where the intricate play of shadow in the unexplored expanse of a forest of adventure is as meaningful as the light shining through the branches. The magicians do more than reveal this world to us: they help us to understand how it came into being. And perhaps the greatest lesson to be learned from them is that what began as an intellectual exercise, as an inquiry into the why and wherefore of originally insignificant episodes, ended as a form of imaginative writing—as an art which

> never pales for weariness
> Of climbing heaven and gazing on the earth.

Woman and Peacock, from the *Aesop* of Joseph Zainer (Ulm, 1475)

ROBERT WORTH FRANK, JR.

Troilus and Criseyde: The Art of Amplification[1]

We can describe *Troilus and Criseyde* in several different ways, depending on what we choose to concentrate upon in that complex poem. Here I wish to describe it in terms of a basic technique it employs. My intention is to approach *Troilus and Criseyde* from a position as close to Chaucer's own as possible: to look at the problem he faced in writing the poem as he might have looked at it, to examine the fundamental technique he used in working through the problem, and to see for what ends the technique was employed.

The *Troilus* is a reworking of a long lyrico-narrative poem in another language, Boccaccio's *Il Filostrato.*[2] It is not merely a translation, as Chaucer piously insisted, but an expansion of his original. The term *amplificatio,* "amplification," from the technical vocabulary of medieval rhetoric, will describe, somewhat crudely, a good part of this process of transformation and expansion.[3] It is a term Chaucer might have known and used; it denotes a rhetorical method with which he unquestionably was familiar.

There is nothing novel in applying the term to *Troilus and Criseyde.* C. S. Lewis has commented on it as a method of the poem,[4] as has Daniel Boughner.[5] Sanford Meech, though not interested in rhetoric as such, has set down a number of ways in which Chaucer expanded Boccaccio.[6] Most recently, Robert Payne has examined critically the process of amplification in *Troilus.*[7] I intend, however, to move in a rather different direction from these writers, and with a different emphasis.

Consideration of the term, we should observe, takes us to the very earliest moments of the poem's inception. Only one critical moment precedes it—when Chaucer decided to use *Il Filostrato,* decided to make an English poem of the Italian. This decision once made, the question of amplification emerges. As his first step in carrying out the decision to use *Il Filostrato,* Chaucer would have to determine his basic method in handling this material. Three primary possibilities were open to him: he could provide a more or less close translation of his original, he could abbreviate it, or he could amplify it. The three possibilities are not mutually exclusive, and Chaucer does in fact make use of all three. At moments he gives us a comparatively straightforward translation, at moments he abbreviates. But his basic technique is to amplify.

The decision to amplify must have been a deliberate one, for the two other methods were equally possible choices. To be sure, faithful translation was not a habitual choice for a medieval poet; but Chaucer was capable of it. His translation of Boethius, for example, and his very close following of Ovid's version of Pyramus and Thisbe in the *Legend of Good Women* are evidence of his willingness to submit his pen to the yoke. We cannot hope to recover his reasons for deciding not to translate, though they are implied by his decision to amplify. At the very least, however, we ought not to listen to C. S. Lewis when he gives us Chaucer's reason: Chaucer, said Lewis, looked at Boccaccio's poem and uttered the Middle English equivalent of "This will never do" [8]—something, I assume, like the words of the gentle tercelet to the duck in the *Parliament of Birds*: *"Now fy, cherl! . . ./ Out of the donghill cam that word ful right! . . ./ Thy kynde is of so low a wrechednesse/ That what love is, thow canst nat seen ne gesse."* Chaucer's primary reason for changing *Il Filostrato,* according to Lewis, was to remove its offenses against the code of love and render it a more orthodox poem. This makes Chaucer's decision not to translate faithfully a rather schoolmasterly action. He was not all that orthodox a poet of love,[9] as the *Parliament of Birds* had already demonstrated; neither is he merely, or strictly, orthodox in *Troilus and Criseyde.* What is worse, Lewis' explanation leaves the bulk of Chaucer's additions unexplained. The "This will never do" thesis will itself not do.

A second possibility Chaucer rejected was abbreviation. It might be argued that there is very little likelihood the possibility so much as occurred to him. Amplification, not abbreviation, was his method and the method of his age—an obsessive medieval practice, not so much a technique as a tic. Certainly Chaucer's earlier work suggests that expansion was the only art he had mastered. He was not working with a source, strictly speaking, in the *Book of the Duchess,* the *House of Fame,* or the *Parliament of Birds,* but in all three it is apparent that he begins with a comparatively simple structure, and that the process in each poem is elaboration upon that simple structure. The amplification is somewhat wobbly but charming and inventive in the *Book of the Duchess.* In the *House of Fame* it is ambitious in the extreme and threatens to split the hull or cause the bark to founder. In the *Parliament* amplification is employed with sure control for the first time, and is exploited for a brilliant development of the poem's theme. But the abortive *Anelida and Arcite* of about the same period is a disaster, and the disaster occurs in part because the technique of amplification is misapplied. The failure might well have given him pause.

The historical sequence in which *Troilus and Criseyde* occurs is, furthermore, suggestive. In the two poems which, so far as we can determine, he wrote immediately after *Troilus and Criseyde,* the Knight's Tale and at least the first several legends in the *Legend of Good Women,* Chaucer did employ the alternate and antithetical medieval method for handling his material, *abbreviation.* So the possibility that he might have considered treating *Il Filostrato* in this fashion is a real one. It seems a safe assumption that the decision to employ amplification as the basic method of procedure in *Troilus and Criseyde* was a conscious artistic choice.

I have so painfully broken what may seem a butterfly because I think the choice Chaucer made was of the greatest importance. The decision to amplify was made, I believe, because Chaucer was impressed not only by Boccaccio's poem and its theme, but also by the possibilities—the unexploited possibilities of the poem. I am perhaps reasoning from effect to cause. But I find the notion that expansion—that mere increase in length—would be valued for its own sake too naive an explanation to apply to a poet like Chaucer. The fact that the poem's basic method is amplification of its original is evidence enough for me that Chaucer wanted to make something *more* of his source material. The question then is, what kind of *more?*

The least attractive answer to that question would be, a more decorated, a more ornamental poem. This is one view of medieval amplification; it makes the device a pastry bag with which the poet squirts pink and blue rosettes of butter-cream icing over his poem. The medieval poets and rhetoricians have largely themselves to blame for this view. C. S. Lewis cites Dante: *Omnis qui versificatur suos versos exornare debet in quantum potest.*[10] And one need not read long in some medieval poetry, especially the Latin poetry, to find rhetorical cadenzas, decorative passages where the ingenious involutions and bravura irrelevance do in fact transform language into a butter-cream baroque. Even Lewis, however, finds beauty and relevance in the passages in *Troilus* he cites as instances of amplification. There are few decorative flights in the poem which are merely ornamental. The method is made to serve a larger and more vital purpose than this.[11]

The purpose, without question, was thematic amplification—to enlarge the range and significance of the poem. More specifically, the purpose was to expand our awareness of both the values and limitations contained within the experience of idealized human love. The range of vision has been enlarged in both directions so that the spectrum of values has been widened and the contradictions contained within that experience have been increased and sharpened. By Chaucer's expansion the poem is made to contain, as it did not before, several value systems related to the experience of love. These value systems clash with one another or with the experience itself, however, and their juxtaposition within the *Troilus* establishes a series of perspectives from which the experience of love is viewed, some of them sympathetic, some antipathetic, some ironic, some condemnatory.

This widening of values is perhaps Chaucer's most notable transformation of his material. Charles Muscatine has observed that the action of *Il Filostrato* springs from "a surprisingly narrow conception of good and evil." Its moral, as he says, is *Giovanne donna è mobile.* The consequence is "a light irony" and a "heavy pathos." [12] If Chaucer was aware of the narrowness of Boccaccio's treatment, as his handling of the poem suggests, he nevertheless accepted love as that secular theme which, in his time, cut most deeply into human experience and exposed most revealingly the nature of that experience. And it is love of which Boccaccio treats, love in some local Neapolitan sense even "courtly." [13] It was, moreover, love acted out with an intensity unadulterated by knightly adventure and unfragmented by the analytical techniques of personification. Whatever Boccaccio's poem does not do, it does dramatize intensity of feeling, of love and joy and sorrow. Chaucer could hardly have found anything to match it for this quality of sustained intensity in the literature of his day. Here is something like the pure thing itself. If we want to see the experience of love for what it is, in its widest possibilities, Boccaccio's story is a fine place to begin. But its possibilities must be brought out. It must be amplified.

Chaucer's plan for his poem dictates his rhetorical method. In what follows I wish to examine some of the kinds of material Chaucer adds in the *Troilus* and to analyze the ways in which this material truly amplifies: that is, enlarges the poem's vision of love. Without for a moment suggesting that the process was mechanical, so much ladled into the poem from vat A, so much from vat B, so much from vat C, I wish to look at three sorts or forms of amplification: material contained normally in individual lines or at most stanzas; extended enlargement of scenes and of the action of the poem; and finally several longish passages added in revision. If this seems unduly schematic, it is only accidentally so. It is, in each instance, the content that interests me. I shall be ignoring a great deal of important matter that Chaucer added, notably the proems and the material given to the Narrator.[14] And I shall not be concerned with Chaucer's changes in the character of Pandarus, or of Criseyde, as such. It is Chaucer's additions, rather than changes, that interest me.

I

I begin with what may seem a trifling matter. Chaucer's poem, to an enormously greater degree than Boccaccio's, makes use of proverbs, sententious sayings, and what R. M. Lumiansky calls monitory examples.[15] Chaucer did this, according to Lewis, because he approached his work as a poet of *doctryne* and *sentence,* found it deficient in this respect, and so amended it. Lewis notices, as have others, that this sententious material is concentrated, much of it, in the speeches of Pandarus and creates some of the comedy of his character—though Pandarus' fondness for proverbs is not *all* a matter of comic characterization, Lewis argues, and quite correctly, I believe.[16] Chaucer's audience, perhaps, as Lewis maintains, would have been edified at moments and, at moments, amused.

But we cannot stop here. The audience's receptivity to proverbial instruction is the instrument upon which Chaucer wishes to play. For one thing, we should not forget that the sententious material is not assigned exclusively to Pandarus. Troilus, on a few occasions, and the Narrator, and especially Criseyde also use proverbs. B. J. Whiting has argued that proverbial material is almost as much a device of characterization for Criseyde as for Pandarus.[17] We tend to be, however, more cautious than we used to be in talking of Chaucer's interest in characterization. It is types of character, rather than individualized character, that seem to have concerned him.[18] And character types are more closely related to value systems than individualized characters.

The use of monitory material in the poem is yet more complex. Pandarus and Criseyde do not speak pure proverbian. They use proverbs almost exclusively when they are trying to determine conduct: Pandarus resorts to them when he is directing Troilus into action in Book I and elsewhere, when he is trying to influence Criseyde in Book II, when he is trying to hearten Troilus after the news of the separation in Book IV. We hear them in Criseyde's speech when she is countering Pandarus in Book II, when she is trying to determine her own mind later in the same book, and when she is urging her plan of action—or inaction—on Troilus in Book IV. Proverbial expressions are largely absent from the consummation scene in Book III, the tragic decline in Book V.

This clustering of the proverbial material and its cumulative effect at moments of decision create one of the value systems within the poem. The monitory matter creates a world of "wisdom" which at times supports and guides the lovers, at times deflates or misleads them. A major preoccupation of the poem is the examination of love in what might be called a prudential context, a world of "wisdom." This wisdom is variously presented as essential, as deflating, and finally as contradictory, self-defeating, and ineffectual.

Wisdom is essential if love is ever to be transformed from feeling to action. The pure, unalloyed extravagance of feeling in Troilus and the self-contained reticence of Criseyde are both submitted to the pragmatic counsels of Pandarus. Though Criseyde possesses her own resources of prudence, these give her divided counsel; they tend to reinforce her reticence and advise inaction as much as they recommend involvement. Under the guidance of Pandarus a way is found which adjusts the inmost desires of each to the pressures and demands of the other. Feeling is bridled, and reticence persuaded to drop its guard. The consequence of prudence's counsels is success, of a kind.

But in achieving success, especially by this means, love suffers a kind of failure. It is coarsened by this contact with prudence. Success itself puts an end to the noblest activity of the game, the faithful wooing, in which the lover's emotion and the lady's reticence are both pure, both faithful to their nature. Even Pandarus can see this impractical ideal gleaming beyond the marketplace and the bedroom:

What? many a man hath love ful deere ybought
Twenty wynter that his lady wiste,
That nevere yet his lady mouth he kiste.

What? sholde he therfore fallen in dispayr,
Or be recreant for his owne tene,
Or slen hymself, al be his lady fair?
Nay, nay, but evere in oon be fressh and grene
To serve and love his deere hertes queene,
And thynk it is a guerdon, hire to serve,
A thousand fold moore than he kan deserve.
(I, 810–819) [19]

Ironically, it is Pandarus alone who remains true to the cult of the pursuit; he alone remains "forever panting" if not forever young. The Higher Prudence he reserves for himself.

What is more critical, prudence contradicts itself and prudence fails. At the threat of separation in Book IV a new course of action must be set. The code grants Criseyde the last word, and a good part of the last word for her is a buzzing of old saws. Prudence wins the day and loses the game. Troilus' foolish, loving heart is wiser than Criseyde's head. If he had obeyed his feelings, they might never have been parted. Emotion, which paralyzed him in the beginning, urges action now. Prudence, which made action possible in the opening scenes, leads to paralysis in the final crisis. Worst of all, though it urged love and devotion in Book I, in Book IV it must recommend faithlessness, muttering, *"And ek, as writ Zanzis, that was ful wys,/ 'The newe love out chaceth ofte the olde . . .' "* (414–415). Where is a guide, if wisdom, which idealistic feeling must attend to, is now right, but now wrong?

II

The process of amplification by which much of this *doctryne* is added is to a considerable degree a patching process, a matter of adding a line or two or a stanza here and there, where it is not part of a larger pattern of revision. Far different is the amplification by which Chaucer transformed the first third of the original so that it constitutes three-fifths of his own considerably longer poem. From the middle of Book I to about line 1300 in Book III Chaucer's poem expands, rearranges, and rewrites *Il Filostrato*.[20] He retains lines and passages here and there, and he preserves the outline of the action in

Boccaccio: Pandarus wins Troilus' confidence, he intercedes successfully with Criseyde, and Criseyde and Troilus become lovers. But
within this scenario a radical transformation is achieved. The first
scene between Pandarus and Troilus is doubled in length, as is the first
scene between Pandarus and Criseyde—and its tone is quite changed.
The scene of Criseyde alone with her thoughts after Pandarus leaves
is quadrupled in length. The dinner party at the house of Deiphebus,
running altogether to about 630 lines, is created either out of whole
cloth or out of an incident near the end of Boccaccio's poem.[21] And
the first part of the consummation scene is completely recast, Boccaccio's 108 lines becoming 812 in *Troilus and Criseyde.*

The compelling question is, Why? Why all this revision? None of
the answers seem quite to satisfy. It is in this section that Chaucer's
Pandarus and Criseyde as opposed to Boccaccio's are created. But it
is difficult to believe the revision was done for this purpose, or exclusively so. Even if we see them as types rather than individuals, their
creation does not seem the primary purpose of the revision. Boccaccio's
somewhat colorless young aide-de-camp becomes the arch-Amis, all
practicality and devotion in the service of his friend's love. Boccaccio's
wanton becomes a lady, *the* Lady *par excellence,* in whom Danger
(standoffishness, reticence), Bel Acoil (friendly reception), and Pity
blend so that the inaccessibly feminine becomes almost accessible. But
do we need the Deiphebus scene or the elaborated maneuvering into
Criseyde's bed for this purpose?

Perhaps we are mistaken to seek a single explanation for the entire
revised section. Perhaps we should take it piece by piece. But is it
really satisfying to say, then, that the dinner at the house of Deiphebus
is introduced to prepare for the bedroom scene? It is a magnificent
trial run, to be sure, but is it necessary, and is that all we get from it?
This scene, and the slow progress in Book III to Criseyde's bed by
that barely ambulatory lover, Troilus, delay Criseyde's acquiescence
to intensify our sense of the lady's "danger" or reticence and to
"heighten" her character—and to intensify our sense of Troilus' joy—
so that when she does fall, the pity of it, Iago, is all the greater. But
somehow this reduces Chaucer to the role of play-doctor, tinkering
with Boccaccio's vehicle in New Haven or Philadelphia to make it go
on West 44th. I do not mean to minimize the importance of technical
improvement. I mean simply to register my feeling that none of these
answers quite satisfies.

We might start with one simple historical observation. This section

of Boccaccio's poem was the portion most vulnerable to change. This
was the part of the story Boccaccio had added to Benoit de Ste.
Maure's *Roman de Troie*. Chaucer knew this, because he knew the
Roman. It was the least traditional, the most novel section, and so he
could change most freely here. But this merely suggests opportunity,
not motive.

The pattern I see running through this extended amplification is
the introduction of contradictions. Criseyde becomes both more delicately or sensitively emotional and more controlled and calculating.
One moment she is the tactician who can react to Pandarus' announcement of Troilus' love by a maneuver to draw his fire:

> Criseyde, which that herde hym in this wise,
> Thoughte, "I shal felen what he meneth, ywis."
> "Now em," quod she, "what wolde ye devise?
> "What is youre reed I sholde don of this?"
>   (II, 386–389)

A moment later she can burst into tears. She can coolly itemize the
advantages and disadvantages of a liaison with Troilus one minute and
the next, at the sight of the heroic, bloodied warrior, gasp, *"Who yaf
me drynke?"* If she can rise to lyric heights in the consummation scene
(and she is removed from all charges of wantonness), she can also
descend to kitchen comedy and backstairs sniggering the morning after
with her uncle:

> And ner he com, and seyde, "How stant it now
> This mury morwe? Nece, how kan ye fare?"
> Criseyde answerde, "Nevere the bet for yow,
> Fox that ye ben! God yeve youre herte kare!
> God help me so, ye caused al this fare,
> Trowe I," quod she, "for al youre wordes white.
> O, whoso seeth yow, knoweth yow ful lite."
>
> With that she gan hire face for to wrye
> With the shete, and wax for shame al reed. . . .
>   (III, 1562–1570)

Almost, but not quite, saved by a blush. The consummation scene also
gives us Troilus' finest and his funniest hours, exalted lover and
mouse's heart, now in a rapture, now in a dead faint.

Chaucer's creation in Books I to III is more than this, I grant you. We are asked to watch love in as complete a realization of the experience as seems possible within a fourteenth-century literary perspective. Perhaps this stretch of the poem does work through the essentials of the code of love, by its marvelous subtlety evading any sense of mechanical orthodoxy or bookish inventory. The subtlety, at all events, comes in great part from the exploitation of the contradictions within the experience. The constant shifting of relationships between characters, the shifting of tone, the shifting of perspectives on love derive from the manifestation of the contradictory elements within the code and among its ideals and its idealized types. Love, like a kite on a mad March day, now soars, now swoops and flutters; now pulls steadily toward heaven, now bangs nose-down in the dirt.

Not the least achievement in this section is the sense of a society, the society in which the lovers move about and against which they plot their private intrigue. There is very little of this sense of society in *Il Filostrato,* and when it emerges, it appears too late, when the poem is almost ended, with the visit to Sarpedon in Canto V and the scene with Deiphebus in Canto VII. Chaucer creates this sense of society in a variety of ways: Criseyde among her ladies reading the Romaunce of Thebes; Criseyde in the garden with Flexippe, Tharbe, and Antigone; Criseyde with her womenfolk at the house of Pandarus. He creates it too with his altered characters of Criseyde and Pandarus. Where these two are gathered together, there is society—social sense, banter, maneuver, the pressure of personality against personality, the knowing mastery of manners and the skillful straining and easing of a relationship and an etiquette. But above all else this sense of society is created by the scene at the house of Deiphebus. It is the creation of this sense that explains, for me, a good deal of the amplification we are discussing, and especially this scene.

All this has been remarked before, but remarked as though this sense of society were created for its own sake, for something vaguely identified as background or added richness. It is created, I would argue, because it, too, is part of the experience of love, and one of the most deeply contradictory aspects of that experience, especially in its courtly form. Love is a private emotion and a public institution.[22] Courtly love intensifies this contradiction. However hypothetical the courtly code may be, as a convention it operates simultaneously to deify love and to outlaw it. Courtly society, presumably, values the experience of passionate love outside marriage but at the same time prohibits it. Antigone will sing love's praises in a song made by *"the goodlieste mayde/ Of gret estat in al the town of Troye,/ And let hire lif in moste honour and joye"* (II, 880–882). But Troilus must hide, watching Criseyde at dinner *thorughout a litel wyndow in a stewe* (III, 601). At its most relaxed, society still is inimical to love, violating its desire for privacy, indifferent to its amazed self-regard, amused by its most cherished emotions. So the dinner talk at the house of Deiphebus swirls and eddies, in its ignorance and indifference a comic reminder that a world exists with other cares and other concerns than lovers' hopes and fears. It diminishes love by its preoccupations, it threatens love by its curiosity, and by its codes it both encourages love and denies it.

So society must be manipulated and outmaneuvered. Ultimately, in the form of the Trojan parliament and Criseyde's father it will work to destroy love, without even an awareness of what it is doing. Before that tragic moment, however, lovers rise from dinner parties to slip on the mask of intimate intrigue. Both at Deiphebus' house and at Pandarus', public, social occasions are necessary for there to be private meetings. The paradox brilliantly dramatizes the contradiction between love and society. Without the scene at the house of Deiphebus and much of the other amplification of Books I to III we would have missed one of love's most significant dimensions. The blandly indifferent, lively, necessary, gossiping world throws into comic relief love whispering its cries from the heart. The chattering ladies with Criseyde when the appalling news of her exchange arrives, the dancing ladies and feasting gentlemen who frame Troilus' heartbreak at Sarpedon's reassert this contradiction with a bitter irony. But this is only possible because the sense of society has been so solidly established in the earlier amplification. We need the charms and prescriptions for fever at Deiphebus' dinner table, and our knowledge that they are for a fever their potions can never cure.

III

The final instances of amplification I wish to consider are those passages which Chaucer appears to have added in revision: Troilus' hymn to Love at the conclusion of Book III, his soliloquy on predestination in Book IV, and his translation to the eighth sphere in Book V.[23] The fact that they all relate to Troilus may suggest some concern by Chaucer about Troilus' role—a desire to give more emphasis to his part in the total economy of the poem. All three passages are in some

sense philosophic, however, and this philosophic character seems equally
their reason for being: a hymn to love, a reflection on predestination,
and a pagan rejection of love and this world—when we line the three
passages up side by side we begin to get some insight into what Chaucer is doing.

Troilus' hymn to love at the conclusion of Book III is not quite so
clearly a later addition as the other passages. And it is not so much
an amplification as a substitution. Boccaccio gives Troilo a hymn to
love at this point, based very generally on the eighth meter of Book
II of Boethius. Chaucer had already borrowed part of this speech,
scrapping the rest, for the Proem to Book III. So the hymn he creates
for Troilus here, following Boethius' eighth meter again but much
more closely, is no more than the hero's due, and in a sense Chaucer
is merely being faithful to his original.[24] The hymn does add to that
original, however. It is the climactic moment of "joy" in the poem.
It transforms the refined sensuality of the consummation scene into
a yet more refined philosophical distillation. It provides an appropriate
parallel to the narrator's praise of love in the Proem to Book III;
opening and closing as they do this book in which love triumphant has
been displayed, these passages give a powerful upward thrust to the
celebration of love's power and glory.

As an apostrophe to love by a character within the poem, however,
it must be ranged beside other such apostrophes in the poem: Antigone's song in the garden and Troilus' own song or complaint, the
Canticus Troili, in Book I. It is like Antigone's song in its expression
of joy, but unlike it in its abstraction. Antigone's song, whose function
is to reassure the hesitant Criseyde, is almost a domestic lyric, celebrating a simple gratitude for the virtues of a particular lover by a
particular person; and while it acknowledges love's power to incite
virtue, it generalizes only to the extent of asserting that love is good
and is to be welcomed, not feared. It is a quiet answer to Criseyde's
doubts, and more distantly, a quiet answer to Troilus' agonized queries
about love in the *Canticus.* By contrast, Troilus' hymn is extravagant.
He identifies his condition with the force that binds the universe and
seems to feel that he and Criseyde have become a philosophical principle. It is the uttermost reach of human passion.

But the hymn contrasts even more forcibly with the *Canticus Troili*
in Book I. It does so, however, not so much because the one expresses
sorrow and the other joy, but because the *Canticus* pictures love as a
chaos, as an impossible conjunction of warring elements, and the hymn

celebrates it as an all-embracing unity, the very essence of concord. We have no reason to doubt the truth of either assertion, but we can hardly affirm that they agree.

The predestination speech seems unquestionably an afterthought. It too is from Boethius, but as with the hymn, philosophical matter in Troilus' mouth seems curiously unphilosophical. He can only speak an emotion. The soliloquy is certainly an utterance of despair from Troilus; in its context, however, it relates to more than a personal condition of feeling. The theme of Book IV might be said to be "choice" or "decision." Troilus' predestination speech merely adds or reinforces one aspect of decision and complicates the problem of choice. Within Book IV we are invited to look at the difficulty of choice, at mistaken choice, at the possibility that there is no freedom and therefore no real choice, and conversely at the possibility that there *is* choice. Difficulty of choice, because of warring considerations, is dramatized in the debate between Hector and the Trojan parliament, in Troilus divided between reason and love, Criseyde burning *both in love and drede,/ So that she nyste what was best to reede* (IV, 678–679), and the debate between Troilus and Criseyde over their course of action. We are aware of mistaken choice in the Trojan decision to exchange Criseyde for Antenor, who will betray Troy (a point which Chaucer comments on at length), in Criseyde's misguided decision to leave Troy, and in Troilus' accession to her wishes. The possibility that there is no choice is communicated by the allusions and invocations to Fortune, Calcas' pronouncement on Troy's fate, Troilus' lack of freedom under the code of courtly love, and his predestination speech.

Contradictions swirl about this issue and about this passage in particular. The speech emphasizes the division of opinion concerning freedom and providence,[25] and Troilus himself is busy trying to make a choice among opinions. He seems to decide against freedom. Yet the inaction of this extended reflective moment, an inaction which is a logical-enough consequence of his reflection and logically should be maintained, is challenged by Pandarus when he finds him in the temple. (The moment recalls the mouse's heart passage in Book III and the attack on the love-stricken Troilus' lethargy in Book I.) *"O myghty God,"* quod Pandarus, *"in trone,/ I! who say evere a wis man faren so?"* And Pandarus proceeds to entertain the possibility of change, and even of choices and freedom: *"Artow for hire and for noon other born?/ Hath Kynde the wrought al only hire to plese"* (IV, 1086–1087, 1095–1096). Elsewhere, Pandarus counsels action. And Troilus, proceeding to Criseyde's room, contrary to his own conclusion, acts as though choice were possible and submits only after debate to Criseyde's decision.

The predestination scene, we should also notice, has been bracketed by a set of decisions on the issue of life and death. Before the scene there is Criseyde's soliloquy in which by a series of comic modifications she first decides to die (but by starvation, for she is afraid of swords), and then decides to dress only in black in token of her sorrow and to found a "religious" order devoted to the memory of Troilus—i.e., she decides to live. The scene between Troilus and Criseyde after the predestination speech begins with Troilus, believing Criseyde dead in her swoon, intent on taking his own life in defiance of Jove and Fortune (IV, 1192–1197). Her timely recovery occurs *as God wolde* (1212), so that the effect of the dramatic moment is to leave the issue of freedom and fate nicely balanced.

Morton Bloomfield has commented on the historical quality of *Troilus and Criseyde,* the fact that we are watching a past and therefore fixed action.[26] But the immediacy of the tale takes it out of the past and into the present much of the time, and we have the sense of choices quite possibly freely taken. We are watching, in other words, actions which are fixed now but perhaps were once free, actions which seem much more flexible and fluid than the rigid historical frame in which they are set.

Into this constantly modulating perspective on choice the predestination speech is inserted. The introduction of the philosophic question of free will and foreknowledge in this context does not provide us, surely, with a final answer. It adds a point of view which casts all in doubt and leaves the issue of human freedom, specifically human freedom in love, yet more deeply unresolved.[27]

And the final flourish. Chaucer's poem has concluded with Troilus' unhappy fate held up as an example of the *"false worldes brotelnesse,"* the adjuration to young people to repair home from worldly vanity, the condemnation of cursed pagan rites, the submissive dedication to Gower and Strode, and the Dantean prayer to the trinity. Surely we have enough. Yet Chaucer must make one more addition. He must borrow from the *Teseide* the passage describing Arcite's ascent to the eighth sphere and apply it to Troilus. Twenty-one lines before his *"Lo here"* dismissal of pagan antiquity Chaucer feels obliged to give us a pagan *de contemptu mundi.* At the very moment when the orthodox Christian view is to be presented, we must have this non-Christian ascent to philosophical awareness. It is certainly not necessary doctrine; Christianity needs no such propping.

What is really reinforced is not Christianity, but rejection. We must have two rejections, from two different and to some extent conflicting value systems. (The rejections, of course, cast an ironic light over all the other ironies of the poem. If the game was not really worth the candle, not because the affair ended unhappily but because it happened at all, what then?) But it is the juxtaposition of the rejections that matters. There is no suggestion that the pagan enlightenment of Troilus after death undercuts the Christian philosophy: this kind of dangerous game Chaucer did not play. But the two rejections do have the effect of reminding us that there are, in history, differences of opinion on the largest issues. Christianity is the final and unchallengeable statement on matters theological for Chaucer. But what of Troilus' vision? Is the implication of the *Lo here of payens corsed olde rites* passage that we must reject his vision, the best to which he can attain? [28] Theologically, perhaps, yes. But as part of the vision of the poem, no. It not only participates in that long withdrawal from involvement in the imaginative world of the poem which is so important a part of the function of the conclusion. It not only serves, with the *yonge, fresshe folkes* passage, to effect some counterbalance to the massive weight of the love poem proper, so that the final irony of rejection may be asserted. Set side by side with the Christian rejection, it offers one momentarily an uncomfortable choice of philosophies. If we are tempted to stop with Troilus, we then become aware that we must move on. What is finally theologically simple has been shown once more to be experientially complex. [29]

IV

Complex, complex. I began with that overworked word, and I find I must end with it. *Troilus and Criseyde* is the most complex medieval English poem on love that we possess. This complexity is the consequence in large part of the technique of amplification which Chaucer applied to his original. Idealized courtly love is examined in *Troilus* with an intensity of feeling and a range of attitudes which exhaust the topic. The method itself has been used with a boldness and an imaginative freedom seldom equaled. There can be few readers of the poem who come away with a sense of possibilities unrealized. No one wishes Chaucer had done more, not out of a sense of tedium, but out of a sense of completeness and fulfillment. Amplification can go no further.

Indeed, the question is, did it not go too far? Is the poem not overloaded, have not too many conflicting attitudes been folded in, does the poem not finally become dropsical and collapse? Is the predestination passage, for example, really necessary? The questions can hardly expect absolute answers, completely independent of individual taste. It does remind us of how far the process of amplification has been carried here. Chaucer's decision to experiment with abbreviation in his next several poems may suggest on his part a suspicion that, for the moment, with this method he had gone far enough. The danger of the method is loss of control, mere decorative elaboration or excessive inflation of an original. Its greatest utility is in the realization of the possibilities of a theme. It is to this method that in large part we owe the poem we have; there can hardly be any question that the method has been brilliantly employed.

The experience of romantic, passionate love, as it is developed by the amplification in *Troilus and Criseyde,* is presented as it is conventionally, though much more simply, in much of the love poetry of the period and by Chaucer in other of his poems of love. It is presented as a contradictory experience. These contradictions are only faintly present in Boccaccio's poem. The trope or figure for expressing this contradictory character of love in the poetry is the *contentio,* oxymoron. The pattern of *Troilus and Criseyde* is of an elaborate oxymoron in which the widest range of contradictory emotions, experiences, attitudes, and value systems is contained within the poem to express and dramatize this oxymoronic character of the experience: joy and sorrow, prudence and folly, passion and reticence, wisdom and half-wisdom, love as comedy and love as tragedy, society as spur and society as bridle, the illusion of freedom and the conviction of fate, philosophy that supports and philosophy that condemns.

The contradictory attitudes of Chaucer himself may be said to spill into the strategy of the poem, so that the intense sympathy for love with which the poem begins and the rejection of love with which it ends reveal the extremes of his own feeling. The somewhat narrower contradictions within the poem may express his own attitude, though primarily they should be taken as a literary view of love. By and large, the poem moves through a series of contradictions, but not beyond them. Oxymoron does not resolve contradictions, it merely asserts them. If there are moments when the contradictions seem resolved, they never last. Where does the poem, and where does the poet come to a final stop? The poem ends with Troilus seeking out Diomede, to kill or be killed—but in vain. Or it ends with Fortune, that arch-figure of oxymoron, triumphant. Or it ends with Troilus laughing from the eighth (?) sphere—he is there, but we are here. Or it ends with the young and lively urged to turn away from what youth and life impel them to. But will they turn? And what of all that joy? And what of all those tears? What, indeed, of life under the moon?

Venetian Woodcut, from Pulci's *Driadeo d'Amore*

DONALD R. HOWARD

Experience, Language, and Consciousness: *Troilus and Criseyde*, II, 596–931

In the *Legend of Good Women* Chaucer says he is writing about women who behaved nobly in love, as a penance for having written about Criseyde; there is a tradition going back to Lydgate that the penance might have been imposed by Queen Ann. Whether or not this is true, we can be pretty sure that his presentation of Criseyde did not go down entirely well with the ladies—Criseyde herself predicts that she will be rolled on many a tongue and that women will hate her most. The resentment against heroine and author is caused by the stark fact that she jilts Troilus. Everyone remembers how she must rejoin her father in the Greek camp: there is no decent alternative; so she goes, promising to return. Among the Greeks she meets Diomede, who escorts her out of Troy. At first coolly and then with cautious interest she agrees to be true "to him, anyway" (as she puts it); she does not return to Troy; in time she writes Troilus a letter, one of the worst of its kind on record.

How are we to react to this apparently treacherous woman? We can, as many do, hate her. The one alternative is to understand her motives, to forgive and pity her. Of course the same can be said of Iago or Milton's Satan; and we live, it is true, in an age when sympathetic understanding of villains is spread around like antiseptic—if only Iago had got to an analyst, if only a social worker had found out Fagin in time. But this is not what I am saying. Criseyde does wrong and so is bad. Chaucer tells us so. He adds that *he* will forgive her out of pity. But does he mean for *us* to do likewise? I say he does— not because he explains why she turns to Diomede (he leaves that for us to imagine), but because he makes us know what it feels like to *be* Criseyde, from the moment she first feels love for Troilus.

173

That moment in her consciousness is what this paper is about. In Book II there is a scene—or a series of four scenes [1]—during which the reader is allowed to participate in Criseyde's mental life. Her uncle Pandarus has just persuaded her to take a favorable view of Troilus, and she has agreed, but with conditions—she cannot love him against her will but only please him from day to day, *"myn honour sauf."* [2] After this she asks Pandarus how he first learned of Troilus' love. Pandarus, seeing his threats and blandishments take root in her fancy, follows with a long, highly romanticized account of Troilus' recent conduct, ending with a hopeful reference to the time *"when ye ben his al hool, as he is youre"* (587). Criseyde breaks in, *"Nay, therof spak I nought, ha, ha!"* He hastens to assure her that he *"mente naught but wel,"* she forgives him, and he takes his leave. Criseyde now rises and goes to her closet where she sits down *as stylle as any ston*:

> And every word gan up and down to wynde
> That he had seyde, as it com hire to mynde.   (601–602)

From here until the end of the scene (596–931) we remain chiefly inside Criseyde's mind. Only about one-fifth of the scene is indebted to Boccaccio's *Filostrato* and that chiefly barebones events; hence we can regard the passage as an original flight of Chaucer's imagination. At its beginning Criseyde is thinking over the conversation just finished; at its end she is asleep and dreaming. We are not told that she makes any decision during this scene, though we sense a drift and settling in her thoughts and feelings. Later (in III, 1210–1211) she will tell Troilus that she has long since yielded, and we are to know then that what we experienced in Book II was the moment of consciousness during which the balance was tipped.

The scene explores a problem often discussed in abstract terms—the relationship between experience (what we do) and consciousness (what we think). One ramification of this problem is the role language plays in the relationship; a second is the role of poetry. A further and perhaps more difficult problem is the place of decisions in this relationship: if every action has something in the way of a motive, experience and consciousness are the area of motives and so the provenance of action. And if language reflects and in some degree shapes our experience, then language, including poetic language, must influence action. I am not sure the problem is much more difficult than this, though it could be made so by spinning out related problems. It can be and often is made a great deal more difficult by introducing an elaborate lexicon of abstractions like "mediation," "intersubjectivity," "vision," "objectification," and the like; but the poet's language, being concrete, has nothing to do with all that.

We honor poets because they are acute observers of human experience, because they have a heightened consciousness of their own experience, and because they have an extraordinary skill and subtlety of verbal expression. Here is a passage by a great poet where the pressures of experience, consciousness, and language interact to produce a determination or action; in it we can perhaps see before our eyes the thing as in itself it really happens—as much (say) as we can see "heredity" happen under a microscope or "phonology" on a sound-spectrograph. We are exploiting the poet as a sensitive instrument, I admit; but in doing so we shall see something no less worth while—Chaucer's skill in depicting Criseyde's mental state. It is hard to find a passage in early literature that equals the present one. It is one of the aspects of the poem which makes it seem, as Kittredge suggested, like a psychological novel. One could compare the great meditation scenes of nineteenth-century novels—those of Isabella in *Portrait of a Lady,* or Clara Middleton in *The Egoist,* or Dorothea in *Middlemarch.* Yet even in the novel, as much preoccupied as novelists are with the inner life of their characters, it is hard to find many passages which show so much instinctive understanding of human nature, so much empathy and dramatic flair. I have tried to show elsewhere how Chaucer succeeded in solving the difficult problem of depicting sexuality in such a way as to enlist rather than alienate the reader's involvement.[3] But his accomplishment in the present passage is greater; in it he does what few men have ever done in literature or life—he sees into the mind of a woman.

I

Experience itself, coming unpredictably from without, first breaks into Criseyde's thought. While she is sitting alone, a cry 'goes up in the streets, men call out *"Se, Troilus . . . ,"* and her ladies echo *"A, go we se!"* Troilus enters the city gate, triumphant, riding an easy pace with his soldiers. Chaucer gives three stanzas to his entrance through the gate of Dardanus; princely, armed save his head, his horse wounded, his helm and shield damaged, *so fressh, so yong, so weldy . . . It was an heven upon hym for to see.* The people cry out, and Troilus **wex a litel reed for shame**: we are allowed to empathize with his modest reaction, then told it was a *noble game* to see how soberly he lowered his eyes. Given this tiny chance to see on our own his princely bearing and blushing modesty, we are then brought back to Criseyde's experience of it. She sees, she lets it sink softly in her heart, and, in an unforgettable moment, she says to herself *"Who yaf me drynke?"*

The line is so striking, and has so delighted all readers of the poem, that I shall try to say nothing about it. Normally glossed as a reference to a love-potion, it could as easily be strong wine which makes the head spin; and this ambiguity is perfect, for the metaphor suggests a feeling as yet undefined. In our pleasure over the exclamation we easily forget its aftermath: she blushes at the thought, remembers that this was he her uncle said loved her, and then, ashamed, pulls her head quickly inside the window! The conflict of impulse and restraint, a major theme in what follows, is here dramatically introduced, and we must pause to ask just what has happened.

Chaucer tells us she *said* the line *to herself,* and in the next line calls it *hire owen thought.* We cannot understand from this that she murmured the words aloud or even formed them with her lips. Yet the thought is more than a mere impulse cloaked in words for the reader's benefit; for Chaucer could have described such an impulse had he chosen to.[4] It will not do to write it off as "literary convention," because no poet worth the name uses literary convention or tradition except as a means of understanding reality. And anyway the convention involved here, soliloquy, is straight realism: like the writer of any soliloquy, Chaucer is reporting, by imitation, the phenomenon of *inner speech,* the inward stream of language which bears our thoughts. He does not of course imitate it with much verisimilitude, for inner speech has, according to Vigotsky's famous description,[5] very special characteristics—it omits the subject of predications, agglutinates word-groups, and combines senses. Inner speech is never articulated except perhaps by scarcely perceptible movements of the vocal cords, and in this it might be compared with the stream of language we experience in very rapid silent reading. We can distinguish the stream of inner speech from *thought,* or what I shall call the stream of imagery. Our thinking really rides on these two inner streams, beneath which Vigotsky said lies the "affective and volitional tendency."[6] How do we know these streams exist? Because they are part of our own introspective experience of the mental life. They occur in our dreams and daydreams; but they are most dramatically present in those moments of semiconsciousness that we sometimes experience just as we drop off to sleep—what are now called hypnagogic phenomena, and were once called (by Macrobius) *fantasma*. In these moments we plunge sometimes very sharply into the stream of imagery, see one single and startling image, a face, perhaps, hovering close to us, a bird, an animal, an automobile hurtling forward. Or we may also be startled by our stream of inner speech—the voices we heard as a child [7] and sometimes strangely hear as adults, which speak some unattached assertion or greeting, or our names. "Inner speech," Vigotsky says, "is not the inner aspect of external speech. It is a function in itself. Inner speech still remains speech—it is thought connected with word. But while in external speech thought is embodied in words—in inner speech words perish and bring forth thought. . . . Inner speech is a dynamic process which moves between two stable poles of thinking-in-words; between words and thought." [8]

Criseyde's stream of inner speech weaves through the present scene. We encounter it first when we see her mulling over her conversation with her uncle. She experiences her own fear and calms herself by reciting inwardly the reassuring precept that a woman does not have to return anyone's love unless she wants to. Her unguarded attraction to Troilus takes shape in the words *"Who yaf me drynke?"* and then,

> "Lo, this is he
> Which that myn uncle swerith he moot be deed,
> But I on hym have mercy and pitee." (653–655)

Then she begins to *caste and rollen up and down* all the good qualities of Troilus, and to think what a pity it was *to sleen swich oon, if that he mente trouthe*. The Narrator, after an interruption to remind us that she did not fall in love with wanton haste, announces that he will tell us *what she thoughte*; and in a long passage (700–812) her inner speech is reported in direct discourse.

Her soliloquy is too familiar to need rehearsing. Its shape and structure are those of consciousness itself, not reasonable or logical in organization, but associative. Her conflict is between what she knows, which is abstract and proverbial, and what she feels, which is concrete and experiential. She can imagine what would happen if she returned Troilus' love, and her imagination of it is based on expediency and circumstance. An alliance with him would be an honor, beneficial to his welfare and her position; if she were to avoid him

utterly he might have her in despite. He is her king's son, and his own
good qualities are self-evident—he is handsome, has *gentilesse,* is not
a boaster, is wise. Anyway, she cannot keep him from loving, and if
people talk of that it cannot dishonor *her;* besides, she is "her own
woman"—at ease in her position, young, and without a husband whose
jealousy she must fear. *"Shal I nat love,"* she argues to herself—
"What, par dieux! I am naught religious." Indeed (though she would
prefer no one knew this thought), she realizes she is one of the fairest
and goodliest ladies in Troy—*"and so* [she adds] *men seyn."*

In all this she is bolstering herself up, indulging in a fantasy, and
rationalizing her desire to make the fantasy real. Then her fears take
over—and like most fears they are spectral and abstract. But they
come upon her with an overpowering reality—like a cloud covering
the sun, Chaucer says, so that *for feere almost she gan to falle.* She
may, first, put her freedom in jeopardy. Then, too, love causes all
kinds of trouble in people's lives—there are the wicked tongues of
malicious and jealous persons and the proverbial fickleness of men.

We grasp Criseyde's thoughts and emotions intuitively throughout
this passage. Soliloquy as a literary convention renders in dramatic
form the phenomenon of inner speech and, especially in poetry, renders
its emotional force; through rhythm, prosody, image, and metaphor
it dramatizes the ineluctable fact that our thoughts and ideas are
charged with feeling. In this, soliloquy relies upon and also dramatizes
the fact that human beings are able to enter into the subjective emotional worlds of others. These two facts about human life can be
labeled *affect* and *intersubjectivity;* but labeling them so makes them
seem less like facts and more like abstractions. And we must keep our
finger on the facts—that every sentence of Criseyde's inner speech is
charged with the "affective and volitional tendency," with feeling; and
that we are able to *feel* her feeling just as we are able to think her
thoughts.

The passage therefore simply cannot be used to show that Criseyde
is "self-centered"—that she is, as some think, vain and self-seeking.
After all, everyone is self-centered in his inner speech, thought, and
feeling [9]—the wonder is that we *can* empathize with others; when we
condemn people for being "self-centered" we really mean that they
cannot. Yet in Book III we are to see Criseyde open her heart to
Troilus, empathize with his jealousy and sorrow, forgive him for not
trusting her—all this, ironically, over a lie concocted by Pandarus with
no protest from his lovesick protégé. Indecisive she may be, weak,

frightened; she may indeed be vain (but women are permitted to be so); she may be looking out for herself, but circumstances have given her the best of causes. She may well be lacking in self-knowledge, a prey to her own feelings; and she is (or so Chaucer tells us) *slydynge of corage.* Yet Chaucer tells us too, *Ne nevere mo ne lakked hire pite,* calls her *tendre-herted* (V, 823–825). That she does wrong none can deny; Chaucer grants the point, adding only that he would excuse her *for routhe* (V, 1093–1099). In studies of the poem Criseyde has, as she herself predicted, been rolled on many a tongue. The justice of the charges against her is one issue, the spirit in which they are made is another. For however we may name her offense, we are meant to understand. Chaucer himself, as Narrator, made the first effort to see her with charitable understanding, with *routhe.* As author he added to his source whatever could help us do likewise. So in the present scene he has made us participate in her conflicted emotions of attraction and fear, recognizing the conflict itself as a phase of human experience known through introspection and empathy.

II

To this inner conflict of attraction and fear Criseyde marshals up a certain kind of wisdom or lore. Ruminating on the question "what-would-happen-if," she can use this lore to rationalize both pro's and con's. On the positive side she exalts the aristocratic virtue *mesure,*[10] using as an example the time-honored case of a mean between drunkenness and total abstinence. On the negative side she can summon up a whole body of lore about men—they are jealous, overbearing, fickle, untrue.[11] This proverbial lore is different from other considerations she entertains, which are for the most part factual or concretely imagined from her own experience. Not that such lore is divorced from experience altogether, but it is based on others' experience, solidified and, as it were, fossilized—not merely expressed in sentences but preserved, transmitted, learned, and chiefly remembered in sentences. And with this body of lore, which itself makes up part of Criseyde's experience and is a notable feature of her mental life, we come into the realm of language, that is, the realm of *external* speech.

Language is articulate and communal, and inner speech could not exist without it; when Chaucer reaches the end of Criseyde's soliloquy he focuses upon this fact. Her last thought is the conventional anxiety of lovers about what people would say: Who, she asks herself, can stop every wicked tongue, or *"sown of belles whil that thei ben ronge?"*

(805). The metaphor is doubly apt. She has been talking about *jangling,* which suggests pointless noise; and it is true that bells, once rung, do go on so. But the comparison, natural enough in itself, was already in Chaucer's time a commonplace,[12] so that his language reflects what it describes: Criseyde's anxiety about people's jangling is expressed with a touch of ordinary colloquial tongue-wagging. Then in the next line he tells us that *hire thought gan for to clere,* and what strikes her in this moment of clarity is a proverb:

> He which that nothing undertaketh,
> Nothyng n'acheveth, be hym looth or deere.   (807–808) [13]

It is the very sentiment Pandarus has tried to persuade her of. The notion—"nothing ventured, nothing gained" as we now phrase it—reflects his philosophy of life. We have seen him urge Troilus to *"seken bote"* (I, 763), to *"don bysynesse"* to his own help (795). We have seen him in his conversation with Criseyde argue that a good *aventure* is shaped for everyone at some point, but that it is up to us to take advantage of it and *"cache it anon"* (II, 281–291). Pandarus has a consistently pagan view of life and a clear opinion about how others should behave; from such a view comes such a proverb.[14] To lovers of any era it is an appealing sentiment, and Pandarus with his charm and wit makes it seem a delight. But its philosophical underpinnings are in fact pessimistic. To Pandarus the world is in a state of flux, controlled by cheerless forces of destiny, capricious and inscrutable, which shape for everyone certain moments of *"good aventure."* Such moments, he explains, will always pass out of our lives as fleetingly as they entered, and it is up to us to seize the day *"lest aventure slake."* At the end we are to learn that this way of thinking is wrong-headed; the "plain felicity that is in heaven above," of which Pandarus can know nothing, makes Christian *contemptus mundi* wiser than pagan *carpe diem.* And indeed this truth is implicit in their own lore if they could but see it.

I have been using the word *lore* to describe the proverbial wisdom which makes up a phase of Criseyde's consciousness. Etymologically, at least, lore is anything learned; but the term is usually associated with popular, anecdotal learning. All Criseyde's lore is unmistakably aristocratic—the notion of *mesure,* the traditional courtly notions about love's woes, her conceptions of jangling, jealousy, men's faithlessness, and her uncle's notion that nothing ventured is nothing gained. Such lore, like spoken language itself, reflects social class; and this raises the question whether we can call it folklore. If "folklore" does not simply mean *peasants'* lore—if, that is, the term is not specifically tied to a sociologist's view of class-stratification—is it feasible to restrict the term to oral tradition? In modern times almost any lore of interest quickly gets "frozen" in writing or through the mass media, and even in medieval times the lore of knights and troubadors came to be written down and then read aloud. It seems too rigid to put such bodies of lore beyond the reach of folklore study merely because they lose "pure" orality. And of course if we do so it means that we have *no* medieval folklore. So, at least, I used to believe and would probably believe still if I had not spent a pleasant evening in 1958 debating the point with Francis Lee Utley. As always in such conversations he dammed up with patience his reservoir of scholarship, loosing on me instead a polite rivulet of ironic questions. But I know I came away convinced that the term folklore does have to be restricted to oral dissemination, that folklore is different in kind from what is frozen in writing or by the mass media—a special phenomenon of oral transmission having a character of its own and requiring a special method of study.[15]

Criseyde's lore is, from this point of view, not *necessarily* folklore. No doubt what these medieval Trojans think about love and life existed in medieval oral tradition; we see them singing songs and listening while someone *tells* the "tale of Wade"—but then we see them listening to a romance of Thebes being read aloud. Pandarus is full of wise saws, but he is not without learning and we cannot be certain he had his proverbs from oral tradition (though we can be fairly certain Chaucer did in many an instance). My point is this: it is customary to talk about Pandarus' "proverbial wisdom" and be amused by his store of old saws; but this lore he possesses does not have to make him like Polonius or Uncle Wiggly. Chaucer's source for the proverbs was perhaps folklore; but in Pandarus' mouth they become part of a consistent view of life which he believes in and presents winningly and indeed learnedly. I have argued elsewhere that this was Chaucer's conception of paganism.[16] We see one phase of it here take root in Criseyde's thoughts. It combines with a body of lore and free-floating opinion which she already possesses. We might conceivably call such opinion *knightlore*—for we know that medieval aristocrats held certain values appropriate to their class, a "chivalric" and "courtly" ethos passed down among them in large part orally.[17] Still, they had the means and motive to patronize poets and to preserve on paper what they liked; they were reverent toward *olde bookes*; they were by no means universally illiterate; and they liked to be read to aloud. Criseyde's knightlore on such subjects as love could have been learned from oral tradition, but might as easily have been learned (allowing for the anachronism) from the *Roman de la Rose*. Hence what she thinks here may well be the product of an imagined literary tradition, the literature of Troy.

The same can be said of the "Trojan song" which Antigone sings (827–875). Criseyde, leaving her room, goes out into the garden, joining the ladies; they walk about arm in arm, they *pleyen, that it joye was to see,* and at last Antigone sings so clearly *that it an heven was hire vois to here.* The song, original with Chaucer,[18] is a characteristic courtly lyric. Antigone identifies its author as *"the goodlieste mayde/ Of gret estat in al the town of Troye"* (880–881). She says the song was *"made,"* and Criseyde speaks admiringly of how lovers can *"faire endite"* (886). There is enough suggestion of poetical composition so that one tends to see the piece rather as literature than as a folksong; we can be sure anyway that it is *not* an instance of *das Volk dichtet*. In content it is exceedingly literary—is almost a compendium of courtly love conventions, embodying the knightlore familiar to all readers of romances and courtly lyrics. But as it emphasizes one tenet or image over another, it chances to light upon the very aspects of courtly lore which most touch Criseyde's mental state. Addressed at first to the God of Love by one of his female servants, it extols love's joy, the virtues of her lover, and the power of love to banish *"alle manere vice and synne."* In its two penultimate stanzas it dismisses the objections against love, in part those aspects of knightlore that have given Criseyde anxiety: whoever says love is vice or thralldom must be envious, foolish, or incapable of loving, for only those defame love who know it not. Then an analogy: the sun is none the worse because men's weak eyes cannot gaze on it direct, and so love none the worse because wretches cry out against it. Two proverbs in the song buttress the analogy: "He deserves no happiness who can endure no sorrow," and, "He who has a glass head should throw no stones in war." The last stanza is a profession of undying love, and it ends—for Criseyde the most telling line—with the couplet

> Al dredde I first to love hym to bigynne,
> Now woot I wel, ther is no peril inne.

This splendid song brings to mind other songs in the *Troilus*. Against the background of a city about to fall, its doomed inhabitants are vibrant with lyricism in all its shades. Troilus himself, once in love, begins composing a song; there are the dawn-songs of the lovers in Book III and the plaintive *Canticus Troili* of Book V. At Pandarus' house they amuse themselves with both lyric and narrative: *He song; she pleyde; he tolde tale of Wade* (III, 614)—as earlier the ladies have been listening while one of them reads from the *Siege of Thebes* (II, 83–84).

So into Criseyde's mind at this point comes the unique quality of lyric poetry, particularly when sung. Lyric submerges the plain sense of language in song and image [19]—we can rarely repeat what a song "says" after hearing it sung; we remember "the words" as a disconnected jumble of image and phrase. Yet song endues words with a measure and intensity of its own which supplants what it takes away in syntax and logical flow. We never have trouble, with a good song, telling what it was *about*; and when we talk about the "haunting" and "moving" qualities of sung lyric we are talking in part of the power lyric has, by suspending normal syntactic and logical relations, to make outlandish notions seem compelling, to make sense out of non-sense. If anyone were to tell me I ought to wear a flower in my hair if I go to San Francisco I should think him mad; but the same sentiment, heard in the song popular a few years ago, managed to take on a pleasant fancy. So it is, I believe, that Antigone's song impresses Criseyde. What had frightened her before loses its terror, seems possible and appealing, takes on the "haunting" quality with which successful lyric cloaks any notion, and helps to convince her, in her feelings, that *"ther is no peril inne."*

We grasp her reaction to this lyric, and the lore it expresses, through a third aspect of language: conversation. Chaucer does tell us explicitly what her reaction to the song is, but not until he has let us see it for ourselves. The conversation (876–898) leaves much unsaid, and this we can see best in paraphrase:

"Now, niece," said Criseyde, "now who made up this nice song?"

Antigone answered, "Madame, I'll tell you—the most wonderful young lady of noble birth in the whole city of Troy, and led her life in the most joy and honor."

"Indeed, so it seems, to judge from her song," said Criseyde; and with that she sighed—"Lord! is there such bliss among lovers, that they can compose so gorgeously?"

"Yes, for sure," said Antigone, "because not everybody that's ever lived could describe the bliss of love. Do you think just any wretch knows about love's perfect bliss? Why, not at all! They think practically anything is love, just if they feel a little glow. Go on, go on, they don't know anything about it. You have to ask *saints* if it's nice in heaven—why? because they can *tell*—and ask devils if hell's ugly."

Criseyde answered nothing, but said "Sure it will be night soon. . . ."

Of course my paraphrase uses novelistic "dialogue," not really the casual spoken style,[20] but what else? Play back a tape-recording of a lively conversation in which you were a participant, and you see to your horror that it was full of awkward pauses, crass interruptions, stammers, repetitions, regrettable lapses. The novelist or romancer tries to capture conversation as heard not by a detached observer but by an active listener. What gives "life" to conversation is our emotional involvement with it, the forward thrust of our expectations, our running efforts to second-guess our interlocutors and frame what we are moved to say. Conversation rides on an eager babble of inner speech, but an exact transcript of a heard conversation monstrously abstracts the one from the other; the artist simulates the experience as a whole. So in the present scene we catch the force of Antigone's emotion in the jumble of her discourse—it breaks out in rhetorical questions, repetitions, broken sentences, little forward-rushing lapses of grammar; it is punctuated by conversational ejaculations—*"Why, nay, iwys!" "Do wey, do wey," "Why? for. . . ."* And what this accomplishes is to suggest the flashing of eye contact, the flickering of facial expressions in others, the tiny movements of hand and eyebrow and shoulder that signal us our listeners' comprehension and response. This non-verbal communication which rides along with all intimate discourse is an acting-out of inner speech—the listener *thinks* "Oh, but . . ." and a tiny furl flickers between his brows. Feeling felt by feeling is the real event which happens in this brief moment of conversation; hence Criseyde's silence speaks so loud. When she answers nothing except *"Ywis, it wol be nyght as faste,"* we *feel* what she is thinking. Then, but only then, Chaucer tells us:

> But every word which that she of hire herde,
> She gan to prenten in hire herte faste,
> And ay gan love hire lasse for t'agaste
> Than it did erst, and synken in hire herte. . . .   (899–902)

III

The greatest poetry is always a miracle, but the miracle here is that of evoking what is itself miraculous, the ability of one mind, closed within its little world of thought, to enter the mind of another. Chaucer makes us experience the reality Criseyde experienced—we see what she saw, heard what she heard. Chiefly he brings to us the experience as it existed for her in various aspects of language—inner speech, colloquialism, proverb and lore, song and poetry, conversation. Language in all these aspects is part of experience, but it is unique among phases of experience because it alone can name, interpret, and so influence those phases, itself among them. While we enter Criseyde's consciousness largely through its content of language, her language—and Chaucer's—brings with it the whole range of human experience from stated cultural values to non-verbal communication.

Language has therefore the *capacity* to become identical with consciousness, to encompass and express all consciousness; but in day-to-day reality, consciousness always races ahead of and runs circles about language. The "inadequacy" of language, about which tongues wag so much these days, is nothing more than the frustrating differential between language and consciousness; but the inadequacy is in us, not in language—the failure is our failure to use language well and to cultivate our gardens of consciousness. That is why it is so extraordinary in the present instance that Chaucer added to this scene a feature that pushes us into the realm of the non-verbal, as far indeed as the edges of consciousness. He makes us experience the *shape* of thought by imitating and rendering it in the scene itself. The structure of the scene, the arrangement and disposition of its parts, expresses the fluctuation and dialectic which we experience in those thoughts which deeply touch our actions. If we ask how the scene is organized, we have to say it has a simple episodic organization, event following event in quotidian fashion. Criseyde is alone thinking; she sees Troilus pass; she pops her head inside and thinks some more; she goes out in the garden, hears a song, and exchanges a few words with Antigone; she goes to bed, thinking more and finally dreaming. But these events are really arranged in alternation: three stretches of inner experience are twice interrupted by outer experiences, one visual and one auditory. This pattern repeats the fundamental alternation of our mental lives, that of stimulus and response. And it carries with it, as if in concentric circles, several other kinds of alternation, which we shall see best if we disentangle them:

(1) *Fear and attraction.* Criseyde is, we know, very much a world-ling—capable of vibrant emotions, sensitive to stimuli,

> Charitable, estatlich, lusty, and fre;
> Ne nevere mo ne lakked hire pite;
> Tendre-herted, slydynge of corage.   (V, 823–825)

We know as well, and have witnessed from the start, that she is the *ferfulleste wight/ That myghte be* (II, 450–451). Fear alternates with her open responsiveness to the world, her attraction to it. Thus when Pandarus leaves her she is *somdel astoned,* but the sight of Troilus trips off a violent reaction—*"Who yaf me drinke?"*—and sets her on a train of thought in which she rehearses all that favors love. Yet midstream in this *a cloudy thought* strikes her (768) *So that for feere almost she gan to falle.* This inner stimulus trips off an opposing train of fears—for loss of her freedom, wicked tongues, betrayal; then she reassures herself *"He which that nothing undertaketh,/ Nothyng n'acheveth"*; then *with an other thoght hire herte quaketh.*

(2) *Insecurity and independence.* Against her vulnerability to fear and attraction we find in her a feeling of self-contained invulnerability. When she is alone with her thoughts, her associations and her stream of inner speech make for her a kind of fortress against the world and foster a conviction of her own independence. Pandarus leaves her and she is *somdel astoned in hire thought*; but presently she is telling her-self that a man can love a woman until his heart breaks *"and she naught love ayein, but if hire leste."* She sees Troilus and is shaken; but pres-ently she can soliloquize the reasons why she is her *"owene wom-man."* She hears Antigone's song and asks, sighing, if there is such bliss among these lovers; but as every word is impressed in her heart *ay gan love hire lasse for t'agaste.*

(3) *Emotion and reason.* Alternating with all these feelings—of fear and insecurity, of attraction, of independence—is a strain of sweet reasonableness, all the good sense and sound lore she possesses. Her initial fear when Pandarus takes his leave is calmed with a generality —that no woman must return a man's love *"but if hire leste."* Her soliloquy after seeing Troilus is full of logical and factual truth—is rationalization in the fullest sense. The *cloudy thought* which makes her almost keel over with fear is put into her mind by knightlore about the ills besetting lovers—and is calmed by a proverb. Stimulus and impulse alternate with common sense and knowledge, as always in

decision-making—the id pushing forward lusts and fears, the superego parading solemn rationalizations and stern prohibitions; or, to put this in medieval terms, the movements of sense being mediated in the will against the moral truth of the higher and lower reason.[21]

This quality of alternation or fluctuation in the mental life, of which everyone has some personal experience, is bolstered by the imagery. Before Criseyde's soliloquy Chaucer tells us she *plited* (turned back and forth) *in many fold*, adding *Now was hire herte warm, now was it cold* (697–698) ; at the end of it she is in the same case:

> Than slepeth hope, and after drede awaketh;
> Now hoot, now cold; but thus, bitwixen tweye,
> She rist hire up.   (810–812)

To this conventional image of hot and cold, which may be found in Boccaccio and almost anywhere in courtly writings, Chaucer adds a far more elaborate imagery of light and dark. Halfway through her soliloquy he introduces her sudden fear with a simile:

> But right as when the sonne shyneth brighte
> In March, that chaungeth ofte tyme his face,
> And that a cloude is put with wynd to flighte,
> Which oversprat the sonne as for a space,
> A cloudy thought gan thorugh hire soule pace,
> That overspradde hire brighte thoughtes alle. . . .   (764–769)

In her thoughts as they follow fast upon, she reminds herself that love is the most stormy life, that always *"som cloude is over that sonne."* And in Antigone's song, about the bliss of love as opposed to its rumored peril, the image of the sun stands for love · is the sun any the worse, asks the song, because a man's weak eyes cannot gaze directly at its brightness? So things stand when at the end of the scene Chaucer devotes a full stanza to the waning sun, the dimming light, and the slow appearing stars:

> The dayes honour, and the hevenes yë,
> The nyghtes foo—al this clepe I the sonne—
> Gan westren faste, and downward for to wrye,
> As he that hadde his dayes cours yronne;
> And white thynges wexen dymme and donne
> For lak of lyght, and sterres for t'apere,
> That she and alle hire folk in went yfeere.   (904–910)

We are permitted to see the sun set and the light fade into ominous dark; in a moment, by a universal irony, she is to experience the clearest illumination of her thought in the darkest hours, and asleep.

The Narrator's appearance here, as elsewhere, is one further way Chaucer dramatizes the alternating shape of Criseyde's thought.[22] Puffed with rhetorical phrases ("day's honor," "heaven's eye," "night's foe") he wheezes in—*al this clepe I the sonne*. The Narrator draws up close to us and joins us in thinking about her—just as before her soliloquy he had lectured us on the way she fell in love with no indecorous haste, adding *And what she thoughte, somewhat shal I write* (699). Then he withdrew and we experienced her thoughts in direct discourse, Antigone's song, and the ladies' conversation. Only now does he pluck us away, just for a breath of fresh air out of sweet rhetoric's windbag. After that, the ladies retire, all is hushed, and Criseyde lying still, thinks more; but, the Narrator adds, he needn't rehearse this to us, *for ye ben wise*. We the audience are suddenly and surprisingly pulled up to attention with the ironic jibe, and our alleged wisdom enlisted for the startling moment to come. Then, in what I have heard called the most beautiful lines in Chaucer, we hear *A nyghtyngale, upon a cedir grene,/ Under the chambre wal ther as she ley*. . . . With that she sleeps and, sleeping, dreams.

The medievals were no less fascinated than we by dreams; but this is not because of their (or our) theories—rather the theories crop up again and again because dreams are and always were our most intense moments of consciousness; in them we grasp by night what we evade and cloak by day, recognizing with unwonted vividness images from a realm beyond our easy reach. The dream-visions of medieval literature may be stiffly conventional, but the successful ones—the *Roman*, *Piers Plowman*, *Pearl*—are powerfully dreamlike all the same; and while Chaucer might make fun of dream *theory* in the Nun's Priest's Tale, no poet who had written *The Book of the Duchess* can have been insensitive to the wonder of dreams themselves. So, with Criseyde's dream of the white eagle, we must admit a degree of psychological realism. We can be aware that birds in medieval literature often suggest human propensities and impulses toward sin or virtue; it will do us no harm to be aware as well that birds, as they occur in the dream-world, often suggest fertility, birth, and rebirth.[23] In the fourteenth century eagles probably suggested gospel truth—for there were lecterns in churches fashioned in the shape of eagles. The eagle is uniformly considered a *noble* bird in Chaucer's works.[24] And his whiteness connotes purity (with perhaps some dread ambivalence at least for readers of Jung and *Moby Dick*). Because the eagle tears out her heart and replaces it with his own, it is easy to suppose he "represents Troilus." But Troilus so far has in no way pursued her or even spoken to her and has been the very reverse of a plundering eagle; besides, the figures in our dreams are never the things themselves as they exist in the real world, but our inner imagination of them. The eagle is Troilus, but Troilus as he exists in Criseyde's inner thoughts, made white by hope and sentiment, made violent and rapacious by expectation and fear—noble, gorgeous, awesome, at once predatory and gentle. Perhaps indeed the eagle is love itself, Criseyde's hopeful and fearful image of it—sexual, lustrous, mystifying—revived in her now by Pandarus' urgings, by the glimpse of Troilus riding in triumph, by the song and talk of love's joy. Her dream can be a *somnium animale* tripped off by anxiety or a *somnium coeleste* foretelling what is to come. Like dreams themselves and the starkest facts, it is inscrutable and intense. The white eagle sets his claws under her breast, tears out her heart, and supplants it with his own, yet she feels no fear or pain. Beneath all the divagations of her thought, behind all the influences on it, is this *fact*—the gorgeous white eagle of her mind's eye, plunderer of hearts.

IV

What have we to learn from this scene about the poem as a whole? In recent years critics have centered attention upon the moral riddle of its ending: a poem which shows love in its highest and most tragic garb ends with the moving counsel against earthly love—*O yonge, fresshe folkes, he or she* . . . . Their attention has thus shifted back to the Boethian element in the body of the poem itself, the slow process by which Fortune makes of the noblest human love another mundane vanity. But the Boethian element in the poem cannot *be* Boethian unless it encompasses what Boethius really said; and Boethius' notion was that while God's foreknowledge of our free choices does not *cause* us to make them, God *does* foreknow our choices and we *do* make them freely. Boethius leaves unanswered the question *how* we make our choices (he has some opinions about how we *should*); and Chaucer really picks up this aspect of the problem when he tries to see into Criseyde's mind.

He thus confronts the timeless riddle of human freedom. Our choices *seem* to happen freely in our consciousness, but consciousness

is a hopeless swirl at the mercy of individual experience, of circumstance and chance occurrence; of language itself and its heritage of
cultural and literary tradition, lore, precept; of reason's shaping dialectic. Our choices *can* happen, as Criseyde's does, in the unfathomed
reaches of consciousness, beneath the stream of inner speech, in a
realm clear to us only through our stream of imagery. In Criseyde's
choice there is thus a subtle determinism and, as we are to learn in due
course, a kind of bondage. As much as she reasons and vacillates, the
choice bursts upon her in sleep, violent and lustrous, as a fact; it is
not God who makes her choice, yet something does—some determinism
of this world which makes us its slaves just as soon as we engage ourselves with it. Living before the time of Christianity Criseyde lacks
that great revealed lore which could save her from the disappointing
flux of her future life; yet as a rational creature she knows it as
through a glass darkly. While Troilus waits outside her chamber she
can say to Pandarus,

> "so worldly selynesse,
> Which clerkes callen fals felicitee,
> Imedled is with many a bitternesse!
> Ful angwissous than is, God woot," quod she,
> "Condicioun of veyn prosperitee;
> For either joies comen nought yfeere,
> Or elles no wight hath hem alwey here."   (III, 813–819)

Yet a few moments later she is to say, embracing Troilus,

> "Ne hadde I er now, my swete herte deere,
> Ben yold, ywis, I were now nought heere!"   (1210–1211)

Later still she is to see with astonishing clarity how she will be *"rolled
on many a tongue,"* how women will hate her most of all. But none
of this stops her—she proceeds with a kind of helpless, perhaps willful,
blindness. Though she has free will and tries to exercise it, she lapses
unconsciously into decision. And Pandarus, glib proprietor of lore and
speech, encourages and misleads her. If we think she would proceed
otherwise were it not for the Fall, we are wrong—that did not, after
all, help Eve. She might proceed otherwise if she were a Christian,
but professing Christianity is not itself a guarantee of right moral
choices. Medieval moralists named rational consent as the test of sin;
but the subtler thinkers, St. Thomas among them, knew the cloudy

area of unreasoning action.[25] Chaucer here explores this irrational
element in our choices and finds that we are not free except in the most
limited way.

This brings us to the reason why Criseyde stays with Diomede and
does not return to Troilus. And the answer must be that it happens so.
Chaucer does not give us a long immersion in her mental life as he
had done before. He presents her regrettable choice with much tongue-
clicking on the Narrator's part and, so he tells us, feels pity for her.
It would be possible to go through the final scenes and glean here and
there a hint of her mental state or psychological fix: we are reminded
of time's passing, her caution, Diomede's persuasive glibness, *His
grete estat, and perel of the town,/ And that she was allone and hadde
nede/ Of frendes help* (1025–1027). But what stands out is the rationalizing and perhaps self-destructive meditation (1054–1085) in
which she castigates and excuses herself all at once—it is too late, she
says; adds *"To Diomede algate I wol be trewe"*; weeping, expresses
what seems earnest praise of Troilus; and concludes that all will pass.
Her two letters to Troilus, written after her decision is a *fait accompli*,
both promise her return; the second, quoted in full, adds a lie about
people's gossiping (1610), casts a subtle doubt on Troilus' good intentions (1614–1617), and puts her return still more vaguely in the future. Troilus sees at once it is *straunge* and soon grasps the truth—
that she/ Nas nought so kynde as that hire oughte be (1642–1643).
I can explain no better than this why she prefers Diomede, whom I
scorn, to Troilus, whom I like. All the same, I feel I do know why she
forsook Troilus. I feel that she did it in the same way and for much
the same reasons that she chose to love Troilus in the second book.
I know, that is, *how* she made this final choice, which I deplore, because I know how she made her earlier one, which I applauded. And I
know this because for a little while, for a space of some four hundred'
or more lines in Book II, I have *been* Criseyde, have experienced the
world as she experienced it, have had my mind and being subsumed
in hers. And having had that experience I can never shake it off.
Chaucer thus gives his reader the ability to understand her falseness,
but it is not the kind of understanding that results from distance. On
the contrary, because we understand through empathy, through entering her mind, our understanding results from our closeness. We get
not a clear overview of her conduct but the muddled sense we might
have of such a choice if it had been our own. And, perhaps for that
reason, her choice seems not at all free or rational; in such choices we

are disposed to decision and action by tangled pressures of culture, lore, belief, habit. Our only freedom is in our conscious awareness of these pressures, in the possibility of doubting them or changing them— which means the possibility of knowing ourselves. Beyond that, our only choice is indifference—indifference to *this world, that passeth soone as floures faire.*

Canterbury Pilgrims

E. T. DONALDSON

The Ordering of the *Canterbury Tales*

Discussions of the order of the *Canterbury Tales,* although some of them are brilliant displays of the scholarly process, seem to share one original sin: a marriage of genuine evidence and rationalization so dearly joined that the reader finds it difficult to distinguish between the two. It is probably impossible for us ever to attain the paradise in which we can be certain of the correct order, but still, as I should like to point out in this paper, we ought to be able clearly to recognize what the real impediments that lie in the path to such a paradise are, even if we cannot surmount them, and even if, in order to do so, we must somehow get over an enormous tangle of rationalization.

Let me first state that, in my opinion, the matter of order is properly an editorial one: that is, in attempting to establish an order, one should make use of the MSS in the same way that one uses them in order to determine the reading of an individual line or word. This involves careful analysis of all variant readings in order to determine what, in the editor's presumably expert opinion, the author originally wrote. In the event that no MS gives a satisfactory reading, the editor cudgels his brains to see if he can find in the preserved readings clues to—one might say ruins of—the original reading; and he may, theoretically at least, come up with a restored reading or conjectural emendation. I say "theoretically" because in the editorial tradition of the *Canterbury Tales* the number of readings admitted to the text that are not in the MSS or even in the preferred MSS is so small as to be almost nonexistent. For instance, while a succession of editors has denied, in the notes, that Chaucer ever intended to assign three priests to the Prioress, to my knowledge none but Professor Pratt has ever dared to let his opinion alter the received text, which (supported, for once, by all MSS) reads *and preestes thre* in A164.[1] Professor Pratt deserves great credit for having the courage of his convictions, even though the resulting incomplete line amounts to a kind of negative conjectural emendation.

Yet—again with the honorable exception of Professor Pratt [2]—editors and other Chaucerians who have taken a conservative position on textual matters have tended to play fast and loose, intellectually if not actually, with the order of the tales. To name only some of the most influential, Furnivall, Skeat, Tatlock, Robinson, Manly-Rickert, Lawrence (originally), and, most recently, Professor Baugh all agree, though not always on the same grounds, that no order represented by the surviving MSS is attributable to Chaucer—indeed, most seem to feel that Chaucer died without having made up his mind about the order.[3] This belief theoretically enables an editor to arrange the tales at will, though actually the latitude it permits, in view of internal references to time and place, is limited. It happens that the order of Ellesmere and eight other MSS, in which the groups appear as A-B^1-D-E-F-C-B^2-G-H-I, provides a broad framework within which all editors have actually operated despite their protestations that the Ellesmere order is not Chaucer's. Manly (in his 1928 edition),[4] Robinson, and Manly-Rickert adhere to the Ellesmere order they specifically reject. Furnivall, whom Skeat reluctantly followed, Tatlock, Manly-Rickert (in the notes), and Lawrence either shifted or proposed shifting the position of two of Ellesmere's groups: B^2, the block of six tales beginning with the Shipman's and extending through the Nun's Priest's, and C, consisting of the Physician's and Pardoner's Tales. Skeat (in his notes) and Baugh settle for the shift of but one group—the shift first suggested to Furnivall by Henry Bradshaw of B^2 from seventh position in Ellesmere to third, following B^1, which consists of the Man of Law's Tale. Only Professor Pratt defends the general authority of Ellesmere, although he believes that Group B^2 has been misplaced from the original Chaucerian order and should follow directly on B^1. His editorial procedure thus involves but a single operation—technically, one alteration in an extant MS-arrangement—while the procedures of the other scholars involve, theoretically at least, ten separate operations: since they eschew all MS-authority, they must start from scratch and place every group in the location they think best.

It is evident that Professor Pratt's method of procedure is by far the most economical, and I believe that it alone is editorially proper, though I disagree with him on the necessity for making the Bradshaw shift. The principal editorial facts are as follows: the fifty-seven surviving MSS analyzed by Manly-Rickert in their discussion of the order of the tales [5] give us a choice of some twenty-seven different orders; yet of this number only the order represented in Ellesmere and its likes is in any way satisfactory: all the other orders raise more problems than they solve. If we are to consider order in the same way that we consider individual readings—as I believe we should—we shall certainly accept the Ellesmere order either as authoritative or as more nearly authoritative than any other: it provides us with a good working base, and has, as a matter of fact, always been used as such even by those who disavow any belief in its authority. Professor Pratt, commenting on Tatlock's statement that the only authority in the MSS is that "of enlightened opinion," observes that in that case "we must wonder at the exceedingly enlightened opinion of the Ellesmere scribe, who, without the aids and benefits of modern scholarship" achieved almost the same order as the one achieved by modern scholars.[6] It is almost as if the scholars were saying, with admirable humility, "If I can produce an order much the same as Ellesmere's, then there is no likelihood that Ellesmere's order is Chaucer's." Of course, the fact is that in many respects the Ellesmere order is inevitable—that is, it generally squares with internal references to time and place—but this does not cast suspicion on its authority. One encounters many readings in Chaucer that might be termed inevitable with regard to rhyme, meter, or sense, but one does not question their authority for that reason. And just as even an inevitable reading is often scribally corrupted, so there are twenty-six orders that lack inevitability to a greater or lesser degree. But fortunately there are good scribes who very often record what we all agree Chaucer must have written. Inasmuch as this is true, I find it strange to reject as wholly unauthoritative a reading that is in general satisfactory—an order which certainly leads us toward the right path if it is not itself the right path.

Before proceeding to examine the reasons for the rejection of the Ellesmere order's authority, one other editorial fact that figures in most discussions must be mentioned: the existence of the link, missing from MSS with the Ellesmere order but present in some thirty-four other MSS, at the end of the Man of Law's Tale (B^1) in which, at one time or another, Chaucer seems to have introduced by name the speaker of the tale to follow. The great majority of the MSS—some twenty-seven—name this speaker as the Squire, an identification that seems wrong, if only because in the universally accepted text the Squire's Tale is neatly introduced with a summons by the Host at the beginning of Group F (which carries on smoothly from Group E). Six MSS (originally seven) identify the speaker as the Summoner, an identification that also seems impossible since in the accepted text the Summoner's Tale is intricately involved in Group D with both the Wife of Bath's Tale and the Friar's.[7] A sole MS, however, Selden,[8] identifies the speaker as the Shipman, and this is an exceedingly significant reading, for the Shipman's Tale is the first in Group B^2, so that Selden's reading might seem to provide a reason for placing B^2 immediately after B^1 (or, in terms of the Ellesmere order, of transferring B^2 from seventh position to third). Unfortunately, though Selden places B^1 and B^2 together, it is considered a very unreliable MS, so that not even those most eager to adopt its sequence are willing to invoke its authority.

The Man of Law's endlink, especially in the Selden form, has figured largely in most discussions of the order of the *Canterbury Tales,* but it is difficult to say what effect it may have had in pre-determining skepticism about the authority of the Ellesmere order. Professor Lee Sheridan Cox in a recent defense of the Ellesmere order which is full of acute observations on the logic employed in discussions of the topic, suggests of scholars who prefer the order B^1B^2 that because "they are adopting the order found in the Selden MS., 'one of the most erratic of all the MSS,' and rejecting what W. W. Lawrence calls 'the best manuscript evidence,' they must constantly reiterate that no manuscript is authoritative." [9] There may be some truth in this statement, but it would be invidious to apply it to any individual: even Tatlock, who was most anxious to establish the order B^1B^2, may have arrived at the conclusion that Chaucer never published the *Canterbury Tales,* and never arranged their order, independently of any concern for the B^1B^2 position—though there is no question that Tatlock made the general and the specific issues cooperate effectively in his rhetoric. And Professor Cox's statement is misleading insofar as it implies that preference for the order B^1B^2 is an invariable motive for skepticism about the authority of Ellesmere, for on the one hand Professor Pratt, who argues for the order, defends Ellesmere's general authority, and on the other, scholars like Manly-Rickert and Robinson are, if possible, even more skeptical about the originality of the reading and sequence shown by Selden than they are about the authority of Ellesmere. Though Robinson prints the Man of Law's endlink in its Selden form, he denies its authority and retains the Ellesmere order; and Manly-Rickert believe that the most likely Chaucerian order would be

B[1]CB[2], specifically denying any validity whatsoever to the endlink in its Selden form.[10]

A review of the discussions of order suggests to me that the overwhelming reason for rejecting the Ellesmere order—whether or not in favor of the sequence B[1]B[2]—is the fact that at D847, at the end of the Wife of Bath's Prologue, the Summoner threatens to tell *"tales two or thre/ Of freres, er I come to Sidyngborne,"* whereas about 8300 lines later in the Ellesmere order, at B[2]1926, the Host remarks *"Loo, Rouchestre stant heer faste by"*; and, of course, anyone journeying from London to Canterbury would pass Rochester some eleven miles before he came to Sittingbourne. With the sole exception of Tatlock,[11] scholars seem to have found this violation of verisimilitude too gross to digest; one indeed suspects that if it were not for this failure of topology to accord with chronology, skepticism about the authority of the Ellesmere order would never have become epidemic. As it is, no matter how sternly a scholar may enjoin the reader not to expect from Chaucer too literal a realism, the outrage he suffers at the misplacement of Rochester and Sittingbourne invariably seems to exempt the scholar himself from his own injunction.[12] On this one point scholars who disagree on most other points seem to agree.

There are, of course, a number of subsidiary reasons that have been offered for doubting the authority of the Ellesmere order. Manly-Rickert, for instance, believe that the time difference between Group H—the brief Manciple's Tale, told in the early morning—and Group I —the Parson's Tale, begun after four in the afternoon—is an equally cogent disproof that Ellesmere represents Chaucer's intention. Moreover, Manly in 1928 cited such matters as the Man of Law's promise to speak in prose, the Shipman's reference to himself as belonging, apparently, to the female gender, and the Second Nun's calling herself an unworthy son of Eve, as proof that when Chaucer died he left many loose ends in the tales, including, by inference, their order.[13] Furthermore, Manly-Rickert believed on the basis of "paleographical and other evidence" that the highly erratic order displayed by the Hengwrt MS represents "the earliest attempt after Chaucer's death to arrange in a single MS the tales and links unarranged by him," while the Ellesmere order represents a later, more successful attempt.[14] Finally, according to Mrs. Dempster,[15] Manly agreed essentially with Tatlock that when Chaucer died he had not prepared the *Canterbury Tales* for genuine publication, and hence had failed to make any firm arrangement of the tales.

Before returning to the Rochester-Sittingbourne contradiction, let us look at these subsidiary reasons for doubting Ellesmere's authority. As far as the time discrepancy between H and I is concerned, it does not seem to have troubled anyone very much except Manly-Rickert: Tatlock, for instance, dismisses it almost casually "in view . . . of the uncertainty as to how much wary though unessential realism we can constantly expect" of Chaucer.[16] Lawrence observes that in the MSS "the order of groups H and I is constant," and places the discrepancy in the same class as the flaws in the Man of Law's and Second Nun's Introductions and in the Shipman's Tale—all obvious indications within the text of the unfinished state of the *Canterbury Tales*.[17] In this he is surely right, for there seems little difference in the quality of the blemishes. I would, however, disagree with Manly (and with Lawrence, insofar as he is in agreement with Manly) that the presence of these blemishes necessarily provides evidence that Chaucer died without leaving any indication of how the tales were to be arranged. For the Parson's Prologue and the Retraction with their emphasis on finality prove that while the *Canterbury Tales* is obviously an unfinished work it is also a work that the author considered finished, if only, I suspect, because he felt that there was little time left for further work. To reject a nearly satisfactory order represented in surviving MSS—one that seems final in the sense of "terminal" if not of "definitive"—because of the existence of blemishes within the text is an arbitrary decision, showing what seems to me an unreasonable skepticism toward the only witnesses we have to the very text of the *Canterbury Tales*.

As far as the history of the MSS between Chaucer's death and the transcription of the earliest copies is concerned, one may suspect, as Professor Cox does about those who favor the B¹B² sequence, that both Tatlock and Manly arrived at their theories about Chaucer's failure to prepare his poem for publication as a consequence of their lack of trust in the Ellesmere order: that is, that their theories are not so much reasons for doubting Ellesmere as rationalizations of a preconceived doubt. But this question is actually irrelevant: what matters is the evidence they were able to produce in behalf of their theories. And here one must sadly concede that they produced almost no evidence: indeed, Tatlock's eloquent article does nothing to make seem more probable the probability with which it begins and ends. For the preserved MSS, which are the only basis of our knowledge of what

Chaucer wrote, tell us almost nothing about their pre-history: we can only conjecture backward from them. Thus when Manly says the Hengwrt MS represents "the earliest attempt after Chaucer's death to arrange" the tales in some sort of order, the evidence actually would permit him only to say that it represents "the earliest (surviving) (detectable) attempt" at arrangement. I can find no evidence in Manly-Rickert or elsewhere for supposing that Hengwrt is an older MS than, say, Ellesmere. Presumably they were both written by the same scribe —although I know of no detailed demonstration of this in print, and my own (admittedly inadequate) experience with MSS causes me to doubt it—and presumably the same scribe would not have been so uncertain about order as Hengwrt is once he had produced Ellesmere. But even if both assumptions are true, there is no evidence at all for supposing that Hengwrt's is the first attempt anyone ever made to arrange the tales, or that Ellesmere's represents a later one. There is no indication in Ellesmere that the scribe was not following a pre-existent order, and no evidence, besides that being discussed here, that this order was not Chaucer's own. We simply do not know anything about the condition of the MSS that Chaucer left or what happened between his death and the transcription of the earliest surviving MSS. MSS are all we have to work with: little as they may tell us about antecedent conditions, they do tell us all we are ever likely to know about the text of Chaucer's poems.[18]

As was suggested above, the existence of the Man of Law's endlink in many MSS and its obvious authenticity have also contributed to scholars' doubts about the Ellesmere order. Indeed, combined with the Rochester-Sittingbourne contradiction, it provides the reason for Professor Pratt's shifting of Group B^2 from its position in the Ellesmere order that he otherwise accepts. But, as I said before, the one MS that juxtaposes B^1 and B^2 and identifies the teller of the first tale of B^2 as the Shipman is deemed highly corrupt and unreliable. Manly-Rickert characterize it as "a bad 15 C edition of no textual authority," whose scribe "had access to MSS of all types." [19] The result is that Selden's reading *Shipman* has proved an embarrassment rather than support to those who would adopt its reading and sequence. Thus Tatlock insists that Selden "gives no *authority* for the solution," but adds that "some scholars speak as if this fact proved the solution wrong: but the removal of one unsound argument *pro* is not an argument *contra.*" [20] Similarly Professor Pratt observes that "the fact that Se[lden] is unauthoritative is not an argument against either the reading or the sequence."[21] While I do not believe that the Selden variants represent Chaucer's intention, I find it extraordinary that those who adopt them reject so summarily what might better be argued to be good MS authority. It is true that Selden is late (Manly-Rickert date it 1450–1470),[22] and that it is heavily contaminated. But there is no reason to exclude the possibility that heavily contaminated MSS have been contaminated from MSS with extremely good readings—indeed, with uniquely good readings that have not elsewhere survived. I suspect that MSS of late date and an untraceable textual tradition are often most helpful to the open-minded editor—at least I know of several examples.[23] Contaminated MSS have bad reputations (note that the term "contaminated" is arbitrarily preferred to "corrected") because, of course, the editor can not find in them neat evidence of genetic relationship; yet the exasperation of the editor is not a factor in determining the originality of a reading, for right readings, not stemmata, are the end-products of editorial work.[24] Furthermore, the lateness of a MS tells us nothing whatsoever *a priori* about the character of its readings. A MS relatively close to the original in time may be much farther removed from it in the number of intermediaries than a MS far removed in time. The opposite opinion depends on a statistical generalization that is of small validity in view of the paucity of the surviving materials providing the sample and of the multiplicity of the unknowns. Both theoretically and actually a scribe or editor in 1470 might copy a poem from a MS that had itself been copied in 1400, or he might make his copy while consulting three or four MSS of varying ages— which is, after all, what most modern editors do. Therefore it seems curious that scholars who accept Selden's "solution" reject the authority of the one editorial fact that exists in support of their decision: one would suppose that they might admit that, for all its faults and lateness, a MS dated 1450–1470 is still far nearer to Chaucer than we are in the twentieth century. Finally, I am not sure that it is humanly possible to reject totally the authority of a MS whose reading one adopts. That is, while if it had not been for Selden I am sure that some Chaucerian would have conjectured its "solution," I am much less than sure that the conjecture would have received general approbation in the absence of any MS support: it is all very well for scholars to repudiate the authority of the MS whose reading they adopt, but I suspect that their readers never cease to derive comfort from the fact that there is apparent MS support for the emendation. When conjecture and fact coincide, it is inhuman to allow the former to destroy the effect of the latter.

The reason I reject Selden's authority is not that I assume all its readings to be inherently unreliable, but because, despite its reading *Shipman* and its juxtaposition of B^1 and B^2, the order of the tales in Selden remains wholly unsatisfactory: $AE^aDE^bF^aB^1B^2GCF^bHI$ (E^a = Clerk's Tale, E^b Merchant's, F^a Squire's, F^b Franklin's). This chaotic sequence suggests, I believe, that Selden's "solution" is nothing more than a laudable attempt to do something constructive with a leftover link. And the fact is, of course, that Selden fails to resolve the Rochester-Sittingbourne contradiction, which remains as in Ellesmere. It should be noted, however, that Selden's repositioning of B^1 (in terms of the Ellesmere order, from second position to seventh) violates no principle of inevitability that is not violated by the majority of the MSS—by all, indeed, except the five that manage to get Group D after Group B^2, Sittingbourne after Rochester. Or, stated differently, since the fragment B^1 contains no decisive reference to time and none at all to place, the only reason for leaving it in second position is the fact that that is where it appears in all but twelve MSS [25]—a point that is insufficiently emphasized by those who insist that no MS order possesses any authority.[26] Again, only Professor Pratt, who accepts as authoritative the Ellesmere order with the exception of the position of B^2, is operating with proper editorial sanction in accepting the second position for B^1: thus it is only with his shift of B^2 that I find myself in disagreement.

This shift—which is represented in no surviving MS—Professor Pratt has defended most ingeniously and persuasively as reproducing Chaucer's final intention. It has, of course, the double advantage of salvaging the Man of Law's endlink (omitted from MSS with the Ellesmere order) and correcting the relative positions of Sittingbourne and Rochester. And Professor Pratt's hypotheses of events are most plausible. He begins with the assumption, which is generally admitted to be a fact, that Chaucer originally wrote the present Shipman's Tale for the Wife of Bath. He then goes on to assume—following the brilliant suggestion of R. F. Jones [27]—that the Man of Law's endlink originally named the Wife of Bath as the teller of the next tale; and that, when Chaucer wrote a new tale (and prologue?) for the Wife of Bath he erased her name from the endlink and wrote in *Shipman,* but did so badly so that later copyists could only make out the initial *S* (hence the reading *Somonour* and *Squier* of the other MSS containing the endlink) ; and that at the same time he added the adverb *heer* in the margin opposite the line in order to remedy the metrical reduction in the speaker's name from a trisyllable to a dissyllable; [28] and finally, that after Chaucer's death Group B[2] became accidentally separated from its original predecessor B[1] and ended up between C and G, with the result that the endlink, no longer having a logical connection with what followed it, was omitted by the scribes employing the Ellesmere order. This is an extremely satisfying series of hypotheses, making excellent use of the actual evidence. Nevertheless, all this amounts only to a conjecture, and one conjecture is, of course, always replaceable by another equally persuasive. Professor Cox has recently tried to provide a conjecture that would counter Professor Pratt's and vindicate the Ellesmere order; and while it is less tidy and perhaps less economical, involving what seem to me serious asperities,[29] I am under the impression that it might be tidied up enough to offer a good challenge to Professor Pratt's, and to appear as likely as his to be true to the actual facts.

My own conjecture concerning the Man of Law's endlink is the very old one, that it was canceled by Chaucer, or at least laid aside until he could find a fitting place for it—which he never did.[30] And I imagine he laid it aside as much because it no longer related to the Man of Law's Tale as because of his uncertainty as to whom he would nominate as the next tale-teller. The speaker variously identified as the Squire, the Summoner, and the Shipman obliquely characterizes the Man of Law's Tale as containing *"philosophie," "phislyas"* (whatever that may be), *"termes queinte of lawe,"* and *"Latyn"* (Latinate vocabulary?), and while these are not entirely irrelevant to the tale of Custance, one suspects that they had more relevance to that tale in prose which the Man of Law still promises to tell. In a critical edition, I suppose the endlink should be printed either in an appendix as representing a passage genuinely Chaucerian but not placeable, or else, within square brackets, in its usual place after the Man of Law's Tale, with the speaker of the next tale identified either as the Summoner (according to Manly-Rickert, the reading of O[1]), or, less conservatively, left blank on the grounds that the three names preserved in the MSS are equally scribal. In a less austere edition, I should do what I already have done: [31] adopt Jones' conjecture and read *Wif of Bathe* as probably the character whom Chaucer once had in mind as the speaker of the next tale. But it seems to me, on the basis of the MS evidence, that all treatment of the Man of Law's endlink must be conjectural, and that its status is too uncertain to affect the matter of order.

Thus the MSS provide us with no evidence for a satisfactory solution to the problem of the Man of Law's endlink; but, in the Ellesmere form, they do provide us with an order of tales which is very nearly satisfactory. Indeed, the only real objection to Ellesmere remains the Sittingbourne-Rochester contradiction. Yet I cannot see that this discrepancy is any worse than allowing (as all editors do) the Man of Law to promise to speak in prose, or the Shipman to speak as if he were a woman, or the Second Nun to speak as if she were a man, or the Manciple to take some eight hours to tell a tale of 258 lines. Is confusion of gender or of time less serious a fault than confusion of place? Perhaps for scholars it is, for the ability to read maps is a kind of symbol of the whole scholarly process: we are permitted to be late for class, or to talk too long and about the wrong assignment, and (especially in these days) to be uncertain which of our students are male and which female, but we mustn't misread maps: the correct interpretation of ink marks on paper is our *raison d'être*. But I doubt that poets should be held up to the scholarly standard. Lawrence feels that the joining of B^1 and B^2 is justifiable because, unlike the other discrepancies, the one involving the two place names can alone "be due to manuscript displacement." [32] But it nevertheless seems a desperate remedy, a huge conjectural emendation involving the transfer of some 3450 lines over an area of 7326 lines in order to correct the reading of a single word. The only advantage that it seems to have is that it is relatively invisible: it leaves no mark upon the text itself, so that the editor can pretend not to be there. This he could not do if he were to proceed in so logical a fashion as also to try to emend the other flaws, which are of equal gravity. Probably there is nothing an editor could do with the Man of Law's promise to speak in prose, or with the time interval between Groups H and I. But the Shipman's Tale could be easily emended by altering the pronouns in $B^2$12–19 from the first to the third person, and the Second Nun could be made to refer to herself as a *doghter of Eve* without metrical impairment, for in this position *doghter* may be monosyllabic. Similarly, there seems no overwhelming need to go to the lengths of shifting the position of Group B^2, thus destroying an order which is in all other respects entirely satisfactory and which is an order handed down by the surviving MSS, merely to

rectify a minor matter of geography. It would be more economical to
emend B²1926 conjecturally to read *"Loo, Osprynge stant heer faste
by!"* or else, imitating Professor Pratt's treatment of the three priests,
to read for D846–847:

> But if I telle tales two or thre
> Of freres, er I come to. . . . [33]

Calendar of Joh. de Gamundia

M O R T O N   W .   B L O O M F I E L D

The Miller's Tale—An UnBoethian Interpretation[*]

Although we cannot always be certain of Chaucer's intentions as to the proper position of some of his tales, inasmuch as the Canterbury scheme was never completely carried out and we have only "fragments" not of a great confession but of a great framed narrative collection, we can be sure of the proper position of the Miller's Tale (MT). The MSS clearly testify to that: the first and beginning fragment to which it belongs was completed. On the one side it follows the Knight's Tale (KT), and on the other it precedes the Reeve's Tale (RT). It has not escaped the attention of scholars that there is a close, often parodic, connection between each of these two tales and the Miller's contribution to the Canterbury journey. There is, however, one point that as far as I am aware has not been made in this triple comparison and which I wish to look into. I think it will take us far afield and ultimately enable us to understand something of MT and the fabliau in general.

Looking at KT and RT with Boethian eyes, we may say that they both present justification for the belief that the world is rational, and governed in some fundamental way by reason and order. This point has certainly been emphasized in studies of KT. The part that Boethian philosophy plays in that tale is writ large. Dr. Herz writes "the real center of the tale is a vision of the noble life where all that happens belongs to a providential order and has its role, even if that role be

[*] It is a great pleasure to dedicate this article to my old and dear friend, Francis Lee Utley, to whom I owe so much that any attempt to repay fully his many kindnesses would be useless. Long may he flourish! I hope he will accept this essay as a token of my appreciation.

205

tragic." [1] The argument that all is for the best in this not too impossible world is openly presented in Theseus' great speech which begins
"The Firste Moevere of the cause above . . ." (I, 2987). The irrationalities of the world such as Arcite's death are only seeming. From
God's point of view all falls into place, all that happens is converted
into his proper will (I, 3037). And throughout we have other less
open but no less convincing Boethian touches. At the end of Part II
and Part IV, we find, for example, set hierarchical scenes with the
king on his throne and the confused actors of the tale, or some of
them, before him.

Theseus settles things in this world just as God settles things in
the cosmos. Ultimately we must all be happy, for the world is sensible
and rational.

The Reeve's Tale, although certainly not a philosophical, pageantlike tale, nevertheless unlike many fabliaux, is based on justice and
fair play. *"A gylour shal hymself bigyled be"* (I, 4321). The duper is
duped and he that does evil must expect evil in return. The cheating
miller has lost his wheat, his pay for lodging and supper, and the
purity (such as it is) of his wife and daughter. We not only enjoy
the joke and trick, but we can glow with a sense that the universe is
on the side of the just. [2]

On the other hand, the central figure of MT, Alison, gets away
with everything. "Alison is the only person who escapes scot-free." [3]
The adulteress successfully cuckolds her husband and receives no
punishment. Even worse, I suppose, is the punishment the kind-hearted
John receives. Besides being cuckolded, he breaks his arm and is the
laughing-stock of his village. Some critics may think that a *senex
amans* like the carpenter deserves anything he gets. In the highly unchristian Christian interpretations of the tale fashionable today, [4] we
find the kind-hearted carpenter's misfortunes considered only just. The
wicked must be punished, and those who are punished must be wicked.
From my point of view, and in my judgment, I think John is unjustly punished. Perhaps only to someone under thirty can the foible
of a *senex amans* call for severe condemnation.

John comes crashing into the story at the end [5] to bring matters to
a close. The narrative is knit up, and the anecdote is properly ended.
But the morality of it all is most unsatisfactory and must seem even
more so when we regard its narrative context—a story of an irrational, unjust world set between two stories of a just and ordered

world. In fact what we have here is a very unBoethian universe, a world which seems rational but is not really so. We are far away from a world which seems irrational but is really rational. It is no doubt with good reason that we are twice warned in the prologue and tale (I, 3163–3164 and I, 3454) of the dangers of attempting to probe *Goddes pryvetee,* God's secrets. We had better not, for we are apt to be made unhappy.

Let us look at MT a little more closely. The plot of the tale is extremely detailed and complex. It is as if Chaucer here was throwing his rhetorical energies into plot rather than into rhetorical ornaments of various sorts.[6] In this intricacy of construction, Chaucer is following in general the common practice of fabliau writers. He differs from them, however, in his use of descriptions and long speeches. The classic descriptions of Alison (I, 3233–3270) and Absalon (I, 3314–3350) and the lesser-known though briefer but no less attractive portrait of Nicholas (I, 3199–3220) have all been sufficiently commented on for us to pass them by. These portraits give an unusual richness of texture to the fabliau.

The basic story (apparently an original combination of three well-known folklore themes—the Second Flood, the Misdirected Kiss, and the Branding) of a successful cuckolding of an old man and the revenge of a discomfited second lover repudiated in the process is fantastic in the extreme. The carrying out of logic and planning to its illogical and unplanned opposite is quietly accepted because of the accumulated realistic detail and because of the extraordinary bawdy of the story. The "realism" wins us to a quick suspension of our disbelief. We think we are witnessing real life. A moment's reflection, which is hard to indulge in while we read the intricate and intriguingly wrought tale, should quickly disabuse us. The story is incredible in the extreme but incredible not as the Clerk's Tale is incredible to a realistic mind, but incredible through its credibility. It is so real that it transcends the reality of life.

The *fabliau* as a genre tends to this slapstick incredibility, and the name itself indicates how it was originally conceived. The term comes from the Latin *fabula,* which was used in rhetoric [7] to describe a narrative that was neither true nor seeming to be true. Even if our own perception does not tell us that these tales are thought of as fantastic and even dreamlike, the etymology should help us to a similar conclusion, at least in the early days of the genre.

Like Machiavelli's play *La Mandragola,* MT is "a hard-boiled, cruel sex intrigue, modeled on the classic fashion in which old men are fools, youths are rogues, and trollops are just what they seem." [8]

Things in the MT world are connected, all right. The shout of water brings John crashing down, the desire to urinate brings Nicholas to the window for his punishment, but the connection leads nowhere and is finally completely arbitrary. The punishment of Nicholas is deserved, but it only leads to the undeserved punishment of John. Besides we are already aware that Nicholas' fun in bed was soon to be permanently over inasmuch as his scheme, though ingenious in the extreme, is a very poor one for continual enjoyment with the fair Alison.

The narrative center of the MT is the climactic night of love, branding, and flood. The tale's story is completely directed to making that night possible and credible within terms of its proper fantasy. We meet the major characters and learn something of them and know their proper locations vis-à-vis each other. Nicholas is a young Oxford student living with John and Alison in the town of Oxford. His reputation as a reader of the skies and as a weather prophet is immediately made clear. John is a carpenter, an old man, married to a young and most attractive wife. She arouses sexual passion and indeed the language used in describing her [9] makes clear her vulgar aspect and her manipulation of her sexuality. We are told of how Nicholas' passion is aroused in a brief encounter. Alison after a show of resistance agrees to grant him her love but points out how difficult a rendezvous will be to arrange with such a jealous husband. She begs him to be careful *"Ye moste been ful deerne"* (3297). Nicholas assures her that he will easily be able to fool her carpenter husband.

Another complication in the triangle is now introduced—a village lover who is also the village dandy, Absalon. He is at a great disadvantage because he does not live in the same house as Alison. *"Alwey the nye slye/ Maketh the ferre leeve to be looth"* (I, 3392–3393).

Now the elaborate scheme of Nicholas must be set afoot. Alison and Nicholas wish to spend a whole night together. They may or may not have already been meeting for amorous purposes: we are not told. In any case the scheme Nicholas proposed would certainly have put an end to his relations with Alison. We are not, however, concerned as the plan unfolds. We are only concerned with the details of this mad scheme.

Nicholas stores food and drink secretly in his bedchamber. There he remains all through Saturday and on Sunday until the evening. John, who obviously is fond of his lodger, begins to worry because he has not seen him for some time. The servant Robin is sent to inquire but is unable to get any answer to his knocking. He then looks through the cat-way and sees Nicholas apparently in a daze of some sort. Robin and John in fear break down the door and rouse the feigning student by shaking and exorcisms.

Having thus established his prophetic credentials for a new prophecy, and after a light reflection, Nicholas then explains to John about a coming flood which will drown the world. However, Nicholas suggests a way of saving him and Alison, for whom John has shown real concern.

The plan is to get three tubs that will hold our three heroes, which can be hung near the roof over the night of the great rain, and which with an ax can be sent off safely on the flood. The artistic imagination of Nicholas reaches a crescendo as he describes the three tubs in the flood with imaginary dialogue between their inhabitants. Nicholas stresses the importance of the separation of husband and wife *"for that bitwixe you shal be no synne"* (I, 3590). One must be chaste for the great event.

The preparations are made and the three ascend to their tubs on Monday night to await the rain. After John announces by his snoring that he is asleep, Alison and Nicholas descend by ladders and speedily make for the bed. In the meantime, Absalon has heard that John is away from home that night and decides to do some wooing at Alison's window. In her good spirits, Alison decides to have some fun and offers a portion of her anatomy to be kissed over the window. Absalon kisses it in the dark and shortly thereafter discovers what he has done.

For revenge, he gets a red-hot poker from the village smith who has prepared his forge early in the morning. This time Nicholas who is near the window decides, on hearing Absalon's second request for a kiss, to repeat Alison's little exploit. This time he receives a red-hot poker in the proper place and yells for water. This shout awakes John who cuts his holding ropes and comes crashing down to the floor to break his arm. The neighbors rush in, and Nicholas and Alison tell the good people that John is mad. All laugh at the poor man, who in vain tries to tell the true story. The tale concludes with a summary of the action and a blessing on the crowd of pilgrims.

Now it is true that the fabliau is normally not concerned with handing out justice in this world. In fact the tradition is clearly amoral and even immoral. The Merchant's Tale and the Shipman's Tale, which belong in varying degrees to the genre, have both been seen as bitter and immoral tales. Sex and surprise are the two great ingredients of the fabliau and, although its characters are often bourgeois or peasants, they are not invariably so. The Merchant's Tale, which deals with a knight, is certainly partly in the fabliau tradition. Both of these tales indirectly glorify injustice. This way of putting it is however profoundly unfair, as the concern of the author is with cleverness and entertainment and not justice. The bitterness of these tales, such as it is, comes from a mistaken expectation.

Now, it is a curious fact that although the injustice and unfairness of both the Merchant's Tale and the Shipman's Tale are frequently alluded to, it is rare to find such a charge leveled at the MT. Its story is equally unjust if we look at it closely. This curious reaction deserves looking into.

The answer, of course, lies in the liveliness of the tale, its wealth of detail, its good spirits, the speed of the narrative, the complexity of the plot, and its general tone. Our attention is drawn away from the basic inhumanity of the tale. The Merchant's Tale and the Shipman's Tale, in spite of the great complexity of their telling, especially that of the Merchant's Tale, do not trouble themselves to hide the fundamentally unjust story of cuckoldry. They are not happy tales even if bitterness is too strong a term to use for the effect they leave.

On the other hand, MT is superficially gay and vibrant. One gets caught up in the movement of the story and in the force of the characters. The unjust denouement is hardly sensed, so catching is the interplay of events, the fascination of the sexual ploys, the wonder of the web of events. The irrationality of it all is buried under the delights of the story and the ingenuity and innocence of the characters. Fortune seems suspended as the characters take control. Events seem to be in hand, and man seems to be master of his destiny.

But there is a sting in the tail of this scorpion of events. All this mastery and control lead to a central nothingness. The world is not controllable, justice is only partially served, and fortune really rules all. Fortune is not the servant of providence at all as she sometimes is or seems to be but the arbitrary creature who cloaks her nefarious activities in a seamless cloak of order. All this order is only a mask for the essential disorder. The universe is, alas, not Boethian at all but irrational and arbitrary. Activity which seems meaningful and pur-

poseful is essentially meaningless and often unjust. The tremendous
effort at organization, especially on Nicholas' part, bespeaks a ration-
ality of means and ends. The universe can be manipulated to attain
certain ends and is therefore to a large extent rational. It is opera-
tionally rational and may even be metaphysically rational as well.

But the universe plays a joke on us. It is only seemingly rational.
It is really deeply irrational and unjust.[10]

Part of the delight of any fabliau, in fact a common feature of its
artistry, is the use of dramatic irony. In almost every case the reader
is in possession of some crucial information which one of the characters does not possess.

In the Shipman's Tale, the reader knows that the merchant has
been cuckolded by his wife and is delighted with the ingenuity with
which the wife and the monk get out of their dilemmas. The merchant
at the end is satisfied in his ignorance and we as readers are pleased.

In the Merchant's Tale, we know Squire Damian is up in the tree;
the blind man, until the miracle occurs, does not. January allows himself to be talked out of the evidence of his eyes, back again into
ignorance, because certain things are not worth knowing.

Sometimes, as in the Merchant's Tale and Reeve's Tale, the gulled
character learns the truth. Sometimes, as in the Shipman's Tale, he
does not. In any case, the audience can have the proper sense of
superiority to the hapless character.

In the Miller's Tale, we are continually ahead of our characters.
We know that Nicholas' elaborate scheme is false and what its true
purpose is. We know what Absalon is about to kiss and what Nicholas
is about to receive. We know what really prompts John to cut the
rope. We are continually superior to the characters and in possession
of the requisite information to understand what is happening. The
universe the audience inhabits seems as rational and controllable as
that in which our four characters live. Yet both assumptions are false.
Events cannot be controlled. Our superior knowledge can do us no
more good than that of the characters, for it leads us into a realization,
if we can think closely on the events, that the universe is as irrational
at heart as we are. *"The man is wood, my leeue brother;/ Every wight
gan laughen at this stryf."* Laughter is all that is left us, except the
blessings of God, which the Miller calls down on us at the very end.

God save al the rowte

Bathers, from the Augsburg Calendar (*ca.* 1480)

STITH THOMPSON

Unfinished Business: The Folktale

After his adventures with Noah and his wife in many parts of the world and in and out of the Middle Ages, no one could be more aware than Francis Utley of the close relation existing between the written literary traditional tale and its oral counterparts. Although this relationship was especially noticeable in the medieval literature of Europe, it has existed everywhere since men began to write down their stories for the edification of their fellows and for future generations. Once, of course, six or seven thousand years ago, there were no written tales, but probably everywhere there was a considerable activity in the telling of stories that were listened to and remembered or forgotten. And even today, if we are to believe the reports of anthropologists, this activity continues everywhere among the unlettered peoples of the world.

Any attempt to study this activity as it appears in all parts of the world and in every type of society, literate and illiterate, is extraordinarily difficult and the path is full of pitfalls. This is not the place to attempt a special discussion of the tales of the present-day unlettered peoples, but any study of oral tales will quickly display the fact that no real line can be drawn to separate the work of the story-teller among such unlettered people from that of the corresponding artist in ancient Greece or Egypt or in medieval Europe. Special problems are presented, however, by the study of the oral tale as it exists side by side with written narrative, because of the continual give and take between the two traditions. These problems are primarily comparative and historical in their nature, and the scholar is above all interested in the life-history of a particular tale, whether told or written. If, however, such a scholar observes the possibilities presented by his subject, he will soon realize that this historic approach is only one of several that

213

the folktale student may well undertake. It is this multiple approach to the study of the folktale with which this discussion is concerned.

Of the stories listened to with wonder or amusement in ancient Sumer and in later Babylonia and Assyria, we have no knowledge except as they may be reflected in the cuneiform records that still exist, and speculation about the relation of these written records to an oral tradition is extremely hazardous. That there developed in these cultures a well-organized series of narratives, some of them spreading over the whole area and beyond and enjoying a life of thousands of years is clear enough, but what we have is usually in a peculiarly stylized poetic form which must have been developed through a long period of time by priests or other intellectuals. Many of these stories are what we would call mythological and have to do with the creation and with the gods and their experiences. We know from the studies of unlettered peoples that such stories are told orally almost everywhere and we can probably assume from such peoples that they were told for a long time in simple prose and that the casting of these stories in the elaborate poetic form in which we now have them was the result of a long development. But the student of the folktale can hardly go further than this in his curiosity to know what the ancient Mesopotamian oral tale was like. Perhaps as these stories are analyzed and brought into ever closer relations to the tales of the whole world, we may be able to approach this question with more assurance than we can now.

We are in similar difficulties when we consider the tales of ancient Egypt. Here we have hieroglyphic records going back into the third millennium before Christ, and some of them show a considerable resemblance to oral folktales as we now know them. A good example is the story of the Two Brothers, where we meet in unmistakable form many motifs that have become a part of the traditional baggage of the modern European teller of tales. This particular story is still well known in the Near East, but in its Egyptian version it has all the peculiarities of a priestly composition. In spite of its general framework and its motifs so familiar in European folklore, the tale belongs in the religious literature of ancient Egypt with its temples and its gods and its peculiar institutions. Shall we assume that this story had already developed among the illiterate story-tellers of the Near East and was then reworked by the Egyptian priesthood to be a part of their sacred scripture? The opposite direction for the spread of this tale can hardly be maintained, since there would seem to be little likeli-

hood that the simple tale-teller of the Near East would have learned
this tale in its elaborate Egyptian form and then subtracted from it
all of the peculiar Egyptian details. This is, of course, primarily a
historical problem and the most we can do in trying to solve it is to
work on a historic-geographic basis.

For these ancient cultures, as also for the ancient Hebrews and
Greeks, we cannot hope really to bring to life even in imagination the
ancient tale-teller and his circle of listeners, but we can as a sort of
archeological investigation ascertain that certain well-known folktales
were in the repertory of all tellers in the Near East during certain
parts of antiquity and we can make lists of some hundreds of motifs
that characterize these tales. But there will always remain certain very
difficult and perhaps unsolvable problems.

Signs of a coexistence between an unrecorded spoken tradition of
story-telling and the narrative products of the great literatures are
everywhere apparent. In the *Mahabharata,* the *Panchatantra,* and the
Jātaka, and the *Sukasaptati* of India ; in the *Thousand and One Nights,*
the *Seven Sages,* the *Iliad* and the *Odyssey,* the Greek dramas and
mythological writings, the Icelandic sagas, *Beowulf,* the Irish epic
cycle, the chivalric romances, the thousands of medieval exempla, the
jest books and fabliaux, not to speak of many other works down
almost to our own day—in all of these the scholar who knows his oral
folktales will find much that is familiar to him. In many of these the
use of the traditional motifs seems almost incidental to the principal
literary work. Such, for example, is the story of Polyphemus in the
Odyssey, and in general the epics and romances.

Certain of these literary forms, however, challenge comparison with
the work of the oral story-teller, for they consist of collections of tales
a great number of which have been collected from unlettered narrators. How much change has occurred in the *Thousand and One Nights,*
for example, between the stories heard in the bazaars of the Near East
and the literary texts as we now have them, must always remain a
problem. And the anecdotes told by medieval priests and handed down
by such writers as Jacques de Vitry or Johannes Pauli or in the novelle
of Boccaccio and his fellows or the ribald jestbook of Poggio—how
many of these were already current in the unlettered world before they
were adapted to the readers of manuscripts or the printed page? The
problem is not simple, because there has undoubtedly been a give and
take between these two traditions. A story like Cupid and Psyche can
be current in the ancient Near East or Greece and then retold by an

author like Apuleius in the second century of our era and later heard in some way by an unlettered story-teller and carried into his repertory of tales.

Of these oral folktales up until two hundred years ago we know nothing except by inference. The problem of their study is historical and geographical. Aside from the literary documents themselves we have now vast collections of tales taken down from story-tellers that permit us to learn much, but not everything, about their relation to written literature.

The collecting of all these oral tales has been a stupendous task and the methods of their collecting have changed remarkably in three centuries. When Basile in the 1630's retold forty-eight of the Italian folktales, he used a baroque style which was a part of the current literary tradition but had no resemblance to the form in which the tales must have been then current in Italy. What influence, if any, his bizarre retellings had on the story-tellers of the next centuries is a folklore problem that can only be solved by comparative historical study. A parallel case is that of Charles Perrault, who at the end of the seventeenth century retold some of the favorite European tales in the form which we still tell or read to our children. The whole general idea of collecting stories as they were actually told hardly dates before the time of the Brothers Grimm, and our modern folklorists realize that although accuracy of collecting was a theoretical ideal of these great folklorists, the tales as we now have them show us only their substance but probably not their form and style.

For the last century and a half the activity of folktale collectors has been prodigious, so that very few places in the world remain unrepresented in our great libraries and archives. From the modern point of view much of this early collection was very faulty. It was done by amateurs of all kinds. In Europe such work was often an avocation of a teacher or lawyer or perhaps a country priest, and it is remarkable that some of these collections are as good as they are. Missionaries and colonial officers published scores of collections made in Africa or Oceania, in the outlying parts of Asia, and among the natives of North and South America. The modern folklorist must discount a good deal as he reads these tales and compares them to more accurate present-day reports, for they are filled with prettifications and elaborations characteristic of the period of literature in which they were recorded and are often reflective of the religious or social ideas of the collector. But as we approach our own time with its trained folklorists and their ideal of complete accuracy, the body of material becomes increasingly worthy of study.

This notable activity in the collecting of folktales has occurred at the very time when many branches of humanistic and literary scholarship were making great advances. It is natural that those interested in linguistics, in the history of religion and of literature as well as of political and social history should approach these tales from a comparative and historical point of view, and until rather recently the principal work of folktale scholars has been the attempt to learn as much as possible about the origin and the life-history of individual folktales; and the study of the tale-teller and his audience, so important to the collector in the field, was left pretty much to our own generation.

Since the traditional oral tale was not collected until within the last two centuries, the only way that we can learn anything of the tale-telling tradition in Europe and Asia before that time is by a historic inference based upon the collections at our disposal. The first scholars to interest themselves in this problem were impressed with the relative stability of individual stories, and they recognized surprising parallels and analogues extending over huge distances of space and time. This is not the place to go into a discussion of some of these early theories, the relation of the tales to ancient myths, the possible explanation of the tales as relics of an Indo-European past, the possibility of a great common source of folktales such as India, or the tales as survivals from a distant past parallel to the present-day unlettered tribes in distant continents. By about 1890 it was pretty well agreed that though there were indeed parallels which could be explained by independent origin, most folktales show definite areas of distribution suggestive of a dissemination from some center.

For the study of these tales as historic phenomena, real progress began before the end of the nineteenth century. Somewhat earlier, there had appeared valuable annotations showing interesting comparisons among the tales of the various countries of Europe and Asia, but this was all rather unsystematic. If large comparative studies were to be undertaken, it was necessary to make available not only the contents of the great national libraries but also of the numerous folklore archives already in existence. This called, first of all, for a checklist of the folktales to be considered; and such a list, based primarily on the Finnish archives, was produced in 1910. This formed the basis for a good deal of indexing, which brought increasingly before the scholar the folktales, at first of Europe, and eventually of many parts of the world. The making of such an index is, it will be agreed, an extremely difficult task, because as much as one may enlarge such an index and include the tales of a larger and larger circle of cultures, he is likely to give a false impression of the content and distribution of particular stories. This can probably not be avoided, but the great archives of folktales in various parts of the world have, nevertheless, found this index practicable for the identification of individual stories in their collections.

Such an index of complete tales in actual circulation within a great culture area like that from Ireland to India has suggested to some scholars the desirability of extending this index to all parts of the world. But except for European and Asiatic tales which have wandered to other continents along with the emigrants, different indexes are necessary for each great tradition area. And we do not yet know just what these tradition areas are. We recognize widespread incidents and ideas, and perhaps the most we can do until our comparative studies become more accurate than they are now is to make a kind of dictionary of traditional motifs extended to all parts of the world. Though such a dictionary has in fact proved valuable in suggesting comparative studies, there is no more reason to suppose that items adjacent to each other in this index have genetic relations with each other than there is in words lying next to each other in the pages of a dictionary. Further collecting and possibly further arranging of materials, through the help of this motif-index or otherwise, will make possible the preparation of special type-indexes for such areas as the North American Indians, several parts of Africa, Oceania, and the like. Whether this may look forward to a combined type-index, as has been suggested, only the future can tell. It will not be easy to make.

With all the work on indexes it has become much easier in recent years to bring together the hundreds of versions of a folktale necessary for historic and geographic study. A focus of such investigations is on an individual tale considered as an entity and its goal is to trace the life history of particular tales. Most of the historical studies of the last seventy years have consisted of the assembling of large numbers of versions, of their analysis, and of attempts through such analysis to learn what has happened to the tale. Many modifications of this system have been suggested and some of them carried out successfully. With the passage of time some mistakes of the early practitioners have been eliminated. It is generally recognized that intensive collections in one area and sparse collections in another invalidate a crude statistical handling of variants, and that even if all proper allowance is made for these inequalities, the so-called archetype arrived at by such studies remains a theoretical construct.

As such, it is valuable as a point of departure and a point of reference in the comparative treatment of the various forms of the tale. It can indicate with some plausibility the general area and time of the beginning of the particular tradition, but it can by no means posit exactly the form of the tale as it was first told. Recent students have a tendency to accept the suggestions made by the critics of the historic-geographic method, and they have undoubtedly improved their techniques by a new acknowledgment of the validity of many of the ideas put forward by the late Dr. Von Sydow, especially concerning *oikotypes* and the nature of tradition-bearers. But generally speaking there is a feeling that he went too far in his opposition to the gradual spread of a folktale. His study of local subtypes covering certain areas and complicating the picture at the edge of these areas has come to be a part of the investigation, which eventually attempts to reach a larger synthesis involving the complete tradition.

Though this general method of investigating individual folktales has resulted in the production of a large number of very competent monographs, there still remains ample material for the investigation of many of the best-known folktales in the world. Perhaps some day it will be possible to learn a great deal more than is now known about the interrelation of the oral tale and its corresponding literary telling. Whether a better knowledge of the stories told in present-day India or Egypt or Mesopotamia will prove to be of value in the study of the ancient literatures is an intriguing problem which has hardly been touched by the comparative folklorist. The historic-geographic method has been largely confined to tales of considerable complication, but how can it be adapted to the investigation of an anecdote consisting of a single motif or of a cumulative tale? It is recognized that several well-known episodes which could be analyzed into five or six motifs appear as a part of a number of well-known European and Asiatic tales. Can such motifs, as for example the Obstacle Flight, which occurs all over the world, be approached in the same manner as a study of Cinderella? How have such clusters of motifs as this or the Swan-Maiden story found their way into so many apparently unconnected cultures?

Up to this point this discussion has been concerned with the comparative and historical investigation of the fictional folktale. On such studies depends any knowledge that we may have of the story-telling activity that may have been contemporary with and influential on our great collections of literary tales and epics. They are a valuable part of the history of human civilization, but they cannot bring to life the generations of tale-tellers nor give us a picture of their audiences. They cannot give us the documents desired by the historian. Their work is more analogous to that of the archeologist and the inferential pre-history which he constructs. And this historic approach to the understanding of the folktales of the world is only one of many on which a lengthier discussion might well elaborate.

The collectors of folktales, especially those who confine themselves to a definite area, are always impressed with the special qualities of the material they work with. From these we have received in recent years some very interesting discussions based upon their intimate knowledge of their area. The conditions of folktale telling in such places as Hungary or Ireland or Siberia, where this seems to be still a living art, have been very adequately described by such authors as Azadovski, Dégh, and O'Duilearga. But these works are only the best-known of a large number of such studies covering various parts of the world. The biographies and character sketches of the tale-tellers and the descriptions of the relation of these tale-tellers to their audience and the function of these tales in their respective societies have been the subject of much attention from folklorists and anthropologists in all parts of the world. We are made aware of the difference between such functions in various cultures. Frequently the approach of such studies is analogous to that of our student of literary history or of literary biography. Sometimes the accounts handle the folktale as a purely social phenomenon and sometimes the interest is in the tale-teller and his relation to the story that he tells. Sometimes the emphasis seems to be primarily upon such questions as why people like to listen to folktales or what are the qualities which go to make the successful tale-teller. It may well be expected that with the activity of anthropologists in all parts of the world, not to speak of folklorists themselves, we may learn a great deal more in the future about many things that concern the student of the oral, fictional tale.

One of the first questions that faced the student of folktales in the nineteenth century was whether folktales had any meaning aside from the obvious tale they were telling. To some of these earlier scholars the tales seemed to be broken-down myths, and their attempt to show the relation of the folktale to what they conceived to be the early forms of myths resulted in some very startling conclusions. But the search for some covert meaning to folktales has not ceased. Sometimes it takes a form that only the disciples of Freud or Jung can accept, but there are other approaches also. Some scholars feel that only a very long and intimate association with a tale-teller and his group will permit us to know just what is behind the seemingly simple story he is telling. These attempts to tell us what the story-teller means are frequently very interesting and undoubtedly many more of them will be made in the future. But the interpretations always run the risk of being purely subjective on the part of the scholar and are often made in a complete vacuum, disregarding all relationships with other peoples in the world and with stories which they share with such peoples. But even so, we need to have a number of studies based upon a thorough knowledge of a particular group.

Not only the students of culture, of psychology, and of history have been busy with the folktale, but also those corresponding in many ways to our literary critics. These have been interested in the formal side of the fictional narrative and have developed structural studies. Just where these will lead is hard to say. Will they merely end in a statement that the folktales of a certain area have a tendency to assume certain forms? Though such a conclusion would not be very meaningful, there is little doubt that these structural studies offer a great deal of material for work in the future. But they must be more definitely focused, so that other scholars can know just what problems are being faced and just how these problems are being solved. They must give more attention to the various genres of folktales and let us know whether their analysis is confined to a particular region or is characteristic of all folktales by their very nature.

Nothing has been said here about the study of myths or of traditions or legends which are subjects of beliefs, nor of ballads, nor epics. The traditional oral folktale furnishes more than enough labor for the scholars of this and coming generations.

From the *Buch der Weisheit* (Ulm, 1483)

ARCHER TAYLOR

The Anecdote: A Neglected Genre

Even the hastiest review, incomplete as it may be, of the genres of the folktale brings to one's attention more than one genre that tempts one to linger. Handbooks of the folktale, whether English, French, or German, differ greatly among themselves, but none, so far as I am aware, names even briefly the genres. They deal primarily with the märchen, cursorily with the Sage, more cursorily with the jest, the saint's legend, and the cumulative tale. They limit themselves to western European narrative and take it for granted that the genres of tales are the same the world over. So risky an assumption may be rejected with very little ado. A generation ago C. W. von Sydow, who was an original thinker about such matters, identified various genres, described them very briefly, and seemed to imply that his definitions had a general validity. Had he cited half a dozen examples of each genre, our thinking about such subjects would be more securely based than it now is. Except for what he has written I can cite no general account of the genres of the folktale.

In any review of these genres the anecdote is ordinarily neglected, but anecdotes are as numerous as the sands of the sea and as easy to find. In compiling *Alverdens anekdoter,*[1] an excellent modern international anthology on which I base my remarks, Henning Fonsmark read fifty thousand texts from which he chose one thousand to reprint in the first volume. In addition, he read perhaps ten thousand more in manuscript collected by and for him from tradition of some sort or other (a definition of his sources is not altogether clear and will shock a folklorist of the strict observance).

An anecdote is a brief narrative current in oral tradition that tells something unusual about a person, an event, or a thing. It may involve quotation of a witty remark or description of a remarkable situation.

There are few collections of anecdotes for the purpose of folklore study. There have been few, if any, studies of the rhetorical form of anecdotes, but one can say, subject to correction, that an anecdote has no introductory or concluding formula (there may be a reference to the circumstances in which the narrator heard the anecdote, but this does not appear to have formulistic quality). It does not appear to be defined by any particular kind of subject matter. "Anecdotes are no one's property. They are common stock. They are an aspect of folklore." [2] I leave the task of a more elaborate definition to another occasion or another hand.

It will be easier to discuss anecdotes if we have some samples before us:

(1) A lady asked the dramatist Sheridan to accompany her on a walk. He excused himself, saying that the weather was bad. She took a walk alone and on her return met Sheridan who also was walking alone. "Well, Mr. Sheridan," she burst out, "the weather seems to have cleared up." "Yes," said he, "only a little, madame, enough for one, but not enough for two."

(2) In *Born in Captivity* [3] Iris Murdoch seems to be quoting from a dictionary of anecdotes arranged alphabetically according to subjects when she writes:

> Most of them [great writers] had shown an uncanny skill in the business of providing material for quotable anecdotes. Pope had been expelled from his first school for writing a satire on the master; Southey for declaring himself opposed to corporal punishment; Tennyson lived in thousands of hearts as the wild-eyed boy crouching in a deserted quarry and staring, long and incredulously, at the stone on which he had scratched the words *Byron is dead*.

This example is interesting for showing how anecdotes are remembered and transmitted. We have no field collections of them, but from this example it appears that anecdotes, like some other forms of folklore, may be transmitted in an abbreviated version.

It is convenient to deal briefly with the collection and study of anecdotes before discussing them as oral tradition. There does not appear to be any treatise on the anecdote and we are limited to articles in encyclopedias and prefaces to collections (a bibliography of collections should indicate what prefaces are important). After reading the pertinent article in several encyclopedias the impression grows that the authors are rehashing the opinions of their predecessors and show more novelty in bibliographical references than they do in ideas. I can cite no bibliography, national or international, of the many anthologies that exist. The task of making a bibliography will not be rewarding unless the compiler includes critical comments. The task is not difficult, for hundreds of titles can be assembled by bringing together those listed in the subject-indexes of large libraries. Henning Fonsmark calls attention to a noteworthy collection in the Hovedbibliotek, Frederiksberg, Denmark, and a remarkable private collection in the library of Gustav S. Bengtsson.[4] A student with bibliographical inclinations will do well to examine these Danish collections or, if he does not care to go so far afield, the collections in the Library of Congress, the New York Public Library, and a very good smaller collection in the library of the University of California at Los Angeles (see the published catalogue). The titles listed in the four volumes of the *Subject-Index of the London Library* offer many suggestions that can be developed without visiting that institution. The list entitled "Anecdotes and Ana" includes, for example, Aelian's second-century *Varia Historia* and thus indicates the scope that a study of the anecdote might have. Fonsmark's short list of books consulted [5] and his instructive comments on them [6] and on the differences among German, French, English, and American collections as well as characterizations of some Danish collections published since 1940 contain a surprising amount of information in few words. He says, for example, that American collections are marked by brevity (of the anecdotes) and ready wit, are practical and unpretentious, and are usually arranged according to subjects: "Amour, Angry, Army. . . ." The correctness of his remarks is to be examined, but he does cite in his bibliography the works that support his reference to the humorous quality of American anthologies of anecdotes.[7] A growth of interest in anecdotes in the 1940's is apparent in countries other than the United States.

The study of anecdotes has not gone very far. The previously cited *Thesaurus* gives a more diversified picture of American anecdotes than I have given and makes some useful remarks on the subject of classification. Daniel George, *A Book of Anecdotes*,[8] an English collection illustrating varieties of experience in the lives of the illustrious and the obscure with excellent introductory comment (pp. v–xii), is a good book with which to start. George reports, for example, his inquiries into the versions of Columbus and the egg, King Alfred and the cakes, Sir Isaac Newton and the apple, and the little Dutch boy who saved the town of Haarlem by keeping his finger in a hole in the dyke—he never existed (p. vii). But there are few investigations of the genre, the collections, or individual anecdotes.[9]

In order to characterize the anecdote more adequately I shall make some comparisons with other traditional narrative genres. The comparisons also include brief mention of investigations in very general terms. Anecdote and märchen have very little in common in either form or matter. The märchen is ordinarily polyepisodic and employs many conventional devices in form: introductory and concluding formulas, a biographical pattern, repetition of acts and scenes. It also exhibits conventions in subject-matter: kings, queens, and suitors; contrasted actors like the good and the bad girl or the hero and the villain. There is nothing in all this in common with the anecdote consisting of a single scene and a single actor, who may be chosen from any level of society, and employing no rhetorical formulas. The scholarly study of märchen suggests little that is helpful in the study of anecdotes. It has dealt with the history and dissemination of individual märchen and groups of märchen and with classifications of one sort and another. These are not directions in which the study of anecdotes is likely to progress.

The comparison of Sage (legend) and anecdote is more fruitful because the Sage is a traditional genre very closely akin to the anecdote. Both are narratives telling a single incident; both are realistic and purport to tell what actually happened; both lack characteristic rhetorical formulas. The Sage is likely to include allusions to the source of the tale; the anecdote does not. The Sage may involve elements intended to emphasize its foundation in fact; the anecdote does not. Sage may be divided into narratives concerned with figures and events in a world different from the everyday world (stories of dwarfs, giants, ghosts, and the like) and narratives of historical or pseudo-historical quality (stories of Alexander the Great, Napoleon, Nasreddin Hoja, Till Eulenspiegel, or Paul Bunyan). The anecdote resembles only the latter category. Sage embraces a category of narratives that are found in various countries and at various times and have been called "migratory legends."[10] As Fonsmark points out[11] there are "migratory anecdotes" like the incident of the Marines at Belleau Wood who were inspired to attack by their leader's cry. Fonsmark does not cite this example. We are very close here to the familiar quotation or *Geflügeltes Wort*. J. P. Marquand remembers the words as " 'Come on, boys,' the sergeant says, 'Do you want to live forever?'" A standard dictionary of quotations reminds us that Carlyle rejected as "pure myth" the story that Frederick the Great uttered almost the same words at Kolin on June 18, 1757. Do we have here Sage, anecdote, familiar quotation, or what C. W. von Sydow calls Memorat?

Both Sage and anecdote involve the human quality of the incident and its significance. In comparison with the vast store of Sagen accumulated in archives investigations have been relatively few. Methods and especially classification are in developmental stages and problems are not as clearly seen as one would like. We need only mention mythical Sagen here because such Sagen and the study of them has little in common with the study of anecdotes. The historical or pseudo-historical legends are not easily differentiated from anecdotes. Is the story of George Washington and the cherry tree Sage or anecdote? Here discussion has been chiefly in the hands of students of history and has dealt with the reliability of these tales as evidence.

Much of what has just been said is true with a little adaptation to a comparison of jest and anecdote. Both are narrative episodes, both direct the hearer's attention to a unique incident (but there are migratory jests just as there are migratory legends and migratory anecdotes), both are likely to give point to the incident by a quotation, both are likely to appear in cycles associated with a famous name and personality. And except for the publication of jests in collections that are often embellished with excellent notes, jests have been rather little studied. The use of one or another jest found in some famous piece of literature has been traced carefully. It is perhaps impossible to separate satisfactorily anecdote and jest. In his very shrewd essay on the Sage, Max Lüthi says, "Like almost every genre Sage can slip into the jest. The almost unbearable tension inherent in it can unburden itself in wit; fantasy often makes mock of the figures of Sage." [12] This calls for further study. As I have said, editions and bibliographies of jests are excellent in quality and are well annotated, but there is much more than this to do.

Comparisons of this sort might be made with other genres of oral tradition, but enough has probably been said to show characteristic features of the anecdote and to emphasize its quality as a genre of oral tradition.

The anecdote has a peculiar position among the genres of folk narrative. It is anonymous and at the same time it is so sophisticated in its expression that we think at once of an author. But tellers of anecdotes are not pointed out for their creative ability. We cannot insist on the authenticity of a text of an anecdote. Study of Near Eastern traditions in which literary elaboration and tradition are inextricably interwoven may help us to understand this situation.

The anecdote is narrative folk tradition of its own special kind. The problems that it presents to the student are varied in the extreme. Even its definition has yet to be written and put to use. Investigation of the anecdote has not gone far. The historian uses the anecdote in his studies or at least he debates whether he dares to use it, but his results are not a contribution to folklore studies. The psychologist investigates fundamental ways of human thinking as exemplified by an anecdote or body of anecdotes and obtains results that are useful to his own discipline. They are only incidentally useful to a folklorist. Few, if any, have endeavored to discover rhetorical form in anecdotes. Such a task would occur to a critic and student of literary history, but the anecdote is a relatively minor literary genre and has attracted few to study it. Someone clearly aware of the nature of folklore can use what other disciplines can contribute to the study of the anecdote in a truly folkloristic manner.

W. EDSON RICHMOND

Paris og Helen i Trejeborg: A Reduction to Essentials

As the raven flies, the distance from Ilium to the site of Trøijborg in Jutland is so great that anyone making the journey in the late Middle Ages would necessarily be a different person when he reached its end. By long ship the distance is even greater, and though the journey was often made during Viking times, so changed were the travelers that often they returned home as strangers, hardly recognizable even to their own families. In subsequent centuries the way was forgotten altogether. It is little wonder, then, that Helen, Paris, and Menelaus, foreigners, traveling as they did by word of mouth, by manuscript, and by cheap broadsides and pamphlets—some of which foundered under them—suffered tremendous sea-change by the time they arrived in Scandinavia and made their appearance in a popular ballad. Indeed, of our ballad heroine we may well seriously ask:

> Was *this* the face that launch'd a thousand ships
> And burnt the topless towers of Ilium?

The answer, of course, is no—at least a qualified no. Like the Helen of Greek epic, our ballad heroine is beautiful and the immediate cause of the destruction of Troy, but she is otherwise undistinguishable from the myriad little Ellens seduced from their fathers' *gårds* by wandering knights and wayfaring strangers in ballad after ballad. The tragedy of her story is not the fall of princes but solely that she loved unwisely. The significant destruction is not that of the city but of the lovers.

It is not at all strange, of course, that the vain and haughty Helen

of the *Iliad* or the romantic Helen of the *Odyssey* became a different
person in the northern ballads. The strange thing is that she reached
them at all. Few are her companions, for in all the ballads of Scandinavia, England, and Scotland there are only three other songs devoted
to classical subjects. In Scandinavia one finds *De to kongebørn* with
its retelling of the story of Hero and Leander and *Jeg ved så rig en
Riddar* which derives from the classical tale of Pyramus and Thisbe,
and in the English language one finds only *King Orfeo*. Thisbe, Hero,
Eurydice, and Helen—by no means such strange bedfellows as they
might appear at first glance, for each was transported by love, literally
as well as figuratively, and this is surely what endeared them to the
composers and singers of ballads.

There is, moreover, no doubt that the Dron[n]ing (Queen) Elen
(or Hél[l]ena as she is called in the texts closest to oral tradition) of
the Scandinavian ballad *Paris og Helen i Trejeborg* is a lineal descend-
ant of Helen of Troy, no matter how mixed her bloodlines, and it is
she and her story with which we are here concerned; the northern
metamorphoses of Thisbe, Hero, and Eurydice belong to a broader
study which must be approached at another time.

A number of texts, perhaps as many as twenty (though exact num-
bering is difficult because of interrelationships and inexact editing), of
Paris og Helen i Trejeborg have been found throughout the Scandinavian linguistic area, but only the three Norwegian texts and one
Danish, a variant collected by Evald Tang Kristensen from one Ane
Jensdotter in Rinde in 1871, are indubitably from oral tradition.[1] The
balance of the texts—Danish, Swedish, and Faroese (the ballad is not
found in Iceland)—are either in manuscript ballad collections (Vise-
bøker) or in the form of "skyllingtrick" (the Scandinavian pamphlet
equivalent of English broadsides). Moreover, with the exception of
one Swedish text published by Arwidsson in 1837,[2] all are closely related and stem undoubtedly from a broadside original, though it is
doubtful whether the earliest form we now know, a broadside labeled
*En Lystig oc skjøn Vise, Huorledis Paris bortførde Helena. Oc huor-
ledis Trøyeborrig bleff vunden* which was printed in Copenhagen in
1581 by Matz Vingaard,[3] is the immediate source for any oral text
despite the fact that it was reprinted with minor variations in 1695,
1706, 1709, 1710, 1711, 1723, 1731, and once without date in Denmark and in nine closely related broadsides in Sweden, one undated
and the rest being printed in 1699, 1772, 1784, 1799, 1802, 1835, and

1844. It is interesting to note, however, that very few Scandinavian ballads appeared in print any earlier than this and that it enjoyed tremendous popularity on the printed page, the initial stanzas of it being introduced into J. Messenius' play *Disa* in 1611 and in N. H. Catonius' drama *Troijenborgh* in 1632,[4] even though evidence for its popularity in oral tradition is slight.

No one can say, of course, why a particular ballad seizes the fancy of the folk and achieves wide oral circulation while another has but a short life in a limited area or is restricted almost entirely to the printed page and never achieves the stature of a truly popular ballad. Certainly artistic excellence in the conventional sense of the phrase has little to do with ballad survival; equally certainly, fitting a conventional narrative pattern does affect survival potential, and to a very great degree the broadside versions of *Paris og Helen i Trejeborg* fit into the pattern of the *burtstolne jomfrue;* indeed, the original Troy story is reduced to this essential but with the addition of another and thoroughly foreign theme so closely and effectively knit to the narrative of the seduction of Helen that it is reminiscent of the artistry inherent in *Sir Gawain and the Green Knight* and Chaucer's Miller's Tale.

The story as it is seen in the longest version from oral tradition, the text collected in 1857 by Sophus Bugge from one Torbjørg Haugen in Skafså, Telemark, a woman who contributed over fifty ballads to Bugge's collection, is remarkably close to the broadside texts, yet shows some signs of variation which appear to result from oral transmission.

The ballad begins with a three-stanza commonplace introduction in which it is pointed out that King Nilaus was a very rich man but Paris was even richer, so rich that he controlled seven kingdoms and served as Nilaus' chamberlain:

1. Kung Nilaus va' så rig en Mand,
   å Paris va' endå rikar hell han.

2. Paris va så rig en Mand
   vel syv Kongeriger så åtte han.

3. Paris va så rig en Svend
   han tjente Kong Nilaus ved sin Seng.

This is followed immediately by three more stanzas which set the scene: King Nilaus is to go on a journey and asks Paris to guard his land until he returns and most especially to guard Queen Elen's bed, to which Paris replies that he will watch over all as if the king were home:

> 4. Kung Nilaus skulde i Ledningen fare,
>   Paris skulde tage Landet i Vare.

> 5. "Du vokter mine Lande til jeg kommer hjem
>   og vokter mest før Droning Elens Seng."

> 6. "Jeg skal vokte dine Riger og Land
>   som du var selv hjemn.ᵃ du kungelig Mand."

The action proper then begins. Paris goes immediately to the smithy and happily makes a harp of silver with gold strings. On this he plays continuously while Elen listens:

> 7. Paris han gjeng at Smiggja,
>   han lader Gullharpan smida.

> 8. Harpen av Sylv og Strenger av Guld,
>   så legde den Herre så frydefuld.

> 9. Han legde i Dage, han legde it två,
>   alt sad Droning Elen og lydde derpå.

So impressed is Elen with the music that she finally asks Paris whether he is an angel or Christ himself come from heaven. Paris insists that he is no angel, and Helen reveals her wish that her husband were half so beautiful. For this Paris rebukes her, saying that a page must not be compared with his master:

> 10. "Enten er dú Paris Engel lig,
>   eller er du selv Kristus av Himmerig?"

> 11. "Ikke er jeg Paris nogen Engel lig,
>   ei heller Kristus av Himerig."

> 12. Det meldte Droning Elen ved sit sind,
>   "Krist give min Herre var halv så ven."

> 13. "Hør du Droning Elen du tal ikke sligt,
>   en Svend må ei være sin Herre lig."

Despite his expression of humility, however, Paris asks Elen if she will follow him out of the land, and she replies that she would do so most gladly were it not that she feared her husband:

> 14. "Hør dú Droning Elen hott eg spyre deg:
>   lyster du fýggje av Lande mæ meg?"

> 15. "Så gjerne som jeg det gjorde,
>   når jeg for min Herren det torde."

Paris quiets her fears by pointing out that Trøiborg is so strong a land that no man can conquer it, that Trøiborg has nine walls so that no man can get within:

> 16. "I Trøiborg der er så fast et Land,
>   der vindes ei over af nogen Mand.

> 17. "I Trøiborg der er dei murane ni,
>   at ingen i Væri hann vinne di."

With this they dig a tunnel from the castle to the strand and Elen dresses in the clothes of one of her maidens in which to flee from the land with Paris:

> 18. Dei grove dæn Løyndegång med sin Hand
>   ifrå Slotte ti Stråndi fram.

> ◄ 19. Droning Elen hun lader sig Jomfruklæder skjære
>   så vil hun af Landet med Paris stræve.

The scene then shifts to the beach itself where the lovers find that King Nilaus is unfortunately just coming to land:

> 20. Men der de kom seg til Strande
>   da lå Kong Nilaus for Lande.

The second principal action begins with the king asking his dear friend Paris whence came the fine maiden who accompanies him. "Never," says Nilaus, "have I seen so attractive a maiden so like unto my dear Queen." Paris replies that it is one of Queen Elen's serving maids. The king then asks Paris to wait where he is while he visits the queen in her bower. Nilaus rides off, but Elen runs through the tunnel and reaches her bower before him:

21. "Hører du Paris kjær Frænde min
    hvor haver du fåt den Jomfru så fin?

22. "Aldrig så jeg nogen Jomfru så deilig
    som var min kjære Droning så lig."

23. "Hør du Kong Nilaus Herren min,
    det er Droning Elens Tjenestekvinde."

24. "Paris, Paris du holder herude
    mens jeg taler med min Dronning i Bure."

25. Kungen rei å Droningji unde Jori rann,
    endå kom ho ti Buri før han.

When the king arrives, Elen proudly awaits him. Nilaus asks Elen the same question he has already put to Paris: whence came the beautiful maiden who will travel back to Troy with Paris? Elen, somewhat ambiguously, replies that the girl was the only payment Paris would accept for his long service; whereupon the king says that he must say farewell to his friend and rides off. Elen again runs through the tunnel and again reaches her goal ahead of the king. Economically no mention is made of the embarkation, but in stanza 32 Paris lifts his high hat, wishing the king a thousand goodnights:

26. Dær han kom sig til Buri
    da sad Droning Elen så prude.

27. "Hør I min Droning faver å fin
    hvor fik Paris den Jomfru så fin?"

28. "Han vilde ei andet have for lange Tjenesten sin,
    jeg gav hannem Tjenestekvinden min."

29. "Hør I min Droning faver å fin,
    nu vil jeg tage Afsked med Frænden min."

30. Kungen rei å Droningji unde Jori rann,
    endå kom ho ti Stråndi fyrr han.

31. Der han kom sig til Strande,
    da stod Droning Elen på Sande.

32. Paris han lyfte på høian Hatt:
    "Farvel Kong Nilaus hav tusind godnatt."

Upon returning to the palace, the king, of course, finds that Elen is gone, and though they search both without and within, she cannot be found. Realization comes to the king at last and he blindly strikes out —and so ends the second act:

33. Der han kom sig til Buri
    burte var Droning Elen så prude.

34. De ledte ude og de ledte inde,
    ikke kunde de Droningen finde.

35. Kongen han slog sin hvide Hand
    "nu er min Droning med Paris af Land."

Though most broadside versions devote a couple of stanzas to Nilaus' successful attempts to raise an army, this element is entirely lacking in our text, and the third act proceeds directly to the end of the siege. An old man who is called King Sakæus appears and says that Nilaus must be a fool to have been repulsed so long, that if he had been there for nine months, Trøiborg would have been his. They then make a copper horse which can carry a hundred knights:

36. Så kom der fram en gamalle Mann
    Sakæus Kungje så kallar dei han.

37. "Hvilke Dosmere mone I være
    når I haver ligget så længe her.

38. "Havde jeg ligget here månerne ni
    så ha' Trøiborg silt vori mi."

39. Så lod de en Koberhest gjøre
    hundrede Ryttere deri føre.

40. Så lode de Skruer i Benene slå
    som Hesten skulde have at stå på.

The climactic fourth act introduces a Helen who is a product of the ballad muse. Paris advises leaving the horse outside the gates, but Elen suggests that it be brought inside. Her advice is followed. The horse begins to snort and spurt fire, then to neigh and to burst the walls asunder. Seeing that all is lost, Paris asks Elen whether she will go back to being Nilaus' wife or along with Paris take her life. She replies that she will be neither Nilaus' maid nor wife, that she will die with Paris, adding that they will open their veins, for there is no easier way to die:

> 41. Ti svåra Paris: "Det er mit Raad,
>   I lader den Hesten for Porterne stå."

> 42. Ti svåra Elen: "Det er mit Sind
>   I lader den Hesten for Porterne ind."

> 43. Hesten for te å grude,
>   så glóandes Ellen sprude.

> 44. Hesten for te å kneggje,
>   dæ rivnar i Murar å Veggjir.

> 45. "Kvori vi' du vera Kung Nilaus Møy
>   hell du vi' hæra mæ Paris døy?

> 46. "Kvori vi' du vera Kung Nilaus Viv,
>   hell dú vi' mæ Paris lata ditt Liv?"

> 47. "Eg vi inkje vera Kung Nilaus Møy,
>   men eg vi helle mæ Paris døy.

> 48. "Nu ville vi lata 'kon Åre slå,
>   lettare Dø kan me alli få."

And the ballad ends with two stanzas which say that it was King Nilaus' greatest vexation that Queen Elen lay dead in Paris' arms, that it was his greatest sorrow that Elen lay dead at Paris' side:

> 49. Det var Kong Nilaus største Harm,
>   Droning Elen lå dø på Paris Arm.

> 50. Det var Kong Nilaus største Kvide,
>   Droning Elen lå dø mæ Paris Side.

The reduction of the Troy story here to a ballad of tragic love is underlined by a refrain which, following his economical custom and the pattern set by early ballad editors, Sophus Bugge wrote in his field notebook only after the first stanza: *Vel upp rósen, um I lyster Paris fýgje.* The first three words are obscure, and, as will become apparent later, they confused singers, but a reasonable translation might well be "Wall up the rose, if you will follow Paris," perhaps intended as an injunction with *fýgje* to be interpreted as "accompany" rather than simply as "follow." It should also be pointed out to the unwary that the word *Ellen* in line two of stanza 43 is not the name of the queen but the definite form of *Eld,* "fire," the spelling of which reflects the strong Danish influence upon the text, an influence which appears in many other words as well.

It is also evident that we have here the linking of two very popular medieval narratives, the Troy story enfolding and being given life by the narrative of a husband deceived and his wife stolen by means of a secret passageway. The earliest known text of our ballad, that of Karen Brahe's folio manuscript, printed in *Danmarks gamle Folkeviser* as number 467Aa, dates from around the year 1550, and as Axel Olrik points out in his notes, it is probably not much older than this.[5] In terms of the Troy legend, this is significant, for though there are literary treatments of the tale in the Scandinavian languages, there is no evidence to show that any of these were circulated widely or even known to anyone except their authors and owners. The Icelandic *Trójumanna saga,* which most certainly built upon a memory of Dares Phrygius' *De excidio Trojae,* with additions from Virgil, Ovid, and Pindar, might seem a possible source, for it certainly enjoyed some popularity and it was written down in the thirteenth century—but it is interesting to note that there are no Icelandic ballads on the subject (though sagas often gave birth to ballads) and that in *Paris og Helen i Trejeborg* there are no signs of Icelandic linguistic influence. Other fugitive materials exist as well. According to the late Professor Knut Liestøl, Bishop Arne of Bergen had in his library at the beginning of the fourteenth century an item listed as *versus de excidio Troie* and another called *truiia saga ok brutus,* but beyond speculation, we know nothing more about these.[6] In 1529 a Swedish translation was made of Guido delle Colonne's *Historia destructionis Trojae,* but it was not printed until the nineteenth century, though it is otherwise perhaps contemporary with the ballad. Almost a century later, in 1623, the Danish poet and priest Christoffer Sivendsøn Glimager translated

Medieval Literature and Folklore Studies

Guido again under the title *Bellum Trojanum, historiske Beskrivelse om den trojanske Krig.* This, however, is younger than our ballad. Thus, though we must certainly conclude that *Paris og Helen i Trejeborg* owes something to the medieval tradition growing from Dares Phrygius, we must also conclude that no immediate connection can be shown to any one piece we now know. The story was in the air.

Equally ubiquitous was the story of the woman who deceived her husband into thinking she was someone else by rushing from one place to another by way of a secret passage. This motif, listed in Thompson's *Motif-Index of Folk Literature* as K1523 is very old indeed, and it appears in the north in a "folkebok" entitled *De syv vise Mestre* as early as 1577. This is a version of the *Inclusa* and it can be traced back through the fourteenth century Latin *Historia septem sapientum* to a French verse text of the twelfth century. In the Scandinavian version, the tale entitled "Keiserindens det syvende eventyr" is remarkably close to this portion of *Paris og Helen i Trejeborg,* and as an examination of the other references in Thompson shows, the motif is common to tales from all over Europe and parts of Asia. But none of these particular tales is knit to the Troy story. Shortly before his death, however, Knut Liestøl ran across references to a medieval Bulgarian manuscript which appeared in large part to be a translation from Greek. Here he found a narrative which, though it contained many themes not found in the ballad and though it employed different names, conjoined the *Inclusa* tale and the Troy legend. It is impossible to believe that the composer of the Scandinavian broadside knew the Bulgarian text or its lost Greek original, but it is also apparent that he was dependent upon far more than momentary inspiration when he composed his song.

Nevertheless, he made his own contribution to the materials, for he so thoroughly relocated the story in the north spiritually that some have searched for a physical relocation as well. As is implied in the opening paragraphs of this paper, the name *Trøiborg* was not unknown in Denmark. According to Axel Olrik it was the name of a place *i det vestlige Sønderjylland, nord for Tonder.*[7] It should be noted, however, that the word *Trojaborg* was a traditional name for structures built in the form of a labyrinth.[8] That this word is related to legends of Troy is certain (even our ballad refers to the nine walls), but it probably has no direct connection with *Paris og Helen i Trejeborg.* Moreover, Olrik quotes four legends collected and written down in the eighteenth and nineteenth centuries which clearly reflect knowledge of the narrative and which tie the story to particular sites in Denmark, though, significantly, the best rounded of these, a text collected by Chr. Rasmussen in Ormislov near Korsør in 1861, tells of infidelity rather than elopement and the returning king eventually besieges and takes his own castle, fooling the lovers by means of a *wooden* horse.[9] This is plainly a reflection of the Troy story alone and probably is entirely unrelated to the ballad.

Paris og Helen i Trejeborg has been relocalized in other ways as well. Some of the names are changed to more typically Scandinavian names, even to the extent of creating an entirely new person in the refrain of the Norwegian B text, and the texts which appear to be from oral tradition have in varying degrees absorbed commonplace material from other ballads and begun to take on the coloring of the truly popular ballad.

The Swedish texts (which neglect the tunnel motif almostly entirely and which in other ways reflect a greater knowledge of the Troy legend than do the Danish and Norwegian texts) show this impregnation of the classical tradition in the names as well. In Swedish A the principal characters are called (drottning) Helena, Paris, and Menelaus, while Paris' father is mentioned and properly called Priamus and the goddess Minerva is named incidentally. Similarly, Swedish B mentions Priamus as the father of Paris, the heroine is called Helena, and her betrayed husband, Menelaus, with references to Kasandra and Hektor being thrown in for good measure. In brief, the Swedish texts have all the appearances of ballad imitations, the retelling of a tale in ballad style.

The Danish texts, however, appear to be at least one step removed from this literate, if not literary, tradition. The name of the hero in Danish A is Parris (Paaris, Paarris, Paarisz), his enamorata (droning) Ellind, and the betrayed husband is called Nillus (Nieellus, Nieelus); Danish B is very similar, using the names Paris (Dronning), Helena, and (Kong) Nilaus (Nilerus, Bi).

An examination of Norwegian A (printed on pp. 231–236 above), a text collected just a few years before Danish B and replete with Danish words, shows it to be very similar. Here Paris is the seducer, Nilaus the king, but Helen has become (Droning) Elen. Norwegian B and C, however, begin to show the effects of oral tradition to a greater degree. Both of these texts were collected by Moltke Moe in the last decade

of the nineteenth century: B from Torbjørg Ripilen in 1890 and again
in 1891 and C from Hæge Bjønnemyr in 1891. These women were
Professor Moe's most prolific informants and most certainly acquainted
with each other. Moreover, Hæge Bjønnemyr was herself the daughter
of one Jorunn Bjønnemyr, a woman who contributed more songs than
did any other single person to Sophus Bugge when he collected in Telemark in the middle decades of the 1800's, though, strangely, Jorunn
did not sing *Paris og Helen i Trejeborg* for Bugge despite the fact that
Hæge says that she got it from her mother. In Torbjørg's text, Norwegian B, the names are Paris, Kong Valdemonn, and (dròning)
Hellena, while in Hæge's text, Norwegian C, they are Paris, kong
Nikelus, and Heléna.

Of the three principal characters, Paris alone retains his name with
nothing more than spelling changes throughout all of our texts of the
ballad. One suspects that this is so simply because even to an un-
schooled peasant woman who had never traveled more than a few
miles from her birthplace the name *Paris* was familiar as a place-name
and so unusual as a personal name as to be especially memorable. Nor
does Helen's name undergo much of a change, being far more constant
than the woman herself. As has already been suggested, there seems
to be a direct relationship between Danish A and Norwegian A, and
the spelling *Elen* represents a perfectly regular shift in pronunciation
in Telemark for the Danish *Ellind,* fortified no doubt by the countless
Ellens who serve as heroines in Scandinavian ballads. The original
conversion of *Helen* or *Helena* to Danish *Ellind* is explainable simply
in terms of the familiarity of the name and its phonetic similarity to
the original.

Nor are the various names applied to Menelaus difficult to explain.
The phonetic relationship of *Niellus, Nialus, Nilaus* to *Menelaus* is
obvious. Moreover, in addition to the fact that *Menelaus* was a totally
foreign name, the names *Niellus, Nilaus,* and *Nikelus* are common in
ballads. King Nielus, for example, appears in *Kong Diderik og hans
Kæmper* (Danmarks gamle Folkeviser VII C) where there is also a
Queen called Elin, a ballad not entirely unrelated to *Paris og Helen i
Trejeborg,* in *Dansk Kongetal* (Danmarks gamle Folkeviser CXV), in
Kongemödet i Roskilde (Danmarks gamle Folkeviser CXVIII), and
in innumerable other ballads as well. *Herr Nikelus* is the title of a ballad
in Landstad's Norwegian collection [10] where it is said of him, as it is
said of Paris in our C text:

Herr Nikelus tener i kongins garð
han tente sjau vetrar og sá eit ár
(Landstad LXXV, stanza 1)

The stanza is a commonplace, and so are the names. Only Norwegian
B has a completely different name: *Valdemonn*. But though unrelated
to the name *Menelaus*, *Valdemonn* is a common-enough name in ballads, often being substituted for *Valdemar* around whom a series of
semi-historical ballads clusters and whose name is itself often substituted for that of lesser known kings in other ballads. Since Valdemar,
too, had problems with his queens, it is not surprising that the ballad
composers and singers made use of a form of his name.[11]

This sort of phonetic and traditional confusion can also be seen in
the refrain as the ballad passes from broadside to oral tradition. In
the Swedish texts the refrain is *Vahler up roser, om J viljen Paris
följa!* (A) and *Väll upp rosor, om J ville Paris följa!* (B). The Danish texts are close to this, as is Norwegian A: *Well op, rosser, om y
well Paaris følgge!* (Danish A), *Vel op, Rosen, om i ville Paris følge*
(Danish B), and *Vel upp rósen, um I lyster Paris fýgje* (Norwegian
A). But as has already been indicated, the first three words, though
common enough in the Scandinavian languages, are confusing in this
context. The oral texts from Norway handle the problem in different
ways, but effectively: in Norwegian B the phonetically similar, but
otherwise nonsensical, *Valibrós søn* is substituted for the first three
words and a relative pronoun added to make the result sensible: *Valibrós søn, som lyster 'en Paris fýgje*. An entirely fictitious and superfluous character is thus created, one who plays no other part in the ballad.
Hæge Bjønnemyr, however, avoids the whole problem in Norwegian
C by simply dropping the first three words, creating thereby a refrain
which seems more appropriate to the narrative than any of the others:
Ho lyster Paris fýlgie ("She wants to follow Paris").

Indeed, all of the Norwegian texts, reflect the process of oral tradition and its effect upon narrative detail. Norwegian A, the text collected by Sophus Bugge from Torbjørg Haugen in 1857, is closer to
the Danish broadside texts in both general language and in specific
detail than are the other two Norwegian variants which were collected
a generation later. As printed in the Appendix (pp. 371–373) following
the notes for this chapter, Norwegian B is a composite collected by
Moltke Moe from Torbjørg Ripilen first in 1890 and later in 1891. It
is interesting to note that the second singing consisted entirely of addi-

tions and corrections to the first, and that these additions (stanzas 1, 2, 7, 25–27, 32, 34, and 35) with the exception only of stanzas 34 and 35 are entirely commonplace. They do, however, serve as a general introduction and as transitional devices between episodes. In short, they are the kinds of contributions which one would expect an accomplished ballad singer to make were she given the opportunity to refresh her memory. But even during the first singing, Torbjørg retained all of the dramatic episodes in exactly the same order as they are found in the broadside originals.

The same thing can be said of Norwegian C (pp. 374–375), the text collected in 1891 by Moltke Moe from Hæge Bjønnemyr. This, the briefest of all known texts whether from broadside or oral tradition, omits nothing essential to the story; yet it has forty-seven less stanzas than the elaborate Danish A, forty-one less stanzas than Danish B, and seventeen less stanzas than Norwegian A. Moreover, it is introduced by an entirely new set of commonplace stanzas, equally satisfactory, but different from those of the other texts:

> 1. Paris han téner i kongens går
>   i vintrane tri å så eitt år.

> 2. Han téner inkje fy ònó løn
>   hell fyr' æ Heléna, ho æ så skjøn.[12]

Indeed, Hæge Bjønnemyr's text is replete with commonplaces. Though many of these appear in other texts of the ballad as well, they are varied in Hæge's text to fit the phrasal and structural patterns common to her singing and, because so much else has been dropped, they appear to overshadow the entire ballad. What one has here, in other words, is the narrative of *Paris og Helen in Trejeborg* reduced to its absolute essentials and told in the idiom of a popular singer—in this instance a singer who is dependent upon memory and who is trying to reproduce what she has heard as closely as possible. Where she has failed, she has fallen back, probably unconsciously, upon her stock of traditional material. Where both memory and traditional materials failed her, Hæge simply left gaps; yet these omissions are insignificant as far as the narrative core of the ballad is concerned.

Of course, were the broadside texts missing and were the names *Paris* and *Helen* changed even as much as the shift from *Menelaus* to *Nikelus,* not to mention *Valdemonn,* it would be difficult to identify this particular narrative with the Troy story as it is commonly known to literature. The principal identifying feature then would be the horse, which is, after all, of a different color from the one we best know. This has become a ballad tale with a typical set of ballad characters completely at home in the remote and rural setting of Telemark. That the Helena-Elen of *Paris og Helen i Trejeborg* resembles more closely the serving-girl she pretended to be than the arrogant Helen of Troy is unimportant for, after all, "that was in another country and, besides, the wench is dead!"

Virgin and Unicorn, from *De Generatione Christi*

The Judgment of Paris, from *Historie van Trojen* (Haarlem, 1485)

DAG STRÖMBÄCK

Some Notes on the Nix in
Older Nordic Tradition

A couple of years ago I was asked to prepare a short survey of the various conceptions of the nix or water-sprite in older Scandinavian traditions. The article was printed in *Kulturhistoriskt Lexikon för Nordisk Medeltid* 1967, vol. XII, s.v. *näcken,* but had to be cut down because of lack of space. The task of describing such a complex supernatural being in a reference work made it necessary to arrange the material according to a scheme. But this systematic arrangement did not permit very much discussion or commentary, although these were sometimes needed. In an essay to an esteemed colleague I now can feel more free to take up arguments and problems concerning this mysterious Proteus-figure in old Scandinavian folk belief and thus also supply a more substantial background to a rather sketchy article.

I

Considering the subject from a philological and historical point of view it seems first of all reasonable to emphasize the conception of the nix (Swedish *näcken*) as a sea- or river-monster in the shape of an animal. This idea must be very old and belong to a common Germanic folk belief. It is reflected in Old High German *nihhus, nichus,* "crocodile," and Old English *nicor,* "hippopotamus," "water-monster," and it is also represented in the later folk traditions both in west Germanic and north Germanic areas, where the water creature has developed into a sea- or river-horse ("kelpie," "river-horse," *vatnahestur, bäckahäst,* etc.).

If we take a look at the Nordic material we find this horse-conception very clearly evolved. In Iceland it is testified already in the *Land-*

námabók where it is told that a dapple-gray stallion comes up from a lake in the vicinity of Snæfellsnes and joins a herd of horses, the owner of which is a man called Auðun stoti. Auðun catches the stallion, harnesses it to a sledge (actually constructed for two oxen) and in one day manages to collect all the hay which he needs for his farm. At noon the stallion is very easy to handle but somewhat later in the day it treads the ground so heavily that the soil comes up to its fetlock, and at sunset it tears its harness and runs away into the sea.[1]

This notion of the nix as a creature in the shape of a horse is a dominant characteristic of Icelandic folklore. For the most part it is associated with certain lakes or tarns. In some of the tales it appears as a captured draft horse, while in others it is described as a superb riding horse which, by standing still, entices people—especially children —to mount it. If they do, it dashes away with them to the closest body of water and drowns them unless they are able to mention its name or call on the name of God.[2]

In Icelandic folklore the motif of the friendly mount luring people but cheating them is probably a later development than that of the nix as a draft horse, and it also shows remarkable resemblances, even in details, to Norwegian and Swedish popular beliefs.

The name of the nix in Icelandic is *nykr* (modern Icelandic *nykur*). In a translated saga from the thirteenth century *nykr* is also used as a name for the hippopotamus (cf. Old English *nicor* with the same sense). Another name is *vatnahestur,* which seems to belong to later traditions,[3] as also does *nennir,* used only in the tales that describe the water-horse as a mount inviting people to ride him. Another special Icelandic name is *kumbur,* which must mean "wooden block," "piece of a log." This sense brings us in touch with an old idea that the nix in the water could, like Proteus, assume almost any shape. According to Norwegian and Swedish folk tradition pieces of wood, logs, and other wooden things floating in the water could be the nix, and in Finnish tradition, where the *näkki*-concepts have come mainly from Sweden, we also come across the same idea.[4]

But this transformation into a lifeless object was just one part of the creature's general and remarkable power of changing shape. This special ability is already alluded to in the Old Norse literature. In the *Third Grammatical Treatise* from the middle of the thirteenth century a certain metrical figure is described and called *nykrat* (a word occasionally formed from a verb *nykr,* "to nix"). This metrical trick implies that the principal word used in a *kenning* in the first half or

helmingr of a scaldic stanza—and through the *kenning* as a whole
denoting a person or a thing—is in the second *helmingr* exchanged for
a completely new word with quite another sense although both kennings
in their entirety actually represent the same object. In a contemporary
commentary to this metrical dexterity it is said that "the figures change
in the same way as the nix shifts form." [5] This is as far as I know
the oldest instance in Nordic tradition for the nix's shape-shifting
power.

Of interest in Old Icelandic tradition is also the name of Iceland in
a *kenning*. The big island in the north Atlantic is called by a scald
from about 1190 *næfrland nykra borgar,*[6] which literally can be translated: "the birch-bark country of the nixes' castle." As a whole it is a
kenning for Iceland. "The nixes' castle" stands for sea, and "the birch-
bark" for the ice cap covering the sea.[7]

II

The nix in horse shape is also to be found in Norway, but, strange
to say, not evidenced by examples from the Middle Ages, although
the Icelandic conception probably emanated from the Icelanders' mother
country. A hint in this direction is given by the Icelandic scientist and
literary man Eggert Ólafsson, when he in his book of travels *Reise
igiennem Island* (1772) mentions the Icelandic water-horse and adds
that also in Norway people have the same fanciful belief about such
a monster in fresh waters. "It is probable," he says, "that Iceland's
first settlers had taken with them this idea from that country." [8]

The Norwegian written traditions about the nix as a water-horse
are generally from the later centuries but reflect, of course, ideas from
much earlier periods. We find them for instance in A. Faye's collection
of folk beliefs and folktales,[9] where it is said that in the upper Telemark a big mysterious horse could be seen in a lake when a storm was
approaching. On such occasions it rose high above the water-surface
and one could even catch sight of its tremendous hoofs.

Likewise the motif of the water-horse as a treacherous mount is
known from Norway, and many instances of its occurrence could be
cited as far as this particular motif is concerned.[10]

III

A very interesting offshoot from Norwegian tradition is the Faroese
nykur, which appears both as draft horse and as a mount.[11] As in later
Icelandic and in Norwegian tradition he is mainly connected with cer-

tain lakes and tarns and does not belong to the open sea where other water-monsters haunt. The Faroese water-horse (*nykur*) is not so big as his Norwegian and Icelandic brothers. According to Hammershaimb [12] he is about the size of a dog.

A very particular feature about him is his tail, which is long and powerful. If a person who pats him happens to touch his tail, he sticks to it and is dragged off.

The *nykur* in Faroese tales is frequently depicted as doing the giant's job at house-building. It drags the heavy stones to the building place by means of its tail. [13] In Faroese folk belief it also sometimes carries a burning light on its tail. [14]

The Faroese *nykur* is able to change into almost any kind of shape— even into that of a handsome young man—but its basic figure is that of a horse. [15]

A rather interesting motif, which needs more investigation, is that in some Faroese tales the *nykur* who captures people and drowns them leaves their lungs floating in the lake. [16] This is very much like Scottish-Gaelic tales. [17] There is an elucidating commentary in J. G. McKay, *More West Highland Tales:* [18]

Even the Water-Horse seems to have shared in the general objection to liver and lungs as food. It was supposed to make away with men, children, and even domestic horses, carrying or dragging them down beneath the waters of the loch or river which it haunted. The presumption was that when in the depths, it devoured its victims, but rejected their livers, for the next day these parts are found floating on the surface of the water.

IV

Like the Faroese *nykur* the Shetland *njuggel* or *sjupilti* is also a rather small creature. "In Shetland," S. Hibbert says, "he took the decided form of a shelty, making his most frequent haunts near watermills, but when observed, hastily withdrawing himself into a burn, or vanishing in a flush of fire." [19] This pony-figure is described by J. Jakobsen in his *Etymologisk Ordbog over det norrøne Sprog på Shetland* [20] as having a wheel-shaped tail and as haunting particularly lakes and small rivers. It enticed people to get on its back and having them there started off at terrific speed for the nearest water. But if its name was mentioned then, it lost its power. It sometimes lived near old watermills and often tried to stop the water-wheel. The name *njuggel* is developed from Old Norse *nykr,* and *sjupilti* comes from an assumptive Old Norse form *sjópiltr.*

A description of how the *njuggel* could stop watermills is given by J. Nicolson in *Shetland Folk Book:* [21]

Some night, when everything was working smoothly [in the watermill], and there was music in the splash of the water from the *fedders* of the *tirl,* then without warning the mill would stop. The person in charge would hasten to adjust the *lichtnin'tree* [appliance for regulating the pressure], but without success. Then he would know what was causing the trouble. The *njugl* was in the *under hoose,* and had taken hold of the *tirl.* Fire was the only remedy. He would take a half-burned peat and drop it cautiously into the *under hoose.* Instantly there would follow a roar of thunder, a blinding flash of bluish flame, and the mill would re-start grinding.

This relation has such a striking similarity to Norwegian and Swedish traditions about *kvernknurren, kvarngubben,* and *kvarnkarlen* that I have quoted it here *in extenso.* Moreover the terminology and construction of the Shetland watermills are very closely related to those of western Scandinavia.

In Orkney there are faint reminiscences of a nix, probably of the same type as in Shetland, but as far as I know there are no tales about it. J. Jakobsen mentions only *"de knoggelvi"* in Hoy,[22] and in J. Hibbert's *Description of the Shetland Islands* there is a reference to Jo. Ben's Description of Orkney, "written A.D. 1529," in which it is said of the nix: *Initus est algis marinis toto corpore, similis est pullo equino convoluto pilis, membrum habet simile equino et testiculos magnos.*[23]

In these Old Norwegian areas the conceptions of the water-horse, although basically of West Scandinavian origin, must be examined as to details and motifs in comparison with corresponding traditions in the Celtic area, especially in Scotland, where there are many evidences of water kelpies and river-horses in tales and folkbeliefs.[24] But this is a special question which demands a thorough investigation of the Irish material as well, and which I am not prepared to take up now. It will only be touched upon in another paragraph of this article.

V

If we now turn to Sweden, where the folklore material concerning the nix is overwhelmingly rich, we are able to detach a large part of the recorded traditions where the nix is definitely conceived as a waterhorse. The dissemination of this conception seems to be limited mainly to the southern and southwesterly parts of Sweden, but in sporadic instances it is also encountered in some northern provinces of the country.[25]

Most of the Swedish provincial names for the water-horse (*bäcka-hästen, vattenhästen, dammhästen, åhästen, strömhästen,* and *sjö-hästen*) indicate the places or surroundings where this demonic horse belongs (rivers, ponds, streams, lakes, etc.). In the tales or the lore about the horse it is most frequently described as a mount enticing people, and in particular children, to get up on its back. This motif seems to belong mainly to the southernmost provinces of Sweden and also to extend into the southwesterly parts of the country.

Although the water-horse is likewise represented as a draft horse, this draft horse concept seems to be favored particularly in the old provinces of the district of Götaland and in the province of Bohuslän. The oldest example known to me is from Bohuslän in a travel report by Pehr Kalm (a pupil of Linnæus) edited in 1742. He writes that:

"in olden days" the nix (*näcken*) in Morlanda (Bohuslän) is said to have transformed himself into a horse and like a horse to have been grazing along the shore. A man had once taken him and put a halter on him and then kept him for spring farming and ploughed all his arable land with him. The halter, however, one day came loose and the horse then dashed "like a fire" into the sea, dragging the harrow with him.[26]

There is a striking similarity between this narrative and the tale in *Landnámabók* about Auðun stoti and his demonic stallion. Since Bohuslän is an old Norwegian province, this instance must be considered as a Norwegian testimony and perhaps the oldest in that area from more modern centuries. But there are also examples from the provinces of Östergötland and Småland (and other parts of Sweden), so the nix as draft horse is fairly well represented in Sweden.[27]

As can be expected, there is a close relationship between the southernmost Swedish traditions about *bäckahästen* (the river-horse), *åhästen,* etc. and the Danish tales and conceptions of the magic mount haunting ponds (*dammhästen*), creeks, and bogs (*mosehesten*).[28]

The nix (*näkki*) in Finnish tradition, according to U. Holmberg-Harva, is the result of western influence, and so far as the water-horse in Finnish tradition is concerned, Harva is of the opinion that it is merely an offshoot from the popular imagination where the anthropomorphized *näkki* is sometimes pictured as having hoofs.[29]

L. Simonsuuri, on the other hand, lists the nix as horse-motif in his motif-index in FFC 182.[30] Still closer to Scandinavian tradition seem to be Esthonian motifs, where we find a multitude of stories about the water-horse enticing people, and in particular children, to mount him.[31]

VI

Regarding this old and fundamental idea of the nix as a water-horse within the Nordic area Dr. Brita Egardt [32] has pointed out that the water-horse traditions in Scandinavia have such a similarity with the Scottish, Irish, and Breton traditions about sea-horses and river-horses that we must attribute a Celtic origin to the Nordic tales of this group. She maintains that the geographical dissemination of this concept in the Nordic area also favors such an opinion. The Nordic material is centered mainly in districts bordering on the North Sea and the north Atlantic.

This theory is well worth considering, but the similarities must be more closely examined than is the case in Dr. Egardt's essay, especially as to details and motifs, before we can be sure of its validity. I should also like to have more of Irish evidences for water-horses haunting lakes and rivers in Ireland.

In the north Atlantic area the resemblances in certain particulars could perhaps be greater in the islands closer to Scotland than in other regions of this wide area from Denmark and Sweden in the south up to Iceland in the north. One essential thing must be remembered in this connection and that is that large parts of Scotland and all the Hebrides were once Norwegian territories. Auðun stoti came, according to *Landnámabók,* from the Hebrides to Iceland, but he was a Norwegian. It is obvious that we also must reckon with west Scandinavian influence as far as folk belief is concerned in the Atlantic islands where Norwegians settled. But certainly there are details in the motifs that must be more geographically examined, particularly where Gaelic influence might be noticeable, as for instance concerning the nix's distaste for liver and lungs, which is unknown at least in Swedish folk tradition.

The fundamental idea of the nix as a water-monster was prevalent on the continent, as we can see from the Old High German glosses, and the nix as water-horse, and particularly draft horse, is not at all unknown in German traditions. We have this conception from Silesia in the southeast up to Pomerania and Mecklenburg in the north.[33] It should be of greatest interest to study this question under a somewhat wider aspect than merely the Nordic-Celtic one.

VII

The nix in anthropomorphic representation in Nordic areas must of course also belong to the very ancient conceptions about this water-demon, although it is not testified in written sources as early as the water-horse.[34] As Aegir and Rán, according to Old Norse mythology, were rulers of the sea and Rán in particular was obsessed by a cruel desire to pull seafaring people down into the depths, so also was the nix the demonic master of lakes and rivers who demanded tribute in the form of human victims.

The Swedish reformer Olaus Petri (d. 1552) says in his Chronicle from about 1540 that people in Sweden believed in the nix and thought that persons who drowned were captured by the nix. In the accounts for the city of Stockholm from 1607 it is said that a cooper was wounded by the nix when he visited the privy at the eastern shore of the city-islet.

In *Historia de gentibus septentrionalibus* (1555) by Olaus Magnus (Book 20, chapter 20) there occurs a paragraph which clearly indicates the concept which also prevailed in later traditions that when the nix turns up in a river or a lake it forebodes a drowning accident. The water-demon claims a human being's life. Referring to a picture in a previous chapter (where he has depicted the castle Nyslott in Finland located at a river where there is a nix) Olaus Magnus says: "So far as the fiddler previously depicted, sitting in the stream and playing his fiddle is concerned, this is a foreboding. His appearing portends namely that the bailiff or the commander of the castle shall be met with a sudden death."

Just to mention a parallel from about the same time, Joen Klint in his "Book of Meteors"—a manuscript from 1599—states that when the nix appears in the Motala ström at Norrköping his appearance is followed by drowning accidents in the river. The nix is also depicted in Klint's manuscript but as a well-dressed gentleman from the upper classes.[35]

As we have seen from an Old Icelandic literary source the nix is already in the thirteenth century thought of as a creature which is able to take almost any shape. This idea is also confirmed in more recent Nordic material about the nix.[36] If he has many shapes he has equally many names. Under the name of *näcken* in Swedish there can in fact be included a large number of sea-, lake-, and river-beings. But these are always solitary beings. The nix's local names are often due to his surroundings. The name *näcken* as a provincial name seems in

Sweden mainly to belong to smooth water (lakes, gently flowing small rivers, etc.) whereas in streaming waters he is usually called by such names as *strömkarlen, strömgubben, forskarlen, forsgubben, kvarn-karlen, kvarngubben,* in Norway *fossegrimen, fossekall, kvernknurr,* and others. It may be added that in *Själens tröst,* an Old Swedish version of a German original from the middle of the fourteenth century, people are admonished against believing in *nek* (nix) and *forsa karla* (*ey thro vppa tompta gudha älla oppa wättir, ey oppa nek, ällir forsa karla* . . .).[37]

The belief in demonic beings of nix-type in waterfalls and streaming waters undoubtedly originates in very old ideas that these natural forces had their own supernatural rulers. Already in *Landnámabók* there is a tale about a pagan settler, Þorsteinn rauðnefr, who was a keen worshiper of a waterfall. He sacrificed to the cataract all that was left of meat and other edibles after the meals. His herd of sheep thrived and increased, but the same night Þorsteinn died all his herd plunged together into the cataract.[38] There is perhaps a connection between this tale and later traditions in Norway and Sweden telling about sacrifices to the nix or *strömkarlen* on certain occasions. Norwegian and Swedish tales from later periods refer to lambs, rams, kids, cats and also pieces of meat as being given to the *strömkarl* or the nix or—in Norwegian areas—*fossegrimen,* but mainly as a sacrifice for receiving from the water-demon the special gift of handling a fiddle with great talent or of learning a certain melody from him.[39]

The association of song and music with water-demons is a very old idea in the northern cultures as well as in the ancient Mediterranean cultures (cf. the sirens in the *Odyssey*). The female water-sprite in Old Norse called *margýgr,* according to the larger Saga of Saint Olaf, had such a lovely voice that she was able with her singing to cause Olaf's men to fall asleep during a sea voyage. In one of the versions of the Saga she is described as having a horse's head and a serpent's body.[40] The siren-resemblance of the female nix is also noticeable in Middle High German *wazzernixe,* which is used *gleichbedeutig mit sirene.*[41]

As to the nix in Scandinavian rivers and streams (Swedish *näck, strömkarl, strömgubbe,* etc., Norwegian *nykk, fossegrim,* etc.), the idea of his skill in playing fiddle or harp must have originated in the melodious sound that comes from cataracts and the rush of streaming water.[42] In the music that the nix was thought to create was such a power that a person who had learned to play from the nix was then by his playing able to force people to dance day and night without break and sometimes also cause inanimate objects to move. This demonic dance which, as far as the nix is concerned, is testified to mainly in later folk traditions, has connections both with the devil legends (in Sweden from the seventeenth century on *näcken* is also a name for the devil) and with the medieval dance tales of Kölbigk-type.[43] About inanimate objects being forced, together with people, to move by magic music, we are informed already in the *Bósa saga*.[44] A similar motif is also to be found in Saxo's *Gesta Danorum*, Book XII.[45]

That a musical instrument was a characteristic accoutrement of the nix, at least at the end of the Middle Ages in Sweden, is evidenced by a church painting. In the church at Häverö in Uppland, among some fabulous creatures on the walls of a vault, appears a nix with something in his hands which resembles a lyre. The painting is believed to date from about 1475.

There is a particular folktale motif connected with the nix's musical activities. Together with other supernatural beings in woods and waters he was considered to be a "fallen angel," belonging to "Lucifer's followers," expelled from heaven and deprived of redemption. In a group of tales from the eighteenth and nineteenth centuries he is described as playing for his redemption and for his reunion with heaven. This motif, that obviously has a learned background and seems to belong to a medieval theological doctrine, can in folktales be traced back to the beginning of the sixteenth century. In a Danish devotional handbook from 1509 there is a tale about a "fallen angel" who plays his stringed instrument under the ground for his redemption—an instrument that he had used for singing the praises of God when he was in heaven and which he brought along with him at his fall. It is possible that this learned tradition as well, which often is reflected in Swedish legends about the fiddle-playing nix, had some influence on the conceptions of the nix as a musical being.[46]

VIII

In the Scandinavian ballads the nix plays a very important rôle. There is a whole group of "nix-ballads" partly of decisively medieval origin and with counterparts in European balladry, partly from later centuries but with elements belonging to earlier stages of balladry.

In "The Might of the Harp" [47] the nix is a sort of river-troll who, according to the oldest variant of the ballad (Karen Brahe folio, about 1580), seizes a bride from her bridegroom when they pass a bridge over a river. The bridegroom, however, is capable of playing his harp in such a fascinating and demonic way that the nix is forced up from the river with the bride. The nix is here called *trold* (*den throld matt op fraa grunde*). Earlier this "troll" has carried away the bride's two sisters, but they are now also given back to the family. In other variants of this ballad the nix is called *havtroll, havmand,* and *vandman* (cf. German *Wasserman*).

In this ballad the nix's nature of real water-monster, greedy for young maids and carrying them off, is clearly displayed. As A. Olrik has emphasized, there is here a basic and very primitive conception of the nix, closer to the old fundamental folk belief than that found in any other Scandinavian nix-ballad.[48]

Quite otherwise is the nix modeled in another medieval ballad called "The Nix's Treachery." [49] He is there pictured as a chevalier who by certain tricks entices a lovely maid to his realm. In the earliest Danish variants of this ballad it is told that the king's daughter dances and sings very arrogantly at a ball in the king's palace. This is heard by the nix who is in the water. He dresses up as a knight, rides to the palace, and makes the proud maid an offer of marriage, promising her golden rings and ornaments. She follows him and he takes her home on his horse. But his home is in "the streaming water" and there he forces her to go down (*den iumfrw sanck neder for striden strøøm*), and people could hear her scream. In another old variant of the same ballad the maid is taken by the nix to a boat, but the boat sinks to the bottom when they get out from land. Her cries are heard from the water.

In Norwegian, Faroese, and Icelandic versions of this ballad the maid escapes from her terrible situation through mentioning the nix by its name—a motif very common in folktales about the nix. In the Icelandic version (*Elenar ljóð*) she involuntarily alludes to the nix's name, Nennir, by saying *"Eg því ekki nenni."* [50] In a Faroese version she calls her seducer frankly *"nykurtröll."* [51] The west Nordic variants, however, are considered to be of later date than the Danish versions.[52]

"The Nix's Treachery" is considered by both A. Olrik and S. Ek to be connected with religious ideas about the dance as a rather dangerous business. Olrik has referred to an old Slovenian parallel in which the water-sprite dressed as a young and handsome gentleman carries off a maid keen on dancing and takes her to his realm in the water,[53] and S. Ek has seen a connection between some of the versions of "The nix's treachery" and the Kölbigk-theme in European folktales. "The ballad," he says, "expresses very early reactions to dancing. Its pagan enchantment is represented by the nix in human shape, and man is defenseless if he not submits himself to the Christian commandments." [54] Professor Ek's viewpoints are applicable only on a few variants, where the dance takes place at a churchyard, but even concerning these variants I find it difficult to follow his subtle argumentation that there should be a connection between the ballad and the Kölbigk-legend. On the other hand his emphasis of the Christian ideas about the dance as a sinful enjoyment seems well founded.

Agnete og Havmannen ("Agnete and the Waterman") [55] is a later nix ballad and obviously influenced by German and Slav ballads on the *Wasserman* or the *Nickelmann* who carries off the maid to his realm under the water where she bears children to her mysterious husband.[56] In the Danish ballad the waterman's appearance is depicted in beautiful colors. He is a man in an embellished shape; his hair is "like the purest gold" and his eyes are sparkling and "joyous." [57] There is nothing of a "water-troll" about him.

This picture of the "waterman" or nix had probably influence also on the molding of the nix-type in later folk traditions and in works of art. He is often described as a handsome young man with golden curls,[58] and in the art of painting he is, in the most famous picture of him, "Strömkarlen" by Ernst Josephson (1884), presented as a young naked man, wearing long golden hair, sitting at a cataract and as in ecstasy playing his fiddle.

In "Agnete and the Waterman" there is also an allusion to the waterman's great treasures on the bottom of the sea, and everything that she gets from him is of gold, even the harp that he, according to one of the variants (D), gives her to play on. This artistic splendor in the nix's hall is a poetic adornment, which also is further developed in literary style by poets, but it is worth noticing that already in the old Scaldic poetry and in Snorri's *Edda* the sea-god *Ægir* had a magnificent hall where gold replaced fire as source of light.

As to the age of this ballad the opinions differ. I think I would join Professor Ek when he attributes its first appearance in Denmark to the time of the Renaissance.[59]

SEÁN Ó SÚILLEABHÁIN

Etiological Stories in Ireland

Professor Francis Lee Utley visited the archives of the Irish Folk-lore Commission in Dublin some years ago, and we later sent him information for some of the articles which he has since written. His detailed studies of stories about Noah, the Ark, and the Deluge have suggested to my mind that a summarized list of origin stories in general, as found in Ireland, may be of interest to students of folklore.

Many of those which I have mentioned will be recognizable as having been listed by Stith Thompson in his monumental *Motif-Index of Folk Literature*. Others will be found absent from that work, as they may be only of Irish provenance or else were not catalogued when the *Motif-Index* was being compiled.

I have included only stories of general interest and relevance. Those which seemed to be of purely Irish origin and provenance have been omitted, such as how the first hens (weasels, maypole, cart, and so on) came to Ireland. Also omitted are legends associated with Irish place-names, with the origins of particular Irish lakes (through the over-flowing of uncovered wells), and with striking natural features of the landscape (such as the Black Pig's Dyke and the Devil's Bit moun-tain).

While I have endeavored to arrange the summaries under what seemed the most suitable headings, it will be seen that some of them might have fitted equally well under some other head. As only about one-quarter of the large collections of folklore has so far been cata-logued in a detailed way, it will be evident that this list of etiological stories found in Irish oral tradition is far from being complete. It will, however, provide a foretaste of what a comprehensive catalogue will ultimately contain.

The manuscript and printed sources which I have used for each section will be found at the end of this essay, pp. 270–274.

A. Nature: The War in Heaven

Lucifer disobeyed God by either sitting on his chair without authority or looking into a mirror which showed the Virgin, who was to be the Mother of God two thousand years later. In the ensuing struggle,

1. The sun sided with God, who blessed it and said that it would always be loved by men.

2. The moon sided with Lucifer, was punished by God, so that it lost half of its former light and has waxed and waned alternately ever since.

3. The sea also sided with Lucifer and was punished, so that ever since it ebbs and flows, is rough and restless, and will, on the last day, shrink into a small shell to hide. Another reason given for the restlessness of the sea is that it promised God never to drown anybody; it broke its promise and was punished. A third reason for its unhappiness is that it gave evidence against Christ during his trial.

4. The wind, too, sided with Lucifer and was punished by God to wander for ever and be disliked by all.

5. The poplar tree refused to bow down to God, as all other trees had done, and ever since has trembled with fear.

6. The angels who sided with Lucifer were expelled from heaven. The Archangel Michael pleaded with God not to empty heaven, and God relented, saying that all things should remain as they then were: the fallen angels in the air and on the earth became the fairies, and those who had fallen into the sea became the underwater beings.

Other folk stories explain:

7. Why the man is in the moon: he was sent there as punishment when found stealing a bush on earth, and can still be seen to carry the bush (or else a sheep) on his back.

8. Why the tips of the rushes (fern), the tips of cows' horns, and the froth of the water are either withered or useless. St. Patrick, tired after a hard day's preaching in Ireland to convert the people, fell asleep; in his sleep, he cursed Ireland three times; his servant, who heard him, transferred the curses to the three aforementioned things. Another reason given for the withered tips of the rushes is the curse of St. Patrick, who tried and failed to peel one of them to form a rush-light so that he could read his breviary. Still another reason

ascribes the withered tips of the rushes to the evil eye of the mythological god, Balor.

B. Adam, Eve, Paradise, the Fall

1. Man's love for woman is due to the fact that Eve was made from Adam's rib.

2. In Paradise, our first parents were covered with *An Scéimh Ainglí* ("The Angelic Beauty"), which they lost when they fell. The only symbol left of this covering is the nails of men's fingers.

3. The *daradaol* (earwig chafer) was the only insect to burrow into the apple of paradise, and ever since it smells of apple.

4. The apple-like lump in men's throats was caused by Adam's eating of the apple (Eve did not taste it).

C. Noah, the Ark, and the Deluge

1. Noah was the first man who was ever drunk, when the Devil, to find out what he was making (the Ark), got Noah's wife to make an intoxicating drink with froth from the mouth of a wild boar as ingredient; Noah revealed the secret.

2. The first mocking laugh ever heard was from one of Noah's sons who had seen his father drunk (or else unclothed); the son was banished by Noah, and from him came the colored races.

3. Noah forgot to take a stallion into the Ark, and forced one of his sons to serve the mare; a stallion was born. Another story says that Noah had to serve the mare himself when Ham refused to do so; Noah, in anger, said that Ham and his descendants should forevermore be the servants of their brothers.

4. Noah had no pig in the Ark, but got one from under a vessel where he had placed something like frog-spawn. (See Section O.)

5. Man's hind parts are cold ever since Noah tried (and failed) to stop a leak in the Ark by sitting on it. His wife stood on the leak (and failed also), so women's feet are ever cold. The dog stopped the leak with its nose, which is cold ever since. (See Section L.)

6. The crow is held in disrepute since, having been sent forth from the Ark by Noah, it stayed to eat carrion flesh rather than return.

7. The kingfisher was also sent forth and flew toward the sun, returning with bright plumage.

8. Stone can emit fiery sparks only since the Deluge—a sign that the world will be ultimately burned rather than drowned.

9. The rainbow is a sign of God's promise never again to flood the earth.

D. Job, Bees, and Flies

1. Job suffered from skin irritation; he scratched himself, and the first insects in the world emerged.

2. Job died after the Devil had failed to make him jealous of his wife's riches. The first bees issued from his sores; ever since the honeycomb resembles human sores.

3. The king of the earth built a tower fifteen miles tall to reach where God was; he then saw that God was still higher; the tower collapsed beneath him; God sent a plague of flies (the first ever) which consumed him.

4. Jesus wept on the cross, and bees were formed from his tears.

E. The Seven Penitential Psalms

King David had many wives but enforced *jus primae noctis,* whereby brides had to spend their marriage night with him. His son, Solomon, resented this (one version says this was because his own wife was involved) and asked his father to pass judgment on the type of man who had many sheep and still would take the only sheep from a poor man. David said that such a man deserved to be buried seven feet underground. Solomon told him that he had passed sentence on himself, so David was buried seven feet deep. He repented when in the grave, composed the seven psalms and rose one foot for each psalm, until he reached the surface.

F. Christ and His Mother on Earth

1. Jealousy first began when Joseph told the Virgin Mary, who was with child and had asked for some cherries, to ask the father of her child for them. The tree bent down miraculously.

2. There was no wheat on earth (only barley) until some wheat grains were found on the hoof of the ass which had carried the infant Jesus to Egypt; ever since, the mark of the ass' hoof can be seen on the wheat grain. Wheat is blessed.

3. When the Holy Family were fleeing into Egypt, they passed a field in which a man was sowing grain. The crop sprang up and ripened as soon as they had passed by. The pursuers asked the man if he had seen the Holy Family, and he replied that they had passed that way on the day he was sowing the crop. They were about to

return from their fruitless search when the earwig said from the corn: *'Iné! Iné!'* ("Yesterday! Yesterday!"), thus betraying the fugitives. That is why one should kill an earwig when one sees it.

4. Jesus slept on green rushes; nobody who does so will ever catch cold.

5. As the Holy Family were traveling along one day, Jesus said to Mary: "You are My love, mother." Mary replied: "You are my seven loves, Son." Ever since, each mother loves her son seven times as dearly as he loves her.

6. Christ was red-haired. Fearing that his followers, who were also red-haired, would be over-proud of this, he decreed that red-haired people would be feared and held in low esteem by all others.

7. The first curds were made from milk by Jesus when he visited the house of a poor woman.

8. The first mushrooms were formed from crumbs of bread that fell from Peter, who was eating a loaf unknown to Jesus.

9. The men who were pursuing Jesus and Mary were told by a man that they were in a house in front of which a tree was growing. Next morning, there was a tree in front of every house, and so the fugitives could not be found. In memory of this, Mary said that she would bless every house which erected a May-bush.

10. Straw crosses, known as St. Brigid's crosses, were woven in Ireland on the vigil of the saint's feast (January 31) to commemorate the manner in which the saint distracted the attention of people on the roadside from Mary, who was with child, by carrying a straw cross on her head as they both went by.

11. Houses are decorated with holly at Christmas since a poor woman, who had no other gift for Jesus, brought him some sprigs of holly.

12. All persons have some physical blemish since Peter remarked on the thin legs of Our Savior.

13. Peter was not a successful fisherman until Jesus taught him to let down his nets from the starboard side of the boat, where the meshes could open.

14. It was Christ who gave the Jews the ability to make money.

15. The elder tree is blessed as it gave shelter to Jesus when fleeing from his enemies.

16. The cock has crowed *"Mac na hÓ slán!"* ("The Son of the Virgin is hale!") since the cock rose miraculously from the vessel in which it was being cooked during the Passion.

17(*a*). The cross of Calvary was made from wild sally (bog myrtle) which had floated around the world during the Deluge; it was the hardest of all woods and could not be cut by any instrument until it was selected for the cross, when it was found to be quite soft. Ever since, the wild sally is stunted.

(*b*) The cross of Calvary was made from a tree that had been growing in the Garden of Eden.

(*c*) The elder tree has a strong smell ever since its wood was used to make the cross of Calvary.

18. The *glúineach* (milkwort) plant has a red mark on it since the blood of Our Savior fell on it; so too has the breast of the robin, which tried to tear out the nails of the cross or the thorns of the crown.

19. A bull drank some of the blood of Our Savior, and as a result, every bull gets mad if he tastes human blood.

20. It is lucky to have a wet funeral day, since Jesus wept on the cross.

21. Jesus was mocked on Good Friday (which was April 1), by being given vinegar to drink; hence the day is known as All Fools' Day.

G. The Origin of Tobacco

There are several stories about this.

1. At the wake of a dead person, the people had no way of passing the time; a stranger (Our Savior) either collected some plants on the nearby hillside or else used some beetles from the shroud over the bed, and showed the people how to make tobacco and snuff—the first ever.

2. When Jesus was to be crucified, the tobacco plant sprang up miraculously; Jesus told the people that it would be thought more of than he would be.

3. The Devil said that he would cause a plant to grow which would be thought more of than God himself. The plant was tobacco.

4. Mary spent a night alone in a house, with no company but a corpse; on a table nearby were three pipes and tobacco, and she smoked some to help her get through the terror of the night; this was the first time tobacco was smoked at a wake, and it has been smoked at wakes ever since.

5. When Jesus was dying on the cross, Mary pulled a plant at its foot, and smoked it to ease her sorrow. Other accounts say that she

found the tobacco plant on the tomb of Jesus and smoked it on the advice of an angel.

6. A man who had promised himself to the Devil at the end of seven years had his soul saved by the Virgin Mary; from his body, which the Devil got, the tobacco plant grew to cause trouble and strife among men.

7. After smoking at a wake, people pray for the souls of the dead, ever since a spirit (*Sprid an Tobac*: "The Tobacco Spirit") was released from purgatory by such a prayer.

H. Smiths, Tinkers, Carpenters, and Tailors

1. The smith refused to make the nails for the Crucifixion; instead he tapped the anvil three times with his hammer, and has done so ever since before striking the iron. The Virgin washed her hands in the forge-water and, when the smith does this, after a hard day's work, his weariness disappears.

2. The tinker made the nails for the Crucifixion, and was condemned to be nomadic for ever.

3. The carpenter helped to make the nails; ever since he must do some of the work of the smith.

4. When a cowherd and a tinker had refused to make a pin for the Virgin's cloak on a windy day, the smith made it and has been blessed ever since. Cowherds have taken over the weariness of the smiths, and tinkers must wander for ever.

5. The smith made a pin for the Virgin's cloak from the tip of one of the arms of his tongs; ever since one arm of the smith's tongs is shorter than the other.

6. St. Patrick wished to have five pounds with which to purchase his freedom; he found a lump of gold and showed it to a tinker, who said that he would take it, although it was of no value; the smith told Patrick of its great value and bought it from him. Since then, smiths are blessed and tinkers cursed.

I. The Twelve Apostles

The miraculous birth of the Apostles (from virgin mothers and a dead father) is described in some Irish folktales. Much has been written about such a theme, *Ignis divinus*, and Milko Matičetov of Ljublana has studied it, using Irish and other versions (see references below, p. 272).

1. Mary, carrying the child Jesus in her arms, was refused assistance by a rich woman, but was helped by a poor woman. Later, Jesus, when asked by his mother, how he would deal with the two women, answered paradoxically that (*a*) the rich woman would have her sons around her deathbed, but (*b*) the poor woman would find her house and her only son burned to ashes when she reached home. Mary was surprised at this. The rich woman got no comfort from the sight of her wayward sons around her deathbed, so it was a punishment rather than a blessing. The poor woman collected the charred bones of her son from the burned house, and placed them in a little bag which she kept in her bosom. On finding work at a house of holy women, she kissed the bag each day when she rested from her work. The holy women got a chance one day to examine the contents of the bag, tasted them, became with child, and so gave birth to the twelve Apostles.

2. The son of a poor widow joined Our Savior and Mary in their travels. He was drowned. His bones were later found by his mother, who kept them. As before, the holy women for whom she worked were made pregnant by the bones and gave birth to the twelve Apostles.

J. How Avarice Entered the Church

Christ and Peter met a poor beggar on their travels. Christ gave him a small coin, but later gave a much larger coin to a sturdy beggar. Peter wondered at this. Christ took him along the road and they found the poor beggar dead; on searching his clothes, Peter discovered that his pockets were full of money, yet he had died of starvation. Christ then told Peter to go into a tavern where he found the sturdy beggar generously spending what money he had on drinks for himself and others. Christ told Peter to throw the miser's money into a river. Peter kept some of it; Christ knew this and told him that the clergy would always be avaricious.

K. The Devil

1. The Devil, vying with God, made the first goat but failed to put life into him. God did so. The goat is regarded as a "limb of the Devil" and cursed.

2. The goat was brought from hell by the Devil (as part of a folktale).

3. The Devil invented money—and bagpipes.

4. The Devil told St. Martin that he would make something new and useful for him if he were given all the souls that would be born during a twenty-four hour period. Martin agreed. The Devil then made a mill from ice, while Martin watched him. Martin prayed to God that no souls would be born during the specified period, and so it happened; the Devil was foiled. Martin then knew how a mill could be made, and made one of lasting materials. It was the first real mill.

5. The Devil knew all trades except carpentry; while trying to learn that, he split his hoof with an adze, and it has been cloven ever since.

6. St. Joseph, the carpenter, had only a knife-like tool with which to cut timber; one day, while Joseph was absent at his midday meal, the Devil, in an attempt to destroy or make useless Joseph's knife, made gaps in the edge of it; Joseph, on returning, had to use the gapped knife and, to his surprise and joy, found that it cut the timber better than before. So he put still more gaps in the edge, and so made the first saw.

7. The Devil once asked a smith to make a razor for him. All the razors he made broke as soon as the Devil tested them. The only razor that proved good was one which had been tempered in men's sweat, which was collected in a trough.

8. Drink was first invented by the Devil to make Noah drunk so that he would reveal the secret of the Ark. Froth from the mouth of a wild boar was an ingredient. Also, poteen (illicit whiskey) came to be made when the Devil spat into the water from which people were trying to make it.

L. Cats and Dogs

1. Long ago the cat had money and with it she bought some "gifts"—usually three, from among the following: ability to see as well by night as by day; silent tread; the forgetfulness of the house-wife; freedom to eat meat on Friday; ability to always fall on her feet from a height; a cosy corner in the house; milk without water mixed in it; permission to go on the king's table or to look at the king, and to sleep in the best bed in the house.

2. The cat has no kidneys as she gave her own away for a desire for milk.

3. The cat never washes her face before eating since a captured mouse asked her to do so and escaped.

4. How black cats originated: a man swallowed a mouse; the mouse, on a doctor's advice, was enticed forth by the smell of cooked meat, but escaped from a cat which followed the mouse into the man's stomach; finally, both the doctor and the patient died; from the latter's grave a brood of black kittens issued each year—the first ever.

5. The cat and the dog ran a race to their master's house to see which of them would have the right to remain indoors. The dog reached the house first but was distracted from entering by a beggar-man who raised his stick. The cat entered the house first, and is still there, while the dog, outside, hates beggarmen and attacks them.

6. The dog's nose is cold (*a*) because the dog was left outside the Ark by Noah; or (*b*) because it was used to stop a leak in the Ark; or (*c*) because, in the race with the cat (see foregoing), the dog got stuck going through a narrow passage and its nose got frozen.

7. The dog, long ago, lent its footwear to the hare, but failed to get it back; ever since, the dog has been chasing the hare and, since the soles of his feet are bare, he must lie near the fire when he can to warm them.

8. Long ago, the hair of the dog stood upright or pointed forward; it has lain smooth toward the tail since Our Savior (or some saint) rubbed his hand to the back of an attacking dog.

9. The dog is the companion of man since it crossed over a trench which separated the animals from Adam and Eve. "The dog will be man's companion for ever," said Adam.

10. The Devil's daughter married a man who did not recognize her; she was banished by a holy man, and their two children, a boy and a girl, were changed into dogs. Ever since, dogs have some of man's nature.

11. The canine king of the dogs bit the king of the people and was punished by death. When the bitten king died from his wounds, all dogs lost the power of speech, which they had had until then.

M. Asses, Mules, Jennets, Goats, and Sheep

1. The ass has a cross on his back since (*a*) he carried the Holy Family into Egypt, or (*b*) Jesus rode on his back into Jerusalem.

2. The ass has long ears since (*a*) Adam pulled them when the ass could not remember its name, or (*b*) a king who was afraid that a plot was being hatched against him pulled them to punish the ass for not disclosing what he had heard the plotters say.

3. The mule kicked Our Savior (or St. Patrick) and, as punishment, can never bear a foal.

4. The mule was unkind to the Virgin Mary; since then, it has had no marrow in its bones, and they will not knit, if broken.

5. The jennet, too, is sterile since it kicked Our Savior. God blessed all animals except the jennet and mule; hence these two cannot breed.

6. The goat was made by (*a*) the Devil, or else (*b*) by God, who created it from pieces left over after the other animals had been created. The goat has been wicked ever since.

7. The goat had a coat of wool originally, while the sheep had only a coat of hair. The goat refused to shelter or hide Jesus, but the sheep helped to do so. As punishment, the goat now has only a coat of hair, while the sheep has a woollen fleece.

N. Hens, Ducks, and Geese

1. The hen ate the butter (grease) which had been given to her, while the duck (goose) smeared her share on her feathers; ever since, the duck and goose are not wet in water or rain, while the hen is.

2. The hen was punished (as above) for refusing to shelter Jesus, but the helpful duck (goose) is blessed (as above).

3. The hen scraped away the clay with which the sow had covered Jesus from his pursuers; ever since, the sow has no pain when farrowing, while the hen has, when laying an egg.

O. How Pigs, Mice, Rats, and Cats Came

Versions of stories to explain the origin of these animals are very numerous in Ireland. They fall into three general categories.

1. The wife of a poor man blamed Eve for their poverty. The man said she herself would have done what Eve had done. They were taken to a fine house by a stranger where ample food and comfort were provided, but they were not to look under an overturned dish. The inquisitive wife did so, and rats and mice emerged. They were banished from the house. (Type 1416.)

2. Jesus and Mary were refused alms at a farmer's house (the farmer was in the fields sprinkling water on his crops during a drought). The servant girl in the house, who was kneading a cake, gave them only a piece of the dough, which the Savior secretly placed in the oven (or in the center of the fire). The dough sprouted into a green sapling. When the girl noticed the miracle, she called her master

(usually St. Martin or some other saint); he suspected who the miracle-workers were and followed them. Flesh (fat) was torn or cut from his body as he ran to overtake them; Jesus healed his wound with a touch of His hand and told the farmer to place the flesh (fat) under a vessel at home; something useful would emerge he was told. He did so, but the servant girl (or his wife) secretly put some of it under another vessel. Later on, when the farmer looked under his own vessel, a sow and piglets came forth; from under the girl's (wife's) vessel came rats and mice. The angry farmer threw his nightcap (mitten) at the rats and mice, and it changed into a cat. Thus, the first pigs, rats, mice, and cats came into the world. In a by-form of this tale, the Virgin was allowed to take from the stingy house only as many grains of wheat as adhered to her damp fingers; miraculous plenty of flour occurred when the grains were ground in a mill; some of this flour was placed under the miller's vessel, and so on.

3. St. Patrick (or St. Brigid) was told in a house at which he called that there was much waste of food, as there was no animal to eat it. The saint put some flesh (fat) from the waste under a vessel; the inquisitive girl did the same, with the usual results in both cases.

P. Wild Animals, Birds, and Fishes

1. The hare has only a stump of tail since a man, who was trapped in a bog hole, pulled the rest off in trying to get free. Similarly, the hind legs of the hare are longer than the front ones, since the same man caught hold of them in trying to get free from the hole.

2. The magpie is a bird of ill omen as he has three drops of the Devil's blood in his veins.

3. The wren, having won the kingship of the birds from the eagle by a trick (Type 221), lost some of its feathers to the angry eagle and can fly only near the ground ever since.

4. The wren was a poor nest-builder, and her eggs were always falling to the ground and getting broken, until her mate taught her to build a round nest with a small opening; since then, her tail is raised aloft as a result of her cramped position in the nest.

5. The jackdaw, wishing to join the choir of singing birds, borrowed feathers from the seagull in order to mislead St. Patrick; the saint detected the interloper and banished him, but the borrowed feathers could not be removed. So came the first magpie.

6. The heron's neck is bent since she was struck by the fox for having helped the pigeon to save her fledglings from him.

7. The seagull borrowed swimming power from the oyster-catcher but refused to return it; since then the latter cannot swim and must perch on firm ground.

8. The flounder has a crooked mouth since it was cursed by St. Patrick (or some other saint) for its discourtesy.

9. The Apostles failed to catch any fish until Jesus pulled three hairs from his beard and threw them into the water; the hairs became herrings, the first ever. They never take a bait, and have the marks of net meshes on their skin.

Q. General Origins

1. The first harp was made in imitation of the ribs of a dead whale through which the wind was musically blowing.

2. The first (endless) story was told by a woman to a king who was about to put her sister to death for unfaithfulness; the story never ended, and the sister was saved.

3. A line to measure how straight a wall was was first used by a woman who suggested to Gobán Saoir (the mythical Irish builder) that he use the unraveled thread of a stocking which she was knitting.

4. Supernatural visitors to the house of a woman who was carding wool late at night demanded admittance. The feet-water could not help them (a live coal had been put in it) nor the cake (a cross had been marked on it). When the tongs was going to the door to admit the unwelcome visitors, the woman pulled its arms apart, and the tongs have been split ever since.

5. Long ago, babies could walk when they were born. This power was taken from them when one of them was maimed by its mother to prevent it from walking (she had some work to do in the fields). Another version puts the blame for this on Cailleach Bhéarra (the mythical Hag of Béarra), who placed her fingers on a baby's kidneys to prevent it from walking, and the marks are still to be seen.

6. Spades and other implements worked of their own accord long ago until a woman interfered or remarked on the work without blessing it; ever since the implements have to be used by man.

7. Foreknowledge of the hour of death was taken away from men when one of them was found putting a temporary guard of rushes around his crops instead of a permanent one.

8. Women cannot throw things straight since the daughter of Balor (the mythical one-eyed Irish giant) threw a halter over her shoulder to his rival, while pretending to throw it to her father.

9. Tailors have been poor, though boastful, ever since one of them told St. Patrick that he was too busy to mend his cloak and said that he worked only for the gentry. Cobblers are always poor and in a hurry for the same reason.

10. Mowers have been poor, and always will be, since one of them, despite payment from a supernatural stranger, continued to mow hay on a Sunday.

11. The smith spills the first portion of every drink he gets in the forge onto the anvil since the wife of one of them tried to poison him.

12. No weavers go to hell since a stuttering member of the craft applied for admittance at the gate; the Devil, thinking that there were many weavers outside, said that he had no room for such a crowd.

SOURCES

(References are to volumes and pages of the manuscripts of the Irish Folklore Commission in Dublin. The letter S. in front of a volume number signifies that it belongs to the Schools' Collection.)

A. Nature: The War in Heaven

1. 809: 469–470; 995: 278–279.
2. 349: 451; 809: 469–470; 995: 278–279.
3. 349: 451–452; 627: 401.
4. 809: 469–470; 995: 278–279.
5. 642: 453.
6. 974: 17; 992: 276–277; 1170: 255, 582–584.
7. 481: 165–166; 736: 531–533, 555; 1176: 64–65.
8. 41: 87a; 56: 392; 560: 141 (for first part); 560: 141 (for second part); 56: 392; 528: 297; 1564: 80; S. 1072: 281 (for third part).

B. Adam, Eve, Paradise, the Fall

1. 1152: 339–341.
2. *Béaloideas*, V (1935), 136.
3. 85: 346.
4. 1176: 211–212.

C. Noah, the Ark, and the Deluge

1. 349: 153–155; 433: 244–252.
2. 976: 499.
3. 303: 514–516; 808: 234–235.
4. 303: 514–516.
5. 738: 334.
6. 303: 514–516; 976: 499.
7. 1127: 109.

C. *Noah, the Ark, and the Deluge* (*Continued*)

8. *Béaloideas,* XIV (1944), 99.
9. S. 273: 31.

D. *Job, Bees, and Flies*

1. 735: 541–542.
2. 978: 71–72.
3. 969: 319, 384–386.
4. 347: 150; 1231: 469.

E. *The Seven Penitential Psalms*

72: 171a–172, 234–235; 303: 512; 1129: 101–102.

F. *Christ and His Mother on Earth*

1. 1014: 283.
2. 1010: 243–244; 1227: 42.
3. 744: 35–37; 1000: 598; *Béaloideas,* V (1935), 249; *Béaloideas,* XIV (1944), 104.
4. 259: 652; 814: 274.
5. 257: 162–163.
6. 992: 272–273.
7. 990: 468–471.
8. S. 774: 138.
9. *Béaloideas,* IV (1933/1934), 205.
10. 990: 468–471, 473–476.
11. 1127: 11.
12. *Béaloideas,* XII (1942), 195.
13. 1242: 153.
14. 1134: 4–5, 27.
15. 642: 454.
16. 738: 305.
17a. 642: 455; *Béaloideas,* IX (1939), 46.
17b. 482: 57–58, 268.
17c. 820: 21.
18. 481: 251 (for first part); 736: 532, 555; 782: 259–260; 814: 269–274; 1159: 14; S. 493: 47–49 (for second part).
19. 814: 271.
20. 347: 150–152.
21. 814: 269.

G. *The Origin of Tobacco*

1. 970: 50–51; 1014: 283; 1101: 206; *Béaloideas,* XI (1941), 100.
2. 481: 80.
3. 483: 187.
4. 227: 92; 1203: 360–363.
5. 782: 241; 814: 273; 1020: 3 (for first part); 970: 190; 1020: 3–5; 1457: 6–7 (for second part).

G. The Origin of Tobacco (Continued)

6. 1247: 175–183.
7. 27: 566.

H. Smiths, Tinkers, Carpenters, and Tailors

1. 744: 36; 815: 50; 990: 468–471 (for first part); 815: 48–49 (for second part).
2. 227: 93; 815: 50; *Béaloideas*, IX (1939), 46; *Béaloideas*, XIV (1944), 104.
3. 744: 35.
4. 42: 352–354; 117: 182–184; 990: 477–478; S. 620: 506–509.
5. 815: 48–49.
6. 289: 112–114.

I. The Twelve Apostles

1. 155: 139–143; 182: 307–309; 191: 232–239; 281: 568–570; 432: 124–126; 601: 567–568; 623: 461–472; 662: 36–37. See Milko Matičetov *Sežgani in Prerojeni Človek (Der verbrannte und wiedergeborene Mensch)* (Ljublana: Academia Scientiarum et Artium Slovenica, 1961).
2. 662: 36–37.

J. How Avarice Entered the Church

790: 376–377, 533; 803: 300–303; *Béaloideas*, III (1932), 6; Douglas Hyde, *Legends of Saints and Sinners* (Dublin: Talbot Press, 1915), pp. 22–25.

K. The Devil

1. 183: 164–178; 433: 254; 782: 437–438; 977: 489; 1168: 442–443.
2. 1239: 10.
3. 434: 201.
4. 1227: 195–196.
5. 744: 270–271.
6. 275: 372–373; S. 321: 77–78.
7. 1134: 54.
8. 433: 244–252; 483: 187; 1168: 442–443; 1457: 6–7; S. 34: 248–249 (for first part); 171: 372 (for second part).

L. Cats and Dogs

1. 26: 134–136; 43: 215, 235; 62: 179; 117: 227; 195: 64–65; 272: 517–522; 779: 433; *Béaloideas*, V (1935), 144, 218, 249.
2. 117: 66; 773: 459.
3. 177: 431.
4. *Béaloideas*, XII (1942), 165.
5. 347: 151; S. 611: 479–481; *Béaloideas*, III (1932), 495–496.
6a. 738: 328.
6b. 349: 153–155; 738: 328, 334; S. 172: 60.
6c. S. 611: 478–479.
7. 1105: 69–70.

L. Cats and Dogs (Continued)

8. 1129: 96; 1187: 447–448; 1203: 55–56; 1227: 195–197; *Béaloideas,* XI (1941), 17.
9. 779: 205.
10. 195: 467–469.
11. 631: 192–193.

M. Asses, Mules, Jennets, Goats, and Sheep

1a. 853: 194; 1052: 99–100.
1b. 632: 447–448.
2a. S. 904: 127.
2b. 1170: 269–272.
3. 117: 185; 433: 12–13; 1169: 1.
4. 1052: 99–100.
5. 433: 12–13; 483: 186.
6a. 809: 506.
6b. 782: 306–307.
7. 117: 66, 184–185; 627: 402–403; 1134: 27; *Béaloideas,* V (1935), 249.

N. Hens, Ducks, and Geese

1. 1014: 282.
2. 349: 450; 481: 82; 736: 532.
3. 349: 219; 481: 80; 736: 531–533, 555; 744: 36.

O. How Pigs, Mice, Rats, and Cats Came

1. See references to Type 1416 in Seán Ó Súilleabháin and Reidar Th. Christiansen, *The Types of the Irish Folktale,* Folklore Fellows Communications, No. 188 (Helsinki: Academia Scientiarum Fennica, 1963).
2. 1227: 195–197; *Béaloideas,* III (1932), 4–5; Hyde, *Legends of Saints and Sinners,* pp. 214–216; 474: pp. 660–663.
3. S. 650: 257.

P. Wild Animals, Birds, and Fishes

1. S. 50: 153.
2. 642: 455.
3. Pat Mullen, *Irish Tales* (London: Faber and Faber, 1938), pp. 126–127.
4. S. 1113: 316; 1013: 340.
5. 323: 286–289.
6. S. 287: 301–303.
7. 1105: 70.
8. 102: 301; 556: 335.
9. 1242: 152–153.

Q. General Origins

1. 54: 369.
2. 1051: 260–271.
3. 347: 395–396.

Q. General Origins (Continued)

4. 914: 334–335.
5. 269: 198–199 (for first part) ; 914: 469–470 (for second part).
6. 269: 98–99; 403: 176; 715: 201–202.
7. 481: 165–166; 1112: 116, 434–436; 1229: 454.
8. 289: 300.
9. 332: 128–129; 977: 405–406.
10. 195: 375–378.
11. 1189: 373–374.
12. *Béaloideas*, V (1935), 53.

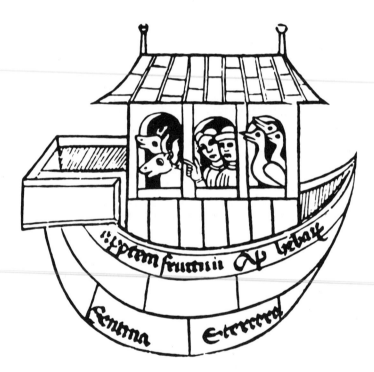

Noah's Ark, from *Fasciculus Temporum* (Cologne, *ca.* 1473)

JAROMÍR JECH

A Bohemian Medieval Fable on the Fox and the Pot

The fox got angry with the pot and decided to drown it. It tied the pot to its tail and let it sink into a well; because the pot was heavy and was filling with water, it dragged the fox under the water and the fox foundered. For a full version of the story see Appendix 1.

That is the short content of the Bohemian verse forming part of a volume of satiric poems called the *Hradecký rukopis* (the Hradec Manuscript), named after the city of Hradec Králové, because it was there that this remarkable work of old Bohemian literature dating back approximately to the second half of the fourteenth century was discovered by Josef Dobrovský, the founder of Slavonic studies. Dobrovský reported on this work for the first time in 1791,[1] and four years later it was the fable, appropriately entitled by its author *O lišcě a o čbánu* (The Fox and the Pot),[2] that was published as the first sample of the manuscript.

Roughly one hundred years after J. Dobrovský's discovery another version (Appendix 2) was published by the Polish representative of Slavonic studies, Alexander Brückner, this time in the form of an exemplum included in a manuscript of the university library in Wrocław (Breslau), IV. Q 126. At the same time he mentioned that in his opinion this Latin annotation was made before the year 1450 by a Czech. His view undoubtedly drew on the poem contained in the *Hradecký rukopis,* but obviously it was based also on other facts: the Wrocław manuscript contains toward the end, from leaf 306 to leaf 356, a *Liber parabolarum* provided with Czech glosses; this collection of fables with detailed moralization, popular with preachers, is known to date back to approximately 1200. Starting as a work by a learned English Cistercian, Odo de Ciringtonia (Sherington), educated in France, the collection was in many respects extended in the subsequent years, many new items being added to it. And it can be assumed that it was in Bohemia where its text was supplemented by the mentioned fable.[3]

Both discoveries aroused enormous interest among research workers. This can well be understood, because it was an epochal text which had not been documented before in medieval literature, as stated in one of the fundamental studies on folktales.[4] It was particularly the *Hradecký rukopis* in numerous editions that enjoyed a general attention. Let us recall at least the first critical edition of Adolf Patera, which is important from the folkloristic point of view chiefly because in the introductory study [5] the variants recorded at that time from tradition are not disregarded and one Russian parallel to the Fox and the Pot is mentioned from Afanasiev's collection.[6] Jiří Polívka viewed the material from a wider international context, mentioning not only the Russian, White Russian, and Ukrainian variants, but also one Epirian-Albanian parallel [7]—i.e., from the territory in the immediate neighborhood of the Greek ethnic group. Polívka's information anticipates, and in fact today supplements, the references made in Aarne-Thompson's catalogue. However, this catalogue includes the 68B type—the Fox Drowns the Pot—only in the last edition (1961) and draws attention merely to the Latvian, Lithuanian, Russian, and Greek variants.

The knowledge of the foreign variants, territorially rather remote, forced Polívka to consider carefully the provenance, even though later on he did not á priori exclude the possibility of the fable's having its origin on Czech soil.[8] Nevertheless, even today any hasty conclusions should be avoided despite the fact that the situation has changed rather substantially and that we no more possess only two medieval records, but two further documents from about the same period (Appendix 3). There is close genetic relationship between the two: either they drew on the same common model, or one is derived from the other one. Collections of Lent preaching, so called *Quadragesimale admontské* (Quadragesimale of Admont), named after the Admontean Cloister in Steiermark where they were deposited, have been preserved in two copies; both the manuscripts, Nos. 550 and 590, are today the property of the University Library in Prague as is the *Hradecký rukopis*. These records of the fable on the Fox and the Pot were made accessible by Jan Vilikovský, first in a version based on manuscript No. 550 [9] and later one based on MS 590.[10] The editor believes that the original of the collection, which is lost, dates back to the seventies of the fourteenth century, i.e., the time of the rule of Charles IV. The numerous bohemisms occurring in the Latin text leave nobody in doubt about the place of its origin.

Although these four documents, not far off from one another as far as the time of their origin is concerned, do not allow us to determine unequivocally the original home of the fable on the Fox and the Pot, they do provide a more reliable clue after all. In their complexity these four variants have remained to this day outside the attention of research workers and they have not been analyzed, therefore, in their mutual relations even from the folkloristic aspects.

From the survey presented it appears that the medieval documents of the fable on the Fox and Pot do not belong to a single literary variety. On the one hand, it is an epic poem; on the other hand, an exemplum. The different genres themselves give a specific form to the text. By this we do not have in mind only the contrast between the verse and prose, but a different approach to the text in principle, a different utilization and effect. While in the conclusion of the poem in the *Hradecký rukopis* there is a mere statement that the unwise fox lost its life and the moral is therefore implicit, the exempla contain explicit moralizing remarks. The different conclusions reflect also different functions. Verse represents a work of art, while exempla present only documentation for illustration, material for enlivening and better understanding the preaching trend. Such differentiation is based naturally only on a rough outline. In fact exempla need not lack artistic ambitions either, especially if such examples should be particularly effective for preaching and if they are expected to have a pronounced effect and influence on the audience, and this is not always achieved by the content of the story alone.

From this aspect the exempla about the fox and the pot have two levels, because at the first sight there exists an evident difference between the Wrocław version presenting mostly only a pattern of the subject matter, and the Admontean versions, which are a much more valuable narration. However, their advantages recede into the background in comparison with the style of the *Hradecký rukopis,* which is greatly superior to the other records. This manuscript, representing the third level, excels chiefly because of the ramification of the story, plasticity, and fine drawing. Moreover, a number of details appear there, e.g., an episode about the cock-chafer, which is not familiar to us from any other sources, or about the fox dropping the pot, which rolls down a hill. This detail gives rise also to another motivation: the pot is rolling too quickly; the fox cannot keep pace with it and thus decides to punish it by drowning. All our other records put it that the fox wished to take water, or was willing to allow the pot to have a drink, too. The Bohemian verse lacks one rather important feature. Although direct speech is amply used, the pot does not speak. On the other hand, we must not overlook certain common characteristics. I have in mind not only the main point, when the fox foolishly dips the pot into water and subsequently drowns, but also the incident when the fox runs into a deserted house and finds the pot there. In the poem of the *Hradecký rukopis* and the Admontean variants the pot is found behind the fireplace.

The last detail suggests that in certain features the links between the exempla are looser than between the exemplum and the Bohemian verse, as will be shown later. We do not intend to deny hereby in any way the correlations and congruencies obvious actually only between the exempla. They are naturally most pronounced between the two Admontean variants. They have a genetic affinity and, thus, have the main features in common: the thematic structure is identical and similarly the individual formulations are conformable. It is in fact a creation of one author, and the person or persons who did the copying adhered to the same basic text and only dared to make minor variations. Being members of the same nation and perhaps equally ill at ease in Latin, they could not help having the same way of thinking in that language. This found expression in the Czech language, although Latin terms predominated. An evidence of this can be found in the following sentence: *Wlpes* [in MS 590, *Wlpis*] *ut scitis, /vocatur a fraude et conveniens nomen habet. . . .* What is the meaning of this sentence? It can be decoded only after being translated into Czech. The relationship between the fox (*vulpes*) and the ruse (*fraus*), after which it is said to have been named, is natural. It is due to folk etymology of fox (Czech *liška*) and ruse (Czech *lest*). This is by no means a unique example of an author in the Middle Ages thinking in his mother tongue and expressing himself in Latin. As far as "Czech thinking in a Latin array" is concerned, it was Albert Wesselski who pointed out that Master Klaret (or his glossarist), Professor of the Charles University in Prague in the second half of the fourteenth century, gave in his works the Czech interpretation of birds' voices in Latin words.[11]

The Czech way of thinking manifests itself often even much more markedly by bohemisms (Czechisms) in the Latin context. However, at the same time an important difference can be observed here, chiefly in the extent to which the bohemisms are used and in the approach to them. In MS 590 bohemisms occur much more frequently, with the one exception in the sentence *Modo omnes exiverunt,* where the Latin verb is not replaced or interpreted by a Czech one. Except for two instances—*domum vacantem* PUSTI and *lusisti, id est* POHRAWALAS— all the bohemisms in MS 590 do not figure as explanatory notes to Latin words or sentences, in contrast to MS 550, but are an indispensable part of the text, assuming in certain places the nature of macaronics. On the other hand, in MS 550 mostly glosses are involved; only in one instance the term *po pustnach* replaces the Latin term.

On the whole MS 590 is more closely linked with the Czech environment. Evidence of this is provided also by the accusative *lysskam,* where the Czech word *lysska* (in the new Czech transcription *liška*) replacing the Latin word *vulpes* was given a Latin ending. There should also be noted an important detail of custom in connection with the period of the Shrovetide: going to town to drink beer belonged to the village pastimes. Nevertheless, it should be likewise stated that both variants retain in their morals a reference to the Shrovetide festivities. In MS 550, therefore, the mention of the domestics having gone to town to have a beer there could simply have been left out. Or, conversely, if such a mention had not been in the master copy, it could have been added later to accentuate the general trend of the story and to place it in the sphere of the typical Shrovetide stories.

With regard to the over-all differentiation it should be emphasized that MS 590 is more concise in the introduction and in the conclusion, while the actual story is presented at greater length, with more stress put on the details and a more vivid sense for dialogue. Otherwise, as stated before, the two variants form one whole and the differences are negligible, particularly when correlated with the next closest variant, the Wrocław Manuscript. Even the different approach to bohemisms seems to be irrelevant here. In the actual record in the Wrocław Manuscript bohemisms are totally absent and in relation to that manuscript the differences between the two Admontean texts completely fade out.[12]

At the same time a comparison of the Admontean texts on the one hand and the Wrocław text on the other makes their differences as well as their conformities more distinct. Both were implicitly mentioned to some extent already, even if not in detail. As far as agreement of the texts is concerned, all variants of the exempla converge, as distinguished from the Hradec Manuscript, in the idea of the fox taking water and in the dialogue with the pot. It is remarkable that the pot speaks in all the instances in the same way. This is another evidence for the well-known fact that dialogues, as far as they occupy more or less a key position in the story, remain unchanged as a rule from the formal aspect and thus show a considerable degree of stability.

Although the brief Wrocław record does not exceed, despite this direct speech, the mere framework of the fable, we could hardly believe that it is only a kind of "decoction" of the Admontean versions, i.e., that it originated from them or from their model. Surely certain links exist here, but apparently they are not direct, but leading through various interlinks. Several factors are indicative of this assumption. First, the designation of the Wrocław text as a mere model of a longer text is applicable only in rough outlines and not in all the details. The Latin version without bohemisms contains, moreover, an extra detail: the pot is big and served for keeping vinegar in it. More important are, however, certain conceptual differences. While in the Admontean variants the actual story about the fox and the pot has an explicatory function, purporting to clarify the proverb "Enough of the game," the Wrocław Manuscript lacks any mention of the proverb, and the resulting moral is completely different. For our purposes it is sufficient to note only the beginning saying that many people place their sins behind their backs as if they were tying them to their tails. This scene could not find a place in the Admontean versions, but it is very appropriate in the Wrocław record, where the fox wishing to take water does not tie the pot round its neck but to its tail. The idea thus realized has here, then, the function of a parable. By this form of the motif and its logical consequence expressed in the moral toward the end, the record moves away from both the varieties of the Admontean exemplum, loses contact with them and, on the other hand, keeps contact with the *Hradecký rukopis* written in Czech verse.

Nevertheless, the situation is not so simple, because realization of the motif retains in the *Quadragesimale admontské* a certain absence of logic. When the pot tied around the fox's neck filled with water and was sinking, the fox turned round to look at it. She could have done so if the pot had been tied to her tail and not round her neck. How to explain this *lapsus?* Probably by an infiltration of the motif from other sources, but naturally an inconsistent infiltration. The new picture did not allow the old picture to disappear altogether, a part of its original version has been retained in the word *retrospiciens*. At the same time this infiltration caused splitting of the motif: first we are told that the fox tied the pot to her *tail* and was running after it here and there across the fields; and then the fox is said to have tied it to her *neck* and lowered it into the well.

It seems, therefore, that the Admontean variants represent a kind of transition between the older records of the fable on the fox and the pot and its more recent records. In other words, most probably more original were those versions in which the fox put into the water a pot tied to the tail, as observed by J. Vilikovský,[13] and only later a change occurred in the formulation, the fox tying the pot round her neck, or rather putting her head into the pot. This variety of the motif eventually prevailed, but not universally, for it does not appear in the Albanian variant.[14] The international draft of the Aarne-Thompson catalogue considers only this form of the motif. Let us compare also Thompson's *Motiv-Index* J 2131.5.7 (Fox trying to drown jug). While this motif is considered as part of a wider group, where mention is made only of the head (J 2131.5 [Numskull gets his head caught] and cf. J 2136.6), here can be included also type 68A (The Jug as Trap), corresponding with our type 68B (The Fox Drowns the Pot) and documented in the international catalogue only by a single variant, the Polish one, although it is undoubtedly well known also in Slovak folk tradition.[15]

From what has been said, certain conclusions can be drawn. It is true that not even now can we claim with certainty that the fable about the fox and the pot has its origin in the Czech lands, but it is beyond any doubt that the fable acquired a distinct form in the Czech environment and that it was closely linked with it, as documented in the Admontean texts both by bohemisms and by the element of the customary "going out to have a beer," especially at Shrovetide. The popularity of the subject matter in the fourteenth and fifteenth centuries is in sharp contrast with its later oblivion. As a matter of fact, it does not appear in the modern records of Czech prose and is registered only from the eastern part of Europe. How to explain this absence? Perhaps we are not far from the truth when we suggest that in the course of time the links between the Czech and east European cultures loosened, while strong links still existed between them at that time, at least as far as folklore is concerned, which seems apparent from a preliminary analysis of the oldest Czech documents and particularly the various Latin manuscripts.[16] On the other hand, links with the other side were becoming stronger, so that we speak today of the Czech culture as a west European culture, and often we fail to examine whether this was always actually so.

By comparing the oldest texts about the fox and the pot from practically the same period we can study the process of variability from several angles, depending on the two variants we compare, namely whether they are genetically or in their genre close to or different from each other. Naturally, we shall not satisfactorily explain the variability only against the background of these four texts, even though they do indicate certain clear trends of development. In order to obtain a more complete and rounded picture it would be necessary to add to the comparative basis all further records; it is those that are today known from people's tradition. Then we would see how even the basic subject-matter is liable to changes and is conceptually totally different, or how the leitmotif of drowning the jug (pot, bottle, etc.) is given in different contexts with the use of other types or motifs. Such an affinity can be observed, among other things, in the variants of other nations: cf. Afanasiev's parallel and the Albanian record. In some cases even another *persona dramatica* makes its appearance: in certain Ukrainian parallels the tasks of the fox are assumed by the hare.[17] However, the coverage of all the variants in the different ethnic areas is beyond the possibilities of this short study.

When comparing the variants we can see at the same time an apparent contrast between the variability and stability of the fable in the general theme and details. Because of their constant, lasting features the variants have different relations. Closest links exist between the two Admontean texts which form a unity as compared with the Wrocław record, and all three taken together represent a larger whole connected by the prevailing genre of the exempla. Yet the relationship cannot be seen only in terms of the framework of the exempla; sometimes the texts of the exempla differ from one another on account of a certain feature, and because of this feature the particular variant resembles the *Hradecký rukopis* in Czech verse. With a slight simplification the relations between the medieval Bohemian records of the fable on the Fox and Pot provide the following picture:

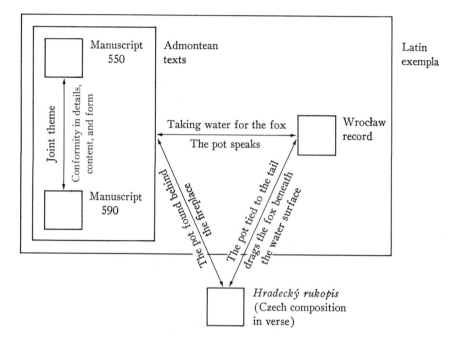

What was the primary form (*Urform*)? We do not dare to determine the original form of the fable on the fox and the pot merely on the basis of four variants. We do not even intend to reconstruct the fictive master copy with all the turnings from which, in a direct or indirect way, links lead to our medieval records. Our objective must be only very modest, and we can attempt to trace only the probable basic theme, the probable subject-matter of the older model. The fox ran into a deserted house and found a pot behind the fireplace. She tied the pot to her tail and was running about with it. She came to a well in order to take water from it. The pot was filling and in the last moment the fox asked the pot in vain not to drag her down. The pot replied: "Enough of the game you had with me! Now it is my turn to play with you," and it drowned the fox.

These are the rough conclusions that can be drawn. Their validity is only very limited, often hypothetical, because they were arrived at only on the basis of scanty documentation. It cannot be excluded that the general mosaic will assume a different or more precise shape if we succeed in discovering further medieval records. Then it would be possible to give a more accurate reply also to the question of the ethnical provenance of the fable on the Fox and the Pot.

APPENDICES

Note: Appendix 1 is taken from Josef Hrabák's edition of *Staročeské satiry* (Ancient Czech Satires), (Prague, 1947), pp. 71–73. Appendix 2 is from Alexander Brückner's publication (cited in footnote 3) and its transcription into classic Latin is reproduced unchanged. Only in one case is the interpretation altered: direct speech is marked and rendered in independent paragraphs, and the initial letters are in capitals. In Appendix 3 both variants are printed to facilitate a parallel comparison. The variants are based on J. Vilikovský's edition (notes 9 and 10); as in the previous appendix, direct speech and the division into paragraphs are slightly modified. I have eliminated the errors pointed out by Dr. Helena Businská of the Department of Greek, Roman, and Latin Studies of the Czechoslovak Academy of Sciences. She has carried out a comparison of published texts with the manuscripts of the *Quedragesimale of Admont*.

Appendix 1: Hradecký rukopis

O lišce a o čbánu

Liška jednú běhajíci,
jésti sobě hledajíci,
uběže do jedněch pústek,
ano v nich jediný chrústek.
Vece: "Pověz mi to, chrúste,
čie jsú toto chýše pusté?"
On jéj tako otpovědě
řka: "Jázt˘ sám nevědě;
teprv sem jedno přišel sěm,
nejmám nice činiti s tiem."
Liška poče sě točiti,
by mohla co uhoniti;
točivši sě sěmo i tam
i uběže k pustým kamnám,
a když sě v niestěji vtoči,
inhed v kamnách čbána zoči.
Vece: "Dobrý večer, čbáne,
kak sě jmáš, mój milý pane?"
Čbán lišce nice nevece
a ona vzemši jej na plece
potěšči sě s ním ven z pústek.
Tu ji potka onen chrústek;
vece: "Liška, co to neseš,
že nohami jedva pleteš?"

Ona vecě: "Nesu čbána,
mého milostného pána."
Zdáše sě jéj nésti těžek;
vznesši jej na jeden břiežek
i pusti jej dolóv opak
řkúc: "Jáz tobě učini tak,"
vecě; "pójdiž dolóv, čbáne,
těžeks mi nésti, mój pane!"
Čbán sě dolóv s hory pokoti,
liška sě po něm běžiec upoti.
Vecě: "Čbáne, proč běžíc prudcě?
Přěsadíš mi skoro srdce."
A když čbán na rovni bieše,
viec sě kotiti nemožieše,
vecě liška: "Kde jdeš, čbáne?
Zdalis ustal, milý pane?
Pakli nechceš se mnú jíti,
jáz chci tobě učiniti,
že pójdeš se mnú bezděky,
kdež sě nevrátíš na věky."
Přivázavši čbán k uocasu,
vecě: "Jáz tě tam donesu,
budeš úpiti na své hoře,
plavaje jako prosěd mořě."
A když přiběže k studnici,
běda liščě hubenici!
mnieše oklamajíc čbána,
nalit sě oblúdi sama.
Vecě: "Čbáne, ké sě modlíš,
zlého úmysle, že tiem dlíš."
Ona nic nepomeškavši,
čbán k ocasu přivázavši,
vzleze vzhóru na ohlubnici
i pusti čbána v studnici;
vecě: "Když sě nechceš modliti,
jáz tě musím utopiti."
Čbán poče svrchu plavati,
poče liška naň volati
řkúc: "Čbáne, brzo viz o sobě,
jižť jest velmi zle o tobě.
Razuť, pokoř mi sě jedinú
a otpustímť vši tvú vinu."

Čbána lzě mluviti nebieše,
nebo z hlíny slepen bieše.
Tehdy sě liška rozhněvavši,
čbána u vodu vrazivši,
vecě: "Jižť sem dosti hověla tobě,
cos uhonil, jměj to sobě."
Čbán sě počě zalévati,
vody sě veň nalévati,
lišky k sobě potáhati.
Liška sě počě ottáhati;
vecě liška: "Ne tak, čbáne,
jázť spíleji, milý pane."
Tehdy čbán počě bobtati,
vody sě veň nalévati,
hlúbe sě pohřižievati;
liška počě vždy volati
řkúc: "Běda, co mi sě chce státi?"
Vecě: "Milý čbáne, otpusť mi to
a jáz tobě slibuji to,
žeť nechci tobě škoditi,
rač mě nebožku živiti."
Ona toho řéci netaže,
až ji čbán k sobě přitaže;
ona sě v studnici vrže,
inhed ji čbán na dno vtrže,
tu jéj neda viec vzniknúti,
musi bezděky utonúti.
Tak sě liška přěmúdřila,
svój život marně ztratila,
ot čbána z hlíny slepeného
zbyla liška života svého.

The Fox and the Pot

A fox, roaming about the fields in search of food, ran into a house and found nobody there but a cock-chafer.

"Tell me, cock-chafer, whom does this deserted house belong to?" asked the fox.

The bug answered: "I don't know. I have just come here."

The fox began to run about until she found a pot behind the oven and said to it: "Good evening, my dear pot, how are you?"

Meeting with no answer from the pot, the fox took it on her shoulders and was off with it. The cock-chafer, encountering the fox, asked her: "What are you carrying? You can hardly drag your legs."

The fox answered: "I am carrying my lord, the pot."

The burden seemed rather heavy. She carried it up a hill and let it roll down. She sighed: "Come down, my lord, you are too heavy."

The pot was rolling down the hill and the fox, running after it, got into a sweat and exclaimed: "Hey, pot, why such a hurry? You ruin my heart."

The pot landed on a plain and stopped rolling. The fox said: "Where are you going, my lord, are you perhaps tired? If you don't want to follow me, I'll force you to go to a place from where you'll never return."

Having tied the pot to her tail, the fox said: "I'll take you there; you'll groan with pain as if you were in the middle of the sea."

She arrived at a well. Alas for the miserable fox who, wanting to fool the pot, punished herself. She said to the pot: "Say your last prayer now."

Instantly she tied the pot to her tail, climbed on the well and began to let the pot sink into the well. "If you don't want to pray, I must drown you." The pot remained for a while on the surface and the fox exclaimed: "I advise you to bow to me humbly once and I'll forgive you."

The pot, being made from clay, could not speak. The fox became angry and pushed the pot under the water, saying: "I have been over-patient with you; now you'll get what you deserve."

The pot began to fill itself with water and started dragging the fox down. The fox tried to disengage herself and said: "My dear pot, I was only joking."

But the pot became fuller and fuller and was sinking lower and lower. The fox began crying: "Alas, what's happening to me! My dear pot, forgive me, and I promise to do no harm to you. Let me stay alive."

Hardly had she said it when the pot began to drag her down the well and did not allow her to escape. Willy, willy, the fox got drowned.

The cunning fox lost her life and was overcome by a pot made from clay.

Appendix 2: Wrocław Manuscript IV. Q 126

Quodam tempore intravit vulpes in quandam domum desertam et invenit ibi amphoram vacuam sed magnam, in qua quondam acetum servabatur, et alligavit sibi amphoram ad caudam et cucurrit cum ea par montes et colles amphoram infestando. Demum pervenit ad unum fontem et immisit ibi amphoram, ut sibi hauriret aquam. Amphora autem impleta aqua ponderavit post se vulpem. Cui vulpes dixit:

"O bona amphora, quare me ita aggravas?"

Respondit:

"Tu mecum satis lusisti, ego tecum etiam ludam."

Et sic vulpem submersit.

Ita multi ponunt eis peccata post tergum, quia ad caudam ea ligantes, sed non ponunt ea ante oculos, ut de eis vellent penitere, quae eos in tantum aggravant et ultimatum post se trahunt et submergunt in inferno. Sed deberent esse sicut avis quae vocatur falco, quae habet in capite etc. etc.

Appendix 3: the Admontean texts

MS No. 550

[S]citis * illud verum † prouerbium vdne venit, quando dicitis: "Satis est de illo ludo" *i. dosti te hry* [enough of that game]; et si nescitis, tunc audite: wlpes vocatur a fraude et conueniens nomen habet, quod sepe multos decipit. Eciam sola a multis decipitur: Ergo ei est dictum istud prouerbium.

Quia vna vice currens per campos et *po pustynach* [over waste land] huc et inde incurrit *i. vbiehla gest* [run into] in vnam domum vacantem *i. pusty dom* [deserted house] et ibi inuenit vnam amphoram retro fornacem et dixit:

"Quid tu hic sola operatis[!]? Modo omnes exierunt *i. wystiehowali sie* [they have left] de domo, et tu sola mansisti."

Et volens sibi facere solacium, ligauit sibi illam amphoram ad caudam et sic cucurrit per campos huc et inde; et quo ipsa cucurrit, ibi eciam amphora, sic quod venit ad vnum fontem et dixit:

MS No. 590

Scitis, unde proverbium istud venit *dosty tee hri* [enough of that game]? Si nescitis, audiatis. Wlpis, ut scitis, vocatur a fraude et conveniens nomen habet, quia sepe multos decipit et eciam decipitur.

Que vna vice currens *po pustynach* [over waste land] huc et illuc *vbyehla* [run into] in vnam domum vacantem *pusti* [deserted]. Et ibi invenit vnam amphoram retro fornacem. Omnis familia de villa exiverat at quandam civitatem *na pywo* [to have a beer there]; et hoc fuit *na masopust* [Shrovetide]. Et dixit ei:

"Quid tu hic sola operaris, Mono omnes exiverunt."

Et volens sibi facere solacium ligando amphoram ad caudam cucurrit per campos dicens:

"Modo *gsu* [are] omnes *weseli* [gay]. Letemur et nos, *myli czbanku!*" [my dear pot].

Et sic in tantum hinc inde per silvas, montes in campos transcurit. Post venit ad fontem quendam et dixit:

---

* Initial letter not used.

† In the manuscript *vm* without abbreviation sign; probably = *verbum* (instead of which the scribe wrote *prouerbium* and forgot to delete ?).

"Modo cum amphora ambulant pro aqua: eciam hauriam aquam."

Et sic ligans amphoram sibi ad collum immisit eam in fontem.

Et dum amphora implebatur aqua, wlpes voluit extrahere et non potuit. Et tunc retrospiciens dixit:

"O amphora, quid facis? Non vis exire?"

Que respondit:

"Iam satis mecum lusisti *i. prze-hrawala* [you have played enough with me]; jam satis de illo ludo. Ego eciam tecum ludam."

Et sic amphora existens plena aqua sua grauedine intraxit in fontem wlpem et submersit.

Quare hoc dixi? Jam satis de peccatis ligastis ibi vobis in carnispriuio et lusistis cum eis, ut voluistis; ergo timendum est, ne uobis dicat peccatum idem ut amphora wlpi: "Iam satis mecum lusisti," et demerget[!] te in infernum, ut amphora wlpem. Ergo confiteamini nunc peccata vestra etc.

"Tamen cum amphora pro aqua ambulant!"

Et sic ligans amphoram ad collum misit ad fontem dicens:

"*Napy sye, myli czbanku* [Drink, my dear pot], et michi etim haurias."

Et dum amphora implebatur, wlpis volebat extrahere. Et dum non potuit, retrospiciens se dixit:

"O amphora, quid facis? Non vis exire?"

Que respondit:

"Iam satis mecum lusisti, id est *pohrawalas* [you have played long]. *Dosty tee hri, lysso!* [Enough of that game, fox!] Ego eciam tecum perludam."

Et sic amphora sua gravedine submersit *lysskam* [the fox].

Ideo hoc dixi: Iam satis cum peccatis in carnisprivio lusistis *giz dosty tee hri* [already enough of that game] ne demergamini in infernum vt wlpis a amphora. Ergo cenfitemini nunc peccata vestra.

February, from a German Calendar (Augsburg *ca.* 1485)

D. K. WILGUS AND BRUCE A. ROSENBERG

A Modern Medieval Story:
"The Soldier's Deck of Cards"

Counting-songs which ascribe religious values to a numerical sequence begin at least in the Middle Ages, and probably earlier; they are sung today. A Latin hymn of this type was recorded in Italy in 1602 and a Hebrew chant, "Echod Mi Yodea," was first printed in 1526. Hungarian versions appear a century later in Catholic hymnarys.[1] To understand ourselves, we see in yet another instance, we must go back through the centuries. What more appropriate tribute, then, can we offer to a man whose scholarship, taste, and sympathies have spanned the centuries and bridged the studies of Folklore and Medieval Literature? Francis Lee Utley has always seen the presence of folk culture in medieval literature as well as in modern. From *Beowulf* to *The Bear* he has illuminated us; we hope in this essay to repay him in part.

Our immediate concern is with a relatively recent modification of the counting song, Thompson Type 1613, best known as "The Soldier's Deck of Cards." On a recent field trip to Bakersfield, California (on June 20, 1967), we recorded as part of an unrelated project the church services of several preachers in the area. Because having one's voice recorded for posterity on tape is a portion of immortality, it is also a matter of some pride in the community: usually the ministers recited their favorite sermons for the visitors, and generally gave spirited performances. One of the ministers we interviewed, the Reverend Rubin Lacy, preached in the Union Baptist Church what he said was his favorite sermon, which he called "The Deck of Cards." In the old days, Lacy told us, this sermon was synonymous with his name and it had always proven immensely popular with congregations around the country.

The sermon itself, as are all sermons preached by Mr. Lacy and most of his colleagues, was spontaneously composed (though the basic outline had been "memorized"), orally delivered, and it was consistently metrical.[2] Although Lacy had memorized—or nearly memorized—small portions of his sermon, the entire piece was recited without the aid of a manuscript or notes of any kind. It was chanted rather than spoken, each line punctuated by exclamations of joy and piety from the congregation and by clearly audible gasps of breath by Lacy. The punctuation of both congregation and minister, almost perfect in their timing throughout, is the one used to break the lines in the following transcription:

Mister Hoyle/ Tryin' his best/ To compare with God/ Look this evenin'/ God made a heaven/ And God made a world/ Mister Hoyle decided/ That he here/ Could compete with God/ That he might draw/ Disciples from God/ Look this evenin'/ Men are always/ Tryin' t'equalize God/ So God/ Made a earth/ A world/ With three-hundred and sixty-five days/ In the year/ Mister Hoyle/ Made a deck of cards/ With three-hundred and sixty-five spots/ In the cards/ Ain't I right about it?/ And God/ Made a year/ With fifty-two weeks in the year/ Mister Hoyle/ Made a deck of cards/ With fifty-two/ Cards in the deck/ Ain't God all right/ And God/ Said there's two ways to go/ Heaven/ Or either hell/ Mister Hoyle/ Made a two-spot/ He called it a deuce/ God from Zion/ And put it in the deck/ And God/ Made the Father/ Son and Holy Ghost/ Ain't God all right?/ And Mister Hoyle/ Made a three-spot/ And called it a trey/ God from Zion/ In Matthew Mark/ Luke and John/ Mister Hoyle/ Made a four-spot/ Put it in the deck/ God from Zion/ Jesus, the lamb of God/ Dyin' on the cross/ Dyin' of wounds/ In His body/ Two in His hands/ One in His side/ And two in His feet/ Mister Hoyle/ Made a five-spot/ Placed it in the deck/ Ain't God all right?/ Mister Hoyle/ 'Membered it took/ Six days/ To make the earth/ Mister Hoyle/ Put a six-spot in the deck/ An' he remembered/ That God rested on the seventh day/ Mister Hoyle/ Made a seven-spot/ And placed it in the deck/ God from Zion/ Then God/ Saved Noah/ And his bretheren/ In the ark/ Eight people/ Saved in the ark/ Mister Hoyle/ Put a eight-spot in the deck/ God from Zion/ And then/ They put a nine-spot in the deck/ Representin'/ Hangin' from the sixth/ To the ninth hour/ Hangin' on His cross/ God from Zion/ And then he put/ A ten-spot in the deck/ Representin'/ The ten commandments/ God from Zion/ Thou shalt not steal/ Thou shalt not commit adultery/ Thou shalt not bear false witness/ God from Zion/ Not over yet/ And Mister Hoyle/ Put a Queen in the deck/ Representin'/ The Queen of Sheba/ Ain't this a good story?/ One day/ Lookin' over God's children/ Not only that/ Said the half had never been told/ Ain't God all right/ Mister Hoyle/ Put a King in the deck/ Representin'/ King Solomon/ Wisest man that ever lived/ And Mister Hoyle/ Put a Jack in the deck/ Representin' black horse—that death/ That rides from home to home/ And from house to house/ Then ya see what he did then/ After a while/ He put a ace in the deck/ Representin' the high card/ The Lord Himself/ Ain't God all right?/

The sermon continued for a few moments longer and ended when Mr. Lacy faded out of the chant and into a gospel song. The sermon is based, of course on Aarne-Thompson Type 1613, Motif H 603.

Before the service Mr. Lacy claimed (with some pride) that the sermon he would deliver was a favorite of his that he had thought up many years ago in Mississippi (his birthplace) and which he had used over the years on special occasions. Being recorded was such an occasion. A certain amount of stylistic originality is prized among Lacy's colleagues, so long as the gospel is kept "straight." Thus his feeling of esthetic pride at having conceived of a clever sermon topic. But on the following week just before the morning service was to begin, one member of the congregation, Sister Mary Olison, mentioned to Mr. Lacy that the first time she had heard the "Deck of Cards" sermon was about "twenty years ago" from "Reverend" T. Texas Tyler. It was Sister Mary's understanding that Tyler was at that time a minister in Texas and that he got his ministerial start by convincing his superiors that the common deck of cards had religious significance. Lacy, seemingly embarrassed at having his real source uncovered, admitted having heard Tyler's version on the radio in Texas somewhere "near Dallas." Thus Lacy's sermon would appear to be a re-creation of a widely performed and recorded professional recitation. Such an impression is false. Mr. Lacy was more likely being polite; he was certainly not making a confession of his source, though he undoubtedly had one, as we shall demonstrate in a brief survey of Anglo-American variants of "The Deck of Cards."

Tale Type 1613 has been widely reported from the continent, the British Isles, and the New World since 1766,[3] and its popularity in the United States continues. Coincidentally, while checking on its popularity at Bakersfield radio station KUZZ, we were interrupted by a caller who requested that the station play Tex Ritter's version on their request program. On the Midwestern Hayride TV program viewed in Los Angeles April 20, 1968, Charlie Gore illustrated a performance of the monologue by flashing oversized playing cards. We agree with Ed Cray's comments introducing his discussion of "The Deck of Cards" that not only is the tale "more widespread than previously thought," but we "have much to learn of the functional interrelationship between oral tradition and the so-called 'popular' arts." [4]

At present the most popular version of "The Deck of Cards" in the United States would seem to be that stemming from the performance of T. Texas Tyler referred to by Sister Mary Olison and printed by Cray.[5] Tyler (David Myrick) was a Country-Western performer of considerable popularity,[6] but Sister Mary's "Reverend" is not mistaken, as Tyler is now an ordained minister and has been evangelizing throughout North America for the last decade. The development and spread of the Tyler version is both interesting and enlightening as an example of the fortunes of traditional material in the modern broadside industry.

In 1938–1939 Tyler was broadcasting on WCHS in Charleston, West Virginia, and in his reading came across "The Soldier's Prayer Book," which he copied.

It had no flowing continuity. . . . I felt it would make a real story if brought up to date—so the common person could understand it. . . . About this time Hitler was making his move. So I desided to place the setting in North Africa. Finally I got it the way I wanted it and started broadcasting the piece on radio. It drew a mild responce—mainly because it wasn't the physcologicial time [*sic*].[7]

The time was right when Tyler recorded "The Deck of Cards" for the Four-Star Record Company in Los Angeles, and the recording (Four-Star 1228) [8] issued in January, 1948, became extremely popular, was "covered" by performers from Tex Ritter to Phil Harris,[9] and was turned into a song by W. F. Stewart.[10] Tyler had not copyrighted the recitation until he "gave it to" American Music in 1947, and he apparently realized very little financial remuneration. But, as he writes, "Most everyone connected with it were like a bunch of sharks after a wounded fish." Industry executives became concerned about copyright when a woman in Seattle wrote Four-Star that she had read the piece in a local newspaper several years previously.[11] Investigation in Seattle yielded no copyright; nor did a subsequent one in Cleveland, based on a similar communication. In March, 1968, Colonel William V. Daum of Cincinnati heard a recording, presumably that of Nelson

King (King 712), played on WCKY and retained patent attorneys, who advised Four-Star that Daum had written the "poem" ten years before and had copyrighted it as "A Pack of Cards, Not Guilty" in 1941. On April 2, 1948, William H. McCall of Four-Star paid Daum $1,250 for the copyright. The account of the transaction in Joseph Garretson's April 8 column in *The Cincinnati Enquirer* resulted in more than 100 letters from readers who had old copies of the piece, recalled hearing it years before, or could furnish a background dating it to the eighteenth century. Some of the texts were said to be identical to Daum's, even to the last comma. Investigation by McCall's attorney located in the Library of Congress the English chapbook "A Pack of Cards Changed into a compleat Almanac and Prayer-Book" dated *ca.* 1790. On September 11, McCall filed suit against Daum for $18,250 in damages. We have been unable to ascertain the outcome of the suit, but tend to agree with Tyler that it was probably settled out of court.

Both the Tyler and Daum texts belong to the dominant English language tradition represented by F, G, and J in Johannes Bolte's study of 1901,[12] while the 1790 chapbook in the Library of Congress belongs to the H tradition.[13] The tradition of H, which we shall call Type I (with no suggestion of precedence), concerns a servant, Jack, denounced to the noble master as a gamester by a fellow servant. When, after his denial of knowledge of cards, a deck is found on his person, Jack cleverly extricates himself by explaining the cards as an almanac and a prayer-book. The references and the sequence of explanation are as follows (items in italics are omitted in abbreviated texts) :

Suits: quarters
Cards in a suit: weeks in a quarter; *lunar months*
Court cards: Signs of Zodiac *or* months
Cards: weeks
Spots (pips): days; *× 24 ÷ 60 = hours and minutes*
Suits: *principal religions*
Court cards: *Patriarchs; twelve tribes; twelve apostles; twelve articles*
King: allegiance to his majesty
Queen: allegiance to her majesty
Ten: *cities of the plains; plaques;* commandments; *tribes*
Nine: *hierarchies;* muses; *noble orders*
Eight: *beauties; altitudes;* persons saved in Noah's ark
Seven: *administering spirits; seals; angels and phials; liberal arts and sciences;* wonders of the world; *planets*

Six: *petitions in the Lord's prayer* (selected as the unique value in the
   H text) ; *work days* (selected as the unique value in the Liverpool
   chapbook)

Five: senses

Four: *theological virtues; evangelists; death, judgment, heaven, and
   hell;* seasons

Three: *Trinity; hours on the cross; hours He lay interred;* days Jonah
   spent in the whale's belly (Liverpool chapbook substitutes the graces ;
   H includes both the graces and Jonah's days.)

Two: *Testaments;* virtue and vice

Ace: God ; *faith, truth, baptism, and master*

Knave: Jack's accuser.

The tradition of Bolte F, G, J, which we shall call Type II, has the
more familiar military setting. A soldier, caught spreading out cards
in church, is taken before a mayor or magistrate. Threatened with
punishment, he explains how the cards serve as his Bible, prayer-book,
and almanac and is rewarded. The following analysis is based on
Bolte's summaries; Edward M. Wilson's Ja and Jb texts;[14] and two
broadsides from the Frank Kidson Collection in Glasgow, Jc and Jd.[15]
Items in brackets do not occur in all texts.

Ace: God
Two: Father and Son
Three: Trinity
Four: Evangelists
Five: wise virgins
Six: days of creation
Seven: day of rest
Eight: persons saved in Noah's ark
Nine: lepers
Ten: commandments
Queen: Sheba [pray for Queen Victoria]
King: King of Heaven [pray for King George]
Knave: sergeant or constable who arrested the soldier
Spots: days
Cards: weeks
tricks: [lunar months] [weeks in a quarter]
Picture cards: [months].

The Daum text, as printed in the April 8, 1948, *Cincinnati Enquirer,*
lacks the detailed introduction (which may have been summarized by

Garretson) but is otherwise identical to Ja, an American songster text circulating at least from the early twentieth century,[16] which is in turn derived from, if not identical to J, "Richard Lee in Glasgow," which we have not been able to examine.

The Tyler text is also related to the JJa texts, but shows significant revision, if not influence from another source. Tyler sets the tale in North Africa, although Cassino, his surrogate for Glasgow, is in Italy. The soldiers have returned from a hike, not a march, and the troops have been on the march for six days instead of six weeks. The accused is taken before the provost marshall instead of a mayor or magistrate. But alterations in the symbolization are more important:

Suits: weeks in a month
Two: Testaments
Queen: the Virgin Mary
Knave: the Devil.

The flexibility of attribution of various "meanings" to the cards makes invention and polygenesis more than possible. The addition of the reference to the suits may be a case in point. But the other changes have analogues worth considering. The one other English language text which contains all three and is not a proven derivative of Tyler's was reported by David S. McIntosh in 1952 from the daughter of a Negro minister in Illinois.[17] It is a bare listing without the narrative "frame." The association of the deuce with the two testaments occurs also in Type I, but the reference to the Virgin Mary has been reported elsewhere only from continental versions (French, Danish, German, Portuguese, Spanish) and in a Negro sermon to be considered later. Furthermore, this would seem to be an unusual introduction into a Protestant tradition. The alteration in the "value" of the Knave is more unusual and important. The Knave (Jack in McIntosh) is equated with the Devil nowhere else in the entire tradition of Type 1613 excepting in "Rattlin' Joe's Prayer," which Austin Fife recently printed from the John A. Lomax Collection.[18] In this recitation, which is a variant of the poem of that title by John W. (Captain Jack) Crawford [19] "Rattlin' Joe" delivers the sequence of symbolizations (omitting the almanac portion) as a funeral prayer for a dead comrade. The referents agree with the Ja tradition except for the identification of the Knave with the Devil. It therefore seems likely that Tyler had multiple sources or that he had access to a source which, by equating the Knave with the Devil, which occurs in an injunction to both the Devil and God to "keep his hands off'n poor Bill," eliminated the incident in which the accused cleverly turns on his accuser.

Professional performances in the wake of the Tyler recording have usually been quite faithful to his version. Tyler personalized the tale by concluding: "And friends, this story's true. I know 'cause I was that soldier" (possibly accounting for Sister Mary Olison's story of Tyler's entrance into the ministry). Tyler's successors.usually change the ending to "I knew that soldier." The "Tyler tradition" has produced three other branches. The first is the Stewart Family song "The Soldier's Prayerbook," previously mentioned, which in versifying the text preserves its substantive essence. The second development shows the continuing influence of the Ja text—or of Tyler's source. "The Bible Deck of Cards" in *Arlen and Jackie Vaden The Southern Gospel Singers Presents Their 1958 Book of Radio Favorites Songs* (KXEL, Waterloo, Iowa) [20] is essentially the Tyler text, but shows influence of Ja in the reintroduction of "Glasgo," "Richard," and "the sincerety of my intentions." (The text concludes: "my brother was that soldier.") The third stream is more complex, involving significant adaptation.

The Billboard (June 26, 1948, p. 31) reported that

Tom Brennan, Los Angeles d.j. known as Tennessee Tom-Tom, has a switch on *The Deck of Cards* utilizing a U.S. History in place of a Bible. It will intro on Ken Curtis's ABS web *Hitching Post*.

This form is not available to us, but we do have that of Red River Dave (McEnery), who in 1952 introduced "The Red Deck of Cards." [21] The scene is a military camp just outside "Freedom Gate" in Korea during an exchange of prisoners. One of the soldiers explains to the others how the "Commies" used a deck of cards to try "to teach us their false doctrine." In this wildly nationalistic version the ace is the one Communist god, the State; the deuce is the two great leaders, Stalin and Lenin; the three great religions would soon be destroyed by the Reds; the hammer and sickle would "soon reign supreme" in the four corners of the earth; the red star had five points, etc.

"The Cowboy's Deck of Cards," composed and performed by the late (Lloyd) Cowboy Copas in 1966 [22] is closer to the Tyler original but changes the scene to the American West and claims that "friends, this story's true, because my grandfather was that cowboy."

Friends, this is Cowboy Copas. I'd like to tell you a story about a cowboy and a deck of cards. During the early years of our great western frontier, a large group of cowboys along with their foreman, were making the big fall roundup and cattle drive from Texas to Abilene, Kansas, and they had been on the trail for many weeks, having seen no one except Indians, prairie dogs, and coyotes. The roundup and drive had been very successful, because they had not lost a single steer and no harm had come to any of the cowboys during the great drive. At the end of the drive the foreman, being a very devout man, suggested to his cowboys that they go to the little chapel in Abilene and offer thanks to the Great Boss in the sky for the success of the drive and for their well-being. When they came into the chapel, most of the boys had their prayer-books except one cowboy who, being the youngest of the group, spread a deck of cards before him. The foreman, seeing the cards, reprimanded the cowboy, saying, "Son, what are you doing with those cards in the chapel? I hope that you have a worthy explanation of this."

"I hope so, Sir," the boy said. "You see, I was orphaned at a early age, and I roamed the country all of my life until I joined you and the rest of my friends here, which gave me a sense of belonging and trying to learn."

And with that, the boy started his story.

(The rest of the story—concerning the meaning of the cards—is almost identical to the Tyler text.)

Undoubtedly the most imaginative version is that of Ferlin Husky (as "Simon Crum"), the "Hillbilly Deck of Cards." Recorded April 5, 1954 (Capitol 3270), this satire at least counterbalances "The Red Deck of Cards."

Friends, this is Simon Crum, with the story about the hillbilly sucker and a deck of cards.

A bunch of boys was playing poker in a little town back home behind the general store, and one little boy kept watchin' 'em, and they said, "C'mon, get in the game." He wouldn't do it. They said, "Why not?" He wouldn't tell 'em. They kept askin' him an' he never would tell 'em. Finally he broke down and he told 'em. He said:

"Ya see, fellers, that ace reminds me of the first and last trip I went to a town called Reno, Nevada.

"The deuce, well that makes me think of the two days and nights that it took me to get to this town of one-armed bandits, card-sharks, and sharpshooters.

"The trey—well that's the three card—that's how many there was in our party, there was three of us, me and my wife and another hillbilly sucker that went along with us to help us drive.

"The four? Well that's the time of day that we got there, four o'clock in the morning and at four o'clock the next morning we were still at it.

"The five—lemme see, the five, oh I don't remember what the five means.

"But the six, well that's after I quit playing poker and tried that other game, you know that long green table and you roll them things with the white spots on 'em down it; well the six is what'd come up on me after I rolled 'em.

"The seven, ha-ha-ha, you guessed it—the seven is what I got.

"The eight? Well that makes me think of all the eight-balls that was up there.

"Nine? That's the number of livestock that I sold to get enough money to get up there: they was four old sows, three white-faced heifers, and two shoats.

"The ten? Well, that reminds me of the ten thousand times I wished that I had stayed at home.

"The Queen? Oh that queen, that was my lovin' wife who stood right by my side and lost twice as much as I did.

"The King? That's what I thought I'd be when I got back home with all that loot that I didn't get in with.

"The Jack? Oh, that was the dirty devil with the diamond-studded tie-pin and the big zircon ring on his finger, that made a pass at my wife and she was sucker enough to fall for him, caused me to knock two of her teeth out and send him rollin' through a plate-glass window.

"There's four suits in a deck of cards, fellers, that's the number of policemen that beat the tar outa me; there was four of 'em. They beat me up and throwed me in the jug.

"Three hundred and sixty-five spots on a deck of cards: well that's how much money I had in my pocket when they throwed me in jail: three hundred and sixty-five dollars, and I paid it to one of those shyster lawyers to defend me, and he didn't even show up at the trial.

"They's twelve picture cards; and that's how many men there was on the jury, they was twelve of them and every dad-burned one of them was as crooked as a barrel of snakes.

"Fifty-two cards in the deck: that's how many weeks that I had to spend in the jug over this little incident.

"So you see, fellers, this deck of cards ain't only to blame for me losin' all of my money an' my wife, my home and all of my livestock, but also is causin' me to go through life as an ex-convict, a jailbird, a criminal, a wife-beater, a peace-disturbiter [sic], and a good-for-nothing low down scoundrel and a gambler. Neighbors, this ain't no fairy tale; I know, because I was that sucker. Ha-ha-ha, ho-ho, well, that's life for ya."

Apparently in the wake of the Tyler version, the tradition of broadside adaptations will continue. In 1968(?) Red Sovine recorded "The Viet Nam Deck of Cards" (*Phantom 309,* Starday SLP 414, 12″ LP), set in Saigon and with slight verbal variation from the Tyler text. It concludes, ". . . my son was that soldier." Another Viet Nam text, "The Deck of Cards" by Bill Wright, Sr. (Decca 31851), ends with the older "I was that soldier." The 1969 "Country Boy's Deck of Cards" (*Bob Kames Plays All Time Country Favorites on Hammond Organ,* Hollywood HLP 506, 12″ LP) deals with a lad who skips Sunday School and whose father discovers him playing cards in the barn. He concludes his lengthy excuse: "And you know, Dad, I know this is a true story, because Uncle Tex told me this happened to him during World War II."

Despite the apparent dominance in the United States of the tradition of Type II, there is evidence of the existence of a possibly flourishing oral tradition of "The Deck of Cards" as an exemplum independent of or at least only influenced by the broadside and songster texts. In addition to the sermon text of Lacy and (probably) that reported by McIntosh, there is the sermon "The Gambler's Doom" by the Reverend J. C. Burnett, assisted by Sisters Grainger and Jackson, recorded in New York, September 21, 1927 (Mx. 144776-2), and released as Columbia 14261-D. In the following transcription we have not been able to render the congregational responses or all the ejaculations characteristic of the Negro sermon-performance.

Uh, I want to talk for my subject this morning, uh, payday. Jesus said in Revelations, the twenty-second and -third verse, that He's coming, uh, with His reward. And reward simply means to pay off. And He's gonna pay off the world, every gambler, every drunken liar. I can see too that the gambler's standin' with his cards in his hand. Represent, the fifty-two cards in the deck represent the fifty-two weeks in the year. And the three hundred and sixty-five spots on the cards represent the three hundred and sixty-five days in the year. And the highest card, my friends, is the ace, represent one God high over all. And the deuce represents Jesus. Lord, you would pick me low, you would cover me. And the, uh, trey represents the three godheads in the trinity, God the Father, Son, and Holy Ghost. And the fourth card represents the four gospel writers, oooh, Matthew, Mark, Luke, and John, ah. And the five spot represents, oh, his five bleeding wounds, ah, on Mount Calvary, ah. Oooh, the six and seven represent, ah, when He told Moses He would be with him in the six trials, ah, and the seventh He'd know why He's forsaken him, ah. Oooh Lord, ah. And the eighth card represent, ah, the eight people was saved in Noah's ark, ah. When the nine represents when Jesus, ah, went to the Kingdom of Galilee, ah, and turned water to wine, ah. Ooooh, ah, oh Lord, ah, when the ten represent, ah, the ten virgins, and five, ah, was foolish and five were wise, ah. Oooh Lord, ah, when they seed this old Jack, ah, represents Jesus, ah, rode a jack from Bethany to Jerusalem, ah. Payday! ah. And the King, ooh, ah, represent Jesus, ah, said in Revelations He was king of kings, that He was lord of lords, ah. Ooooh, ah, I hear the (moon fail?), ah. And the four Queens, the first one, ah, representin' Mary, the mother of Jesus, ah, and the second represents Queen Esther, ah, because she saved a nation of people, ah, and the third represents, ah, the Queen of Sheba come, ah, from the uttermost parts to hear the wisdom of Solomon, ah, and the fourth represents Queen (Mes . . . ?), ah. Oooh, payday, ah! Is you gonna be paid up? Oooh—one more amen. Amen.

The extent to which some of Burnett's associations are in the tradition of Type 1613 or are "creative" is difficult—in fact impossible—to determine. It is more than possible that the arbitrary length of the 78 rpm disc resulted in the omission of elements "normal" to the sermon. The "values" of the six, seven, and nine cards are unique to the reported tradition, and the association of the ten card with the virgins seems transferred from the usual reference of the five card. But Burnett's use of the five card to symbolize the wounds of Christ agrees not only with Lacy's text, but with a wide continental tradition. Similarly Lacy's association of the nine with the hours on the cross occurs also in Scandinavian tradition, while the use of the deuce as a symbol of heaven and hell is unique. Burnett's equation of the Jack with the biblical jackass would seem as normal a development as Lacy's association of the King with King Jesus in a 1968 version of his sermon. Furthermore, in his more recent performance, Lacy added to his deck the Joker, which he used as a symbol for the extra leap-year day.

Lacy's alterations and additions are no more testimony to the flexibility of the Negro sermon and of the Type 1613 tale than are the uses to which he and Burnett put the story. In the Type I and II traditions the cards become symbols to extricate a clever man from a difficult situation, or they are a valid and pious substitute for the Bible. To Burnett, the cards suggest the approaching punishment of transgressors. But Lacy uses the cards to argue that man is always trying to compare himself to God. "Mister Hoyle" is Lacy's synedoche for man's presumption throughout the sermon, and for all we can tell he thinks that Hoyle did invent playing cards. "Mister Hoyle" observes

God's creation and devises playing cards to imitate and rival him—to "compare" with God and His works. The deck of cards becomes, for Lacy, a symbol of man's impudence and pride.

We may conclude by agreeing with Edward M. Wilson that recent broadside tradition must be examined for the origins of such tales as the "Deck of Cards" and that we may well look back to a medieval sermon writer for ultimate sources; and the still flourishing tradition of the oral sermon will provide not only "texts," but a "living laboratory."

A Game of Cards (German, *ca.* 1450)

RICHARD M. DORSON

Esthetic Form in British and American Folk Narrative

While the folk ballad has won its way into the canon of English and American literature, the folktale remains as yet outside the pale. Literary histories and anthologies pay their early respects to "Sir Patrick Spens," "Young Hunting," "The Four Marys," and other illustrious specimens of English and Scottish popular balladry. Instructors in English department courses discuss stylistic and compositional elements of Anglo-American ballads to familiarize students with "leaping and lingering," the dramatic use of dialogue, dependence on commonplaces, and other techniques of the traditional ballad. Courses on the folktale are much rarer, and emphasize European and primitive rather than British and American folktales. The fact is that no one is quite sure about Anglo-American oral narratives. They suffer in contrast with the highly visible and esthetically proven ballads, so clearly and proudly a possession of the English singing world. But where are the folktales of English speakers? What are their forms, esthetic or otherwise? Do they deserve consideration from the literary historians?

Unlike the clear-cut Child ballads, permeating Scotland, England, and the United States, the folktales of the three countries tell three separate stories. In his *Type and Motif Index of the Folktales of England and North America,* published in 1966, Ernest W. Baughman abstracted some 13,000 tales, exclusive of the American Indian, the American Negro, and foreign-language groups in the United States and the Celtic peoples in Great Britain. Here arises the first question in our inquiry: which folktales do we include as part of English and American literature? I would unquestionably include the American Negro and exclude the American Indian, and with less assurance divide the Gaelic tales of Scotland from those of Ireland to bring Scottish traditions within the English realm. Negro story-telling takes place inside the frame of American language and civilization, but tribal Indian narratives belong to another world. Gaeldom unites the Highland and Hebridean Scot with the Irishman, but political boundaries now set them apart. Campbell of Islay presented English translations with the Gaelic texts of his famous *Popular Tales of the West Highlands* and addressed his work primarily to an English-speaking audience. The ample store of West Highland folktales contains a high incidence of the märchen or magical fictions uncovered first by the Grimm brothers and ever since the primary object of interest for folktale scholars. Among the genres of folk narrative, the märchen lends itself most easily to the case for esthetic form, with its firm structure of thrice-repeated episodes, its dramatis personae of peasant heroes, royal princesses, demonic ogres, and supernatural helpers, and its happy resolution of the hero's quest. But the märchen is a rarity in England and the United States. Of all the countries of Europe, England has proved leanest in wonder tales, and consequently had few to transmit to the American colonies—although we must recognize the surprising finds in the southern Appalachians, from the 1920's on, of the so-called Jack tales. Still, Baughman's tables prove that the märchen must take a back seat to other oral narrative forms. Even in Scotland, the balance in favor of märchen is receding with the publication in 1964 of *The Dewar Manuscripts,* a collection of local history chronicles recorded under the supervision of Campbell of Islay but lying in file drawers for the past century.

While the narrators both in England and the United States tend to shun märchen, their repertoires still differ noticeably from each other. English oral narratives run heavily to local legends of supernatural and spectral beings, but legends of elves and bogles are not told in the States—perhaps because, as immigrants say half in jest, spirits cannot cross the ocean. Conversely, the lying tale or tall tale so abundantly collected in the United States is a stranger in England. Baughman arrives at a twenty-five per cent correspondence between English and American tale types, a figure that might be stretched to fifty per cent if narratives not reported from England but found in sections of the United States settled by the English are counted.

We come to the question, what are the main forms of Anglo-American oral prose traditions? and for an answer we must rely on imprecise terms: local legend, ghost story, anecdote, yarn, joke, shaggy dog, protest tale, animal and bird stories, numskull or noodle tales, dialect stories, tall tales or lies. None of these forms are sharply defined. By and large they tend to be short narratives, as opposed to long wonder tales and romances, and their characters and content often determine what names they possess. A dialect story may be told as a terse anecdote or an extended recital but it always hinges on ethnic stereotypes who speak in accents contrasting humorously with standard English. A ghost story involves a spectral experience but this may be a fragmentary report of an eerie sight or sound or a local adaptation of a hardy tale type, such as the now famous account of the Vanishing Hitchhiker. In lieu of any acceptable replacement, the vague label "legend" continues to designate the large body of believed narratives that circulate in our society. We can distinguish certain sub-groups of legendary tales revolving around persons, places, or events, according to the focus of the tradition. One of the most popular species of American story-telling is the anecdote about a village or neighborhood character, and this may be called a personal legend, or legendary anecdote, or anecdotal legend.

The idea of legend involves a communally shared tradition possessed and credited by a cohesive group—geographical, occupational, ethnic. Legends are usually told in conversational and reminiscent fashion. Vance Randolph's collections of Ozark folktales take the form of breezy local legends. In spite of the wide latitude accorded the concept of legend, the word still does not satisfactorily cover all varieties of believed oral traditions. The Swedish term *memorat* denotes individual reports of encounters with supernatural creatures, and is making its way into English usage. Still it does not apply to the richly detailed autobiographical stories and recollections of W. H. Barrett, the raconteur from the Cambridgeshire fens, whose wry and mordant *Tales of the Fens* bear a distant likeness to Icelandic family sagas.

Then there are jokes or jocular tales, the prime story form of our times, dispersed in town and country social circles, through the mass media, by public speakers of every hue from politicians to clergymen, and via professional and parlor entertainers. In preparing his expanded edition of *The Types of the Folk-Tale* (1961), Stith Thompson found that the section on "Jokes and Anecdotes" had grown far more substantially than any other category. No one has yet taken the humble jest and the lowly anecdote seriously as oral art, although they surely deserve as much consideration as any other kind of folktale. Jokes seem so ephemeral, topical, and trivial that the literary and folk critic

may well be excused for scorning them. But some have shown remarkable staying power, enduring from Greece of the fifth century
B.C. to America of the mid-twentieth century. Athenian contemporaries of Pericles laughed at the unworldly behavior of the absent-
minded pedant who vowed, after a narrow escape from drowning,
that he would never go near the water until he had learned how to
swim; and who cut his horse's feed daily to teach him how to live
without eating, and grieved that, just as the animal was learning to
do so, he died.[1]

A genre only recently baptized is the protest tale, whose humor,
often grim and biting, turns on racial prejudice and social injustice.
The Negro repertoire is especially rich in protest tales, which mingle
with better known genres such as the Brer Rabbit fictions of speaking
animals. Some humorous stories mock social protest itself, such as
dialect jokes told by Jewish story-tellers ridiculing excessive sensitivity
to anti-Semitism.

We turn from the question of the genres of British and American
story-telling to the problem of their texts. The text of an oral tale
includes a good deal more than spoken words. There are facial expressions, intonations, chanted phrases, onomatopoetic sounds, gestures,
bodily movements, pauses, emphases, eye contact and interplay with
the audience, the use of props, noises made by banging on the table
and slapping of the palms—all adding up to a small theatrical performance. The term performance is indeed now commonly used by folklorists to describe a story-telling situation. Even the electronically
recorded recital conveys only a portion of the scene. Once when I was
discussing the matter of textual fidelity with Vance Randolph, he
admitted to some editing of his Ozark folktales, but contended that
literally transcribed texts still took no account of silent intervals; and
he told an illustrative tale. One time he met an Ozark friend limping,
and asked the cause of the lameness. The hillman said, "I went to a
dance, and a feller stepped on my foot." Pause. "He was from Chicago." Without the pause, said Vance, the written words would lose
their humorous effect based on the Ozarker's disdain for the outlander
from the big city.

Furthermore, any written representation of an oral tale reproduces
but one variant text. Even the same speaker telling the same story
varies his text with each delivery. There is no fixed text. Even the
single variant is difficult to trap in print, for the exact words, including the hems and haws and confusing pronouns and incomplete sen-

tences of transcribed oral speech need a little pruning and sprucing before they meet the reader's eye. The question is, how many small adjustments can an editor make before the text ceases to be oral? I scarcely trust my own printed texts, and go back to the field notebook or tape if I want to be thoroughly certain of the original wording.

On the other hand, the literary text is not all that definitive, what with variant editions, misprints, and censorship from authors' wives. Francis O. Matthiessen brilliantly explained the symbolic meaning of the phrase "soiled fish of the sea" in *White Jacket,* unaware that Melville had written "coiled fish of the sea." [2]

Still the point needs to be underlined that the oral text, slippery as it may be, differs wholly from a literary text based on an oral tale. The sketches in the New York *Spirit of the Times,* brought to the attention of literary historians in 1930 by Franklin J. Meine in his *Tall Tales of the Southwest,* are not folktales but sophisticated literary compositions. A writer seeking to convey the rhythms and manner of oral delivery is still a writer addressing readers. Ever since the Grimms first published their Household Tales and drew a line between the spoken and written story, collectors polishing their narratives and authors emulating village bards have crossed the line, including the Grimms themselves, and blurred the distinction. But oral art and literary art are separate productions.

The classic statement on this score was made by the eminent Danish folklorist Axel Olrik in his essay of 1909 on "Epic Laws of Folk Narrative." [3] Olrik formulated a number of principles governing oral compositions, such as the need of the narrator to present the story-line clearly and simply, even repetitively, without subtleties or subplots, since listeners had no opportunity to reread the text and ponder over its meanings. In particular he emphasized the law of concentration of character, the restriction of the characters to two strongly opposed figures, and the construction of the narrative around peak tableaux readily visualized by the audience. Olrik generalized for the European oral literature he knew best, the heroic epics, Sagen, märchen, and ballads, and our purpose is to see how well his conclusions hold for Anglo-American forms.

Traditions of Single Combats

With these preliminary matters of genre and text in mind, we will present three oral narratives that come from widely scattered sources but reveal common patterns of composition. The first is a portion of a Highland Scottish tradition about the battle of Culloden, collected in the 1860's by John Dewar and translated from the Gaelic by Hector Maclean.

AFTER THE BATTLE OF CULLODEN

After the day of the battle of Culloden many of the Highlanders were taken prisoners, and they were put in pens until the intentions of the Duke of Cumberland regarding them should be known. John Campbell of Mamore was General under the Duke of Cumberland on the side of King George. It was he who had the command of the Highland regiments. The Duke of Cumberland was going around to see the prisoners, and he took General Wolfe and General John Campbell with him. They were going from pen to pen, and they reached a place where there was a pen resembling a sheepfold. There were fifteen young Highland lads inside waiting for the Duke's sentence. There was a fire in the middle. One of the prisoners whom the rest called Fierce John was sitting at the side of the fire. The hand was off him a short distance from the wrist and his blood was shedding. He had a sword in the whole hand which he was heating in the fire and applying to the wound to staunch the blood. The three Generals stood for a short time observing the poor prisoner's manner of staunching the blood. Someone remarked, 'It must be that that little man has an exceedingly strong heart.' 'He, the paltry fellow!' said the Duke of Cumberland. 'It must be that Prince Charles is an exceedingly silly blockhead of a man when he took such trifling creatures for soldiers.' 'You do not estimate these men correctly,' rejoined General John Campbell. 'Although they are but little, they are as good soldiers as any in England.' 'These paltry men are not at all to be compared with the English,' observed the Duke. 'One Englishman is better than three of them.' 'Remember,' said General John Campbell, 'that these men are for a long time on bad food and without enough of it, enduring cold and hunger, and without much sleep. That would give a bad appearance to any men.' 'These men had never the appearance of soldiers,' replied the Duke of Cumberland, 'and I do not know who the devil would take the despicable creatures for soldiers.'

Although General John Campbell was on the side of the Duke of Cumberland in the battle he took it very ill to hear his countrymen dispraised, and notwithstanding that he was against the prisoners in the battle, he said, 'There are not there but fifteen young lads altogether, and although they are as tired as they are, I could choose one out of these who would fight with anyone that you could choose from any regiment under your command.'

'I will wager so many bottles of wine,' said the Duke of Cumberland,

'that you will not choose out of these anyone who will fight the Englishman that I should bring against him.' General John Campbell observed,
'I am not much inclined to hazard men's lives for wine, but wager you
the men and I will wager the wine. If the Englishman shall win the fight
I will pay you a dozen bottles of wine, but if the Highlander shall van-
quish the Englishman, let the wager be that the Highlander and the rest
who are in the pen with him shall get free leave to go home to their own
place.' The Duke consented that if the Highlander won, he and his com-
rades should get their freedom to go to their own home.

The wager was laid, and the Duke of Cumberland sent an officer to the
Colonel of a cavalry regiment which he considered the best under his
command, for a man to fight a Highlander. A swordsman was got as good
as they thought was to be found in the English army, and brought into the
presence of the Duke of Cumberland. The English soldier was brought to
see the Highland prisoners. When he saw them he was asked if he would
fight one of those men. 'Yes,' said he, 'and it is my opinion that I could
fight every one of them, if I got them one after the other.'

General Campbell was then asked again, if he would stand to his wager.
He said he should. The wager was laid anew. Then General Campbell
went into the pen where the prisoners were and said, 'Is there any one of
you at all who are here that would engage to fight with an accomplished
English fencer, if all of you who are in this pen got your liberty to go
home for winning victory over the Englishman?' The prisoners were silent
and looked at General Campbell without saying a word. Fierce John was
sitting at the side of the fire, and although the one hand was off him and
the blood not yet being full stanched [*sic*], he rose and said, 'Let me to
him. I will do business on him.' There was not one in the pen that did not
say that he would engage him. General Campbell said, 'Take care what
you are about, men! This is a weighty business. Take heed that the life of
every one of you depends upon the man's hand, whichever he may be who
goes to fight the Englishman. If the Englishman will kill the Highlander,
every one of you here shall be put to death; but if the Highlander will win,
every one of you here shall get leave to go home.' A brother of Fierce
John walked a step or two apart from the rest and said, 'Let me to him.
I will make use of him.' 'You are yourselves acquainted with one another,'
said General Campbell, 'and I should like that you would choose the best
swordsman among you.' 'I am of opinion,' remarked the brother of Fierce
John, 'that I am he.' General John Campbell put it to the opinion of the
rest, and that was Fierce John's brother was the best swordsman among
them except Fierce John himself, who was now wounded and had also
lost one of his hands; and as that was so, that they would trust the hand
of his brother. It was the brother of Fierce John that was chosen for the
combat.

He asked a sword, which was got for him. He was brought on level ground and the English champion was brought against him. They did not resemble each other in appearance. The Englishman was a big, stalwart man and seemingly very strong. The Highlander was but a chip of a slender, sallow stripling, very bare of flesh, but tough and brawny, and slightly under middle size. The two fencers were placed opposite each other, the word of combat was given, and the play began. The Englishman was violent at first and struck fiercely, but the Highlander sought to do nothing further than defend himself. 'You must draw up better than that, lad,' said General Campbell to the Highlander, 'much is entrusted to your hand.' 'Is it death?' said the Highlander. 'Death undoubtedly,' replied the General.

The Highlander closed up with the Englishman then, and it was but a short time until he struck him with the sword and killed him. When General Campbell saw that the Englishman had fallen, he went where the Highlander was, clapped him on the shoulder, and said to him, 'Go home now and thank your mother, because she gave you such good milk.'

All who were in the pen got leave then to go home, but the Duke of Cumberland was so full of wrath because the Englishman whom he thought to be the bravest in the whole English army was killed by a little Highlander, that he gave orders to persons of his to kill every Highlander who was found wounded in the battlefield and every prisoner who should be made after this to be hanged without mercy.[4]

This text may be called an historical legend. It derives a good deal of its dramatic power, in the first place, from its setting in history. The battle of Culloden on April 16, 1746, brought to an end the Jacobite uprising of 1745, staged by the Highland forces of Bonnie Prince Charlie, the Stuart pretender, against the royal army of George II in the last battle fought on British soil. Culloden signified the doom of the Highland cause and the extirpation of Highland culture. Anecdote, ballad, oral and written history, and documentary film all bear witness to the impact of Culloden on the imagination of Englishmen and Scotsmen. In 1964 a stirring television film of the BBC, produced by Peter Watkins, reenacted the battle scene and the desperate charge on foot of the Highland clans, whose parts were played by citizens of Inverness living close to the battle site, some themselves descendants of the survivors. Culloden is a highly charged historic name, conjuring up the final conflict of Stuarts and Hanoverians, of kilted clansmen and soldiers of the Crown, of Highland and English ways of life. It conjures up, too, the sadistic figure of the Bloody Duke of Cumberland, general of the king's army, and a heartless butcher in countless legends.

The episode of traditional history here presented thus gains considerable drama at the outset from its cast of characters, the commanders and soldiers of Culloden. It develops its own drama with the wager between the Bloody Duke and the defecting Highland general, John Campbell, who recognizes the valor of his countrymen. A classic David and Goliath duel ensues in the epic tradition of single combats between opposing champions.[5] Our sympathies are already enlisted on the side of the underdog Scots, vanquished, underfed, outnumbered, and are further moved by the injury and stoicism of Fierce John and the audacity of his small brother. In the narration the Highlander's anticipated victory is scanted, contrary to the Hollywood movie script which would have given it extended emphasis. Rather than emphasize the obvious, the narrator dwells on the Highlander's reticence and his quick dispatch of his opponent when he sees he must take his enemy's life to save those of his fellows. By contrast, the cruel vengeance on other Highland prisoners taken by the Bloody Duke accords with the known character and legendary cruelty of the English general.

This selection illustrates the artistic power that oral traditional history can achieve. The action marches surely to its climax, the language is sinewy and taut (allowing for some fluff in translation), the dialogue simple and crisp, and the heroic mood of valor and honor sustained from first to last. In place of any vainglorious taunt after the Highlander's triumph, his sponsor, General Campbell, softly lauds him with a homely adage. All four protagonists fall at once into place. The Highland general and soldier duplicate each other in manly virtue as do the English general and soldier in contemptuous bluster. Cumberland and Campbell debate the merits of the Highlander in a verbal joust enacted out physically by the combatants. The heroism and tragedy of Culloden are felt from the initial prison scene through the wager, the selection of duelists, and the combat, to the final bitter order of slaughter.

In its form, this historical legend resembles other traditions in *The Dewar Manuscripts* and in clan chronicles. These oral annals are straightforward accounts of raids and feuds and tricks between rival lairds and their men, of varying length, filled with names of families and localities unfamiliar to the outsider. Frequently the sober statements are lit up with marvelous dreams and shocking acts and bizarre events. One unusual tradition describes the imprisonment of two High-landers in Boston during the American Revolution and their rescue by a countryman they accidentally discovered, Duncan Stewart, who then himself had to flee to Britain. There Stewart encountered the Camp-bells whom he had saved, and they now intervened with King George III to help Stewart recover his hereditary land. The train of events is astonishing and the coincidences, escapes, and just conclusion heart-warming for a Highland audience. As a specimen of oral art it ex-hibits some of the same qualities as the Culloden narrative, but without achieving its tautness and tension.[6]

The second text represents a contemporary example of urban Ameri-can story-telling. It was first told me on June 14, 1967, during my Harvard 30th Reunion at Martha's Vineyard, by an old friend and classmate going back even to preparatory school at Exeter, William B. Gresham, Jr. "Gresh" resides at Tampa, Florida, where he is in the pest control business, and I telephoned him from Bloomington, In-diana, on June 22 to re-collect the story verbatim. He remembered his source as Tom Dowd, the traveling secretary for the Boston Red Sox, who had spoken to the local branch of the American Personnel Asso-ciation at the Commerce Club in Tampa in March, 1967.

THE POOR COLORED BOY AND LEO THE LION

There was a poor little old colored boy in Jackson, Mississippi, who had just gotten his driver's license. The first day he was driving he was ar-rested by a motorcycle cop for speeding 25 miles an hour in a 20 mile an hour zone. The white cop hauled him before the white judge who glared down at him from high on his bench and, peering over his glasses, frowned and said, "Nigger boy, you have committed a heinous sin and a serious crime, and I am going to have to give you the maximum penalty. But I will give you a choice. You can either be hung by the neck until you are dead at 8 o'clock in the morning or fight Leo the lion in Ole Miss Stadium tomorrow afternoon at 2 o'clock."

The little colored boy thought fast, and hanging by the neck sounded awful sure, awful fatal, and awful dead. He looked up at the judge and he said, "Judge, suh, Ah chooses to fight Leo the lion." The judge said, "Take him off to the jail cell till tomorrow."

Next afternoon Old Miss Stadium was filled with 56,000 white people cheering and hollering, bands playing, the cheerleaders urging them on, because they had seen this kind of spectacle before. Two deputies brought the little colored boy out with his hands manacled behind his back. They walked him out to the middle of the field and lowered him into a hole on the 50-yard line. They filled the hole up with dirt until only his head was showing.

Then at the far end of the field where the football teams usually came in appeared a jeep hauling a lion's cage containing Leo the lion. Leo was getting anxious. They opened the cage door at the goal line and out leaped Leo. He spied the little colored head up on the 50-yard line which reminded him of his carefree days back in the jungle. He set out at full speed. By the time he reached the 40-yard line, he realized he was going too fast. He put on the brakes, and when he came to a stop his body was over the head of the poor little colored boy.

The boy looked up and right above him were the tenderest parts of Leo the lion's body. He saw his only chance, reached up with his teeth and sank them into the tenderest parts of Leo the lion.

Meanwhile the crowd was hooping and hollering and calling out, "Come on Leo, come on Leo!" But Leo the lion was in trouble. He was roaring in pain, beating his paws on the ground, thrashing his tail back and forth in agony. The little colored boy held on for dear life 'cause he knew it was his only chance.

The crowd quieted, seeing that Leo was in trouble. After a moment they realized what was going on. A hush settled over the stadium. Then a solitary voice boomed out, "Fight fair, nigger, fight fair."

The first point to observe is that the central motif of this tale exists in tradition. On a field trip in 1953 to Pine Bluff, Arkansas, located in the Mississippi Delta, I heard from a Negro the related story of "John in Alabama." In this narrative a colored man from Arkansas named John was visiting in Alabama and was informing his friends how much better the colored were treated in Arkansas, when a white man passed by, heard him, and knocked John down. John struck back, and was winning when the police arrived, arrested John, buried him in the ground up to his shoulder, and turned two bulldogs loose on him. John nodded his head so fast the "laws" stopped the dogs and told John to hold his head still and fight fair.[7]

Here is a clear example of a protest tale, and in fact it was told to me by John Courtney drinking coke in his home after I had been refused curb service by a teen-aged white girl because I had "colored" in my car. We may further note that the skillful dodger appears in the Negro but not in the white version, and that the dodger clearly belongs to Negro tradition. In still another tale type, of which I collected three variants, a Negro defies a white man to beat him up and then simply dodges his blows.

Immediately following the delivery of this paper (September 7, 1967), I was told an intermediate variant by Donald Stoddard of Skidmore College, in which the lion rushes three times at the colored boy, who the third time seizes the tender parts. Mr. Stoddard heard this in June, 1966, in Boston from a maintenance supervisor at Northeastern University.

The white text has combined the protest tale of racial injustice, recently surfacing on the American scene, with the honored American tradition of the poker-faced tall tale. Usually tall tales deal with backwoods and agricultural themes—remarkable feats of hunting and shooting, enormous vegetables, extraordinarily rich or poor soil, changeable weather. Such "windies" are amusing but lack any emotional charge. The marriage of exaggeration and protest has produced a potent offspring, a tale funny and grim, articulating the deep anxieties of a racially divided nation.

Both the protest tale and the tall tale are anecdotal in form. That is, they purport to relate actual incidents about real people in brief, conversational narrations. Supernatural beings do not enter into the dramatis personae. The protest tale characteristically makes use of irony and inversion, rather than overt social criticism, by having colored folk accept the white man's code and extend it to the point of absurdity. The tall tale too contains only natural phenomena and traps the listener by a sudden leap from the possible to the impossible. Tall tales soon become monotonous, and while they can and are still collected today, the repetitious lies about giant pumpkins and lucky hunting shots mean little to contemporary Americans. In the above text the impulse for creative exaggeration has fastened onto new and more immediate themes. The form remains anecdotal; this is a supposedly factual incident occurring to an actual person in a specific locality, the fearsome one of Jackson, Mississippi, and introducing familiar situations: the appearance of a traffic violator before an implacable judge, a spectacle in a crowded football stadium. As Negroes tell tall tales, so whites tell protest tales, and the shift from a colored to a white narrator has brought an added awesomeness to the ordeal of the victim. The private incident has become a public entertainment, recalling the punitive ritual of primitive Christians thrust before the lions in the Roman amphitheater. Helpless, friendless, accused, and accursed, the poor little colored boy is the Christ-figure, reviled when he uses his last means of defense to protect himself from his would-be killers.

Platitudinous sermons delivering the message of racial injustice do not circulate among secular Americans, who consume with relish the same preachment hid in a mocking story capped with the customary joke-ending punchline. As befits the mood of the tale, the narrator maintains a solemn tone and a somber rhythm—"awful sure, awful fatal, and awful dead"—along with the deadpan mien of the older frontier Münchausens. But the laughter of this anecdote borders on tears.

In the central scene where the poor colored boy faces Leo the lion in the football stadium, we see reenacted the single combat of heroic legend, as in the duel between Fierce John's brother and the British champion. Traditionally the hero battles not only other champions but also monsters, dragons, and wild beasts. The single combat provides one of the visual tableaux defined by Axel Olrik as narrative peaks and perfectly illustrates his law of two to a scene. What episode can more readily stir and imprint itself on a listening audience than the duel to the death between an underdog hero and a powerful ogre before opposing armies or a bloodthirsty throng?

While the Scottish tradition faithfully conveys the heroic mood of classical epic and medieval romance, the American folktale is told in a mock-heroic spirit of parody and irony. Single combats did take place in American life, although not under conditions of chivalry; the Crockett almanacs set forth encounters between Davy and assorted rapscallions of the backwoods, and in Michigan's Upper Peninsula I collected lurid descriptions of eye-gouging, groin-butting affrays between whiskey-inflamed lumberjacks in bar-room melees. The third text in this group reflects the violent and reckless spirit of the Upper Peninsula. Its narrator is a Swedish immigrant, Swan Olson, who specialized in autobiographical yarns in which he outwitted and outfought highway robbers, crazed lumberjacks, and murderous tramps. Yet audacious Swan, a gentle old man of seventy-three when I met him in 1946, scarcely looked the part of the swashbuckler portrayed in the following personal narrative, which I printed in *Bloodstoppers and Bearwalkers*.

SWAN OLSON AND ERIC ERICSON

I came from Stockholm, Sweden, when I was just confirmed, about 1890. I was seventeen. I landed at Quebec and went to Litchfield, Minnesota. I came there in harvest time, and worked for a farmer, Eric Ericson. He drank clear alcohol with a dipper. No one would work for him more than two or three days; he would go crazy and threaten to murder them, and his wife, and me.

We took some big barrels of eggs thirteen miles into town to sell for three cents a dozen. The storekeeper sold them for five cents, but Ericson could only get two cents. Well, he went into a saloon and told me to get three cents for the eggs or take them back and bury them in a hole in the manure pile. I couldn't sell them, so I went back to the saloon, and he was dead drunk—couldn't walk.

So I had a couple of fellows help me lift him up into the wagon, alongside me, and let the curved iron side hold him in place, slumped against it. So we started back, and I let the horses go as fast as they wanted to. It was a spring wagon, with springs under the seat, which fitted over the sideboards. The wagon hit a deep rut, and gave a big bump from the spring, and he went from the bloody wagon clear up in the air, and landed plunk in the bloody sluice alongside the clay road.

It took me a while to slow up and go back, and I couldn't figure out how to get him up—he was like a dishrag. So finally I unhooked one of the lines from the horse's bit and tied it under his arms, and then I went up in the wagon and began pulling him up. I got hold of him by the neck and the collar and pulled him the rest of the way. Then I put him under the bloody seat and left him there the rest of the trip.

So we got back to the farm and drove up to the front door. Then I went into his room, looked under his pillow and pulled out his gun, emptied all the cartridges and put them in my pocket. Then I went out and unhitched the team and put them in the barn. I had one harness off, and was just hanging the other up on the peg when he came in the barn holding the gun.

He said, "You son of a bitch!" and pointed the gun right in my face, and clicked the hammer—click, click, click.

Then he said, "Don't you drop? You son of a bitch."

I said, "Not for your gun or you either." Then I dropped the harness, grabbed his gun and hit him right in the mouth, and the blood squirted all over him and right in my face. I knocked out one of his teeth. He fell backwards over the doorway, and I thought I killed the bugger. I listened to his heart, heard it beat. So I got a pail of cold water from the galvanized trough and poured it over him, and he began to hiccup. Then I helped the bugger up to the house and seen him get undressed and get to bed.

Then I went back to the barn, after wiping off and feeding the horses. I couldn't sleep up in the attic of the log house—only two rooms in the whole place—so I slept in the barn in the hay. I slept with two blankets and a pillow, and in the morning I was covered with snakes, ice-cold snakes. They wanted my heat, so they curled up all around me, up to my neck and my face. When I'd wake up I'd take one of the bloody buggers by the tail, when his head was under my neck, and break his neck. They were slippery and cold, but not poisonous. (One time when I was pitching hay, I pulled on one's head, and he just squeezed tighter round my neck, and I had to grab his tail with my other hand.)

About three o'clock in the morning I heard a holler of "Murder" from the house. So I threw off the snakes and put some overalls on and ran up to the house. Eric was standing over his woman (his second wife—his kids ran away 'cause he said he'd kill them) with a stove handle in his hand, ready to kill her. She was lying down on the floor stretched out. He had hit her once, was going to finish her up. I grabbed the stove pipe from behind him and hit him over the head, right on the coconut, so he dropped down on the floor. Then I picked him up and put him over an Old Country chest he had in the corner (I got two of them at home—they're rounded at the top) and laid him across it on his stomach, and pushed the trunk against the wall with all my strength, so his head was caught between the trunk and the wall. Then I took the iron rod from an old muzzle-loader he had, about four feet long, and pulled it out over the barrel, and beat him with it on the hind end and the legs and all over.

The woman said, "Just keep it up."

When I was finished, I was all perspired. He fell over the side of the trunk on the floor, and I picked him up and put him back in the bed.

That was Saturday night. I got up early in the morning, milked the cows, fed the horses. Then at breakfast the woman said he wanted to see me. So I went up into the bedroom, and he showed me all his bruises; he was black and blue and green.

So I said, "Well, that's what you get when you go to town. They was going to beat you up in the saloon, and I saved your life."

Then he asked me to hand him his pants. They were on the chair right alongside the bed, but he couldn't reach them, he was so weak. (He stayed in bed for a week.) And he took a silver dollar out of his pocket—they had no paper dollars then—and gave it to me for saving his life.

That was the only time he paid me all the time I was there.[8]

Whatever the content of fact in this narration, it is a well-told tale and a red-blooded slice of Americana. Although allegedly a personal experience, Swan's account does adhere to Olrik's laws of oral narrative. Two central characters dominate the actions, a dark villain and a shining hero, the teller himself. No subtleties obscure the plot; Olson clobbers Ericson again and again and again, but with imaginative variations. A tension persists throughout the recital, for Ericson is a madman and Swan is continually in danger. Swan knows his man and anticipates his moves, but the listener cannot, as in conventional folk-tales, anticipate the next episode. Throughout the story Swan plays the role of the faithful hired hand, attending to the chores and mauling Eric only under provocation. The graphic scenes move from one thrashing to another: Swan dumping Eric from the buggy, knocking him out in the barn, whaling him with the muzzle-loader as he lies draped across the Old Country chest. But Swan triumphs by wit and strategy rather than by muscle; he is the clever hero. Details of farm routine are sketched in with the precision of an archival historian. Some matters are inserted with a sure sense of their shock value: the low price of eggs, the snakes clasping Swan in the barn. A number of casual references build up the portrait of the arch villain: Eric drinks straight alcohol, has driven his children away, beats his wife, shoots at all and sundry, and never pays his help. The marvelous O. Henry ending ties together the opening visit to town with the last episode in the bedroom as the now impotent ogre rewards his sly emasculator, who triumphs intellectually as well as physically.

These three narratives come from quite unlike tellers: a Scottish Highlander, a Harvard graduate living in Florida, a Swedish immigrant in Michigan's Upper Peninsula. One story deals with a famous battle, another with an imaginary public spectacle, a third with employer-employee relations on a farm. They seem to have little in common. Yet generically, esthetically, and traditionally they all conform to the same pattern. Each is told on the plane of sober fact as a realistic occurrence. Each portrays a single combat in which the underdog hero emerges triumphant against a bully or monster. The Swiss folklorist Max Lüthi stresses the pervasive theme in folk narrative "of the defeat of the great by the small, the mighty by the apparently powerless," and cites examples:

The intelligence of the dwarfs, the stupidity of the giants, the victory of David over Goliath, of Odysseus over Polyphemus, of the clever peasant girl over the king, of Hänsel and Gretel over the witch, of the divine child over the monsters sent by his enemies (Hercules strangles Hera's serpents), the power of the Christ-child over the giant Christophorus, representing the power of the Crucified who took upon himself the form of a servant, the power of God in meek and lowly guise—all this testifies to the same insight present in all types of folk narrative, fairy tales, legends, as well as in the farces and saints' legends, based upon both faith and experience, and which tells of the possible victory of the small over the great, the weak over the strong.[9]

Lüthi sees the same theme displayed in the written literature of Kafka, Thomas Mann, Rilke, Shakespeare, Goethe, and French comedies of manners, but of course in highly complex form. We may extend Lüthi's examples to American literature, folklore, and history. There come to mind the triumphs of Brer Rabbit over the bear and the fox, clever John the slave over his Old Marster, and Signifying Monkey over the lion in Negro tradition; of Davy Crockett over b'ars, panthers, and armies of Mexicans and cannibals in frontier legend; of Jack the giant-killer in the southern Appalachians; of Ahab's conquest of the great white whale; of the perilous odyssey of Huck Finn; of Thoreau's defiance of the State; of Horatio Alger's novels celebrating the rapid rise of Ragged Dick, the bootblack; of the success stories of Ben Franklin, Abe Lincoln, Andrew Carnegie. It is the same tale of a determined underdog hero vanquishing powerful foes or subduing a hostile society.

Our three texts are variations on this theme. From disparate materials the narrators have fashioned dramatic compositions intended to be told. They have followed a construction, presented characters, and employed speech in the manner of universally successful prose traditions. These tales have not accidentally come into existence and endured by chance. They are products of individual oral artists working within a time-honored folk tradition.

Other genres of folk narrative possess stylistic and compositional elements that contribute to their traveling power and staying power. The lowliest of Anglo-American folktale forms, the anecdote of local characters, proves on closer examination to follow a fixed story line that ends with the dupe lamenting his deception at the hands of the trickster. Folktales have to fight for approval from fresh audiences at each new telling, and their long survival testifies to the persistent appeal of oral fiction.

Now that written literature is receiving such intensive and subtle analysis, perhaps more critical attention will be directed to oral literature, its precursor and constant supplier.

The Notary, from Cessolis *Scaecspul*
(Delft, 1483)

WAYLAND D. HAND

Hangmen, the Gallows, and the Dead Man's Hand in American Folk Medicine

The mystery that surrounds the life processes, including the inevitable cessation of life, has given rise to the rich and abundant folklore of the life cycle: birth, marriage, death.[1] Inextricably connected with the life cycle at all three main life crises, or rites of passage, as van Gennep denominated these changes,[2] are folk medical notions and practices appropriate to each new condition.

It is one of the ironies of folk medical practice that things connected with the realm of the dead should by some inexplicable logic be employed to combat sickness and sustain life. Perhaps this is part of the religious and philosophical dilemma expressed by a tenth-century theologian and philosopher in the famous dictum, *in medio vitae mortuus sum.* It is more likely, however, that the offices of hangmen, *Leichenwäscherinnen,* gravediggers, and even knackers, in caring for the sick, and the use of parts of the coffin, appurtenances of the gallows, graveyard earth, and even parts of the dead, rest on more primitive modes of thought than the theological aphorism stated by Notker of St. Gall. It is hard to see, however, on what this special healing efficacy of agents and things connected with death is based, and why things that would normally be shunned are, by some mental quirk, especially sought out for curative practices. It is clear, of course, that the principles of decay and dissolution associated with death and the dead fit readily into frames of thought and logic looking to removal and dying off of warts, wens, moles, and other excrescences, as well as to the shrinking and disappearance of goiters, tumors, and other kinds of swellings. Accordingly, it would be more to the curing of such diseases as ague, convulsions, epilepsy, fits, fever, hiccoughs, and the like that the paradox really applies. At work, in any case, are principles of both homeopathic and contagious magic. Perhaps even more important in a strictly medical sense would be rudimentary notions of immunology and other considerations of antithetical vital forces summed up in the magico-medical prescription of *contraria contrariis*.

A possible resolution of this dilemma—the use of parts of the dead to cure the living—is seen in the case of people who have died violently, and ahead of their appointed time, or, better still, those whose lives have been forcibly taken. It has been argued, for example, that people hanged, or otherwise executed, continue to exert a vital force beyond the gallows or the executioner's block—a tenacious prolongation of life,[3] with the thought that this vital force and magical power continues to operate until their normal life span would have run out. Belief in the magical power of the bodily parts and products of executed criminals as remedies and amulets was known in classical antiquity, as attested by Pliny,[4] and these old superstitions, nurtured during the Middle Ages, have lived on until the present time. Important in these old beliefs and customs, of course, was the hangman himself. Some scholars believe that a sacral function attached to his office, holding, in a sense, that in taking a human life he represented deity in a sacrificial act.[5] The hangman's reputation as a healer, and as a trafficker in splinters from the gallows, as well as in pieces of the hangman's rope, the clothes and other chattels of the executed criminal, goes back many centuries.[6] In former times executioners openly advertised themselves as healers.[7] As payment, in part, for their grisly work went the clothes of the criminal,[8] which were disposed of without difficulty for medical as well as other magical purposes. It is interesting to follow in eighteenth-century England the transfer of the magical power of the hanged criminal to the hangman himself. This is seen in the curing of warts, wens, and other excrescences, in the first instance, merely by having the sufferer touch his afflicted part to the hand or other parts of the defunct.[9] As a result of his traffic with the dead, and by contagious magic, the hangman himself also rubbed people afflicted with warts, receiving at one time a fee of 2/6d. for his services.[10] Traffic in bodily parts of hanged criminals, particularly skulls, fingers, and the notorious dead man's hand, or "hand of glory," [11] whether by sale or theft, continued unabated throughout the nineteenth century, and the practice has lived on pretty much to our own time.[12] A "collector," for example, is supposed to have offered £600 for the rope from which von Ribbentrop swung at the Nuremberg trials after

World War II.[13] Unfortunately, little lore about hangmen has been reported in America, even though one may assume that dealings of the kind mentioned were resorted to in parts of the country where hanging was still practiced.[14] Executions in public, one of the main reasons for hanging when this method of execution was originally instituted, are now pretty much a thing of the past,[15] with the result that only a few people are ever allowed to witness such a spectacle. Under these circumstances active traffic in items of gallows magic is impossible, even though reports of the use, or the recommended use, of these products still continues today.

With the natural limitations of the subject—particularly in the matter of unrecorded and uncodified data—I shall nevertheless essay in these pages a sketch of folk medical curing in America by means of certain things connected with the dead, whether bodily parts of the dead or funerary objects of various kinds immediately connected with the dead and with death. Executed criminals constitute a special phase of this subject; and with this subject we shall begin, even though the data are scanty.[16] In Pennsylvania it is believed among people of German extraction that a wen will be carried away if it is passed across the head of a criminal just hanged.[17] Although the hand of a corpse, as we shall see later, has been used for a variety of ailments in America, the specific use of the hand of a dead criminal is apparently not reported in the literature I have examined.[18] Neither has there been reported the use of the powdered skull of criminals,[19] the rendered down fat of humans,[20] nor the drinking of fresh blood set free by the headman's axe.[21] The use of the hanged man's tooth for toothache is rare, even for Europe, but there is an instance of this unusual practice in Siena, Italy, in 1435.[22]

The use of the hangman's rope for medical and other purposes is well known in Europe.[23] In the United States its use seems limited to Pennsylvania, where it is encountered in both the Anglo-American and German-American traditions.[24] The North Carolina entry in the Brown Collection, submitted by a student from Indiana,[25] would seem to be a copying of a Pennsylvania text. The hangman's rope is also used for fits in Pennsylvania,[26] whereas people suffering from headache could be cured, it was believed, by tying around their head the halter wherewith a person had been hanged.[27] The King's Evil, or scrofula, was also treated with bits of the hangman's rope, but I do not find American examples.[28] Magical power was thought also to attach to the rope with which a person had committed suicide. The use of such a rope in the treatment of epilepsy is reported from Pennsylvania.[29] Convulsions in children are also treated in this way.[30]

Equally rare with the use of the hangman's rope in America for curing purposes, is the use of parts of the gallows or the gibbet. This is no doubt for the same reason—rarity of hanging at a time when folklorists, local historians, and other antiquarians came on the scene to report such happenings. Resort to contemporary police and warden's accounts of a former day, and particularly to diaries, family books of all kinds, and rare local histories, would perhaps add notably to our poor knowledge of American gallows lore.

Whether the reference to the use of a fragment of a gibbet or gallows on which people had been executed to cure ague, as reported in *The Casket* of Philadelphia for 1833 deals with American material earlier than the *Virginia Museum* from which it was taken,[31] or whether it rests on such earlier well-known sources as Aubrey's *Remaines of Gentilisme and Judaisme* (1686–1687),[32] cannot be learned. In a disease related to ague, namely, fever, the use of gallows wood goes back to the time of Pliny.[33]

The use of splinters from a gibbet as a sovereign remedy for toothache, whether carried in the pocket, or used to probe the aching tooth, is well known in England and elsewhere,[34] but I do not command instances from America.

If the use of the hand of an executed criminal is little known in American folk medicine, the custom of treating various kinds of ailments with the touch of an ordinary dead man's hand is much better known. There is an important reason for this over and above the sharp decline in hangings in America in recent times, as indicated above. In Europe, where the corpse was gibbeted, and left for birds to consume, folk medical practitioners could get at the corpse to sever the hand, as could thieves, who also appropriated the so-called "hand of glory," to make themselves invisible as they burglarized, and also to render the victims deaf to any possible noise.[35] Under less notorious conditions it was not difficult for sufferers to go to the house where the dead was laid out, or even to the undertaker's, when such mortuary establishments later came into general use. Examples of both circumstances, each involving the supposed cure of goiter, are seen in accounts from Ontario (1908) and from the Ozark country (1940's).[36] The practice of using a dead man's hand in the treatment of goiter is found not only in Pennsylvania (Anglo-American tradition as well as in the Ger-

man tradition),[37] but also in New York State.[38] This cure is encountered in Ontario in both the Anglo-American and German-American
traditions,[39] and also in the South.[40] Indiana entries run true to form,[41]
as do two references from Illinois.[42] Two further accounts, both from
Hyatt's great collection, add interesting details. The first tells of a
fourteen-year-old girl going to the place where the dead person was
laid out, taking the dead person's hand, and rubbing her goiter with
it three times, after which she placed the hand back exactly as it was.
Within a year her goiter was gone.[43] The second account is a *memorat*,
telling of the use of the corpse's left hand for a goiter on the left side
and the right hand for one on the right side, and the unsuccessful use
of the left hand for a goiter on both sides of the neck: "and her goitre
got well on the left side and never did get well on the ride side."[44]
This cure for goiter has not been reported west of Nebraska.[45] The
use of a dead man's hand for goiter is, of course, well known in the
British Isles and elsewhere in Europe.[46]

Similar procedures to those used for the cure of goiter were employed also for other kinds of tumors and swellings. Once more, the
Pennsylvania German country is involved.[47] A variation on the treatment of tumors involved the use of a *Zwischenträger*, string or intermediate agent, namely, a string that had been tied around the finger
of the dead man's hand was later tied around the tumor, and as the
string rotted the tumor was supposed to disappear.[48] The method of
curing swellings by the touch of a dead person's hand is as old as
classical antiquity,[49] and as modern as the 1960's, as a recent report
from Somerset shows.[50] Belief that a dead man's hand touched to a
cancer will cure it was reported from Salt Lake City as recently as
1960.

The charming off of warts by means of touching or rubbing, a folk
medical practice which is known in Europe,[51] is encountered not only
in the Pennsylvania German country,[52] as one might suspect, but also
in such widely separated places as Tennessee,[53] the Ozark country,[54]
and Iowa.[55] The dispelling of wens, reported in *The Casket* of Philadelphia as early as 1833,[56] was, of course, known in England at a much
earlier time.[57] In modern times this cure, among other places, has been
reported from Suffolk (1895), Lincolnshire (1896), and Herefordshire (1912).[58] More recent American references to this practice, involving several southern states, as well as Pennsylvania, are to be
found in the Brown Collection.[59] The removal of wens is also accomplished by Louisville Negroes who place a string around the neck of

a deceased friend, and afterward wear it around their own necks with wens on them.[60]

"The touch of a dead man's hand," writes Randolph, "is popularly supposed to discourage moles, blackheads, enlarged pores, and other facial blemishes. I have seen a little girl, perhaps three years old, dragged into a village undertaking parlor and 'tetched,' in the belief that a large red birthmark on the child's face might thus be removed." [61]

Contact between the person seeking relief and the dead man is not limited to the latter's hand; it may extend to the fingers, to the face, and to other parts of the body; also it may involve the skull and the bones of the deceased, and even linen and cloths of various kinds that have been in contact with the dead person. The Alabama folk medical practice, around 1900, of putting the finger of a dead person in one's mouth for toothache,[62] is reported from Europe at an earlier day.[63] The application of the finger of a corpse to a wart, rather than the hand, as noticed above is reported from Norway.[64] Warts and moles are removed by rubbing the excrescences of the dead person's face, rather than bringing them into contact with his hand, according to an attestation from Illinois in 1935,[65] and a less certain report from California almost thirty years earlier.[66] In Illinois, likewise, the warts may be rubbed on the body of the corpse, the exact spot not being specified.[67] In other items from the same state interesting details are included, with a woman rubbing her wart on the corpse of a man three times, and vice versa.[68] The patient's own hand is rubbed over the corpse and then touched to the wart. This should be done as the full moon begins to decrease.[69] Tumors were treated in much the same way in Illinois: "If you have a tumor on the outside of your body, take it and rub it over a corpse of a dead person three times and it will go away. I know this is true, because when my father died, our neighbor had a tumor on her arm and she came and rubbed her tumor over my dead father three times, and in no time the tumor was gone." [70]

The drying and powdering of moss found on human skulls, as reported in *The Casket* (Philadelphia, 1833),[71] and then taken as snuff to cure headaches, doubtless is a carry-over from European practices.[72] The grating of the skull itself, and administering it, with or without ginger, to infants and others suffering from fits, seems not to be known in America.[73] Drinking from a skull to prevent scrofula is reported in an American popular journal of 1869,[74] but I can find no ready parallels. In another unusual practice, reported from Norway, a bone is used in a curious way: "For sudden gout or paralysis, which is called 'dead man's grasp,' stroke the sufferer with a bone from a corpse." [75] Instructions are given to get the bone back to the graveyard before nightfall, and it is recommended that someone, who knows about these matters, and not a relative, be entrusted with the job.

Contact with the corpse by means of bed linen, shrouds, washrags, and the like, rather than by direct touch or rubbing, is noted for warts, as one might expect. Disposing of the washrag which has been used to wash a corpse by placing it under the eaves is noted from Pennsylvania.[76] A more involved ritual is recorded from Illinois: "If you have a wart, go where they are laying out someone that is dead and take that piece of cloth that is over the dead one's face and rub that piece of cloth over your wart. Then you must put that piece of cloth in the coffin with that dead one and let it be buried with the dead, and your wart will go away." [77] Toothache cures of this sort are reported from Norway, where a cloth that has been in contact with a corpse, is placed over the mouth; [78] or the gum over the tooth is probed with a pin which has been fastened to the sheet in which the corpse has been wrapped. Similarly, in Norway, a cloth which has been used around the jaw of the corpse to keep the mouth closed, is tied around the head of a sufferer from headache.[79] In Portugal, scrofula is cured by scratching the affected part until it bleeds with a toenail from the left foot of a corpse and wiping away the blood with a cloth which is then placed in the coffin.[80]

Even though material introduced in this short discussion is little more than an adumbration of the scope and variety of material which exists, I trust that it will stimulate workers in the field to dredge up data for a fuller account at some later date.

Since completing this paper, I have been able to turn up additional data in the Newbell Niles Puckett Collection of Ohio Popular Beliefs and Superstitions, which has come to me for editing. A cursory search of the folk medical holdings shows that the touch of a dead man's hand was recommended not only for the cure of goiter, but also for the removal of birthmarks and warts. Recommended cures for epilepsy include the use of rope with which a person has committed suicide and a broth made from the skull of a dead person. Headache was to be treated by hanging around the forehead a piece of rope with which a criminal had been hanged. These dozen items were collected from different parts of Ohio between 1929 and 1962 and stem from people of continental as well as British ancestry.

Ars Moriendi

TRISTRAM COFFIN

Folk Logic and the Bard:
Act I of *Macbeth*[1]

When DeQuincey wrote in *The London Magazine* of October, 1823,

Oh! mighty poet!—Thy works are not as those of other men, simply and merely great works of art; but are also like the phenomena of nature, like the sun and the sea, the stars and the flowers—like frost and snow, rain and dew, hail-storm and thunder, which are to be studied in the perfect faith that in them there can be no too much or too little, nothing useless or inert—but that, the further we press our discoveries, the more we shall see proofs of design and self-supporting arrangement where the careless eye had seen nothing but accident!

he was rationalizing the "Knocking at the Gate Scene" (II, iii) in *Macbeth*. This paragraph, which has become a symbol of the Romantic attitude toward Shakespeare, might not be so effusive had DeQuincey taken a really critical look at Act I. For Act I shows a Shakespeare not only quite mortal, but even quite naively mortal at that. It shows Shakespeare to be as close to rustic simplicity in structure as he has been recognized to be in imagery. Act I, at least as we have it from the First Folio, is bluntly folk-like in its lack of concern with motivation or consistency and in its concentration on plot economy at any cost. And it, along with other acts from other plays by Shakespeare and his contemporaries, shows the Elizabethan theatre to reflect folklore and the technique of folk literature in a way that has not, to my knowledge, been discussed before.

In Act I we find a writer who is satisfied by the logic of a plot that would be perfectly satisfactory to a folktale-teller, but that would irritate a more sophisticated and scientific mind. In fact, Act I of

331

Macbeth cannot be made logical to the twentieth-century mind, unless one uses information that his imagination, not the text, supplies or unless he recognizes that Shakespeare has simply used the sort of "logic" that is common to most folktales—"folk logic" as I will call it.

Before going on to a detailed discussion of Act I, it would be wise to discuss the whole problem of plot "logic" at the various literary levels. In our society, consistency of time, sequence, detail, and motive has become a fetish.

Novelists, dramatists, movie and TV script men have become so conscientious about these matters that almost all of them are willing to sacrifice pace to make sure no critic will accuse them of a logical inconsistency or a failure to tie up a loose end. The result is a body of self-conscious, over-disciplined expression in which the main purpose of narrative (telling a story) gets lost. Nor is the weakness confined to the poorer writers. It is as common in the Henry James novel where the relationships of character and action are so involved the book becomes a magnificent technical exercise, as it is in the musical show which forgets its central appeal of glamor and song to make tediously sure that boy meets, loses, and gets girl. It is evident in the elaborate symbolisms and narrative patterns of Hemingway, Joyce, and Faulkner, in the feverish accuracy of the historical movie or the Book-of-the-Month Club novel, even in the stage sets and costuming of the Broadway play. One is reminded of the centipede who was asked which leg he used when.

The best works of the best writers succeed in spite of all this, just as Alexander Pope wrote successfully under the handicaps imposed by eighteenth-century culture. Nevertheless, I suspect our literature is reflecting a foolish by-product of our recent technological advances. Primitive and folk stories do not concern themselves with scientific, logical accuracy. A typical Indian tale could stagger the modern critic who took it seriously.

The Theft of Fire [2]

Many people lived around here, but they had no fire. They had only a heated stone. I don't know how they heated it, but there was no fire. The people were always hunting rabbits. Coyote was on the edge of the hunter's line. He saw the ashes of a fire coming from somewhere and dropping to the ground. He yelled to the others, and they came, gathering round in a circle to watch. While watching they said, "Some of us shall go up into the air and find out where it comes from." Eagle said, "Let me try first to see whether I can get high enough to see." He went up and out of sight, but returned without having seen it. A Chickenhawk set out next, but he did not go out of sight. Woodpecker also did not get very far, they were able to see him. All the birds tried, but none could go far enough. Only fish was left. They said, "You have no wings; how are you going to go up?"—"Let me try for fun whether or not I can fly." He started up. He went out of sight, and when he returned he said: "Not very far from here are flames of fire, by a snow-topped peak near Las Vegas." Coyote said, "Let us go and get it, that is not far." All started, Coyote leading, and Woodpecker, Chickenhawk, Bluejay, Roadrunner, Jackrabbit, and others following. They went toward the place where fire had been seen and made firedrills to take along so as to deceive the fire-owners and prevent them from guessing what their visitors were seeking.

When they arrived Coyote made a speech: "We have merely come for fun to gamble and play with you." The hosts gave all the animals the kind of food they were used to eating, to each bird a different kind of seed, to the Crested Jay good hard pinenuts. To Coyote they gave cedar berries. After they had eaten, they began to play at a game. They made three piles of dirt and hid something in one of the piles. If the guesser hit the right pile with a stone, he won the game. All night they played. The hosts said, "These people have not come to gamble, they have come to steal our fire." Coyote replied, "No, we have fire ourselves," and showed them their firedrills. Towards morning Coyote had some cedarbark tied to his hair and let it stick out. When he tied it on, all were watching him circle around. "We know what they have come for," they said. At daylight Coyote bent over the fire, then the bark caught fire and he jumped away over the crowd and ran off followed by his people. Before very long the Crested Jay was caught and killed by the pursuers. One after another carried the fire. When they reached the Colorado River, all the rest were tired and Roadrunner said, "Let me carry the fire." He put it on each side of his head. Then he tore his feet in different ways so that they could not see the direction he had taken and made lots of sand. The pursuers tracked him, some backwards, others forwards, and did not know which way to go. He arrived in the Shivwits country. They tracked him. He built a big fire on the top of a mountain. Looking up, the pursuers saw the big fire. Then they went back.

In the evening Coyote's people saw clouds. It was going to rain. Coyote carried together plenty of wood. His people went into a cave for shelter. After dark it rained. They built a big fire, but the water put it out. They saved one charcoal, and in the morning they told Jackrabbit to hold it. He took it into the rain. Coyote bade him not let it go out or he would shoot him. But Jackrabbit kept it under his tail and saved it. The rain ceased, then Jackrabbit brought the coal back and it was still alive. Everything was wet, however, and they could not find any tinder. Rat said, "I have a dry nest to make fire with." He gave it to them and they had a big fire. Coyote said to his followers: "Let us give heat and fire to all the trees and shrubs and to all the rocks." So he gave fire to every one of them so they could burn thereafter. Then he dried his bow and arrows, and called Rat to come by imitating his noise. When Rat came, Coyote shot and killed him, and roasted him in the fire. After that he killed Jackrabbit, skinned him, and made a blanket of the skin. He killed nearly all of those with him and ate them. "Hereafter people shall do thus," he said.

It becomes obvious at once that statements in this tale that trouble the modern mind are of no concern to the Indian teller at all. The people have no fire, but they are able to heat stones. (Even the narrator, undoubtedly influenced by White education, is disturbed over this point.) The animals see fire and recognize it, although they have never known it. Fish flies even though he has no wings and doesn't know if he can. The fire is not far off, but none of the birds are able to spot it. The animals make firedrills in anticipation of an incredibly astute question they must answer, although they have never had fire. The hosts realize that Coyote and the rest have come to steal fire, although they have no reason in the world for such suspicions. They also watch Coyote's whole deceit aware of what he is going to do, but without attempting to prevent his doing it. Nor is Coyote grateful for his friends' aid: he kills nearly all of them. (Admittedly, these killings are related to ritualism and the roles the victims must play in Shoshone life.) However, the real point with this tale is that it is functioning a-logically or on a completely different logical system from the one we are accustomed to use. The important thing seems to be *what happened*. The teller knows what happened, and the actors are made to know that what happened *must* come to pass. The conclusion is, thus, inevitable; so events that *are to be* in the narrative are referred to as *actually being*. Everything—logic, time sequence, et cetera—is subordinated to the tale itself. That is what the folk focus on, often to the exclusion of what we hold dear. The result is good stories, lacking perhaps in characterization, but certainly not in precision and pace.

This way of handling a tale bothers the twentieth-century reader, but it is not unknown to him. Older literature, produced when the writers were closer to the folk, shows similar characteristics. Aeschylus allows Agamemnon to arrive in Greece only a few uninterrupted minutes after the beacons have flashed the news of Troy's fall. Seneca's Thyestes tells his children of his fears for them should they return to Atreus' kingdom, but he turns them over to their doom just the same.

Today, the only haven for such inconsistencies is the little nonsense literature we have, where concern with "proper technique" can by definition be excused. The following advertisement cartoon by Al Capp for Wildroot Cream-oil Hair Tonic[3] uses essentially the same technique as "The Theft of Fire" tale. The script, minus the appropriate drawings, proceeds as below:

Panel 1:
    Sexy Girl: Help! I'm being kidnapped by a fire-hydrant!!
    Police Chief: That's silly!! Nobody's ever been kidnapped by a fire hydrant!!
    Fearless Fosdick: Wait, Chief!! That's no hydrant!! That's "Anyface" Master of 1000 Disguises!!

Panel 2:
    Police Chief: That hydrant's got a g-gun!! —Save me, Fosdick!! —Remember!! —I'm your b-beloved chief!!
    Fosdick: I'll try to save the girl, too —if you don't mind, sir!!

Panel 3:
    Fosdick: Chuckle!! —I cleverly absorbed all his bullets in my body!! Drop that girl, Anyface!! —I'm going to run you in!!

Panel 4 (In which the hydrant squirts Fosdick's hair):
    Anyface: Haw!! —You can't!! —This water will dry out your hair, and you'll look a mess!! —The boys at the police station will laugh at you!!

Panel 5:
    Fosdick: Gulp!! —So they will!! —I just can't run you in with my hair looking like this!! Oh, what will I do.
    Girl: Get Wildroot Cream-oil, Charlie!!

Panel 6:
    Fosdick: That would be illegal!! —My name is Fosdick!!
    Girl: No matter what your name is, Wildroot Cream-oil relieves dryness!! —Keeps hair neat, but not —ugh!! —greasy!!

Panel 7:

Fosdick: Well, bless my well-groomed head!! Wildroot Cream-oil did the trick!! —And, now —Anyface—I'm going to lock you up!!

Girl: Lock me up, Fosdick—in your arms!! —I just love men who use —sigh-h!! —Wildroot Cream-oil!!

The obvious absurdities of the situation are utilized for humor here, but the narrative method is quite similar to the one put to serious use in "The Theft of Fire" tale. The action is illogical. The plot, such as it is, hinges on a preposterous fact. The police chief needs no convincing that the hydrant is really a man. Fosdick's body, full of holes in one panel, has absorbed the bullets in another. Fosdick regards his name as a legal barrier to the use of the hair-tonic. For us, the spontaneous nature of these episodes would be permissible only for nonsense. (W. S. Gilbert, for example, successfully hangs the plot of *Patience* on the fact that Bunthorne threatens Grosvenor with a curse.)

I am convinced that Act I of *Macbeth* will make sense to those modern readers who are not overwhelmed by Shakespeare's reputation only when it is recognized that it is proceeding according to the principles outlined above and not like an act from a modern drama.

There are six passages in Act I that are germane to our discussion: iii, 130–141; iv, 48–53; v, 1–30; v, 39 f.; v, 60–71; vii, 1 f.[4] There is no way these passages can be made consistent with each other, unless the reader goes beyond the text into his imagination. The trick then is not to supply "missing" speeches and "missing" ideas, but to harmonize the inconsistencies that exist in the text as we have it.

In iii, 130–141, Macbeth and Banquo have just been told by the witches of their future. Macbeth admits in an aside (127) that "two truths are told," and he has no reason to doubt that if he but waits the third will come to pass and he will be king. His reaction to this possibility is hard to believe:

> This supernatural soliciting
> cannot be ill; cannot be good. If ill,
> Why hath it given me earnest of success,
> Commencing in a truth? I am Thane of Cawdor.
> If good, why do I yield to that suggestion
> Whose horrid image doth unfix my hair
> And make my seated heart knock at my ribs
> Against the use of nature?

Certainly, were any of us to be told that he were to be the next king of England, his first reaction would not be to consider murdering Elizabeth. Such a reaction would have to be the result of impatience after a long wait—and especially if one's information had come from clairvoyants who had just been proved doubly reliable. Macbeth, we are forced to conclude, has planned to kill Duncan before he met the witches. Shakespeare's sources verify such a conclusion, but we have to read it into Banquo's observation (51–52) when Macbeth hears himself referred to as "king hereafter!"

> Good sir, why do you start and seem to fear
> Things that do sound so fair?

At any rate, the idea of murdering Duncan is thoroughly fixed in his mind in scene iv when the king names Malcolm, Prince of Cumberland, next in line. Again, a normal reaction to this event would be to wonder what was going to happen to Malcolm in order that the witches' prophecy might come true, not to speak as Macbeth does (48–51):

> The Prince of Cumberland! That is a step
> On which I must fall down, or else o'erleap,
> For in my way it lies. Stars, hide your fires!
> Let not light see my black and deep desires.

Scene v adds confusion. Lady Macbeth, who has not appeared in the play before and has not seen her husband since he and Banquo met the witches, is found reading a letter in which Macbeth informs her of the fortunate prophecy. The tone of the letter, and we hear only the last part, reflects Macbeth's simple exhilaration at this good luck he is anxious to share with his wife. He never mentions murder. Nevertheless, she puts the letter down and speaks directly of murder (16–21) as though that were a path long since chosen:

> Glamis thou art, and Cawdor, and shalt be—
> What thou art promis'd. Yet do I fear thy nature.
> It is too full o' th' milk of human kindness
> To catch the nearest way. Thou wouldst be great;
> Art not without ambition, but without
> The illness should attend it.

This scene shores up the idea that Macbeth and Lady Macbeth have made previous plans to murder the king, but we have to know the sources to be sure of this point. Shakespeare never lets us know for certain that the witches' prophecy has re-ignited an old plan, nor does he ever concern himself with Macbeth's impatience, with his inability to wait out the witches' forecast.

Subsequent action offers further confusion. At the end of scene v, Lady Macbeth makes it clear (39–44) that she is going to grasp the first possible opportunity to dispose of Duncan, who by fate comes to visit that very night:

> The raven himself is hoarse
> That croaks the fatal entrance of Duncan
> Under my battlements. Come, you spirits
> That tend on mortal thoughts, unsex me here,
> And fill me, from the crown to the toe, top-full
> of direst cruelty!

However, when her husband (using, incidentally, the double chronology of stage convention) enters at the conclusion of her speech, he seems to have put aside any plans for murder (59–62):

> *Macb.*   My dearest love,
> Duncan comes here tonight.
> *Lady.*   And when goes hence?
> *Macb.* To-morrow, as he proposed.
> *Lady.*   O never
> Shall sun that morrow see!

In fact, Macbeth does not seem particularly stirred by the whole idea. "We will speak further" he says (72), and they go out.

Nevertheless, when scene vii opens, Macbeth is set on murdering Duncan (1–7):

> If it were done when 'tis done, then 'twere well
> It were done quickly. If th' assassination
> Could trammel up the consequence, and catch,
> With his surcease, success; that but this blow
> Might be the be-all and the end-all here,
> But here, upon this bank and shoal of time,
> We'ld jump the life to come.

Shakespeare does not tell us when his wife convinced Macbeth that they must act, nor does he explain Macbeth's reluctance or obtuseness in scene v. Either the dramatist is letting Macbeth hesitate in scene v for cheap dramatic effect or he forces us to assume his wife has been talking to him between scenes when we can't hear what's going on. Either way, Shakespeare nods. And he lets himself in for more criticism later in the same scene when Lady Macbeth says to her husband (47–54):

> What beast was't then
> That made you break this enterprise to me?
> When you durst do it, then you were a man;
> And to be more than what you were, you would
> Be so much more the man. Nor time nor place
> Did then adhere, and yet you would make both.
> They have made themselves, and that their fitness now
> Does unmake you.

At this point, scene v becomes impossible. Either Lady Macbeth's speech after reading the letter or Macbeth's naiveté when she asks him when Duncan "goes hence" is illogical and inconsistent. Furthermore, no matter which way one turns, one can't excuse Shakespeare from sloppy organization and sloppy motivation.

Not that the Bard's admirers have failed to excuse him. There are a dozen rationalizations centering on such things as the previous plan to kill the king; the desire of the Macbeths to kill Duncan for fear the witches may be wrong or be satanically inspired; Macbeth's being overly cautious in scene v; Lady Macbeth's acting "just like a woman" when she blames her husband in scene vii; the fact that the whole play depends on Macbeth's inability to trust the witches; and so forth. But none of these rationalizations can take the place of demonstrable consistency of action and clear-cut motivation. The fact remains, if we wish to see Act I of *Macbeth* as a first-rate act opening one of the world's great tragedies, we have to find better explanations than these.[5] And, to be sure, "folk logic" offers them.

The historical Macbeth [6] ruled Scotland from 1040 to 1057. He seems to have been an ordinary king and quite unlike the Macbeth of the play. In 1385, however, John of Fordun was referring to him as a tyrant and by 1424 Andrew of Wyntoun had added the embellishment of the "thre werd systrys who pronounce prophesies to Macbeth in hys dremyng." Banquo and Fleance enter the tale in 1526–1527 in

Boece's *Scotorum Historiae,* as does the non-historical Macduff who becomes the character Shakespeare used. Ralph Holinshed followed John Bellenden's 1536 translation of Boece, as it had been adapted by William Harrison, and Shakespeare used Holinshed.

In Holinshed, accounts are presented of Macbeth's meeting with the witches, the death of Duncan in an ambush planned by Macbeth, Banquo, and others, and the subsequent years during which Macbeth ruled Scotland. In Holinshed, it is not certain that Macbeth actually is the slayer of Duncan, but he does have a claim to the throne. He turns to tyranny only near the end of his rule, when he realizes that Banquo's and not his issue will take over Scotland. The murder of Duncan, as it appears in the play, comes from a separate account in Holinshed in which King Duff is slain by Donwald, who was urged on by his wife. Duff is Donwald's guest, and Donwald is a reluctant killer with too much imagination for his own good.

The crux of this semi-literary legend is, of course, the fact that Macbeth engineers Duncan's death, regardless why, how, or where it is done. This is the central and inevitable event on which the story's existence hangs and this is, therefore, "what must come to pass." If one conceives of the plot in terms of the "logic" of folk literature, everything naturally subordinates itself to the inevitability of the murder. Thus, the witches can prophecy Macbeth's inevitable succession to the throne, though Macbeth will ignore this inevitability and be compelled to gain that throne through murder—simply because the tale is about Macbeth's murder of Duncan and, really, nothing else. Thus, also, the narrator can make the assumption that Macbeth planned to kill Duncan, and his wife knew he planned to kill Duncan, before meeting the witches, even if the witches' prophecy introduces him to the idea of becoming king for the first time.

So the scenes can be made to make sense. Macbeth and Banquo meet the witches and are told of their futures. Macbeth, who is determined by the story-line to kill Duncan and become king through murder, at once focuses on the crime he is to commit. When Cumberland is placed in his way, he again thinks only of the predetermined crime, as does his wife when she reads the letter. When Duncan fortunately comes for the night, Lady Macbeth is ready to move. Macbeth hesitates; he wants to talk things over. However, he is ready when scene vii opens, and his wife is free to blame him for sowing these ideas in her mind by line 47.

The witches' prophecies are not original to the story anyhow. These

sisters, whether old women who have traded themselves to the Devil
or Norns of destiny, are first recorded in the legend of Macbeth's rise
to power by Andrew of Wyntoun. They are an embellishment, and
when they come into the legend they do not change the already established motivation of the story-line. Of course, they lend the story
supernatural status, give it mystery, and philosophical overtones, but
they are introduced as part of the normal urge of the folk and the
folk-influenced chroniclers to decorate their material in standardized
ways.

Nor is it of real importance to my arguments that George Buchanan's *Rerum Scoticarum Historia* (first printed in Edinburgh in 1582)
states that Macbeth, before he met the witches, *regni spem occultam
in amino alebat*. Perhaps Shakespeare knew Buchanan, although there
is no proof of this. Possibly, too, Macbeth murders Duncan because
he does not trust the prophecies of the devilish sisters, who may, at
the bidding of their master, be trying to incite him to murder. But if
this doubt is present, Macbeth gives no indication of it. In fact, one
of the powerful things about the tragedy is that the witches always tell
the truth, and Macbeth believes them until he despairs his charm at
the end. These points both become academic once one realizes the possibilities of Shakespeare's using what I have called "folk logic."

Because Shakespeare and his contemporaries were such great writers,
and because we think of ourselves as far more demanding in matters
of logic than we really are, many of the folkloristic elements in the
Elizabethan dramas have gone ignored. London of 1600 was very,
very close to the folk culture of Britain. Tales, songs, superstitions
from oral tradition were everywhere; what veneer the urbanite had
was not deep. The Shakespearean audience hesitated to disbelieve the
Ghost of Hamlet's father, the reality of Faustus' temptation, the alchemy of Friar Bacon.

Much becomes clear, if we will only stop overestimating Shakespeare, if we will only stop giving him a mind like ours. For example,
the "I know you all" speech that Prince Hal makes at the close of
Act I, scene ii, in *Henry the Fourth, Part I* has bothered scholars for
years. Pages have been written rationalizing these lines, which make
Hal appear to be a calculating, possibly hypocritical, politician, in
spite of the fact he is not such a fellow anywhere else in the play.
Yet it is obvious that the same sort of thing that occurs in *Macbeth*
occurs here. The legend is about Hal's reform. As Hal must reform
for the narrative to exist, the author is free to use this fact before it

actually takes place in the story-line. Hal is not a hypocrite, and he does not speak inconsistently at the end of Act I. Hal, like Camillo in Act IV, scene iv, of *The Winter's Tale* and like many others, is simply a character in a tale that is being told by a narrator to people who have heard tales handled this way all their lives, as their forefathers did before them.

Shakespeare, it is true, is a "mighty poet"—and his works, in one sense, are not as the works of other men. But at the same time they are as those of other men, the folk—of whose literary heritage he and his audience still seem to have been a part.

Notes

BEOWULF: ONE POEM OR THREE?

1. L. L. Schücking, *Beowülfs Rückkehr* (Halle, 1905).

2. R. W. Chambers, *Beowulf: An Introduction to the Study of the Poem,* 2nd ed. (Cambridge: Cambridge University Press, 1932), pp. 118–120.

3. Magoun, *"Béowulf A',* a Folk-Variant," *Arv, Tidskrift för Nordisk Folkminnes forskning,* XIV (1958), 95–101; *"Béowulf B:* a Folk-Poem on Béowulf's Death," in *Early English and Norse Studies Presented to Hugh Smith,* ed. Arthur Brown and Peter Foote (London: Methuen, 1963), pp. 127–140.

4. *"Béowulf A',"* 100–101.

5. *Beowulf,* ed. Fr. Klaeber, 3rd ed. (Boston: Heath, 1950), pp. lvii–lviii.

6. In *The Art of Beowulf* (Berkeley: University of California Press, 1959), pp. 79, 223.

7. *"Béowulf A',"* 95–96.

8. See Eduard Sievers, *Angelsächsische Grammatik,* 3. Aufl. (Halle: M. Niemayer, 1921), Par. 270 and *Anm.* 2.

9. W. W. Lawrence, *Beowulf and Epic Tradition* (Cambridge, Mass.: Harvard University Press, 1928), pp. 126–127.

10. *"Béowulf A',"* 96.

11. *"Béowulf A',"* 96.

12. *The Art of Beowulf,* pp. 92–93.

13. *"Béowulf A',"* 97. But see Adrien Bonjour, *Twelve Beowulf Papers* (Neuchatel, 1962), p. 65.

14. *"Béowulf A',"* 98.

15. *"Béowulf A',"* 98.

16. *Beowulf,* note to 1. 2152b.

17. *"Béowulf A',"* 98.

18. *"Béowulf A',"* 98.

19. *"Béowulf A',"* 98.

20. *"Béowulf A',"* 99.

21. *"Béowulf A',"* 99.

22. *"Béowulf A',"* 97.

23. *The Art of Beowulf,* pp. 237–238.

24. *"Béowulf B,"* 127.

25. *"Béowulf B,"* 128–129.

26. *"Béowulf B,"* 129.

27. *"Béowulf B,"* 131.

28. J. R. R. Tolkien, *"Beowulf*: The Monsters and the Critics," Proceedings of the British Academy, XXII (1936), 271–272; Kemp Malone, "The Old English Period," in *A Literary History of England,* ed. Albert C. Baugh (New York and London: Appleton-Century-Crofts, 1948), p. 94. See also my *Art of Beowulf,* pp. 72–74.

29. *"Béowulf B,"* 130.

30. *"Béowulf B,"* 130–131.

31. *"Béowulf B,"* 131.

32. *"Béowulf B,"* 131.

33. "The Monsters and the Critics," 271–272.

34. *"Béowulf B,"* 132.

35. Adrien Bonjour, "The Technique of Parallel Descriptions in *Beowulf"* and "The Problem of Dæghrefn," reprinted with later Comments, in *Twelve Beowulf Papers,* pp. 51–65, 77–88.

36. *"Béowulf B,"* 132–133.

37. *"Béowulf B,"* 134.

38. Bonjour ("Beowulf and Heardred," *Twelve Beowulf Papers,* p. 72) doubts that the killing of Dæghrefn was an act of vengeance for Hygelac's death, since we are not specifically told that Dæghrefn was Hygelac's slayer. But presumably Beowulf, in killing Dæghrefn, was carrying out his duty to avenge his lord and kinsman.

39. *"Béowulf B,"* 134.

40. *"Béowulf B,"* 135.

41. *Beowulf,* p. 278 and note 2.

42. *Beowulf: An Introduction,* p. 120.

43. See *The Art of Beowulf,* Chapter I.

44. *"Béowulf B,"* 135–136.

45. Lawrence, *Beowulf and Epic Tradition,* pp. 213 ff.

46. Malone, "Notes on *Beowulf,"* *Anglia,* LXIX (1951), 296.

47. Bonjour, "Young Beowulf's Inglorious Period," *Anglia,* LXX (1952), 339–344; *Twelve Beowulf Papers,* pp. 91–93.

48. *Beowulf,* p. xxvii, note 6.

49. Adeline C. Bartlett, *The Larger Rhetorical Patterns in Anglo-Saxon Poetry* (New York: Columbia University Press, 1935), p. 88.

50. *"Beowulf B,"* 136.

51. *The Art of Beowulf,* pp. 238–239.

52. "Notes on *Beowulf,"* 295–300; "Young Beowulf," *JEGP,* XXVI (1937), 21–23.

53. Malone, "Notes on *Beowulf,"* 299; Bonjour, *Twelve Beowulf Papers,* p. 90.

54. *Twelve Beowulf Papers,* p. 95.

55. *The Art of Beowulf,* p. 237.

56. *"Béowulf B,"* 137–138.

57. C. Schaar, "A New Theory of Old English Poetic Diction," *Neophilologus,* XL (1956), 302–303; Benson, "The Literary Character of Anglo-Saxon Formulaic Poetry," *PMLA,* LXXXI (1966), 334–341.

58. *"Béowulf B,"* 138–139.

59. *"Béowulf B,"* 138–139.

60. A. Heusler, *Die altgermanische Dichtung* (Potsdam, 1926), pp. 14–15, 109.

61. *The Art of Beowulf,* pp. 1, 16–17.

A SYMBOLIC WORD-GROUP IN *BEOWULF*

1. Stanley B. Greenfield, *A Critical History of Old English Literature* (New York: New York University Press, 1965), p. 86.

2. Lines 3180–3182. All citations will be made from Fr. Klaeber's 3rd ed. (Boston: Heath, 1941). As to the *"Beowulf* poet" see especially Dorothy Whitelock, *The Audience of Beowulf* (Oxford: Clarendon Press, 1951), pp. 4–5.

3. *Beowulf,* Introduction, p. li.

4. Miss Whitelock, *The Audience of Beowulf,* pp. 19–20, proposes, only to reject, the important possibility that *Beowulf* was written for an audience of ecclesiastics alone. Something very close to this I hope to defend before too long.

5. M. L. W. Laistner, "The Library of the Venerable Bede," in *Bede: His Life, Times, and Writings,* ed. A. Hamilton Thompson (Oxford: Clarendon Press, 1935), pp. 237–266; J. D. A. Ogilvie, *Books Known to the English, 597–1066* (Cambridge, Mass.: Mediaeval Academy of America, 1967).

6. "Quid Hinieldus cum Christo?" in a letter to Hygebald, Bishop of Lindisfarne, A.D. 797. Alcuini Epistolae 81, in *Bibliotheca Rerum Germanicarum,* VI (Berlin: Weidmann, 1873).

7. F. P. Magoun, "Bede's Story of Caedmon: The Case History of an Anglo-Saxon Oral Singer," *Speculum,* XXX (1955), 49–63. The argument (pp. 58–59) that Caedmon must have known the method of song long before the time of his miraculous experience seems reasonable. In effect, it denies priority to Caedmon as a religious poet on the ground that "under observable conditions formulas are created only slowly and no one singer ever invents many, often none at all, finding the available supply quite adequate for his needs." Even if this was true of the traditional (pagan) oral formulas of unlettered singers, it is very unlikely to have been true when lettered poets were adapting the oral-formulaic method to Christian purposes. Working pen in hand and without the immediate pressure of extemporizing before a live audience, they could be more deliberate—freer to vary old formulas and to create new ones. A further implication is that this adaptation began before Caedmon. The first adapters adopted at least the *form* of Anglo-Saxon verse and many existing formulas; they may well have taken some *substance* from Latin sources too: see note 8.

8. Ambrosius, *Hexaemeron,* IV. i. 1; in Migne, *Patrologia* (1845), XIV, 188C: *Oculus est enim mundi, jucunditas diei, coeli pulchritudo, naturae gratia,*

praestantia creaturae. This work was one "well known to Bede, who used it in his own commentary on *Genesis* in his dedicatory epistle to Acca." Ogilvie, *Books Known to the English,* p. 59.

9. See the very penetrating paper of Morton W. Bloomfield, *"Beowulf* and Christian Allegory," *Traditio,* VII (1949–51), 410–415.

10. *Beowulf,* note to l. 95.

11. Luke 2: 32. In the Old English version: *leoht to þeoda awrignesse*—a light for revelation to the nations. J. W. Bright, *The Gospel of Saint Luke in Anglo-Saxon* (Oxford: Clarendon Press, 1893).

12. *Dies solis* = Late Greek ἡμέρα ἡλίου, "day of the sun."

13. Dorothea Forstner, *Die Welt der Symbole,* 2nd ed. (Innsbruck: Tyrolia, 1967), p. 102.

14. So Proclus, Oratorio IV (*in Natalem Diem Domini*), *Patrologia,* LXV, 714. The "Sun of Righteousness" is from *Malachi* 4: 3—see note 20.

15. André Grabar, *Christian Iconography,* Bollingen Series XXXV (Princeton: Princeton University Press, 1968), pp. 143–144: "Iconography was intended to reveal the secret but essential meaning within sacred history of certain events related in the Old Testament, to make that meaning specific by showing that the given events of the Old Testament were direct and individual antetypes of events of the New Testament, and to show that the correspondences existing between such symmetrical facts extended also to the history of the Church, whose sacraments have their prefigurations in the Old Testament. Iconography rises here to the level of theological commentary. . . . Clearly, the methods that [verbal] image-makers of the age of scholasticism were to use constantly already have their beginnings here."

16. Forstner, *Die Welt der Symbole,* p. 100.

17. Oskar Doering (revised by Michael Hartig), *Christliche Symbole* (Freiburg im Breisgau: Herder, 1940), p. 37.

18. Grabar, *Christian Iconography,* p. 117.

19. For further detail on iconographic representations of the *aureole,* the *nimbus,* symbolizing pagan, then Christian deity, see Grabar, *Christian Iconography,* pp. 116–118; also plate 285, the sun (Christ) in his chariot, Vatican grottoes, and plate IV, Enthroned and standing gods [with aureole], Karanis, Egypt, second century.

20. *Et orietur vobis timentibus nomen meum sol iustitiae et sanitas in pennis eius.* See note 14, Proclus' allusion to it. Also Ambrosius, *Hexaemeron* IV. ii. 5, Migne, *Patrologia* (1845), XIV, 189D, referring to *Genesis* 1: 14: *Deus ergo Pater dicit: Fiat sol; et Filius fecit solem. Dignum enim erat, ut solem mundi faceret Sol iustitiae.* Gildas, in the sixth century *De Excidio et Conquestu Britanniae,* Chapter 8, uses it for missionary purposes: the cold of pagan Britain will be counteracted by this sun. (J. A. Giles, *Six Old English Chronicles* [London: Bell and Daldy, 1872], p. 302.)

21. Cf. the common epithet for Christ: Old English *Hælend,* Old Saxon *Heliand,* etc.

22. *Psalms* 103: 2: *Deus . . . amictus lumine sicut vestimento.* In the Vespasian Psalter: *God . . . biswapen lehte swe swe mid hregle* (Sherman M. Kuhn, ed. [Ann Arbor: University of Michigan Press, 1965], p. 99). In the

Vitellius Psalter: *God . . . ge*[ ] *of leohte swaswa of hraegle* (James L. Rosier, ed. [Ithaca: Cornell University Press, 1962], p. 254).

23. *Isaiah* 60: 19–20, etc.: *Non erit tibi amplius sol ad lucendum per diem, nec splendor lunae illuminabit te; sed erit tibi Dominus in lucem sempiternam, et Deus tuus in gloriam team.* On the moon as a symbol of resurrection and of the Church, see Forstner, *Die Welt der Symbole,* p. 107. Also Ambrosius *Hexaemeron* IV. ii. 7, Migne, *Patrologia* (1845), XIV, 190C: *Est ergo in diei potestate sol, et luna in potestate noctis, quae temporum vicibus obedire compellitur, et nunc impletur lumine, atque vacuatur: licet plerique hunc locum mystice de Christo et Ecclesia videantur accipere.*

24. See *John* 1: 4, 5: *In ipso vita erat, et vita erat lux hominum; et lux in tenebris lucet . . .* ; also *Epistle of John* 1: 5: *Deus lux est,* etc.

25. *Tacen* is used of the sun also in *Andreas* 88 and *Phoenix* 96, the latter equated with *beacen* in l. 107.

26. Klaeber's note, in *Beowulf* (to 572 f.), suggests the other saying "Fortune favors the brave," in which *wyrd* is more literally translated and without Christian suggestion. But he continues, "Frequently God is substituted for fate," giving four examples from *Beowulf,* one from *Andreas,* and four supporting references to scholarship.

27. See F. Anne Payne, *King Alfred and Boethius* (Madison: University of Wisconsin Press, 1968), Chapter III, especially the first 3 sections. Alfred concerns himself with the question "whether Wyrd rules the world independent of God's permission. Even though it is quickly established that it does not, . . . 'wyrd' has the distinction of naming the only force other than God whose extensive influence Alfred recognizes" (p. 79).

28. Lines 569b–570a. In *Phoenix* 107 *beacen,* unmodified, translates *sol*: see lines 35 ff., Mary C. Fitzpatrick, *Lactanti de Ave Phoenice* (Philadelphia, 1933).

29. *Beacna beorhtost* is a favorite formulaic epithet, used in *Andreas* 242 of the sun, in *Crist* 1085 of the cross.

30. T. Wright and R. P. Wülcker, *Anglo-Saxon and Old English Vocabularies* (London: Trübner, 1884): *tacnbora* translates *signifer* (117.29, 142.10, 332.27, 549.30) and in the first two also *vexillifer; segnbora* translates *vexillarius* and *signifer* (225.14) ; *seign* translates *vexilla* (52.37).

31. Hygelac fought under a *segen* (1204a, 2958b) but it is not described. Scyld Scefing's (47) is golden and stands high over his head. The first of Hroðgar's gifts to Beowulf is a *segen gyldenne . . . hroden hildecumbor* (1021a, 1022a).

32. Compare the heavenly light, *wuldres tacn,* that floods the prison (Andreas 88) and out of which God speaks; similarly in *Guðlac* 1256–1257. One may compare also the light accompanying Christ when he harrows hell: suddenly there comes a brightness "as if a golden sun were kindled there." Satan and his band are afraid of the light. Adam and the highfathers and prophets declare, *þys leoht ys ealdor þaes ecan leohtes, eallswa us Dryhten behet, þaet he us þaet ece leoht onsendan wolde.* Isaiah says, *þys ys þaet faederlice leoht, and hyt ys Godes sunu,* the fulfillment of his prophecy. St. Simeon tells them to glorify *Dryhten Cryst, Godes Sunu, þone þe ic baer on mynum earmum into þam temple.* Thunder is heard and a voice speaks, etc. S. J. Crawford, ed., *The Gospel of Nicodemus* (Edinburgh: Hutchen, 1927), pp. 17–18.

33. G. P. Krapp, *The Vercelli Book* (New York: Columbia University Press, 1932).

34. G. P. Krapp and E. V. K. Dobbie, *The Exeter Book* (New York: Columbia University Press, 1936).

35. So Bosworth-Toller. The references are to Bede's *Ecclesiastical History,* ed. Thomas Miller, EETS, 95, 96 (1890–1891), 5. 23: *beacniendlic;* and to Wright-Wülcker, *Anglo-Saxon and Old English Vocabularies,* I, 401: *beacnung.*

36. We can only hope, in Francis Utley's words, to "prefer St. Augustine or Philo Judaeus to Friar Dollenkopf." See his remarkable review "Robertsonianism Redivivus," *Romance Philology,* XIX (1965), 260.

37. *Tacen* did not always have religious significance; indeed, of Bosworth-Toller's seven senses only two would seem to be necessarily of this kind. On the other hand, it does mean Christ's cross in *Elene* 164, 171; *Juliana* 491; *Homilies of Aelfric* 62.12 (ed. B. Thorpe for the Aelfric Society, I [1844–46]); it also enters into a number of compounds meaning the same: *sigetacen* (*Blickling Homilies* 97. 13); *sigortacen* (*Guthlac* 1089)—cp. (*Elene* 85) *sigores tacen.* Note also for the cross *sigebeacen* (*Elene* 168, 887, 974) and *sigorbeacen* (*Elene* 984).

A READING OF *BEOWULF* 3169–3182

1. *Bjowulfs Drape* (Copenhagen, 1820), p. 312.

2. See his *Illustrations of Anglo-Saxon Poetry* (London, 1826), p. v. The collation itself is given on pp. 137–155.

3. *The Anglo-Saxon Poems of Beowulf, the Traveller's Song, and the Battle of Finnes-Burh* (London: William Pickering, 1837), p. 224.

4. *The Anglo-Saxon Poems of Beowulf* . . . (Oxford: Parker, 1855), p. 214, note.

5. See my discussion in the Magoun festschrift *Franciplegius,* ed. J. B. Bessinger, Jr. and Robert P. Creed (New York: New York University Press, 1965), pp. 122 f. and cf. *Early English Manuscripts in Facsimile,* XII (Copenhagen, 1963), p. 109.

6. Beowulf may well have been called the king who was *his mannum mildust,* "mildest to his men," but the poet would hardly have spoken of him as *his manna mildust,* "mildest of his men," a turn of phrase unknown in English before Milton. But whether the MS originally had *his* or not, it has a mark of abbreviation (sloping downward from left to right, it is true) over the last letter of *mann?* and we are justified in replacing the question mark with *u,* since *mannā* would yield good Latin (*mannam,* accusative of the biblical *manna*) but impossible English. There is no space in the MS for the *his* if we take it to have come at the end of line 20, but it might have been squeezed in at the head of line 21. Or was it set in the margin as a correction? In view of its presumably damaged state we need not be surprised that both A and B overlooked the marks or skipped them.

PROBLEMS OF COMMUNICATION IN THE ROMANCES OF CHRÉTIEN DE TROYES

1. Herbert Kolb, *Der Begriff der Minne und das Entstehen der höfischen Lyrik* (Tübingen: Niemeyer, 1958), *passim.*

THE SUGGESTIVE USE OF CHRISTIAN NAMES IN MIDDLE ENGLISH POETRY

(References to Chaucer are to Robinson's second edition [Boston: Houghton Mifflin, 1957, abbreviated Robinson]; Skeat's six-volume edition [Oxford, 1894–1897, abbreviated Skeat, *Chaucer*] has been consulted for his notes. References to the B- and C-texts of *Piers Plowman* are to Skeat's two-volume edition [Oxford, 1886, abbreviated Skeat, *Piers Plowman*], and references to the A-text are to George Kane's edition (London: Athlone Press, 1960). The editions in the series of the Early English Text Society have been used for the mystery plays; the edition used for the York plays is that of Lucy Toulmin Smith [Oxford: Clarendon Press, 1885].)

1. "An Experiment with Proper Names," *Language and Society* (Copenhagen, 1961), pp. 27–36; reprinted in *C. A. Bodelsen: Essays and Papers* (Copenhagen: Nature Method Centre, 1964), pp. 169–178.

2. *A System of Logic, Rationative and Inductive,* I (London, 1862), 37.

3. A few studies dealing with the subject: English names—Ph. Aronstein, "Gebrauch von Eigennamen als Gattungsnamen im Englischen," *Englische Studien,* XXV (1898), 245–258; supplemented by J. Koch, *"Bemerkungen . . . ,"* *Englische Studien,* XXVI (1899), 152–153; Thomas Stenhouse, *Lives Enshrined in Language, or Proper Names Which Have Become Common Parts of Speech* (London: Walter Scott, 1922); Josef Reinius, *On Transferred Appellations of Human Beings, Chiefly in English and German: Studies in Historical Sematology,* I (Gothenburg dissertation, 1903). Scattered remarks on the development are to be found in Ernest Weekley's *The Romance of Names,* 3rd ed. (London: John Murray, 1922), *Words and Names* (London: John Murray, 1932), and *Jack and Jill: a Study of Our Christian Names,* 2nd ed. (London: John Murray, 1948). On Romance names see Bruno Migliorini, *Dal nome proprio al nome comune,* Biblioteca dell' "Archivum Romanicum," Serie II: Linguistica, XIII (Geneva, 1927). For French names see Alfred Kölbel, *Eigennamen als Gattungsname* (Leipzig dissertation, 1907); Axel Peterson, *Le passage populaire des noms de personne à l'état de noms communs dans les langues romanes et particulièrement en français* (Upsala dissertation, 1929); and Friedrich Cramer, "Die Bedeutungsentwicklung von 'Jean' im Französischen," *Giessener Beiträge zur romanischen Philologie,* XXIII (1931). For German names see Othmar Meisinger, *Hinz und Kunz: deutsche Vornamen in erweiterter Bedeutung* (Dortmund, n.d. [1924]).

4. An excellent comprehensive treatment of the subject is Georges Doutrepont, *Les types populaires de la littérature française,* Mémoires de l'Académie

royale de Belgique, Classe des lettres et des sciences morales et politiques, XXII, 2 parts (Brussels, 1926).

5. *Les origines de la poésie lyrique en France au moyen âge,* 3rd ed. (Paris, 1925), p. 425.

6. MS Bibl. Nat., Paris, fr. 12,483 (2nd half of the fourteenth century), fol. 98v; see Arthur Langfors, "Notice du ms. fr. 12,483 de la Bibl. Nat." *Notices et extraits,* XXXIX (1916), 576.

7. Ed. Richard Morris, *An Old English Miscellany,* EETS 49 (London, 1872), pp. 186–191.

8. *Gibbe* comes from *Gibert,* a common Old French variant of *Gilbert.*

9. *Water* for *Walter* is the result of French influence and reflects the vocalization of preconsonantal *l* in Old French (as shown by Anglo-Norman *Wauter*). *Water* was the normal pronunciation of *Walter* throughout the Middle English period, and it still prevailed in early modern English.

10. *The Pedigree of 'Jack' and of Various Allied Names* (London, 1892).

11. *The Oxford Dictionary of English Etymology* (Oxford: Clarendon Press, 1966), s.v. *malkin.*

12. *Grundzüge der englischen Semantik,* Wiener Beiträge zur englischen Philologie, LXX (Vienna, 1967), p. 92.

13. *Words and Names,* p. 86.

14. *A Dictionary of English and Welsh Surnames* (London: Henry Frowde, 1901), pp. 508–509, s.v. *Malkin.*

15. *English Surnames: their Sources and Significations,* 9th imprint (London: Chatto and Windus, 1915), p. 77, note.

16. The information given in this paragraph is based on Eilert Ekwall, *Early London Personal Names* (Lund, 1947).

17. Taken from Karl Michaëlsson, *Études sur les noms de personne français d'après les rôles de taille parisiens (rôles de 1292, 1296–1300, 1313),* Vol. I (Upsala dissertation, 1927), p. 60.

18. The following slightly inaccurate translation is reproduced from Thomas Fuller's *Church-history of Britain* (1655), Book IV, p. 139:

"Tom comes thereat, when called by Wat, and Simm as forward we find,
Bet calls as quick to Gibb and to Hykk, that neither would tarry behind.
Gibb, a good whelp of that litter, doth help mad Coll more mischief to do,
And Will he does vow, the time is come now, he'll join in their company too.
Davie complains, whiles Grigg gets the gains, and Hobb with them does partake,
Lorkin aloud in the midst of the crowd conceiveth as deep is his stake.
Hudde doth spoil whom Judde doth foil, and Tebb lends his helping hand,
But Jack the mad patch men and houses does snatch, and kills all at his command."

Watte stands for *Walter, Thomme* for *Thomas, Symme* for *Simond, Bette* for *Bartholomew, Gibbe* for *Gilbert, Hykke* for *Richard, Colle* for *Nicholas, Geffe* for *Geoffrey, Grigge* for *Gregory, Dawe* for *David, Hobbe* for *Robert, Lorkyn* for *Lawrence, Hudde* for Old English *Hudda, Iudde* for *Jordan,* and *Tebbe* for *Theobald.*

The passage is taken from G. C. Macaulay, *The Complete Works of John Gower*, IV : *the Latin Works* (Oxford: Clarendon Press, 1902).

19. Quoted from Kenneth Sisam's *Fourteenth Century Verse and Prose* (Oxford: Clarendon Press, 1921; imprint of 1955), pp. 160–161.

20. *Purnele, Pernel,* from Old French *Perronnele, Perrenele,* Latin *Petronilla. Felice,* Old French *Felise,* Latin *Felicia.* The male name *Bette* is from *Bertelmew, Bartholomew. Beton* is a diminutive of the female pet name *Bette,* which probably goes back to *Betrys, Beatrice.*

21. *Sesse, Cesse, Cisse,* from *Cecilie,* Latin *Caecilia. Houwe, Huwe,* from *Hugh. Claryce,* French *Clarice, Claricia* in Latin records. *Peeres, Piers,* Old French *Piers, Pers,* Peter. *Rose,* originally from Germanic *Hrodohaidis,* recorded after the Norman Conquest as *Rothais, Rohese, Roese, Rose;* the last-named form came to be regarded as if it had been derived from Latin *rosa.*

22. Printed by Rolf Kaiser, *Medieval English,* 3rd ed. (Berlin, 1958), pp. 441–443, from Harley MS 5306 (fifteenth century).

23. Printed by Thomas Wright, *The Political Songs of England* (London: Camden Society), pp. 155–159, and R. H. Robbins, *Historical Poems of the XIVth and XVth Centuries* (New York: Columbia University Press, 1959), pp. 24–27, from Harley MS 2253 (c. 1340). Wright's translation of the passage: "There stands up a yellow man and jogs with a rod—and shouts out aloud that all the assembly heard—and calls Mag and Mal; and she comes be-mothered as a moor-hen . . . and say, 'By my gabbing, it shall not go so—and that be on you all—that thou shalt wed me and have me to wife.'"

24. These two names exemplify a widespread linguistic phenomenon—alliterative and reduplicative word-pairs often implying some degree of polarity and frequently having *and* or some other connective word as a link. Other conventional name-pairs of this kind are *Degon and Dobyn* in *Mum and the Sothsegger, Jack and Jill* and *Tom and Tib* (these two last-named pairs characterized by the vowel gradation *a-i* [*o-i*], Finnish *Matti and Maija,* "Matthew and Mary," etc. These are comparable to such word-pairs as *this and that, here and there, now and then, up and down, off and on,* etc., and there is also a connection with such asyndetic groups as *Humpty-Dumpty, willy-nilly, clap-trap, tick-tack,* and *zig-zag.* The occurrence of such repetitive patterns in medieval poetry was briefly discussed in the present writer's article, "Middle English With an O and an I," *Neuphilologische Mitteilungen,* LVI (1955), 161–173; a recent comprehensive discussion is Nils Thun, *Reduplicative Words in English* (Upsala dissertation, 1963).

25. Names of the type *sir Robert* and *sir Huwe* are discussed briefly on p. 68.

26. For this name see Friedrich Cramer, "Die Bedeutungsentwicklung von 'Jean' im Französischen," cited in note 3.

27. For this name see Othmar Meisinger, *Hinz und Kunz: deutsche Vornamen in erweiterter Bedeutung,* cited in note 3.

28. Printed by Richard L. Greene, *Early English Carols* (Oxford: Clarendon Press, 1935), pp. 260–261.

29. John Heywood, *Dialogue Containing Proverbs,* xi, 142, ed. B. A. Milligan, *John Heywood's Works and Miscellaneous Short Poems,* Illinois Studies in Language and Literature, 41 (Urbana: University of Illinois Press, 1956).

30. See Robinson, p. 689, and Skeat, *Chaucer,* V, 128.

31. Carleton Brown, *Religious Lyrics of the XIVth Century* (Oxford: Clarendon Press, 1924), p. 48.

32. "By *Robert* is very sufficiently indicated *a robber;* and by *Richard,* with much fitness, a *rich hard* man; *Gilbert* is not without reason called a *guiler;* and *Geoffrey* is, if we come to the point, changed into *jo frai* (i.e. I will do it)." (Wright's translation.)

33. Printed by Wright, *Political Songs,* pp. 69–71, and by Bruce Dickins and R. M. Wilson, *Early Middle English Texts* (London, 1951), pp. 10–12.

34. This account is reproduced in Wright's *Political Songs,* p. 354.

35. Also quoted in Sisam's *Fourteenth Century Verse and Prose,* p. 255.

36. A little later in that passage the same line of thought is taken up again in "so rewe on this robbere that *reddere* ne haue" (B-text, V, 475); the A-text (V, 241) has *on þis Robert* (*Robyn* W, *robber* JH³, *rybawde* K), the C-text *on me, Roberd* (VII, 322).

37. "Simkin's Camus Nose: a Latin Pun in the *Reeve's Tale?*" *Modern Language Notes,* LXXV (1960), 4–8.

38. "Sym(e)kyn/*simia:* the Ape in Chaucer's Millers," *Studies in Philology,* LXV (1968), 44–50.

39. Meisinger, *Hinz und Kunz,* p. 84.

40. See Weekley, *Words and Names,* pp. 26–27; see also Skeat, *Chaucer,* V, 325, and Robinson, p. 705. Robinson, echoing Halliwell-Phillipps, suggests that a play on the Latin words *vetula* and *vidula* is also involved.

41. "The disastrous effects of this sin are made more widely apparent on festival days than on working days . . . when Robin leaves his ploughing and Marion her spinning. . . ." *The Complete Works of John Gower,* ed. G. C. Macaulay, IV (Oxford, 1899–1902).

42. "I do not know who is dancing, who is jousting, but I do know that when a monk is holding in his hands his large flagon full of wine, he presses it against himself with infinite joy and says that *that* is the right kind of rule. I do not believe at all that it is what Saint Augustine meant; rather it is the rule of Robin, who leads a gluttonous, raven-like life."

43. Printed by Richard L. Greene, *The Early English Carols* (Oxford: Clarendon Press, 1935), p. 309, and Robbins, *Secular Lyrics of the XIVth and XVth Centuries,* 2nd ed. (Oxford: Clarendon Press, 1955), pp. 21–22, from the early fifteenth-century MS Sloane 2593.

44. Printed in J. A. W. Bennett, G. V. Smithers, and Norman Davis, *Early Middle English Verse and Prose* (Oxford: Clarendon Press, 1966), p. 128, from Merton Coll., Oxford, MS 248.

45. Printed by Peter Dronke, "The Rawlinson Lyrics," *Notes and Queries,* CCVI (1961), 245–246.

46. Printed, e.g., by Skeat, *Specimens of English Literature . . . 1394–1579,* 6th ed. (Oxford, 1892), pp. 24–27.

47. Printed by Robbins, *Secular Lyrics,* pp. 22–24.

48. Robbins, *Secular Lyrics,* pp. 24–25.

49. Greene, *Early English Carols,* p. 278.

50. Greene, *Early English Carols,* p. 278, and Robbins, *Secular Lyrics,* pp. 6–7.

51. Robbins, *Historical Poems,* pp. 186–189, Nos. 75 and 76. See *NED,* s.v. *Jackanapes.*

52. Robbins, *Historical Poems,* pp. 164–165.

53. Printed by A. de Montaiglon and G. Raynaud, *Recueil général et complet des fabliaux,* I (Paris, 1872–1890), 168–177, from Bibl. Nat. MS fr. 837.

54. Ed. by A. W. Pollard in *Representative English Comedies: from the Beginnings to Shakespeare* (New York, 1903), pp. 61–86.

55. *Scenes and Characters of the Middle Ages,* 6th ed. (London: Simpkin, Marshall, 1926), p. 247, note.

56. Robbins, *Secular Lyrics,* pp. 19–21 (Nos. 25 and 26); the former was also printed by Greene, *Early English Carols,* p. 309; his comment is on p. 448.

57. Printed by W. C. Hazlitt, *Remains of the Early Popular Poetry of England,* III (London, 1866), 44–53.

58. The names in this passage are used in a vaguely generic sense. In a short poem entitled *A Schoolboy's Wish,* printed by Robbins, *Secular Lyrics,* p. 105— & þow sire Robert, with his cloke,/ Wold þe helpe & be þi poke . . .—*sire Robert* is the devil.

59. Robbins, *Secular Lyrics,* pp. 15–16.

60. On this name see Skeat, *Piers Plowman,* II, 92. At least one MS of the A-text reads *Gruffith,* i.e. *Griffith,* a common Welsh name.

61. Printed, e.g., by Wright, *Political Songs,* pp. 237–240, and Robbins, *Historical Poems,* pp. 77–79, from Harley MS 2253 (ca. 1340).

62. Printed by Mabel Day and R. Steele, EETS 119 (London, 1936), and Skeat, *Piers Plowman* (under the title *Richard the Redeless*).

63. *"Hankyn or Haukyn?" Modern Philology,* XXVI (1928–1929), 57–61. The continental origin of the first element, *Hann(e),* is contested by Reaney (*A Dictionary of British Surnames,* s.v. *Hann*), who believes that in some cases *Han-* goes back to *John,* in some to *Henry.* It is possible, since the first element in *Haukyn* obviously goes back to Henry too, through *Hal,* that a confusion arose between *Hal-kin* and *Han-kin,* which must have been promoted by the habit of writing *u* and *n* in the same way.

64. "The Name of Chaucer's Friar," *Modern Language Notes,* LXX (1955), 169–172.

65. In the poem beginning *Ichot a burde in a bour ase beryl so bryht* in Harley MS 2253, for example, there are several names which seem to be echoes from a remote past, such as *Regnas, Tegeu, Wyrwein, Wylcadoun,* and *Hilde;* see Carleton Brown, *English Lyrics of the XIIIth Century* (Oxford: Oxford University Press, 1932), pp. 226–228. Two further names connected with literary tradition and folklore are *Felyce* and *Rosamounde* in *Piers Plowman* ("Felyce hir fayrnesse fel hir al to sklaundre"; and "Rosamonde riȝt so reufully bysette," B-text, XII, 47–48); see Skeat's notes, *Piers Plowman,* II, 181.

66. *Les origines de la poésie lyrique en France au moyen âge,* p. 425.

67. Greene, *Early English Carols,* p. 309, and Robbins, *Secular Lyrics,* pp. 21–22.

68. The most recent edition is that of Bennett-Smithers-Davis, *Early Middle English Verse and Prose,* pp. 197–200.

69. "The Merit of Malkyn," *Modern Language Notes,* LXIII (1948), 52–53.

70. *Dialogue Containing Proverbs,* ed. Milligan, XI, 62.

71. The most complete text is that printed by Peter Dronke cited in note 45 above.

72. Printed by A. Jubinal, *Nouveau recueil de contes, dits, fabliaux et autres pièces inédites des XIIIᵉ, XIVᵉ et XVᵉ siècles,* II (Paris, 1842), 28–39.

73. For the printed text see preceding note.

74. *Piers Plowman,* II, 265.

75. *The Good Wyfe Wold a Pylgremage,* printed in *Annales Academiae Scientiarum Fennicae,* B LXI, 2 (Helsinki, 1948), pp. 173–175, line 15.

76. "Callet, Minx, Gixie," *Englische Studien,* XXII (1896), 325–329. *Callet* is discussed on pp. 327–328.

77. Ed. of Jonson's works by C. H. Herford and P. and E. Simpson, VIII (Oxford: Clarendon Press, 1941), p. 573.

78. Ed. Milligan.

79. *Piers Plowman: the Evidence for Authorship* (London, 1965), Chapter IV.

80. *Piers Plowman as a Fourteenth-century Apocalypse* (New Brunswick, N.J.: Rutgers University Press, 1962), p. 7.

81. One is inevitably reminded of the very short jacket of Chaucer's Squire, particularly as it appears in the marginal illustration to the Ellesmere text.

82. *Memorials of London and London Life in the XIIIth, XIVth, and XVth Centuries . . . A.D. 1270–1419* (London, 1868), p. 535.

83. *Ibid.,* p. 535.

CAXTON AND MALORY: A DEFENSE

1. *The Life of Mayster Wyllyam Caxton* (London, 1737), preface.

2. *The Amenities of Literature* (London, 1840).

3. *William Caxton* (London: Robinson, 1933).

4. Leon Kellner, ed., *Caxton's Blanchardyn and Eglantine,* EETS 58 (London, 1890); W. Wright Roberts, "William Caxton, Writer and Critic," *Bulletin of the John Rylands Library,* 1930; A. T. P. Byles, "William Caxton as a Man of Letters," *The Library,* 4th Series, XV (1934–1935); Curt Bühler, *William Caxton and His Critics* (Syracuse, New York: Syracuse University Press, 1960).

5. William Blades, *The Biography and Typography of William Caxton* (London, 1882), p. 92; Nellie Slayton Aurner, *Caxton, Mirror of Fifteenth-Century Letters* (Boston: Allan, 1926), p. 205; Byles, "William Caxton as a Man of Letters," 25; Bühler, *William Caxton and His Critics,* p. 15.

6. Ranulph Higden, *Polychronicon,* ed. C. Babington and J. R. Lumby, Rolls Series (London, 1865–1886).

7. *Godeffroy of Boloyne,* EETS 64 (London, 1893), p. viii; *The Book of Fayttes of Armes and of Chyualrye,* EETS 189 (London, 1932), p. liii; *Caxton's Mirrour of the World,* EETS 110 (London, 1913), p. vii; H. S. Bennett, *Chaucer and the Fifteenth Century* (Oxford: Clarendon Press, 1947), p. 212.

8. He may have been thinking of the doubts expressed in Higden's *Poly-chronicon,* which he published three years before.

9. J. A. W. Bennett, ed., *Essays on Malory* (Oxford: Clarendon Press, 1963), p. 143.

10. Eugène Vinaver, ed., *The Works of Sir Thomas Malory,* I (Oxford: Clarendon Press, 1947), xxix–xxxv.

11. See William Matthews, *The Ill-Framed Knight* (Berkeley, California: University of California Press, 1966).

12. Vinaver, *Works,* I, xxx.

13. William Caxton, *Godeffroy of Boloyne,* ed. Mary N. Colvin, EETS 64 (London, 1893), p. 2.

14. I think the omission must be related to the reduction and rewriting of the Roman War episode (Caxton Book V) and that involved with it is the problem of who made the new version. It is always assumed that Caxton did it. This I doubt, but the matter is too complicated to discuss here, and I shall be dealing with it in another essay.

15. How literally Caxton followed his copy in this matter may be judged by the fact that he was led by a "colophon" to divide Book IX from Book X in the middle of a sentence.

16. It is barely possible that the last four words in this quotation hark back to "redeth the book."

17. Vinaver, *Works,* I, 56.

18. In his note on this passage (*Works,* p. 1298), Vinaver says it is uncertain whether the reference is to the French *Mort Artu* or to the last tale in Malory. In the latter case, he maintains, the reference should be attributed to one of Malory's early copyists, since at the time Malory completed the first part of the *Tale of King Arthur* he had not yet begun his own *Death of Arthur.* It may be remarked however that the French *Mort Artu* does not contain the matter referred to in Malory's passage, and that to invoke copyists for Malory's explicits and cross-references undermines all argument based on them. In the new (1967) edition, Vinaver has changed his opinion, not very satisfactorily.

19. Gaston Paris and Jacob Ulrich, eds., *Merlin,* Société des Anciens Textes Français (Paris, 1886), I, 206.

THOMAS USK AS TRANSLATOR

1. In part of an article entitled "The Two Styles of Thomas Usk," for a volume of studies dedicated to Professor Vachek of the University of Brno, Czechoslovakia, to appear in 1969.

2. "Usk's *Testament of Love* and St. Anselm," *Speculum,* XVII (1942), 69–73.

3. Citations from this text are taken from the edition of Migne, *Patrologia,* CLVIII, 507–540. Those from Usk are taken from his *Testament* as edited by W. W. Skeat in *Chaucerian and Other Pieces* (Oxford, 1897). Skeat has normalized punctuation and spelling according to London usage in the fourteenth century.

4. The copy in the British Museum was reproduced in facsimile with an introduction by W. W. Skeat (London, n.d.) after the publication of *Chaucerian and Other Pieces.* This reproduction has been used to check some doubtful readings. The *Testament* will be referred to as *TL,* St. Anselm's work as Anselm. Page and column numbers refer to the editions mentioned in the previous note.

SOME OBSERVATIONS ON KING HERLA
AND THE HERLETHING

1. *De Nugis Curialium,* ed. M. R. James (Oxford, 1914), pp. 13–15; translated by F. Tupper and M. B. Ogle (London: Chatto and Windus, 1924), pp. 15–18. It is difficult to distinguish between the Wild Hunt and the Wild Host. Sometimes the spectral company is depicted as hunters, sometimes not, but they are always accompanied by clamorous noises. Since the motif is classified in Stith Thompson's *Motif-Index of Folk Literature,* revised ed. (Bloomington, Indiana: Indiana University Press, 1956), E.501.3.1–10, as the Wild Hunt, it will be convenient to use this title. On the Harlequin legends and related matters, see O. Driesen, *Der Ursprung des Harlekin* (Berlin, 1904); H. M. Flasdieck, "Die Reduplizierenden Verben des Germanischen," *Anglia,* LXI (1937), 241–365; H. Plischke, *Die Sage vom Wilden Heere im deutschen Volke* (Leipzig, 1914).

2. "Walter Map's *De Nugis Curialium*: Its Plan and Composition," *PMLA,* XXXII (1917), 75.

3. *De Nugis,* p. 9.

4. *De Nugis,* p. 15.

5. *De Nugis,* p. 17.

6. *De Nugis,* p. 18.

7. *De Nugis,* p. 186. The Latin text reads: *Cetus eciam et phalanges noctiuage quas Herlethingi dicebant. . . .* The translation of Tupper and Ogle (p. 233) includes the interpretative phrase "followers of Herla," for Herlethingi, which is misleading. See discussion below.

8. *De Nugis,* p. 16.

9. But Gervase of Tilbury reports that the Wild Hunt led by King Arthur appeared sometimes at noon. Cf. R. S. Loomis, *Wales and the Arthurian Legend* (Cardiff: University of Wales Press, 1956), p. 45, note 45.

10. Ordericus Vitalis, *Historia Ecclesiastica,* Book VIII, Chapter xvii, ed. A. Le Prévost, III (Paris, 1838–1855), 367–377. For demonstration of the English provenance, see Kemp Malone, *Studies in Heroic Legend and in Current Speech* (Copenhagen: Rosenkilde and Bagger, 1959), p. 192. This study was first published in 1935.

11. Driesen, *Der Ursprung des Harlekin,* pp. 30–31; Malone, *Studies,* p. 194.

12. *The Science of Fairy Tales* (London, 1890), Chapters VII–IX, pp. 178–180.

13. Hartland, *Science of Fairy Tales,* pp. 161–169; Loomis, *Arthurian Tradition and Chrétien de Troyes* (New York: Columbia University Press, 1949),

pp. 166 f.; "The Spoils of Annwn," *PMLA,* LVI (1941), 917 f.; V. J. Harward, Jr., *The Dwarfs in Arthurian Romance and Celtic Tradition* (Leiden: Brill, 1958), pp. 10–13.

14. In the Welsh Mabinogi of *Branwen Daughter of Llŷr,* composed at the end of the eleventh century or the beginning of the twelfth (P. MacCana, *Branwen Daughter of Llŷr* [Cardiff: University of Wales Press, 1958], p. 181), a similar tradition is recorded. Bran's followers are instructed not to open a particular door after they settle in Gwales, a place where they remain free from care and the memory of sorrow for four-score years. But someone disobeys the prohibition, and becoming again aware of their afflictions, they can no longer rest, and they resume their wanderings (pp. 84–86). No one suggests any direct connection with the story of Herla, especially since the incident in *Branwen* has been greatly modified and adapted, but it shows that such a tradition existed in Wales at an early date.

15. Thompson, *Motif-Index of Folk Literature,* E.501.3.1–10; Loomis, *Folklore,* LXIX (1958), 12.

16. *De Nugis,* p. 322.

17. Malone, *Studies,* p. 194; Flasdieck, "Die Reduplizierenden," pp. 276–339; M. Delbouille, *Etymologica: Walther von Wartburg zum siebzigsten Geburtstag* (Tübingen, 1958), pp. 167–185, and references in note 11, p. 180.

18. Malone, *Studies,* p. 195; *wine* has this sense in Old English.

19. *Studies,* p. 195.

20. R. W. Chambers, *Widsith* (Cambridge: Cambridge University Press, 1912), pp. 28–36.

21. C. Brady, *The Legends of Ermanaric* (Berkeley, California: University of California Press, 1943), pp. 156 f., 205–221.

22. Chambers, *Widsith,* p. 33; Malone, *Studies,* p. 195.

23. Thomas Jones, *The National Library of Wales Journal,* VI (1950), 132–139.

GAWAIN'S GREEN CHAPEL AND THE CAVE
AT WETTON MILL

1. Lines 2163–2200 and 2217–2222, *Sir Gawain and the Green Knight,* ed. J. R. R. Tolkien and E. V. Gordon, revised by Norman Davis (Oxford: Clarendon Press, 1967), pp. 60–61.

2. I am indebted to Alfred L. Kellogg of Rutgers University for suggesting that the green chapel may depend in part on the *mirabilia* tradition, exemplified in the Nennian *Historia Brittonum,* VII, ed. Theodor Mommsen, *Chronica minora, saec. IV. V. VI. VII* (MGH, Auct. antiquiss., XIII; Berlin, 1898), III, 213–222, and particularly in Gervais of Tilbury's *Otia imperialia,* ed. Gottfried Wilhelm von Leibnitz. *Scriptores rerum Brunsvicensium* (Hanover, 1707–1711), I, 881–1004; see also Felix Liebrecht, *Des Gervasius von Tilbury Otia imperialia in einer Auswahl . . .* (Hanover, 1856), pp. 117–123, n. 44. Such a dependence, which seems to me likely enough, would be quite compatible with the argument that follows.

3. Introduction to *Sir Gawain and the Green Knight*, EETS 210, ed. Israel Gollancz (London, 1940), p. xx. In the Ordnance Survey One-Inch Map of Great Britain, Wetton Mill is on Sheet 111, "Buxton and Matlock" (National Grid SK), 0956.

4. E.g., Dale B. J. Randall, "Was the Green Knight a Fiend?" *SP*, LVII (1960), 488.

5. *The Natural History of Stafford-Shire*, IV, 40 (Oxford, 1686), p. 172.

6. It is so glossed in the unrevised edition by Tolkien and Gordon (Oxford: Clarendon Press, 1925), pp. 113, 158; and in the edition by Gollancz, p. 149. Norman Davis, in his revision of Tolkien and Gordon, pp. 125–126, explains it as "presumably OE *furh*, 'furrow,' used in the sense of watercourse."

7. *Natural History*, IV, 41, p. 172.

8. "A New Approach to Middle English Dialectology," *ES*, XLIV (1963), 5–6. Though in general *Sir Gawain and the Green Knight* seems not to be significantly related to the surviving medieval iconography of the surrounding area, it may be worth noticing that the Anglo-Saxon or Norman lintel over the south doorway in the Church of St. Mary the Virgin at Tutbury (Staffs.), about eighteen miles southeast of Wetton Mill, preserves the outlines of a spirited boar-hunt; and that the Norman tympanum over the blocked north doorway in the Church of St. Leonard at Linley (Salop), some forty-five miles southwest of Wetton Mill, contains the figure of a "green man."

9. In the Ordnance Survey One-Inch Map, Lud's Church is on Sheet 110, "Stoke-on-Trent" (National Grid SJ), 9865.

10. "Sir Gawain in Staffordshire: A Detective Essay in Literary Geography," *London Times*, May 21, 1958, p. 12. Further evidence will appear in Professor Elliott's forthcoming book, *The Gawain Country: A Study of the Topography of "Sir Gawain and the Green Knight,"* which may eliminate some of the criticisms that follow.

11. Plot, *Natural History*, IV, 41, p. 173, refers to "the stupendous cleft in the rock between *Swithamley* and *Wharnford* commonly call'd *Lud-Church*, which I found by measure 208 yards long, and at different places 30, 40, or 50 foot deep; the sides steeped and so hanging over, that it sometimes preserves *Snow* all the *Summer.* . . ."

CONVENTION AND INDIVIDUALITY IN THE MIDDLE ENGLISH ROMANCE

1. "Improvisation in the Middle English Romance," *Proceedings of the American Philosophical Society*, CIII (1959), 418–454. See especially pp. 440–454.

2. See the article referred to above, p. 432.

3. *Der anglonormannische Boeve de Haumtone*, ed. Albert Stimming, Bibliotheca Normannica, VII (Halle, 1899).

4. EETS ES 46, 48, 65.

5. Ed. Karl Vollmöller, Altfranzösische Bibliothek, III (Heilbronn, 1833).

6. Both versions are edited by G. Sarrazin, Altenglische Bibliothek, III (Heilbronn, 1855).

FROM MOTIVE TO ORNAMENT

1. *Erec et Enide,* ed. W. Foerster (Halle: Niemeyer, 1890), line 14.

2. *Erec et Enide,* lines 9–22: *Por ce dist Crestiens de Troies/ Que reisons est que totes voies/ Doit chascuns panser et antandre/ A bien dire et a bien aprandre,/ Et tret d'un conte d'avanture/ Une mout bele conjointure,/ Par qu'an puet prover et savoir/ Que cil ne fet mie savoir/ Qui sa science n'abandone/ Tant con Deus la grace l'an done./ D'Erec, le fil Lac, est li contes/ Que devant rois et devant contes/ Depecier et corronpre suelent/ Cil qui de conter vivre vuelent.*

3. E. R. Curtius, *Europäische Literatur und lateinisches Mittelalter* (Bern: A. Francke, 1948), p. 484: *begrifflicherweise widmen sie der* amplificatio *mehr Raum als der* abbreviatio; *über jene war mehr zu sagen.*

4. "Morgain la fée and the celtic goddesses," *Speculum,* XX (1945), 183. Reprinted with some additions in *Wales and the Arthurian Legend* (Cardiff: University of Wales Press, 1956), pp. 105–130.

5. It survives in two French manuscripts, British Museum Add. 38117 (originally known as the "Huth MS") and Cambridge Add. 7071. The only existing edition is the one published by Gaston Paris and Jacob Ulrich on the basis of the Huth MS (cited below). On the origins and significance of this work see Fanni Bogdanow, *The Romance of the Grail* (Manchester: Manchester University Press, 1966), *passim,* and her article in *Arthurian Literature in the Middle Ages,* ed. R. S. Loomis (Oxford: Clarendon Press, 1959), pp. 325–335.

6. *Merlin, roman en prose du XIIIe siècle,* ed. Gaston Paris and Jacob Ulrich, Société des Anciens Textes Français, II (Paris, 1886), 174 ff.

7. *"Et comment vin ge cha? le sés tu?" "Nennil voir, che dist li nains, fors que che sont des aventures de Bretaigne ou des enchantemens de ceste terre"* (p. 180).

8. *". . . il fust mors sans recouvrier, a chou qu'il se laissast anchois occhirre qu'il criast mierchi, se ne fust la damoisele dou lac, qui fu la por aidier le roi, se elle veist que Merlin n'i fust"* (p. 206).

9. Edmond Faral, *La Légende arthurienne,* III (Paris, 1929), 274–278.

10. Ivor Arnold, ed., *Le Roman de Brut de Wace,* Société des Anciens Textes Français (Paris, 1940), lines 13223–13255.

11. Cf. Jean Frappier, *Étude sur La Mort le Roi Artu* (Paris, 1936), pp. 201–226.

TROILUS AND CRISEYDE: THE ART OF AMPLIFICATION

1. In its original form this paper was presented at a conference on *Troilus and Criseyde* at the English Institute, held at Columbia University in September, 1966.

2. The question of what sources in addition to *Il Filostrato* Chaucer used and of whether or not he used a French translation of Boccaccio's poem is irrelevant to my discussion here. *Il Filostrato* gave him the basic material he worked with.

On these matters, however, see Karl Young, *Origin and Development of the Story of Troilus and Criseyde*, Chaucer Society, 2nd Series, No. 40 (London, 1908) ; Sanford B. Meech, *Design in Chaucer's "Troilus"* (Syracuse, New York: Syracuse University Press, 1958) ; and Robert A. Pratt, "Chaucer and *Le Roman de Troyle et de Criseida,*" *SP*, LIII (1956), 509–539.

3. See Edmond Faral, *Les Arts poétiques du XIIᵉ et du XIIIᵉ siècles* (Paris, 1924), pp. 61–85; J. W. H. Atkins, *English Literary Criticism: The Medieval Phase* (London: Methuen, 1952), pp. 102–106, 167.

4. "What Chaucer Really Did to *Il Filostrato,*" *Essays and Studies*, XVII (Oxford: Clarendon Press, 1932), 61–62, 63.

5. "Elements of Epic Grandeur in the *Troilus,*" *ELH*, VI (1939), 200–202.

6. *Design*, pp. 6, 423–424, and *passim*. On rhetoric, see p. vii.

7. *The Key of Remembrance: A Study of Chaucer's Poetics* (New Haven and London: Yale University Press, 1963), pp. 176 ff.

8. "What Chaucer Really Did," p. 59.

9. On this see Roger Sharrock, "Second Thoughts: C. S. Lewis on Chaucer's *Troilus,*" *Essays in Criticism*, VIII (1958), 123–127.

10. "What Chaucer Really Did," p. 61.

11. See, for example, John Bayley's analysis of what would seem at first a purely decorative passage in *Troilus* (III, 1415–1421) : *The Characters of Love* (New York: Basic Books, 1960), p. 59. Bayley's comments on Chaucer's rhetoric in the Troilus are most suggestive: pp. 58–66.

12. *Chaucer and the French Tradition* (Berkeley and Los Angeles: University of California Press, 1957), p. 128.

13. As Karl Young pointed out many years ago: "Chaucer's 'Troilus and Criseyde' as Romance," *PMLA*, LIII (1938), 47–49.

14. On the proems, see Kemp Malone, *Chapters on Chaucer* (Baltimore: Johns Hopkins University Press, 1951), pp. 104–123; and especially Morton Bloomfield, "Distance and Predestination in *Troilus and Criseyde,*" *PMLA*, LXXII (1957), 20–21. The Narrator has been much discussed: see Bloomfield, "Distance and Predestination," 14–26; Robert M. Jordan, "The Narrator in Chaucer's *Troilus,*" *ELH*, XXV (1958), 237–257, and *Chaucer and the Shape of Creation* (Cambridge, Mass.: Harvard University Press, 1967), pp. 64–107; Dorothy Bethurum, "Chaucer's Point of View as Narrator in the Love Poems," *PMLA*, LXXIV (1959), 516–518; and E. Talbot Donaldson, "The Ending of Chaucer's Troilus," in *Early English and Norse Studies Presented to Hugh Smith*, ed. Arthur Brown and Peter Foote (London: Methuen, 1963), pp. 26–45.

15. "The Function of the Proverbial Monitory Elements in Chaucer's *Troilus and Criseyde,*" *Tulane Studies in English*, II (1950), 5–48. See also Bartlett Jere Whiting, *Chaucer's Use of Proverbs*, Harvard Studies in Comparative Literature, XI (Cambridge, Mass.: Harvard University Press, 1934), 48–75; and Grace Frank, "Proverbs in Medieval Literature," *MLN*, LVIII (1943), 508–515.

16. "What Chaucer Really Did," pp. 64–65.

17. *Chaucer's Use of Proverbs*, pp. 61 ff., 74–75.

18. See, for example, Wayne Shumaker, "Alisoun in Wander-Land: A Study in Chaucer's Mind and Literary Method," *ELH,* XVIII (1951), 77–89, especially 88–89.

19. All quotations from Chaucer are from *The Works of Geoffrey Chaucer,* ed. F. N. Robinson, 2nd ed. (Boston: Houghton Mifflin, 1957).

20. There is a convenient summary of the changes Chaucer makes in Boccaccio's poem in R. D. French, *A Chaucer Handbook,* 2nd ed. (New York: Appleton-Century-Crofts, 1947), pp. 179–182. For a listing of the main parallels between the *Troilus* and *Il Filostrato,* by lines and stanzas, see Robinson, *Chaucer,* Notes, p. 813.

21. *Il Filostrato,* VII, 84–103.

22. Though concerned with a somewhat later period, John Stevens, *Music and Poetry in the Early Tudor Court* (London: Methuen, 1961), provides a stimulating discussion of the social aspects of courtly love and some of its anomalies (pp. 154–202, especially p. 187). A somewhat different view from mine, however, of the social sense created by the *Troilus* is expressed by Father Dunning, who compares its "evocation of life in a court," to its disadvantage, with the *Roman de la rose*: T. P. Dunning, "God and Man in *Troilus and Criseyde,*" in *English and Medieval Studies Presented to J. R. R. Tolkien . . . ,* ed. Norman Davis and C. L. Wrenn (London: Allen and Unwin, 1962), p. 167. If Father Dunning's stress is on "court" rather than "society," then perhaps there is no real disagreement.

23. See Robert Kilburn Root, *The Textual Tradition of Chaucer's Troilus,* Chaucer Soc., 1st Ser., No. 99 (London, 1916), pp. 155–157, 216–220, 245–248. For a perceptive analysis of the additions, see Charles A. Owen, Jr., "The Significance of Chaucer's Revisions of *Troilus and Criseyde,*" *MP,* LV (1957), 1–5.

24. See Root's discussion of the opening and the close of Book III (1–38, 1744–1771) in his edition, *The Book of Troilus and Criseyde by Geoffrey Chaucer* (Princeton: Princeton University Press, 1945), pp. 463–466, 493–495.

25. The range of opinion on these issues at the scholastic level is documented and discussed in Gordon Leff, *Bradwardine and the Pelagians: A Study of His "De Causa Dei" and its Opponents* (Cambridge: Cambridge University Press, 1957).

26. "Distance and Predestination," pp. 14–15, 21–24.

27. An interesting discussion of the passage is given by Peter Elbow, "Two Boethian Speeches in *Troilus and Criseyde* and Boethian Irony," in *Literary Criticism and Historical Understanding,* Selected Papers from the English Institute, ed. Phillip Damon (New York and London: Columbia University Press, 1967), pp. 84–107.

28. On the "paganism" of the poem and Troilus's "natural religion," see T. P. Dunning, "God and Man," pp. 164–182, especially pp. 172–176.

29. See E. Talbot Donaldson, "The Ending of Chaucer's *Troilus,*" pp. 41–44.

EXPERIENCE, LANGUAGE, AND CONSCIOUSNESS:
TROILUS AND CRISEYDE, II, 596–931

1. See Francis Lee Utley, "Scene-division in Chaucer's Troilus and Criseyde," in *Studies in Medieval Literature,* ed. MacEdward Leach (Philadelphia: University of Pennsylvania Press, 1961), pp. 109–138.

2. II, 470–489. *The Works of Geoffrey Chaucer,* ed. F. N. Robinson, 2nd ed. (Boston: Houghton Mifflin, 1957).

3. "Literature and Sexuality: Book III of Chaucer's *Troilus*," *Massachusetts Review,* VIII (1967), 442–456.

4. Medieval literature had an elaborate iconography for suggesting nonverbal impulse, which Chaucer used in describing Troilus' first sight of Criseyde. In I, 206–210 Troilus is struck by Love's arrow; we are told *his herte wax a-fere* (229), and on seeing her that *he wax therwith astoned* (274). Only then do we get inner speech reported in direct discourse (276–277). On the passage see Robert M. Jordan, *Chaucer and the Shape of Creation* (Cambridge, Mass.: Harvard University Press, 1967), pp. 76–79.

5. L. S. Vigotsky, "Thought and Speech," in *Psycholinguistics,* ed. S. Saporta and J. R. Bastian (New York: Holt, Rinehart, Winston, 1961), pp. 509–535.

6. "Thought and Speech," p. 533.

7. On this phenomenon see the very interesting story or essay by Peter Taylor, "Demons," in *The New Yorker,* August 24, 1963, pp. 30–63.

8. "Thought and Speech," p. 532.

9. Indeed Vigotsky shows that inner speech develops from the "egocentric speech" of childhood: "Thought and Speech," pp. 514–524.

10. See lines 715–718. On moderation or *mesure* as an aristocratic virtue, one can cite its frequent appearance in romances. Pandarus himself believes in it—see I, 687–689. See Lynn White, Jr., "The Iconography of *Temperantia* and the Virtuousness of Technology," in *Action and Conviction in Early Modern Europe,* ed. Theodore K. Rabb and Jerrold E. Seigel (Princeton: Princeton University Press, 1969), pp. 197–219.

11. Lines 755–756, 786–791. In the earlier passage she is using it as encouragement—she has no husband who will be fickle and jealous.

12. OED and MED cite Gower, *Confessio Amantis* I, 2391 and V, 4640. *Jangle* and *clap* referred to any noise; but *clapper* was generally used to mean the "tongue" of a bell ("tongue" is not cited in this usage until the sixteenth century).

13. See Robinson's note for parallels in English proverbs.

14. Later, in V, 784, the opportunistic Diomede uses the same proverb.

15. His ideas on the subject appear in a later article, "Folk Literature: An Operational Definition," *Journal of American Folklore,* LXXIV (1961), 193–206.

16. *The Three Temptations: Medieval Man in Search of the World* (Princeton: Princeton University Press, 1966), pp. 135–138, and cf. 127–135. Pandarus twice mentions his reading, in I, 788 and II, 108; on his bookishness see also

David I. Grossvogel, *Limits of the Novel* (Ithaca, New York: Cornell University Press, 1968), pp. 44–73.

17. See Ernst Robert Curtius, *European Literature and the Latin Middle Ages,* trans. Willard R. Trask, Bollingen Series No. 36 (New York: Pantheon Books, 1953), pp. 519–537.

18. But inspired, as Kittredge noted (*MLN,* XXV [1910], 158), by Machaut's "Paradis d'Amour."

19. Cf. Northrop Frye, *Anatomy of Criticism* (Princeton: Princeton University Press, 1957), pp. 270–281.

20. I have in mind here the detailed analysis of Martin Joos, *The Five Clocks,* Indiana University Research Center in Anthropology, Folklore, and Linguistics No. 22 (Bloomington, 1962), especially pp. 22–23. Joos shows that a characteristic of the casual style is the participation of the listener and the assumption of a common frame of reference. The ladies do *not* speak in the intimate style, where emotion is unexpressed because habitually felt; Antigone expresses enthusiasm openly while Criseyde tries to check and conceal her response.

21. On this phase of medieval psychology, see D. W. Robertson, Jr., *A Preface to Chaucer: Studies in Medieval Perspectives* (Princeton: Princeton University Press, 1962), pp. 71–76; and cf. Howard, *The Three Temptations,* pp. 56–65.

22. On this general function of the Narrator, see Morton W. Bloomfield, "Distance and Predestination in *Troilus and Criseyde,*" *PMLA,* LXXII (1957), 14–26.

23. Cf. for example C. G. Jung, *Symbols of Transformation,* Bollingen Series No. 20, 2nd ed. (Princeton, 1967), pp. 347–348.

24. So also in Thomas of Cantimpré, *De natura rerum* in British Museum MS Roy. 12. E. XVII, fol. 73–74.

25. See Odon Lottin, *Psychologie et morale aux XIIᵉ et XIIIᵉ siècles* (6 vols. in 8, Louvain and Gembloux: Abbaye du Mont César, 1942–1960), especially I, 220–221, 393–424; II, 493–496, 588–589.

THE ORDERING OF THE *CANTERBURY TALES*

1. *Selections from The Tales of Canterbury and Short Poems,* ed. Robert A. Pratt (Boston: Houghton Mifflin, 1966). For the simultaneous rejection and retention of the three priests, see, e.g., *Canterbury Tales,* ed. J. M. Manly (New York: Holt, 1928), pp. 153, 507–508; *The Works of Geoffrey Chaucer,* ed. F. N. Robinson, 2nd ed. (Boston: Houghton Mifflin, 1957), pp. 18, 655 (citations from Chaucer in this paper are from Robinson); *Chaucer's Major Poetry,* ed. Albert C. Baugh (New York: Appleton-Century-Crofts, 1963), p. 241. Manly and Edith Rickert, *The Text of the Canterbury Tales* (Chicago: University of Chicago Press, 1940), naturally retain the priests in their text as present in O¹, but issue the usual rejection in their notes (III, 9, 422–423).

2. "The Order of the *Canterbury Tales,*" *PMLA,* LXVI (1951), 1141–1167, especially pp. 1160–1161.

3. F. J. Furnivall, *A Temporary Preface to the Chaucer Society's Six-Text Edition of the Canterbury Tales* (London: Chaucer Society, Second Series,

1868), Pt. I, 9–41, *passim;* W. W. Skeat, *The Complete Works of Geoffrey Chaucer* (Oxford: Clarendon Press, 1870), III, 434 (remarks on order), IV (tales); J. S. P. Tatlock, "The *Canterbury Tales* in 1400," *PMLA,* L (1935), 100–139; Robinson, *Works of Chaucer,* p. 2; Manly-Rickert, *Text of Canterbury Tales,* II, 474–494; W. W. Lawrence, *Chaucer and the Canterbury Tales* (New York: Columbia University Press, 1950), pp. 90–118 (Lawrence was later persuaded to Professor Pratt's point of view: see "Order of *Canterbury Tales,"* 1160, n. 34); Baugh, *Chaucer's Major Poetry,* pp. 231–233.

4. *Canterbury Tales,* pp. 77–82.

5. *Text of Canterbury Tales,* II, charts following p. 494.

6. Pratt, "Order of *Canterbury Tales,"* 1160–1161; Tatlock, *"Canterbury Tales* in 1400," 131. Professor Pratt's phrase "the Ellesmere scribe" is not strictly accurate, for despite the impression given by Manly-Rickert, *Text of Canterbury Tales* (II, 479), there is no concrete evidence that the Ellesmere scribe invented the order rather than inheriting it, and while some of the other MSS with the Ellesmere order may have picked it up from Ellesmere, there is no evidence that others did not come by it independently from a prior source. The point is important to the present discussion in that I defend the Ellesmere order because it is a good order and not because Ellesmere is presumably a good MS. Throughout I use the phrase "Ellesmere order" merely to identify the order and not to suggest that it is peculiarly Ellesmere's invention.

7. There are, of course, critical objections to identifying the speaker as either the Squire or the Summoner, but in view of the textual situation it hardly seems necessary to advance them.

8. Professor Baugh's statement (*Chaucer's Major Poetry,* p. 333) that four MSS read *Shipman* seems based on a misinterpretation of Manly-Rickert's sigils in the apparatus for B1179 (*Text of Canterbury Tales,* III, 230).

9. "A Question of Order in the *Canterbury Tales,"* *The Chaucer Review,* I (1967), 229.

10. Robinson, *Works of Chaucer,* p. 696; Manly-Rickert, *Text of Canterbury Tales,* II, 492.

11. Professor Pratt, "Order of *Canterbury Tales,"* 1164–1165, remarks that Tatlock along with Manly "rejected the a-El order as unauthoritative because of the geographical inconsistency." But Tatlock, *"Canterbury Tales* in 1400," 132, says that "the mention of Sittingbourne earlier than Rochester . . . would trouble few but Kentishmen." It is, however, true that Tatlock's position is not entirely clear.

12. Thus Manly-Rickert's discussion begins by dismissing the Ellesmere order as non-Chaucerian on the grounds of the Rochester-Sittingbourne reversal and the time discrepancy between Group H and I (see below), but ends by announcing (in a different context, to be sure) that "the whole conception of a series of tales told while riding by so large a group of pilgrims is, however entertaining, entirely unrealistic" (*Text of Canterbury Tales,* II, 474, 494). Lawrence, *Chaucer and the Canterbury Tales,* on p. 43 says that "accuracy and consistency in the details of the journey must not be expected and . . . this does not matter"; but on p. 102, he says the misplacement of Sittingbourne and Rochester "seems less like a slip than a somersault."

13. *Canterbury Tales,* pp. 77–78.

14. *Text of Canterbury Tales,* II, 477, 479.

15. Germaine Dempster, "Manly's Conception of the Early History of the *Canterbury Tales,*" *PMLA,* LXI (1946), 379–415, especially p. 383.

16. *"Canterbury Tales* in 1400," 124.

17. *Chaucer and the Canterbury Tales,* pp. 102–103. Lawrence's appeal to the order of the groups in the MSS is illustrative of how hard it is, even with the best of intentions, to deny the authority of the MSS. Note the Manly-Rickert argument for the sequence CB²: C is "always placed before B² by the early scribes, and, although there is no reason to believe that they were informed of Chaucer's plan, there is no objection to accepting this position" (*Text of Canterbury Tales,* II, 492). But despite the effort of the left hand to take away what the right hand has just given, the fact remains that there is no reason for the order CB² except what is provided by the MSS. Tatlock performs a similar feat with the sequence AB¹; see *"Canterbury Tales* in 1400," 130.

18. A not entirely extinguished sense of piety prompts me to apologize for dismissing so lightly the conclusions reached by scholars of so formidable learning and experience as Tatlock and Manly. Yet the rules of scholarship dictate that credibility must emanate not from the reputation of the scholar, but from the evidence he produces.

19. *Text of Canterbury Tales,* I, 496.

20. *"Canterbury Tales* in 1400," 118.

21. "Order of *Canterbury Tales,*" 1154.

22. *Text of Canterbury Tales,* I, 495.

23. One of the B-text MSS of *Piers Plowman,* Corpus Christi College, Oxford, 201, seems, at first glance, so horrendously erratic in its text that no editor would be willing to trust it: yet it offers a large number of uniquely good readings, of which Skeat gives a single example on p. xxviii of his edition of the B-Text (EETS OS 38, 1869). See also my note on D117 of the *Canterbury Tales* in *Speculum,* XL (1965), 626–633.

24. This point is dealt with more fully in my paper "The Psychology of Editors of Middle English Texts" in *English Studies Today,* Fourth Series (Rome: Edizioni di Storia e Letteratura, 1966), pp. 45–62. The position of those who adopt Selden's reading while rejecting its authority seems a classic example of what I refer to (p. 54) as "the torment of a genetic editor facing the prospect of having to admire and perhaps introduce into his text a reading from a MS which could not possibly have come by it through honest inheritance."

25. These figures are based on Manly-Rickert, *Text of Canterbury Tales,* II, charts following p. 494.

26. See, e.g., Tatlock's reasons for leaving B¹ after A, referred to above, n. 17.

27. "A Conjecture on the Wife of Bath's Prologue," *JEGP,* XXIV (1925), 512–547.

28. It is perhaps a slight flaw in the elegance of Professor Pratt's demonstration that the assumption that an initial "S" alone remained legible after Chaucer's alteration of B¹1179 (*Seyde the S———; "heer schal he nat preche"*) suggests more reasonably an imperfect erasure of an original word beginning with "S" than the overwriting of such a word upon an original *Wif of Bathe.*

On the other hand, the shifting position in the MSS of the word *heer* logically suggests that *heer* was added to the line marginally after a trisyllabic phrase such as *Wif of Bathe* had been replaced by a dissyllable such as *Shipman.* I do not understand Professor Cox's explanation (*Chaucer Review,* I [1967], 235, n. 15) that the "preponderance of Squire entries, by the way, could stem from the fact that if the original deleted entry was *Wife,* an insertion of Squire could create no metrical problem." In Chaucer's metrics *wif* (*wife* does not exist) is always monosyllabic, and *squier* dissyllabic.

29. Professor Cox argues that the Man of Law's endlink reading *Wif of Bathe* in 1179 and followed by Group D represents Chaucer's final intention; but her assumptions that the Hengwrt scribe once had the Man of Law's endlink before him but let it pass from him without transcribing it and that Ellesmere's lack of the endlink is somehow attributable to the Hengwrt's scribe's loss of it are a long way removed from the available evidence. The most sanguine statement I can find on a close relationship between the Hengwrt and Ellesmere orders is Mrs. Dempster's dampening conclusion ("The Problem of Tale Order in the *Canterbury Tales,*" *PMLA,* LXIV [1949], 1139) that "all we can say is that the *a*-El order may not be as entirely independent of Hg's as has hitherto been assumed." As far as the textual relationship between Ellesmere and Hengwrt is concerned, aside from the assumption that they had the same scribe, which does not necessarily affect textual matters, the chief apparent evidence for a close relation seems to lie in shared right readings—which, of course, in the genetic system is no evidence of close relationship. It should be said of Professor Cox's theory, however, that the inelegance of a conjecture involving human activity may be far more damaging to its credibility than to the historical truth of what is conjectured.

30. For references, see Robinson, *Works of Chaucer,* pp. 696–697.

31. *Chaucer's Poetry* (New York: Ronald Press, 1958), p. 150.

32. *Chaucer and the Canterbury Tales,* p. 102.

33. I am aware that I have ignored a vast body of material devoted to the topic of the order of the tales. I have done this in an endeavor to limit my comment to those discussions that seem to be most influential on current opinion and that deal, on the whole, most directly with the actual MS evidence (though I have ignored most of the scholarship that conjectures backward from the MS evidence or that deals with problems of order in MSS other than Ellesmere). There is, of course, a wealth of literary criticism justifying one order or another, but most of this seems to me to consist of *ex post facto* demonstrations of the literary effects—"resonances"—that occur after a given order has been adopted. My trouble is that I am almost equally persuaded by them all: as much, for instance, by Professor Pratt's analysis of the effects produced by placing B^2 next after B^1 as by Professor Cox's rehearsal of the advantages achieved with the Ellesmere order. Unfortunately, resonances tend to work equally well in either direction: for instance, Lawrence admires the effect produced on the Wife of Bath's Prologue when the Nun's Priest's Tale is made to precede it ("Order of *Canterbury Tales,*" 1160, n. 36); but I have always found the Nun's Priest's Tale much enriched because it follows the Wife of Bath. I should also

acknowledge that critical attempts have been made to justify almost all the discrepancies noted in the *Canterbury Tales*: for my purposes, the most alluring of these points out that in the Summoner's threat to tell two or three tales before he gets to Sittingbourne, Sittingbourne may be understood to be well in the future, and not necessarily this side of Rochester (see Stanley B. Greenfield's note, *MLR*, XLVIII [1953], 51–52) ; but it has been my experience that most readers find this interpretation unnatural, and so I do not employ it as a justification of the Ellesmere order, though I accept it as a likely interpretation once the Ellesmere order has been adopted.

THE MILLER'S TALE—AN UNBOETHIAN INTERPRETATION

1. "Chaucer's Elegiac Knight," *Criticism*, VI (1964), 223. Even those like Westlund ("The *Knight's Tale* as an Impetus for Pilgrimage," *PQ*, XLIII [1964], 526–537) who stress the failure of attempts to impose order in the KT give order a major significance in the tale. "I suggest that the Knight's Tale presents the continual subversion of noble efforts to bring order out of disorder" (p. 526). I do not agree with this interesting interpretation.

2. Paul A. Olson ("The *Reeve's Tale*: Chaucer's *Measure for Measure*," *SP*, LIX [1962], 1–17) argues that the Reeve's Tale disguises "revenge as justice." I have my doubts about this point, but even if correct, Olson's point of view is psychological. He is concerned not so much with the tale itself as with Oswald's motivation in telling it.

3. J. Y. T. Greig, *The Psychology of Laughter and Comedy* (New York: Dodd, Mead, 1923), p. 104.

4. E.g., Paul A. Olson, "Poetic Justice in the *Miller's Tale*," *MLQ*, XXIV (1963), 227–236. Like all moral and Boethian interpretations of the Miller's Tale, Olson ignores the fact that Alison is unpunished.

5. See Robert Jordan, *Chaucer and the Shape of Creation* (Cambridge, Mass.: Harvard University Press, 1967), p. 196.

6. A suggestion made orally to me by Professor Robert O. Payne of the University of Washington.

7. E.g., Cicero, *De inventione*, I, 19, 27. See K. Barwick, "Die Gliederung der narratio in der rhetorischen Theorie und ihre Bedeutung für die Geschichte des antiken Romans," *Hermes*, LXIII (1928), 261–287.

8. Karl F. Thompson, "Machiavelli in Bloomsbury: The Anglicized Italian," *Italica*, XLI (1964), 312.

9. See the splendid essay by E. Talbot Donaldson, "Idiom of Popular Poetry in the Miller's Tale," *English Institute Essays*, ed., Alan S. Downer (New York: Columbia University Press, 1950), 116–140.

10. Needless to say, the interpretation put forth here is diametrically opposed to that put forth by Helen Storm Corsa in *Chaucer Poet of Mirth and Morality* (Notre Dame: Notre Dame University Press, 1964), pp. 108–115, which may be summed up by the following quotation. "In unambiguous and unequivocal terms this Tale [MT] reveals that as you reap so shall you sow, as you do so

shall you be done unto, as you pretend so shall you be fooled, as you deserve so shall you get. In short, the Miller's world is in essence the same world as the Knight's; its differences are accidents only" (pp. 109–110). In order to sustain this thesis, Alison is considered to have been "more sinned against than sinning" and "no more subject to moral judgment or social criticism than is the weasel"; and the carpenter is a fool "naive and presumptuous, jealous and old" and deserves his cruel punishment.

THE ANECDOTE: A NEGLECTED GENRE

1. I, 3rd ed. (Copenhagen, 1958); II, 2nd ed. (1964).

2. Edmund Fuller, ed., *Thesaurus of Anecdotes* (New York: Crown, 1942), p. ix.

3. (New York, 1954), p. 42.

4. See *Alverdens anekdoter,* I, 8.

5. *Alverdens anekdoter,* I, 347–348.

6. *Alverdens anekdoter,* I, 8.

7. Bennett Cerf, *Anything for a Laugh* (New York: Bantam, 1946) and *Laughing Stock* (New York: Grosset and Dunlap, 1945); Irvin S. Cobb, *A Laugh a Day Keeps the Doctor Away* (New York: George H. Doran, 1923); Ed Ford and others, *Can You Top This?* (New York: Didier, 1945); and L. Laursen and P. N. Buck, *The World's Best Humorous Anecdotes* (New York, 1930).

8. London: Hulton Press, 1957, n.p.

9. See, as examples, Isaac D'Israeli, *Dissertation on Anecdotes* (London, 1793) and Robert Birley, *The Undergrowth of History* (London: George Philip and Son, 1955). Louis Brownlow, a noted raconteur, began *The Anatomy of the Anecdote* (Chicago: University of Chicago Press, 1960) as a treatise but allowed it to pass almost immediately into a collection showing the social use of anecdotes. See also James M. Osborn, ed., Spence's *Anecdotes,* I (Oxford: Clarendon Press, 1966), xvii–xxi, "Ana and Anecdotes as Literary Genre." All of these books have rather more of the historian than the folklorist about them. The student will do well to note the specialization of collections. An excellent example is Dr. Minime, ed., *La Médecine anecdotique historique littéraire. Recueil à l'usage de médecins, chirurgiens et apothecaires érudits, curieux et chercheurs. . . . Estampes, dessins, gravures et fac-simile,* 3 vols. (Paris, 1906) in more than a thousand pages.

10. See R. Th. Christiansen, *The Migratory Legends. A proposed list of types with a systematic catalogue of the Norwegian variants,* FFC 175 (Helsinki, 1958). Christiansen does not include migratory legends of historical or pseudo-historical quality. He does not, for example, include the story about the Marines mentioned below. For this see J. P. Marquand, *Thirty Years* (Boston: Little, Brown, 1954), p. 456 (written in 1945); Archer Taylor and B. J. Whiting, *A Dictionary of American Proverbs 1820–1880* (Cambridge, Mass.: Harvard University Press, 1950), p. 226; Burton Stevenson, *The Home Book of Quotations,* 5th ed. (New York: Dodd, Mead, 1947), p. 67:5.

11. *Alverdens anekdoter,* I, 6.

12. *Sagen und ihre Deutung* (Göttingen, 1965), p. 25.

PARIS OG HELEN I TREJEBORG: A REDUCTION TO ESSENTIALS

1. The Norwegian texts have never before been printed. The text collected by Kristensen was first printed in Evald Tang Kristensen, *Jyske Folkeminder,* X: *100 gamle jyske Folkeviser* (Copenhagen: Gyldendal, 1889), 328–331, No. 81, and as a variant text combined with broadside texts from 1581, 1674, and 1710, a text from Bröms Gÿllemärs Visbok, and four Faroese texts, one of which may be from oral traditions, by Axel Olrik in *Danske Ridderviser,* Danmarks gamle Folkeviser VIII (Copenhagen: Gyldendal, 1919), 8–10, No. 467B.

2. Adolf Iwar Arwidsson, *Svenska Fornsånger,* II (Stockholm: Norstedt and Sons, 1837), 335–341, No. 151B. This copy derives from Per Brahes Wisbock which dates probably from the 1620's. The author of this certainly built upon the widely circulated broadside versions, but was equally certainly aware of many elements in the Troy story which do not appear in other texts.

3. According to Olrik (*Danske Ridderviser,* p. 11a) an earlier edition also printed by Matz Vingaard in 1572 has been noted by W. H. F. Abrahamson and R. Nyerup, but it is now lost.

4. Bengt R. Jonsson, *Svensk Balladtradition I: Balladkällor och balladtyper* (Stockholm: Svenskt Visarkiv, *Svenskt Visarkivshandlingar* I, 1967), 765.

5. Axel Olrik, *Danske Ridderviser,* p. 2. He bases his belief upon the manner in which the narrative is developed and, more certainly, upon certain foreign words and their glosses, concluding that though it necessarily is as old as 1550, it is not much older than the beginning of the century.

6. This material is taken from notes left by Professor Knut Liestøl in materials brought together for a definitive edition of Norwegian ballads which death prevented him from completing.

7. *Danske Ridderviser,* p. 3, note ††. The place is shown even on modern tourist maps as an historical site, approximately eleven kilometers northwest of Tønder which itself lies near the west coast of Jutland just north of the present German border.

8. *Gyldendals store konversasjons leksikon.* 2d ed. (Oslo: Gyldendal Norsk forlag, n.d.), V, column 2244: TROYABORG: *folketradisjons navn på labryntformede konstruksjoner, ofte av stein, lagt i konsentriske sirkler eller spiraler. Finnes over hele Europa, også i Norden. Muligens har de vært brukt til kultiske riddeleker.*

9. Axel Olrik, *Danske Ridderviser,* pp. 3–4.

10. M. B. Landstad, *Norske Folkeviser* (Christiania [Oslo]: Tönsberg, 1853), LXXV, 594–595.

11. See, for example, *Valdemar og Tove* (Danmarks gamle Folkeviser, CXXI) as well as the entire series of ballads beginning in Danmarks gamle Folkeviser with *Kong Valdemar og hans Soster,* Danmarks gamle Folkeviser CXXVI, and running through *Mettelille og Dronning Sofie,* Danmarks gamle Folkeviser

CXXX, all of which deal with Valdemar's problems as a husband, and the group beginning with *Dronning Dagmar og Junker Strange* (Danmarks gamle Folkeviser CXXXII), and continuing through *Dronning Dagmars Død,* Danmarks gamle Folkeviser CXXXV, which sympathetically treat of Valdemar's courtship of and marriage to Margrete, called Dagmor by the Danes, daughter of King Priemysl Ottokar I of Bohemia, one of Denmark's most popular queens whose supposed sympathy for the common people contributed to the popularity of her royal husband.

12. Compare, for example, *Rullemann og Hildeborg*:

> 1. Rullemann han tener i kongins garð
>   i nie vetrar og så eit ár.
> 2. Han tener kvárgin fer kost hell' lön
>   men berre for Hildeborg, hon var så skjøn.
>   (Landstad, No. LXX, stanzas 1–2)

Or, perhaps more significantly, *Herr Nikelus*:

> 1. Herr Nikelus tener i kongins gárð
>   han tente sjau vetrar og så eit ár.
> 2. Han tener inki for onno lön
>   hell' fer liti Kjersti, hon var så ven.
>   (Landstad, LXXV, stanzas 1–2)

And there are countless other examples.

APPENDIX

The Texts

The Danish Texts

The Danish texts are all printed with full editorial notes in Axel Olrik, *Danske Ridderviser,* Danmarks gamle Folkeviser VIII (Copenhagen: Gyldendal, 1919; reprinted in photo-offset by Det Danske Universitets-Jubilæets Samfund, 1967–1968), 5–13. However, both Danish A and Danish B are composite texts, and Danish Bi is the closest to oral tradition. It is printed in Evald Tang Kristensen, *Jyske Folkeminder,* X: *100 gamle jyske Folkeviser* (Copenhagen: Gyldendal, 1889), 328–331.

The Swedish Texts

The Swedish texts, though less easily available in American libraries, have not been printed here (partly for lack of space and partly because their relationship to the Norwegian texts with which we are concerned is less significant than that of the Danish texts). Both Swedish A and Swedish B are printed in Adolf Iwar Arwidsson, *Svenska Fornsånger,* II (Stockholm: Norstedt and Sons, 1837), 329–341. The editorial notes are superficial and should be supplemented by references to Bengt R. Jonsson, *Svensk Balladtradition I: Balladkällor och balladtyper* (Stockholm: Svenskt Visarkiv, *Svenskt Visarkivshandlingar* I, 1967), especially pp. 765 ff.

The Norwegian Texts
The Norwegian texts have not been previously printed.

Norwegian A
Printed in pages 231–236 above.
Collected by Sophus Bugge from Torbjørg Haugen in Skafså, Telemark, in 1857.
Manuscript source now available: Norsk folkeminnesamling Manuscript S. Bugge k, pp. 41–47. This is a field notebook.
Textual variations and other manuscript peculiarities: Stanza 3^1 consists merely of the words *Paris—Svend.* 14^1 has simply *Dr. E.* for *Droning Elen.* 44^1 consists only of the following: *—kneggje.* 46^1 is simply the word *—Viv.* 47^1 employs merely the initials *K.N.* for *Kung Nilaus.* Stanza 50 is noted merely as *—Kvide—mæ—Side.*

Norwegian B
Collected by Moltke Moe from Torbjørg Ripilen in Mo, Telemark, in 1890 and 1891.
Manuscript source now available: Norsk folkeminnesamling Manuscript M. Moe 25, pp. 125–129 (September, 1890) and M. Moe 27, pp. 22–24 (April, 1891). These are both field copies. The second is not complete and consists merely of additional stanzas and variations, all retranscribed in Moe 25.

1. Kong Valdemonn va so rik ein mann,
   å Paris va endå rikare han.
   — Valibrós søn som lyster 'en Paris fýgje.
2. Paris han va so rik ein mann,
   sjou kongeríkji so hadde væl han.
3. Dér kåm eitt bò frå eitt anna land,
   at kongen sille seg avatt lédingen.
4. Kongen sill' seg avatt ledingen fara,
   Páris si' véra heimi taka landi i varé.
5. "Du vòktar mitt kvæg, du voktar min hest,
   men voktar dròning Héllena allerbest."
6. "Ja eg ska' vokte dròning Hellena så væl som eg kann,
   som du sjave ha' vóri heimi, du kungelege mann!"
7. Horpa av sylv å strænggin av gull
   so va den horpa so frydefull.
8. Paris han reiste seg avatt smidja,
   den røde gullhorpa han smia.
9. Han leika i dagar, han leika i två,
   dròning Héllena stó å lydde derpå.
10. "Anten æ du Paris, selv ænglerne lik,
    hell' å æ du Kristus av himmerik!"
11. "Nei eg æ inkji Paris, selv ænglerne lik,
    å inkji Kristus av himmerik.
12. Høyrer du dròning Héllena, eg talar ti deg:
    Lyster du kji fygje ti Trøyeborg mæ meg?"

13. "Så gjerne eg dæ gjorde,
    når eg for min herre det torde."
14. "I Trøyeborg dér æ dei murane fem,
    slett ingjen i værden kan vinne over dem.
15. I Trøyeborg dér hev eg dei murane ni
    slett ingjen i værden kan vinne over di."
16. Ei halv mil av slòtti av néatt ti strand,
    dér gróv selv Paris med hvidan hånd.
17. Dæ va ei løyndegòng han gróv, å so skifte ho
    klæi mæ terna si å gjekk mæ 'en igjænom løyndegangji.
17. Når Paris å droningji kåm seg at strand,
    kåm båten ti kongjen skriand ti land.
18. "Høyrer du dæ Paris, min tjener so trúgjen,
    hòr hev du no fængjé deg so skjøn ei jomfruve?"
19. "Eg ville kji hava anna for lang' tjenesta min,
    so gav ho meg tjenestekvinden sin."
20. "Eg hev alli sét noko jomfru so deilig,
    eg sønest, du æ mi dròning so lik!
21. Høyrer du Paris, hòt eg spyrje deg må:
    no vi eg av heim i buri å sjå."
22. Kongjen han rei å dråningje rann,
    endå va ho fyrr inni buri hell han.
23. "Høyrer du dæ, dròning Hellena mi fruve so fin,
    eg vi 'né, taka avskjé mæ Paris, langténaren min!"
24. Kongjen han rei å droningji rann,
    endå va ho né at strand fyrr hell han.
25. Han sette dråning Hellena på båtebor
    sjav'e sette Paris seg fyr årin å ró.
26. Paris han lyfte på høian hatt:
    "Farvel kong Valdemonn, hav nò tusen gó natt!"
27. Kongen han kom seg riand i går,
    han kunna 'kji dråningji att'e sjå.
28. Han leita uti å han leita inni,
    han kunna inkji dròning Hellena finne.
29. So gjóre han bò ivi alt sitt land,
    "so mange som sværi béra kann!
30. Dei som inkji hava sønner i krogen at stå,
    skò lata datteren for sønine gå."
31. Når dei kåm seg på vegjen fram,
    so møtte dei seg ein gammel trollmann.
32. "Å høyrer du dæ, du gamle trollmann,
    du lyt rå meg ei rå, dæ beste du kann!"
33. "Du skò deg ein kåpårhest gjøre
    å trædive ryttarar déruti føre."
34. Ti tala dråning Hellena: "Dæ æ mitt sind,
    dé leier den hesten av pórten inn."

35. Å so tala dråning Hellena: "Sæ æ mitt rå
    dé læt'e hesten for porten stå!"
36. For uden av kåber, for inden av gull,
    så æ den hesten så frydefuld.
37. Så tala dråning Hellena, ei jomfru så fin:
    "No stænd dæ ein hest'e for portens dør."
38. Då hesten tok ti å kneggja,
    dæ rivna bå' i murar å i væggjar.
39. I òtte dage monn' Trøyeborg brenne
    å ingjen mann konna skái kjenne.
    Paris siger da han ingen udvei ser:
40. "Kvår vi du héra mæ Paris døy,
    hell fygje kong Valdemonn sør ónder øy?"
41. "Eg vi hell'e hera mæ Paris døy,
    hell' fygje kong Valdemonn sør ónder øy."
42. "Då vi' mé lata kòss årine slå
    for lettare dø kann me alli få!"
43. Å dæ va kongen ti største kvide,
    at dråningji låg dø mæ Paris's side.
44. Å dæ va kongen ti største harm,
    at dråningji låg dø på Paris's arm.
    Kongen:
45. "Ha eg visst, ho ha' havt Paris så kjær,
    so ha' alli Trøyeborgji silt brunni her!"

So va dæ 'kji berre ei tvo-tri vers ti, som eg inkji kjem ihug. Dæ va so at han sette ell på Paris's skóg, å den va so vi'e at 'en brann i åtte dagar, fyrr-hell nokon kjende dæ,—so vi' va han.

Textual variations and other manuscript peculiarities: MS M. Moe 25: For stanza 6 there is written the following variant: *So væl sko eg vokte ditt rikje å land/ som du vøre heimi, du kunggelege mann.* 8^1 corrects the last word to *smidjen.* 9^2 is corrected to *sto (jamt) å lydde.* 11 is rewritten as *Nei enkji æ eg selv ængglerne lik/ å enkji Kr. av himmerik.* 13^1 is rewritten *Så gjerne (såmænd) eg dæ (jeg det) gjorde;* 13^2 writes *jeg* for *eg.* 14^2 (*so*) *slett ingjen.* 15^2 is rewritten *alt ingjen.* 17 is rewritten *Når dei kom seg neatt ti strand/ då kåm kungg Valdemunns båt skriand for land.* 22^1 changes *rann* to *sprang.* 22^2 is rewritten *men fyrr'e va ho énni buri hell han.* 24^1 is rewritten *Kongjen (han) rei å dr. spring.* 24^2 is rewritten *fyrre va ho rié at stranda hell han.* 28 is rewritten *Han leita uti, han leita inni/ han kunna kji dråninggji att'e finne.* 29^1 has the word *Kunggen* scratched out and *han* inserted. 30^1 is changed to *Den som inkji hev.* 30^2 is rewritten *skò lade datteren for sønnen gå.* 33^1 is rewritten *Å eg skò deg ein kåpårhest gjøre.* 36^1 changes *av kåber* to *den kåber.* 37^2 corrects *portens* to *porternes.* 38^1 has a notation that the first singing employed *kneggje* but that it was lacking in the second. 39^2 is changed to *å man konna slet ingjen skai kjenne.* 40^2 changed to *fygje konggen søv.* 41^1 changed to *Hell'e vi eg.*

41^2 changed to *fygje K. atte sør.* 42^2 changed to *lettare døe kann me ikkje få.*
43^1 changed to *dæ blei kunggen.*
    M. Moe 27 has the additional stanzas 1, 2, 7, 25, 26, 27, 32, 34, and 35. These
are not in M. Moe 25, but are printed above. The corrections in M. Moe 25 are
made from M. Moe 27.

Norwegian C
    Collected by Moltke Moe from Hæge Bjønnemyr in Mo, Telemark, in 1891.
Hæge said that she had learned the song from her mother, Jorunn Bjønnemyr.
    Manuscript source now available: Norsk folkeminnesamling M. Moe 25, pp.
288–291.

1. Paris han téner i kongens går
   i vintrane tri å så eitt år.
   — Ho lyster Paris fylgje.
2. Han téner inkje fy ònó løn
   hell fyr' æ Heléna, ho æ så skjøn.
3. Å kongen han skulde at ledingen fare,
   å Paris sill' vér' hjemme, tak' landet i vare.
4. "Den voktar nå uti, du voktar nå inni,
   du voktar Helena, den dydige kvinne.
5. Du voktar min' åker, du voktar mi æng,
   du voktar 'a Helena alt førii si sæng!"
6. "Å høyrer du Helena, hòt eg spyr'e dig:
   Å lyster du av lande at fygje mæ mig?"
7. "Så gjønne så lyster eg av lande å fygje mæ dig,
   når eg visste hòr me sill' freden få."
8. "Trejeborg dæ æ så fast eitt land,
   at alli nokon kristen mann vinne dæ kann."
9. Dei gróve då på den myrke gong,
   alt òma lofti å ne-at strånd.
10. Å når dei kom seg dér neat strand,
    då lae kong Nikelus snekkja for land.
11. "Vælkòmen kong Nikelus, eg talar ti deg:
    Å no vi eg flykja mæ tjenestkvinden dén!"
12. "Så gjerne må du flykkja mæ tjenestkvinden min,
    når eg hev vòri heimatt te dròningen min."
13. Å kongen han rei, å Helena onde jóri rann,
    men ho bleiv no fyrr'e uppi lofti hell han.
14. "Å vælkomen kongen, eg talar ti deg:
    å no vi Paris flykja mæ tjenestkvinden mén!"
15. "Å eg hev no alli sét likare viv
    hell den né på stråndi å dròningen min!"
16. "Min nådige herre, du snakkar ei slik:
    dæ æ så mangt kvårannas likt!"
17. Å kongen han rei, å Helena ónde jóri rann,
    men ho blei no fyrre at stråndi hell han.

18. Å Helena ho lyfter på Paris hatt:
    "Hav farvæl, kong Nikelus, å tusen gó-natt!"
19. Dei leita uti å dei leita inni,
    inkji så kónne dei Hélena atte finne.
20. Så fant dei den myrke gòng,
    alt òma lofti å né at strònd.
21. Dei brænde på Treieborg i åtte år
    å ikkje så konna dei dæ atte sjå.
22. Dei brende på Treieborg i åri ni
    å ikkje dæ søntes i alle di.
23. Å dér kom då inn så gamall ein mann,
    Simon sáttan så kalla dei han.
24. "Me sko gjéra ein hest av kåpar å inkje av stål
    å lata så den innfor porten gå."
25. "Heléna, Heléna, å dæ æ mitt rå:
    me vi lukke atte porten, lat' folen uti stå!"
26. "Å Paris, å Paris, å dæ æ mitt sinn:
    me vi lukke upp porten, lat' folen gå inn!"
27. Den hesten han for då ti frøse,
    han frøste 'kji ana ell å gløse.
28. Å den hesten han for då ti gjeispa,
    han gjeispa 'kji ana ell å neistar.
29. "Kvår vi du fygje kong Nikelus sør ónder øy,
    hell du vi no hera mæ 'en Paris døy?"
30. "Å hell'e vi eg mæ 'en Paris døy,
    hell eg vi fygje 'en kong Nikelus sør ónder øy!"
31. "Me sko drikke mjø å lata konn årebló slå,
    å lettare dø me kann inkje få."
32. Dæ va kong Nikelus's støsste kvie,
    at Heléna låg dø'e mæ Paris's sie.
33. Dæ va kong Nikelus's støsste harm,
    at Heléna låg dø'e på Paris's arm.
    — Ho lyster Paris fylgje.

Textual variations and other manuscript peculiarities: 7^2 uses *når* for *hòr*. 13^2 adds the *bleiv* printed in the text above. 33^1 is written *Dæ va ——— harm*.

SOME NOTES ON THE NIX IN OLDER NORDIC TRADITION

1. *Landnámabók I–III*, ed. F. Jónsson (Copenhagen, 1900), pp. 30, 151.
2. For these two types of traditions, see for instance J. Árnason, *Íslenzkar þjóðsögur og æfintýri*, I (Leipzig, 1862), 135 ff.; Ný útgáfa, II (Reykjavik, 1954), 207 ff.; Oddur Björnsson, *Þjóðtrú og þjóðsagnir*, I (1908), 203 ff.; Sigfús Sigfússon, *Íslenzkar þjóðsögur og -sagnir*, V (Reykjavik, 1945), 77 ff.; and Ólafur Davíðsson, *Íslenzkar þjóðsögur*, III (Reykjavik, 1945), 35 ff.

3. *Vatnahestur* is, for instance, used by J. Árnason, I (1862), p. 135. In the margin of the first printed edition of *Landnámabók* (Skalholt, 1688), there is a note to the Auðun stoti episode, which says: *vatnshestur, er nú kalla sumir nikurhest*. See further *Íslendinga Sögur,* I (1843), 93.

4. Except to the written material of the folklore archives, I refer to T. Norlind, *Studier i svensk folklore* (1911), p. 108; U. Holmberg-Harva, *Die Wassergottheiten der Finnisch-Ugrischen Völker* (Helsinki, 1913), pp. 191 ff.; and L. Simonsuuri, *Typen- und Motivverzeichnis der finnischen mythischen Sagen,* FFC 182 (1961), L 212 (*Nixe als . . . Baumstumpf*). In Esthonian traditions *Klotz, Balken, Krummholz* are also mentioned among the things that the nix could transform himself into (O. Loorits, *Grundzüge des estnischen Volksglaubens,* II [Lund, 1949–1960], 263.

5. B. M. Ólsen, *Den tredje og fjærde grammatiske Afhandling . . .* (Copenhagen, 1884), pp. 80, 191, and 315.

6. *Nóregs konunga tal,* stanza 75.

7. Parallels can be found in H. Meissner, *Die Kenningar der Skalden* (1921), pp. 97 and 100. Ice is, for example, called *hvals búðar húð,* the whale's booth's hide, *Ránar ræfr,* Rán's roof, *hœings hallar næfri,* the salmon's hall's birch-bark.

8. I, 55.

9. *Norske Folke-Sagn,* 2nd edition (Christiania, 1844), p. 49.

10. See for instance J. T. Storaker, *Elementerne i den norske folketro* (Christiania, 1924), pp. 126 ff. and *Naturrigerne i den norske folketro* (Christiania, 1928), p. 101, and further *Norsk folkminnelags Skrifter,* No. 11, pp. 44 f.; No. 61, p. 39; No. 74, pp. 15 f.

11. V. U. Hammershaimb in *Antikvarisk Tidsskrift* (1850), p. 200, and in *Færøsk Anthologi,* I (1891), 334 f. See also J. Jakobsen, *Færøske Folkesagn og Aeventyr* (1898–1901), pp. 197 f., 227 f.

12. *Antikvarisk Tidsskrift,* p. 200.

13. V. U. Hammershaimb, *Færøsk Anthologi,* I (1891), 334 f., and J. Jakobsen, *Færøske Folkesagn,* p. 227.

14. According to information by Dr. Åsa Nyman (Uppsala) who is working on Faroese folktales.

15. Hammershaimb, *Antikvarisk Tidsskrift,* p. 334.

16. J. Jakobsen, *Færøske Folkesagn,* p. 198.

17. See for instance J. G. Campbell, *Superstitions of the Highlands and Islands of Scotland* (Glasgow: J. MacLehose and Sons, 1900), pp. 204–208.

18. (Edinburgh, 1940), p. 206.

19. *A Description of the Shetland Islands* (Lerwick: Manson, 1891), p. 233.

20. II (1921), 571 f.

21. (Lerwick, 1947), pp. 11 f.

22. *Etymologisk Ordbog,* II, 572.

23. P. 233.

24. See for instance J. F. Campbell, *Popular Tales of the West Highlands,* IV (Edinburgh: Edmonston and Douglas, 1862), 330 ff., 337 f., and further N. MacDonald in *Arv,* XIV (1958), 129.

25. Maja Bergstrand in *Folkminnen och Folktankar,* XXIII (1936), 15 f., and Brita Egardt in *Folkkultur,* IV (1944), 124 f.; cf. also C. W. von Sydow in *Vetenskaps-Societetens i Lund Årsbok* 1922, pp. 85 ff.

26. P. Kalm, *Westgötha og Bohusländska Resa* (1742), p. 200.

27. References to printed sources in T. Norlind, *Studier i svensk folklore,* p. 105.

28. J. M. Thiele, *Danmarks Folkesagn,* II (Copenhagen, 1843), 291 ff.; E. T. Kristensen, *Danske Sagn,* II (Aarhus, 1892–1901), 163 ff.; Ny Række II Afd. (Copenhagen, 1929), 112 f.; J. Kamp, *Danske Folkeminder* (Odense, 1877), p. 118.

29. U. Holmberg-Harva, *Die Wassergottheiten,* pp. 161 f.

30. (1961), No. 211 (*lockt Kinder auf ihren Rücken*).

31. Holmberg-Harva, *Die Wassergottheiten,* pp. 161 f. and O. Loorits, *Grundzüge,* p. 263.

32. *Folkkultur,* IV (1944), 119 ff.

33. Cf. H. Bächtold-Stäubli, *Handwörterbuch des deutschen Aberglaubens* (Berlin and Leipzig, 1927–1942), IX, col. 131 f.; VI, col. 1635.

34. I am here leaving out the *marmennill,* which is a specific dwarf-like sea-being in human shape, very wise if it is caught and forced to talk, a soothsayer according to Icelandic sources (*Landnámabók I–III,* pp. 23 and 146; *Hálfs saga ok Hálfsrekka,* Chapter 7) and also well known from West Scandinavian tales and traditions.

35. Picture in *Svenska folket genom tiderna,* ed. E. Wrangel, III (Malmö, 1938), 280.

36. See for instance T. Norlind, *Studier,* pp. 106 ff., L. Simonsuuri, *Typen-und Motivverzeichnis,* L 201–300, and (for Esthonian material that must be very much influenced from the West) O. Loorits, *Grundzüge,* pp. 263 f.

37. *Själens Tröst,* ed. S. Henning (Stockholm, 1954–1957), pp. 30 f.

38. *Landnámabók I–III,* pp. 22 and 110.

39. See for instance T. Norlind, *Studier,* pp. 117 f., and M. Bergstrand, *Folkminnen,* pp. 26 f.

40. *Flateyjarbók,* II (1862), 26.

41. J. Grimm, *Deutsche Mythologie,* 4th ed., I (Berlin, 1875), 404.

42. Cf. J. Sahlgren in *Namn och Bygd,* XXIII (1935), 47, and M. Bergstrand, *Folkminnen,* p. 22.

43. Cf. D. Strömbäck in *Arv,* XVIII (1962), 1 ff.

44. Ed. O. Jiriczek (1893), pp. 45 ff.

45. Ed. A. Holder (Strassburg, Darmstadt, 1886), pp. 404 f.

46. This theme is dealt with in detail in my essay "Näcken och förlossningen" in *Varbergs Museums Årsbok* 1963, pp. 77 ff. To the tales quoted there I should now like to add also N. L. Hallender's legend about the nix in *Svenska Landsmål,* Bd. II (1880–1887), pp. lxxvi f., which is closest to the example from 1509.

47. *European Folk Ballads,* Danmarks gamle Folkeviser XL, ed. E. Seemann, D. Strömbäck, and B. Jonsson (Copenhagen: Rosenkilde and Bagger, 1967), pp. 20 ff.

48. *Nordens trylleviser* (Copenhagen, 1934), pp. 63 ff.

49. Danmarks gamle Folkeviser XXXIX.

50. *Íslenzak Fornkvæði,* I (1854–1858), 15.

51. V. U. Hammershaimb, *Færøsk Anthologi,* I (1891), 13.

52. A. Olrik, *Nordens trylleviser,* p. 58.

53. A. Olrik, *Nordens trylleviser,* p. 58.

54. *Folkminnen och Folktankar,* XXIII (1935), 73.

55. Ed. S. Grundtvig, Danmarks gamle Folkeviser XXXIX.

56. See my introduction to "The Might of the Harp" in *European Folk Ballads,* p. 20.

57. Cf. A. Olrik, *Nordens trylleviser,* p. 58.

58. A. A. Afzelius, *Svenska Folkets Sagohäfder,* II (Stockholm, 1842), 153 f.

59. *Folkminnen och Folktankar,* XXIII (1935), 3.

A BOHEMIAN MEDIEVAL FABLE ON THE FOX AND THE POT

1. *Abhandlungen der königlichen böhmischen Gesellschaft der Wissenschaften,* Geschichte der böhmischen Sprache, I (Prague, 1791), 331–332.

2. Antonín Jaroslav Puchmajer, *Sebrání básní a zpěvů* (Collected Poems and Songs), I (Prague, 1795), 147–150.

3. Aleksander Brückner, "Die böhmische Fabel von Fuchs und Krug," *Archiv für slavische Philologie,* II (1888), 471–472.

4. Bolte-Polívka, *Anmerkungen zu den Kinder-u. hausmärchen der brüder Grimm,* V (Leipzig: 1913–1932), p. 122: *Daneben kann sich die altčechische Literatur auch einiger Stoffe rühmen, die sich noch nicht in anderen Literaturen jener Zeit vorfinden. So lesen wir in der Königgrätzer Hs die Fabel vom Fuchs und dem Krug, welche nur in einer späteren lateinischen Breslauer Hs. aus der Mitte des 15 Js. belegt ist.* ("Furthermore, we can find in ancient Czech literature several themes not encountered in other literatures of that period. Thus, we read in the Hradec [Königgrätz] Manuscript the fable about the Fox and the Pot, evidenced only in a later Latin work, the Wrocław Manuscript, dating from the middle of the fifteenth century.")

5. *Hradecký rukopis* (Prague, 1881), p. xvii.

6. *Narodnyje russkije skazki* (Russian Folk Tales), III (Moscow, 1860), 24, No. 4. (Edition of V. Y. Propp, I [Moscow, 1957], 40, No. 26. Here, on p. 111, the Russian variant is compared with the ancient Czech composition.)

7. Jiří Polívka, "O srovnávacím studiu tradic lidových" (The Comparative Study of Folk Traditions), *Národopisný sborník českoslovanský* (Czechoslovak Ethnographical Journal), II (Prague, 1898), 6.

8. Jiří Polívka, "O českých pohádkách" (Czech Folk Tales), in Jan Satranský's edition of *Národní pohádky* (Folk Tales), (Prague, 1911), p. 204: "One may assume that this fable, too, had originated on Czech soil, but its spreading as far as Albania should warn us before any hasty conclusions."

9. Jan Vilikovský, "Nová latinská verse bajky o lišče a džbánu" (The New Latin Version of the Fable about the Fox and the Pot), *Listy filologiské* (Journal of Philology), LVI (1929), 246–247.

10. Jan Vilikovský, *Staročeské satiry* (Ancient Czech Satires), (Prague, 1942), p. 93.

11. Albert Wesselski, *Klaret und sein Glossator* (Claret and his Glossator), (Brno, 1936), pp. 46–47, 125–126.

12. We are faced here with the well-known problem of the relativity of variability and stability, typical of medieval literature, especially of folkloristic compositions. Cf. Jaromír Jech, "Relativitätsaspekte bei der Beurteilung der Variabilität und Stabiltät" in *Volksüberlieferung—Festschrift für Kurt Ranke zur Vollendung des 60. Lebensjahres* (Relativity Aspects in the Appraisal of Variability and Stability, published in *Folk-Reproduction—Memorial Address on the Occasion of the Sixtieth Jubilee of Kurt Ranke*), (Göttingen, 1968), pp. 115–131.

13. Nová latinská verse, p. 247.

14. Jiří Polívka, *"O srovnávacím studiu tradic lidových,"* p. 6.

15. Jiří Polívka, *Súpis slovenských rozprávok* (Survey of Slovak Tales), (v Turčianský Sv. Martin, 1931), pp. 142–143.

16. A more profound analysis will be found in a special work to be published by me. For the time being, I should like to refer to the concluding chapter of my edition *Tschechische Volksmärchen* (Berlin, 1961), pp. 481 ff.

17. Cf. Jiří Polívka, Review of *Ukrajinski narodni bajky* (Ukrainian Folk Tales), *Národopisný věstník českoslovanský* (Czechoslovak Ethnographical Bulletin), XIII (1918), 109.

A MODERN MEDIEVAL STORY: "THE SOLDIER'S DECK OF CARDS"

1. Alexander Scheiber, "Hungarian Parallels of the 'Twelve Numbers,'" *JAF,* LXIII (1950), 465–467; Leah Rachel Clara Yaffie, "Songs of the Twelve Numbers and the Hebrew Chant of 'Echod Mi Yodea,'" *JAF,* LXII (1949), 382–411. Professor Bruce Rosenberg was assisted by a fellowship from the American Council of Learned Societies.

2. The oral sermon is old in American tradition. An early account is in Clarence Deming, *By Ways of Nature and Life* (New York, 1884), p. 361; James Weldon Johnson also discusses the phenomenon in *God's Trombones* (New York, 1948), pp. 1–5.

3. To the references in *The Types of the Folktale,* add Alexander Scheiber, "A Hungarian Encyclopedia of Cards," *Midwest Folklore,* II (1952), 93–100; Flavio de Toledo Piza, "Estudo Sôbre o Romance do Soldado Jogador," *Revista do Arquivo* (São Paulo, Brazil), CLXV (1959), 71–116; Ed Cray, "'The Soldier's Deck of Cards' Again," *Midwest Folktales,* XI (1961), 225–234; Austin Fife, "The Prayer Book in Cards," *Western Folklore,* XXVII (1968), 208–209; Ed Cray, "The Soldier's Deck of Cards Once Again," *Western Folklore,* XXVIII (1969), 211.

4. "The Soldier's Deck of Cards Again," 225.

5. "The Soldier's Deck," 230–231.

6. Judith McCulloh, "Some Child Ballads on Hillbilly Records," *Folklore and Society: Essays in Honor of Benj. A. Botkin,* ed. Bruce Jackson (Hatboro, Pennsylvania: Folklore Associates, 1966), p. 128.

7. Tyler's account is from a letter, March 26, 1968.

8. Tyler's recording was reissued as Four-Star 1709. Other releases and reissues by Tyler are Capitol T/ST 2344; Design 607; King 660, 664, 807; Starday SLP 229, SLP 374.

9. The following list of recordings subsequent to Tyler's may not be complete: Alladin, Dot 25570; L. Burton, Universal U-114; Rex Cross (The Roaming Philosopher), Musicraft 566; Rusty Draper, Mercury 16243; Phil Harris, RCA Victor 20-2821; Nelson King, King 712; Wink Martindale, Dot 150, Hamilton HLP 12128; The Rainbow Four, Rainbow 60005; Tex Ritter, Capitol 6018, 40114, T/ST 1623, DT 2595; Riley Shepard, Banner 559; Tex Williams, Decca 7-4090, 9-28809, DL 4090, Boone 1210. Harvey Leeds apparently recorded the piece for Bell; but Ed Cray's conjecture that there was an issued recording by Ernest Tubb seems groundless, though we have heard Tubb perform "The Deck of Cards." The recitation was printed in the song folio *Country and Western Favorites* (Charles Hansen [1963?]), 80–81; *Country Song Roundup,* May, 1954, p. 29; and Austin Fife has printed a text from the files of the Pacific North West Farm Quad (pp. 211–212).

10. The Stewart Family, King 687; printed by Ed Cray, "The Soldier's Deck," 232.

11. The account of the copyright dispute is drawn from *The Cincinnati Enquirer,* April 8, April 22, and September 3, 1948; *The Billboard,* September 11, 1948, pp. 4, 30.

12. "Eine geistliche Auslegung des Kartenspiels," *Zeitschrift des Vereins für Volkskunde,* XI, 376–406.

13. In addition to the 1790 chapbook, there are two other editions in the Library of Congress. An identically titled edition with an 1802 imprint has but slight textual differences. "A Pack of Cards, A Complete Almanack" (C. Wosencroft, Liverpool) greatly abbreviates the tale, particularly by giving single rather than multiple references for cards, suits, etc. It thus resembles Bolte's H text. Excerpts from a J. Pitts chapbook of the H tradition are printed by H. T. Morley, *Old and Curious Playing Cards* (London: B. T. Batsford [1931]), pp. 218–219.

14. "The Tale of the Religious Card Player," *Folk-Lore,* L (1939), 263–272.

15. Mitchell Library, Glasgow, Folio vol. 1, p. 125 (Jc: Leeds: G. Buchan); Folio vol. 3, p. 74 (Jd: Leeds: Barr).

16. Wilson's text is from *Gems of Inspiration, Comic Songs, Funny Stories and Recitations* (Chicago: Max Stein, 1928). Ed Cray, "The Soldier's Deck," 228–230, prints an identical text credited to *Comic Songs, Funny Stories and Recitations* (Chicago: Max Stein, ca. 1915).

17. *Midwest Folklore,* II, 219–220.

18. "The Prayer Book in Cards," 208–211.

19. *The Poet Scout* (San Francisco, 1879), pp. 44–47. Although in most ways the Lomax text seems derivative from Crawford's published poem, it includes a couplet furnishing symbolizations for the nine and the ten which is missing

in *The Poet Scout* text. We have not been able to examine the 1904 reprint of *The Poet Scout*. If the couplet is missing there also, we would suspect that the Lomax text derives from a newspaper publication by Crawford. It may be worthy of note that the text of "California Joe" printed in Lomax's *Cowboy Songs* and credited to Crawford does not agree exactly with the *Poet Scout* text. Another of Crawford's texts which seems to have become at least pseudo-traditional is "The Burial of Wild Bill," recorded in 1929 by Frank Jenkins' Pilot Mountaineers and released on Conqueror 7270 under the pseudonym of Alex Gordon.

20. Ed Cray noted the occurrence of this variant, "The Soldier's Deck" (232, 234), and we are grateful for his loan of the song folio.

21. Red River Dave, Decca 29002, 9-29002; Pee Wee King, RCA Victor 20-25587, 47-5587; Tex Ritter, Capitol 2686, F 1665; Jimmy Wakely, Coral 61112. Ed Cray has printed a text from *Arlen and Jackie Vaden The Southern Gospel Singers Presents Their 1958 Book of Radio Favorites* (KXEL, Waterloo, Iowa), *Midwest Folklore*, XI, 232–234.

22. Starday 750, SLP 2-355.

ESTHETIC FORM IN BRITISH AND AMERICAN FOLK NARRATIVE

1. *The Jests of Hierocles and Philagrius,* newly translated from the Greek by Charles Clinch Bubb (Cleveland: Rowfant Club, 1920. Wittol Series No. 1).

2. David Dempsey, "Refurbishing American Authors," *Saturday Review* (June 10, 1967), 30.

3. In *The Study of Folklore,* ed. Alan Dundes (New York: Prentice-Hall, 1965), pp. 129–141.

4. *The Dewar Manuscripts,* I, *Scottish West Highland Folk Tales,* collected originally in Gaelic by John Dewar, translated into English by Hector Maclean, edited with introduction and notes by John Mackechnie (Glasgow: William MacLellan, 1964), pp. 233–236.

5. The relevant motif in Stith Thompson, *Motif-Index of Folk Literature* (Bloomington, Indiana: Indiana University Press, 1955–58) is H 1561.2, "Single combat to prove valor."

6. *The Dewar Manuscripts,* pp. 218–224.

7. Richard M. Dorson, *Negro Tales from Pine Bluff, Arkansas and Calvin, Michigan* (Bloomington, Ind.: Indiana University Press, 1958), p. 110.

8. (Cambridge, Mass.: Harvard University Press, 1952), pp. 251–254.

9. "Parallel Themes in Folk Narrative in Art and Literature," *Journal of the Folklore Institute,* IV (1967), 3–16.

HANGMEN, THE GALLOWS, AND THE DEAD MAN'S HAND IN AMERICAN FOLK MEDICINE

1. Well-known folkloristic approaches to the life cycle, or life crises, have been made by Paul Sartori in his standard work, *Sitte und Brauch* (Handbücher

zur Volkskunde, V–VIII, Leipzig, 1910–1914) under the rubric "Hauptstufen des Menschendaseins," and by Arnold van Gennep in his *Manuel de folklore français contemporain,* 9 vols. in 4 (Vol. II never appeared) (Paris, 1937–1958), and in his various collections of provincial French folklore under headings in most volumes, *du berceau a la tombe.*

2. Cf. Arnold van Gennep, *Les rites de passage* (Paris, 1909). This work is now available in English translation (*The Rites of Passage,* trans. Monika B. Vizedom and Gabrielle L. Caffee [Chicago: University of Chicago Press, 1960]).

3. *Handwörterbuch des deutschen Aberglaubens,* IV (Leipzig, 1927–1942), 39. (Hereinafter cited *HDA.*) Cf. also *HDA,* III, 1455. The reader will also find excellent material in the general area of this study in Mabel Peacock, "Executed Criminals and Folk-Medicine," *Folk-Lore,* VII (1896), 268–283. The British author has brought material together not only from the British Isles, but from other countries of Europe as well. For a general statement on the magical power of an executioner in medical matters, see O. v. Hovorka und A. Kronfeld, *Vergleichende Volksmedizin: Eine Darstellung volksmedizinischer Sitten und Gebräuche, Anschauungen und Heilfaktoren, des Aberglaubens und der Zaubermedizin,* I (Stuttgart, 1908–1909), 377–379.

4. *Natural History,* XXVIII, 2; cf. *HDA,* III, 1455.

5. *HDA,* III, 1439–1440, 1454–1455, *passim;* cf. Werner Danckert, *Unehrliche Leute: Die verfemten Berufe* (Bern und München: Francke, 1963), pp. 25, 30, 42, *passim.*

6. Danckert, *Unehrliche Leute,* p. 34.

7. Danckert, *Unehrliche Leute,* p. 43.

8. Ersch und Gruber, *Allgemeine Encyclopädie der Wissenschaften und Künste,* Zweite Section, H-N, Fünfter Theil, p. 321, s.v. "Henker." This custom is also alluded to in "Robin Hood Rescuing Three Squires" (Child Ballad, No. 140).

9. Alfred Marks, *Tyburn Tree: Its History and Annals* (London, n.d.), p. 48, as cited from the *Gentleman's Magazine,* XXXVII (1767), 276. "A man having been hanged at Tyburn on May 4, 1767, 'a young woman, with a wen upon her neck, was lifted up while he was hanging, and had the wen rubbed with the dead man's hand, from a superstitious notion that it would effect a cure.'"

10. John Deane Potter, *The Fatal Gallows Tree* (London: Elek, 1965), p. 70.

11. E. and M. Radford, *Encyclopaedia of Superstitions,* edited and revised by Christina Hole (London: Hutchinson, 1961), pp. 179–180, s.v. "Hand of Glory"; cf. also "Dead Hand" (pp. 124–126). (This work is hereinafter cited as Radford-Hole.) T. F. Thiselton Dyer, *Strange Pages from Family Papers* (London, 1895), pp. 154–161.

12. For Germany, see *HDA,* IV, 46, *passim;* Potter, *The Fatal Gallows Tree,* pp. 70–71.

13. Potter, *The Fatal Gallows Tree,* p. 71.

14. As of fifteen or twenty years ago only six states prescribed hanging as a means of capital punishment, namely, Idaho, Iowa, Kansas, Montana, New

Hampshire, and Washington; in Utah hanging is optional. *Encyclopaedia Britannica* (Chicago, London, etc., 1962), XI, 152, s.v. "Hanging."

15. The last "public" hanging in the United States took place in Kentucky in 1936. *Encyclopaedia Britannica,* XI, 152, s.v. "Hanging."

16. To stimulate further search, and to make available "jury texts," I shall cite references from the British Isles and the continent.

17. Thomas R. Brendle and Claude W. Unger, *Folk Medicine of the Pennsylvania Germans. The Non-Occult Cures,* Proceedings of the Pennsylvania German Society, XLV (Norristown, Pa., 1935), p. 68; John Graham Dalyell, *The Darker Superstitions of Scotland* (Glasgow, 1835), p. 129; E. and M. A. Radford, *Encyclopedia of Superstitions* (London, n.d. [1947]), pp. 98, 256; William George Black, *Folk-Medicine: A Chapter in the History of Culture,* Publications of the Folk-Lore Society, XII (London, 1883), pp. 100–101.

18. European examples, of course, are numerous; a few references will suffice: Thiselton Dyer, pp. 157–158 (for smallpox); *HDA,* II, 1176 (epilepsy), 1455 (goiters, warts); IV, 44–45 (various); John Symonds Udal, *Dorsetshire Folk-Lore* (Hertford, 1922), p. 186 (skin complaints); Dalyell, *Darker Superstitions,* p. 129 (scrofula).

19. *Folk-Lore,* VII (1896), 270–271 (Denmark); *HDA,* III, 1455 (Amsterdam [1693]).

20. *Folk-Lore,* VII (1896), 269–270 (scrofula: France); *HDA,* III, 1455 (Bohemia [1613]).

21. *Folk-Lore,* VII (1896), 270–271 (epilepsy: Denmark; also wens: Denmark and Sweden); Danckert, *Unehrliche Leute,* pp. 42–43. In the Swedish-speaking part of western Finland an account is given of a woman who ran up with a little bit of bark when the head fell at an execution, and drank the blood to cure herself of epilepsy (V. E. V. Wessman, *Folktro och Trolldom.* 3. Människan och Djuren, Finlands Svenska Folkedigtning, VII [Helsingfors, 1952], 49–50). An instance from 1696 is also reported (p. 50). Cf. *HDA,* II, 1176, s.v. "Fallsucht." Epileptics are also reported to have drunk the blood of performers killed in the circus in ancient Rome (Danckert, *Unehrliche Leute*), p. 43.

22. *HDA,* III, 1455.

23. Radford-Hole, p. 181, s.v. "Hangman's rope"; *HDA,* III, 262 ff., s.v. "Galgen"; cf. Index under "Galgenstrick," "Armsünderstrick," "Strick," etc.

24. Henry Phillips, Jr., "First Contribution to the Folk-Lore of Philadelphia and its Vicinity," Proceedings of the American Philosophical Society, XXV [1888], 164, No. 20 (epilepsy); *Folk-Lore,* VII (1896), 268 (epilepsy: Lincolnshire).

25. *Frank C. Brown Collection of North Carolina Folklore* (Durham, North Carolina: Duke University Press, 1952–1964; Vols. VI–VII, *Popular Beliefs and Superstitions from North Carolina,* ed. Wayland D. Hand, 1961–1964), VI, 179, No. 1348.

26. Phillips, p. 164, No. 20; cf. Brown Collection, VI, 193, No. 1478 (text possibly unreliable). Cf. *Folk-Lore,* XLIV (1933), 202 (fits: Lincolnshire—noose as well as rope).

27. *The Casket,* VI (Philadelphia, July, 1833), 264, No. 2. This reference was taken from the *Virginia Museum,* but without more precise details, and I am unfortunately unable to trace this publication, which appears to be a contemporary journal. Cf. Dalyell, *Darker Superstitions,* p. 128 (who says that the use of the noose dates from the time of Pliny) ; Black, *Folk-Medicine,* p. 100; George Lyman Kittredge, *Witchcraft in Old and New England* (Cambridge, Mass.: Harvard University Press, 1929), p. 142; Thomas Joseph Pettigrew, *On Superstitions Connected With the History and Practice of Medicine and Surgery* (London, 1844), p. 64; Radford, *Encyclopedia of Superstitions,* pp. 141, 146; Ella M. Leather, *Folk-Lore of Herefordshire* (Hereford: Jakeman and Carver, and London: Sidgwick and Jackson, 1912), p. 79. Since writing this article I have come upon an entry containing a recommended cure for headache, employing the halter of a man who has been hanged. This is found in the *Farmer's Almanac* for 1832 (Boston: Willard Felt & Co.), p. 34. With the widespread failure in early days to credit sources in almanacs and other media of cheap print, it is not unlikely that the *Virginia Museum* may have copied the item which originally appeared in the *Farmer's Almanac.*

28. *Folk-Lore,* XI (1900), 217 (Devonshire) ; XXVII (1916), 415 (Herefordshire) ; Kittredge, *Witchcraft,* p. 142.

29. Brendle and Unger, *Folk Medicine,* p. 106; cf. Edwin Miller Fogel, *Beliefs and Superstitions of the Pennsylvania Germans,* Americana Germanica, XVIII (Philadelphia, 1915), No. 1548.

30. Fogel, *Beliefs and Superstitions,* No. 1772.

31. *The Casket,* No. 6 (June, 1833), 264, No. 7.

32. Ed. James Britten, Publications of the Folk-Lore Society, IV (London, 1881), p. 118. This was repeated in the standard work on English folk medicine in the nineteenth century, Thomas Joseph Pettigrew, *On Superstitions Connected With the History and Practice of Medicine and Surgery* (London, 1844), p. 68. Cf. also Black, *Folk-Medicine,* p. 100; Kittredge, *Witchcraft,* p. 142.

33. *Natural History,* XXVIII, 30. (I have been unable to verify Professor Cyrus L. Day's reference, which he takes from Heckenbach [*Western Folklore,* IX (1950), 238, n. 31].)

34. Radford, *Encyclopedia of Superstitions,* p. 242; Kittredge, *Witchcraft,* p. 142.

35. Radford-Hole, pp. 179–180; cf. *HDA,* s.v. "Diebsdaumen," "Diebsfinger," etc. (Index).

36. *Journal of American Folklore,* XXXI (1918), 137, No. 23: "The cure by stroking or rubbing the goitre with a dead man's hand was tried quite recently in East Oxford township, the woman who had it coming from some distance to where the corpse lay"; Vance Randolph, *Ozark Superstitions* (New York: Columbia University Press, 1947), p. 148: "a small town undertaker tells me that an old woman in the neighborhood is always coming to his place, wanting to try this" [rubbing her goiter with a dead man's hand].

37. *Journal of American Folklore,* IV (1891), 124 (rubbing the neck three times) ; II (1889), 31; Brendle and Unger, *Folk Medicine,* p. 79; E. Grumbine, *Folk-Lore and Superstitious Beliefs of Lebanon County* (Papers and Addresses of the Lebanon County Historical Society, III, 1905–1906), p. 278.

38. Emelyn E. Gardner, *Folklore from the Schoharie Hills New York* (Ann Arbor, Mich.: University of Michigan Press, 1937), p. 267, No. 27; *New York Folklore Quarterly,* VIII (1952), 89.

39. *Journal of American Folklore,* XXXI (1918), 22, No. 288; W. J. Wintemberg, *Folk-Lore of Waterloo County, Ontario,* National Museum of Canada, Bulletin, No. 116, Anthropological Series, No. 28 (Ottawa, 1950), p. 12.

40. Daniel Lindsey Thomas and Lucy Blayney Thomas, *Kentucky Superstitions* (Princeton, N.J.: Princeton University Press, 1920), No. 1218 (rub a dead person's hand over it [the goiter] three times; as the body decays the goitre will disappear [Louisville Negroes]); E. Horace Fitchett, "Superstition in South Carolina," *The Crisis,* XLIII (1936), 360.

41. *Hoosier Folklore,* IX (1950), 9; *Indiana History Bulletin,* XXV (1958), 126, No. 155 (Marion and Noble Counties); No. 156 (Clinton County).

42. *Journal of American Folklore,* XXXI (1918), 205; Harry Middleton Hyatt, *Folk-Lore from Adams County Illinois* (New York: Hyatt Foundation, 1935), No. 5277.

43. Hyatt, *Folk-Lore,* No. 5278.

44. Hyatt, *Folk-Lore,* No. 5279.

45. Pauline Monette Black, *Nebraska Folk Cures* (University of Nebraska Studies in Language, Literature, and Criticism, XV, Lincoln, 1935), p. 36, No. 42.

46. *Folk-Lore,* VII (1896), 268–269 (England and France); XL (1929), 119 (Norfolk); XLIV (1933), 203 (Lincolnshire); Black, *Folk-Medicine,* p. 101 (rubbed nine times from east to west and nine times from west to east); Radford, *Encyclopedia of Superstitions,* pp. 133, 142 (make a cross over the goiter with a dead man's hand); Hovorka und Kronfeld, II, 17–18; W. G. Soldan, *Soldan's Geschichte der Hexenprozesse.* Neu bearbeitet von Heinrich Heppe, I (Stuttgart, 1880), 68 (ancient Rome).

47. Fogel, *Beliefs and Superstitions,* No. 1566 (stroke the tumor with the hand of a corpse and it will disappear with the decomposition of the corpse); Brendle and Unger, *Folk Medicine,* p. 80; A. Monroe Aurand, Jr., *Popular Home Remedies and Superstitions of the Pennsylvania Germans* (Harrisburg, Pa.: Aurand Press, 1941), p. 13. European references: Black, *Folk-Medicine,* p. 101; Radford, *Encyclopedia of Superstitions,* p. 245 (placing the hand of a man who has committed suicide will cure tumors on the skin); James Napier, *Folk Lore: or, Superstitious Beliefs in the West of Scotland Within This Century* (Paisley, 1879), pp. 92–93; Kittredge, *Witchcraft,* p. 142 (especially if the person has been hanged).

48. Brendle and Unger, *Folk Medicine,* p. 80; Fogel, *Beliefs and Superstitions,* No. 1479.

49. Pliny, *Natural History,* XXVIII, 11.

50. R. L. Tongue and K. M. Briggs, *Somerset Folklore,* Publications of the Folklore Society, CXIV (London, 1965), p. 136 (a dead hand passed nine times over a swelling dispels it).

51. Radford, *Encyclopedia of Superstitions,* pp. 142, 249; *HDA,* III, 1393, s.v. "Hand"; VII, 621, s.v. "reiben."

52. Fogel, *Beliefs and Superstitions,* No. 1686; Aurand, *Remedies and Superstitions,* p. 13.

53. *Tennessee Folklore Society Bulletin,* XIX (1953), 54.

54. Randolph, *Ozark Superstitions,* p. 151.

55. Earl J. Stout, *Folklore from Iowa,* Memoirs of the American Folklore Society, XXIX (New York, 1936), No. 741.

56. No. VI (July 1833), 264, No. 4 as reported in *Western Folklore,* XII (1953), 29.

57. Cf. John Aubrey, *Remaines of Gentilisme and Judaisme,* Publications of the Folk-Lore Society, IV (London, 1881), p. 198; Kittredge, *Witchcraft,* p. 142.

58. *Folk-Lore,* VI (1895), 124–125; VII (1896), 268–269; Leather, *Folk-Lore of Herefordshire,* p. 84.

59. Vol. VI, No. 2703. An additional reference, one from Illinois contains a first-person account of this curative procedure: "I had a wen on my hand. I tried several things and it would always come back. A negro man got burned in a fire and died. I went to see him and took his hand and rubbed it over my own, and it left and never came back" (Hyatt, *Folk-Lore,* No. 3964).

60. Thomas and Thomas, *Kentucky Superstitions,* No. 1546.

61. *Ozark Superstitions,* pp. 163–164. Cf. *HDA,* III, 1393 (rashes and sores).

62. *Southern Workman,* XXIX (1900), 443; cf. Joh. Th. Storaker, *Sygdom og Forgjørelse i den Norske Folketro,* Norsk Folkeminnelag, No. 41 (Oslo, 1938), No. 124.

63. Kittredge, *Witchcraft,* p. 142; cf. *Folk-Lore,* XXXIII (1922), 396.

64. Storaker, *Sygdom og Forgjørelse,* No. 377.

65. Hyatt, *Folk-Lore,* No. 4110.

66. Fletcher Bascom Dresslar, *Superstition and Education,* University of California Publications in Education, Vol. 5 (Berkeley, 1907), p. 111.

67. Hyatt, *Folk-Lore,* Nos. 4108, 4109 (rub it over the corpse three times). Also known in Nebraska; see Black, *Nebraska Folk Cures,* p. 28, No. 76.

68. Hyatt, *Folk-Lore,* Nos. 4111 (woman on man), 4112 (man on woman).

69. Hyatt, *Folk-Lore,* No. 4114.

70. Hyatt, *Folk-Lore,* No. 5661.

71. Vol. VI (1833), 264, No. 3, as reported in *Western Folklore,* XII (1953), 29.

72. Black, *Folk-Medicine,* p. 96; Radford, *Encyclopedia of Superstitions,* pp. 146, 220; Kittredge, *Witchcraft,* p. 142.

73. Cf. Black, *Folk-Medicine,* p. 97; Radford, *Encyclopedia of Superstitions,* pp. 123–124; Kittredge, *Witchcraft,* p. 142; *Journal of American Folklore,* XXII (1909), 123.

74. *Appleton's Journal of Literature, Science, and Art,* II (1869), 139.

75. Storaker, *Sygdom og Forgjørelse,* No. 261.

76. Fogel, *Beliefs and Superstitions,* Nos. 1699, 1737; Brendle and Unger, *Folk Medicine,* p. 65.

77. Hyatt, *Folk-Lore,* No. 4104. Disposal of disease by means of a *Zwischenträger* placed in a coffin is very common in Europe and is also somewhat known

in America. Cf. *North Carolina Folklore,* XIII (1965), 84–85, for a discussion of *Zwischenträger,* or intermediate agent.

78. Storaker, *Sygdom og Forgjørelse,* No. 125.

79. Storaker, *Sygdom og Forgjørelse,* No. 36.

80. Rodney Gallop, *Portugal* (Cambridge: Cambridge University Press, 1936), p. 62; cf. Kittredge, *Witchcraft,* p. 142 (wear a napkin from the dead man's face around the neck and then drop it on his coffin in the grave).

FOLK LOGIC AND THE BARD: ACT I OF *MACBETH*

1. A small portion of this essay appeared in the *Southern Folklore Quarterly,* XXIII (1959) under the title "The Tale is the Thing."

2. Quoted from Robert H. Lowie, "Shoshonean Tales," *JAF,* XXXVII (1924), 117–119, No. 8.

3. Printed, among other places, in *Life,* March 1, 1954.

4. Act, scene, and line citations refer to the George L. Kittredge edition of *The Complete Works of William Shakespeare* (Boston: Ginn, 1936).

5. It is of course possible that the First Folio text represents an abbreviated or poorly edited version of Shakespeare's script. Shakespeare may also have had an earlier play to work from. But we cannot be certain of such things and must rule them out as a means of rationalizing problems in Act I until citable evidence appears.

6. Surveys dealing with the sources of the Macbeth legend are numerous. E. K. Chambers "Introduction" in the Arden Shakespeare *Macbeth* (Boston: D. C. Heath, 1901) gives a great deal of information. See especially pp. 148–163. More modern is Henry N. Paul, *The Royal Play of Macbeth* (New York: Macmillan, 1950), especially pp. 183–225. See Ronald Berman's *A Reader's Guide to Shakespeare's Plays* (Chicago: Scott, Foresman, 1965), pp. 112–113, for bibliography.

Index

abbreviation, 148–49; Chaucer's use of, 156–57, 170

Abélard, Peter, 75

Accalon, 149–50

Adam, in Irish folklore, 259, 266

Admontean Cloister, Steiermark: Fox and Pot MS in, 276, 277, *278*, 279–81, 282, 288–89

adnominatio, 100, 103

advertising copy, logic and, 335–36

Aegir, 252, 256

Aelian, 225

Aeneid (Virgil), 39, 78–79

Aeschylus, 334–35

Afanasiev, Fox and Pot fable and, 276, 282

Africa, 216, 218, 294, 297

"After the Battle of Culloden," 310–13, 314

Agamemnon, of Aeschylus, 334–35

Agnete og Havmannen, 256

ague, cures for, 323, 326

Alabama, 315, 328

alba, the, 44

Albania, 276, 281, 282

Alcuin, 28

Alexander (figure), 123

Alexander (Chrétien de Troyes character), 42, 45, 46, 49

Alfred, king of England, 225; *Boethius* of, 31, 347n27

Alger, Horatio, 321

alliteration, 37, 38, 58–59, 101, 102; name pairs and, 69, 72–74, 75, 351n24

Alverdens anekdoter (Fonsmark), 223

Ambrose, saint, cited, 28

American Indians, 216, 218, 305–306, 332–34

American Negroes, *see* Negroes

American Revolution, 314

amplificatio, 148–49, 151; Chaucer's use of, 155–71, 174

Andreas, 24, 38

Andrew of Wyntoun, 341; quoted, 339

anecdote, 223–28, 306, 307, 316–17

Anelida and Arcite (Chaucer), 157

Anglo-Americans, folk medicine of, 325, 326–27, 329

Anglo-Norman literature, 71–72. *See also* French

animals: foster-parent motif, 140, 141, 144; speaking-animal tales, 308, 332–34; as water spirits, 245–52, 253. *See also specific animals*

Ann, queen of England, 173

Anselm, saint, 97–103

Antigone, in Chaucer's *Troilus and Criseyde,* 164, 166, 182–84, 185, 187, 188, 363n20

aphaeresis, 54

apocope, 54

Apostles, The: in Irish folklore, 261, 263, 264, 269; in Soldier's Deck of Cards exemplum, 292, 296, 301

Appalachian Mountains, 306, 321

apple, in Irish folklore, 259

April Fool's Day, 262

Apuleius, 216

Arabic languages, Romance borrowings from, 63

Ark, The, 292, 295, 296, 302; in Irish folklore, 257, 259, 265, 266

cherry tree legend, 260

Cheshire, England, 119

Chevalier de la Charrette (Chrétien de Troyes), 44, 50; *see also* Lancelot

Child ballads, 305

Chrétien de Troyes, 39–50, 121, 140, 141, 147

Christianity, 346*nn*15, 19; Beowulf and, 27–34, 345*n*4; *Bevis of Hampton* and, 130, 138; Chaucer and, 168–69, 180, 190; counting songs and, 291; Irish origin-stories and, 258–70; the Nix and, 254, 256; in *Octavian,* 140, 142; Scandinavian ballads of Troy and, 232; Soldier's Deck of Cards and, 291–303; Wild Hunt tradition and, 109

Christian names, 51–76

Christian Remembrancer, 79

Christmas, 29, 261

Chronicle, of Olaus Petri, 252

Cincinnati, Ohio, 294

Cincinnati Enquirer (newspaper), 295, 296–97

Cinderella theme, 219; in *Beowulf,* 21, 22

"Clerk's Tale, The" (Chaucer), 201, 207

Cleveland, Ohio, 294

Cligès (Chrétien de Troyes), 42–44, 46, 49, 50

Climent le vilain, in *Octavian,* 141–42, 144–45

cock, in Irish folklore, 261

cockchafer, in Fox and Pot fable, 277

Codex Regius, 14

Coffin, Tristram, 331–42

Coke, Sir Edward, 62

Columbus, Christopher, 225

Colvin, Mary Noyes, quoted, 82

comedy: advertising and, 335–36; anecdotes and, 224, 225; in *Bevis of Hampton,* 131–32; Chaucer and, 159, 163, 165, 168, 170, 205–11; in *Octavian,* 141, 142, 143, 144, 145, 146; protest tales and, 314–17

Concordia praescientiae et praedestinationis, De (St. Anselm), 97–103

Confessio Amantis (Gower), 60, 78

consciousness, 173–92

Constantine, emperor of Rome, 32

contentio (oxymoron), 170–71

contraria contrariis, 323–24

convention, 123–46, 207, 214, 217, 218; of courtly love (*see* courtly love); of dream-visions, 188; folktale motifs and, 207, 214, 217, 218, 238; of the märchen, 226; name connotations and, 51–76; of soliloquy, 176, 178; topographical, 121

Conybeare, J. J., 36, 37

"Cook's Prologue, The" (Chaucer), 61

Copas, (Lloyd) Cowboy, 298–99

Corsa, Helen Storm, quoted, 367*n*10

corselet, in *Beowulf,* 11–12

counting-songs, 291

"Country Boy's Deck of Cards," 301

courtly love: Boccaccio and, 158, 187; Chaucer and, 156, 164–65, 167, 169, 170, 180–81, 182, 187; Chrétien de Troyes and, 41, 42–43, 44, 46–48, 49

courtly tradition: *Beowulf* and, 25–26; Criseyde and, 180–82

Courtney, John, 315

"Cowboy's Deck of Cards, The," 298–99

cowherds, in Irish folklore, 263

cows, 258

Cox, Lee Sheridan, 198, 202, 366*nn*29, 33; quoted, 196, 365*n*28

coyote, Indian tale of, 332–34

Crawford, John W. (Captain Jack), 297

Cray, Ed, quoted, 294

creation, 214; Irish origin stories, 257–74; sun imagery of, 28–34

Criseyde, in Chaucer's *Troilus and Criseyde,* 159–70, 173–92

Crist (Cynewulf), 24, 32

Crockett, Davy, 317, 321

Crooked Rib, The (Utley), 76

Lüthi, Max, quoted, 227, 320–21
Lydgate, John, 66, 173
Lystig oc skjøn Vise, Huorledis Paris bortførde Helena, En, 230

Macbeth (Shakespeare), Act I, 331–42
McCall, William H., 295
Machiavelli, Niccolò, 208
Macduff, in *Macbeth,* 340
McEnery, Red River Dave, 293
McIntosh, Angeus, quoted, 119
McIntosh, David S., cited, 297, 301
McKay, J. G., quoted, 248
Macrobius, Ambrosius Theodosius, quoted, 177
magic: in *Bevis of Hampton,* 125, 136; medicine and, 323–29; of Morgan le Fay, 149–50, 153
Magnus, Olaus, 252
Magoun, Francis P., Jr., on *Beowulf,* 3, 4, 6, 7, 8–9, 10–11, 12, 14–15, 16, 17, 18–22, 23–24, 25
magpies, 268
Mahabharata, 215
Maid Marian, 53, 55, 63–65
Mainerus, quoted, 62
Malachi, 30
Maldon, 38
Malone, Kemp: on *Beowulf,* 15, 21, 22, 23, 35–38; on the Herlething, 109
Malory, Thomas, 77–95
"Manciple's Tale, The" (Chaucer), 197, 203
Mandragola, La (Machiavelli), 208
Manifold River, Staffordshire, 113, 114, 118
"Man of Law's Introduction, The" (Chaucer), 71
"Man of Law's Tale, The" (Chaucer), 140, 194, 198; endlink of, 195, 196–97, 199, 201–203, 365n28, 366n29
Manly, J. M., 194, 195, 196, 197, 198, 202; quoted, 199, 364n12, 365n17
man-in-the-moon, origin of, 258
Man in the Moon, The, 69
Mann, Thomas, 321

Map, Walter, 105–10
märchen, 223, 226, 306, 309
Margaret of Burgundy, 82
Margrete of Bohemia (Dagmor), queen of Denmark, 369n11
marmennill, described, 377n34
Marquand, J. P., cited, 226
Martin, saint, 265, 268
Matičetov, Milko, cited, 263
Matilda, daughter of Lord Fitzwalter, 55
Matthew, 29–30
Matthews, William, 77–95
Matthiessen, Francis O., cited, 309
May-bush, origin of the, 261
measuring lines, origin of, 269
Mecklenburg, Germany, 251
medicine, 323–29
Meech, Sanford, cited, 155
Meine, Franklin J., 309
Melville, Herman, 189, 309, 321
memorat, 227, 327; defined, 307
Memorials of London (Riley), 75
"Merchant's Tale, The" (Chaucer), 201, 210, 211
Meredith, George, 175
Mery Play betwene Johan Johan the husbande, Tyb his Wyfe, and Syr Jhan the Preest, 67
Mesopotamia, 219
Messenius, J., 231
meter: A-verse, in *Beowulf,* 19–20, 24; Chaucerian, 365n28; conventional phrases and, 123; the laisse form, 126; *nykrat,* 246–47
Meyer, Richard, cited, 26
mice, in Irish folklore, 265, 266, 267–68
Michael, Archangel, 258
Michigan, 317, 320
Middle English Dictionary, 72
Middle English: Christian names in, 51–76; romance conventions of, 121, 123–46
Middle High German, 253
Middlemarch (Eliot), 175